Competition: · Understanding - the 1998 Act

FOR RET

Competition:
· Understanding ·
the 1998 Act

James Flynn
Barrister

Jemima Stratford
Barrister

Foreword by
The Right Hon the Lord Slynn of Hadley

Palladian Law Publishing Ltd

© James Flynn & Jemima Stratford 1999

Published by
Palladian Law Publishing Ltd
Beach Road
Bembridge
Isle of Wight PO35 5NQ
www.palladianlaw.com

ISBN 1 902558 06 5   1001897508

Typeset by Cheryl Zimmerman
Printed in Great Britain

To our families

· Contents ·

· Foreword ·

For years the European Commission has been advocating that national authorities and courts should be more involved in the application and enforcement of Community competition law – an aspect of Community law which has perhaps the greatest role in legal practice. It has not proved easy. At the same time Member States have come to realise the importance of having national rules which reflect, or at least are not inconsistent with Community law and most Member States now have competition legislation and procedures far more effective than anything which existed even a relatively few years ago. In the United Kingdom there has been much discussion as to how our restrictive practice law should be changed; what should be the guiding principles, what the structure of control.

Currently the legal (and even the wider) press constantly reminds us that the Human Rights Act 1998 is to come into force in 2000 and that judges, lawyers and businessmen must prepare for it. Seminars and training courses flourish, books appear all the time. For the business world and its lawyers the significance of another 1998 statute coming into force in 2000 is no less, indeed is greater. The Competition Act 1998 will have an enormous impact on trading and commercial practices and thereby on trade. It is complex, deriving much from European Union law but as far as domestic law and procedures are concerned is innovative. A book clearly and authoritatively analysing and explaining the provisions of the Act and its derivation before the Act comes into force is not only desirable but essential. This is that book.

The authors, well experienced in this area of the law, naturally concentrate in the first place on the substantive law. Echoes of the Restrictive Practice Acts and Article 81 (old 85) are to be found in what they regard as the "fussily" (uninformatively?) named "Chapter I Prohibition". They explain in direct language without frills the important terms – concerted practices, undertaking, the notion of appreciable effect, the relationship between parent and subsidiary in regard to prohibited agreements. They consider the sort of questions which will quickly arise once the Act is in force – can damages be obtained for breach of a prohibition by someone who suffers in consequence of the breach, European Union law not giving a clear answer; what effect will be given to Commission decisions of different kinds to which "regard" must be had; how far will the European Court accept an Article 234 (old 177) reference in respect of a phrase in the Competition Act which is the same as the one in Articles 81 and 82 (old 85 and 86) in view of the stated purpose of section 60 of the Act to achieve consistency "so far as possible" and "having regard to any relevant differences"; what is the scope of the exceptions? And many others.

Then there is the second head of substantive law imaginatively dubbed "The Chapter II Prohibition" more familiar as the prohibition of conduct which amounts to the abuse of a dominant position. Again an explanation of terms, concepts and the scope of the second prohibition – dominance, relevant market, market share, predatory pricing.

I find valuable in this part of the book in particular (a) an awareness that the Court's jurisprudence and the Commission's decisions have to be known and taken into account coupled with a warning of pitfalls – too easy an assumption that aspects of the two prohibitions are on all fours with decisions in Articles 81 and 82 (old 85 and 86); and (b) the tracing of the development of the concepts involved coupled with detailed references to Office of Fair Trading Guidelines and Department of Trade and Industry explanatory material.

The procedural chapters are of immediate value for those likely to be affected by the Act – the difference is between notification for guidance and notification for a decision, the effect of comfort letters and of a decision. The new powers of investigation and enforcement both for the purposes of the Act and to aid the European Commission in investigating alleged breaches of Articles 81 and 82 (old 85 and 86) under the Commission's procedures have more force than under earlier legislation and businesses will need to be aware of them. Then there is the new appeals procedure and the Competition Commission which will have a most important role in interpreting and administering the new Act.

It is very valuable to have the text of the Act with its schedules and of Articles 81 and 82 (old 85 and 86), the Office of Fair Trading Guidance Directions and the various forms of Notification, EC Commission notices on cooperation between national authorities and courts and the European Union, all included as appendices to the text.

This could have been either a very stodgy book or a mere tabulation. It is neither. It is a clear, readable exposition of an area of the law which (not only because of the very large penalties which can be imposed for breach of the Act) is about to become of much increased practical importance. The authors have done a valuable service to commerce and industry and to the allied professions in getting it out so early.

Slynn of Hadley

· Preface ·

This book appears in the middle of a revolution and perhaps on the eve of another.

The Competition Act 1998 will enter into full force, unless present expectations are confounded, on 1 March 2000. It will revolutionise competition law in the United Kingdom by adopting the EC model, deriving from Articles 81 and 82 (old Articles 85 and 86) of the EC Treaty.[1]

However, the United Kingdom has not gone as far as the EC Commission considers essential: the competition authorities in the United Kingdom (like those of six other Member States of the European Union) have not been given the power to apply Articles 81 and 82 directly. The reason for the United Kingdom's reticence is that the Commission currently has, and has hitherto wished to retain, a monopoly of exemption for agreements which satisfy the criteria contained in Article 81(3) (old Article 85(3)). This has been the principal stumbling block for the Commission's desires to see the national authorities relieving it of some of the burden of day-to-day case handling.

The Commission has now grasped the nettle and proposes radical changes to EC competition law. It has made a complete intellectual volte-face. The changes it now urges[2] would involve renunciation of its exemption monopoly, and the conversion of the Article 81(3) (old 85(3)) criteria from a basis for administrative exemption of notified agreements to a directly applicable legal standard. Contracting parties and complainants could then rely on Article 81(3) (old 85(3)) in any context, including proceedings before national competition authorities and national courts.

If this radical text from the Commission inspires an actual revolution, it may be that the Competition Act 1998 will turn out to have been merely a step along the road to a fully integrated set of rules

---

1 We adopt the numbering introduced, for better or for worse, by the Treaty of Amsterdam with effect from 1 May 1999; old and more familiar numbers are given in brackets.
2 In its White Paper on Modernisation of the rules implementing Articles 81 and 82 of the EC Treaty (old Articles 85 and 86), issued on 28 April 1999. This important document is available from the Commission's web site at the following address:
http://europa.eu.int/comm/dg04/entent/other.htm#dgiv_pdf_wb_modernisation.

stemming from that visionary document, the Treaty of Rome. An essential part of the reform which the Commission envisages would be the empowering of the UK competition authorities to apply Articles 81 and 82 directly. That would require a new Act of Parliament. The ability of the courts to apply Article 81(3) directly, on the other hand, would not require national legalisation: it would arise as a matter of law from the legal changes which the Commission proposes.

In the meantime, business in the United Kingdom will have to adapt to the harsher conditions which the Act will usher in. There is no practice under the Act yet, and the transitional period has only recently begun. The broad lines of the regime can be seen in the Act itself. But a certain amount of detail remains to be filled in. At the time of writing, we had available to us many of the Guidelines which the Office of Fair Trading proposes to issue, most in final form but some still in draft. The Procedural Rules for the Director General of Fair Trading are still awaiting approval from the Secretary of State and the important statutory instruments excluding vertical and land agreements from the Chapter I prohibition are still in draft. The rules of procedure for the Competition Commission Appeal Tribunals are no more than a gleam in the eye of their newly appointed President.

In some ways, then, it is premature to be writing a book about the Act. However, given the importance of the revolution it heralds, we hope that it will be useful for those who wish to ready themselves for the Act's introduction to have a survey of its aims and likely impact.

A word about gender. All references to "he" or "him" are intended, in more than a merely formal sense, to include "she" and "her". A number of the key players in government and in the relevant competition and other regulatory authorities are, or have been, women, and no doubt more will be in the near future. Furthermore the Act uses the masculine (to include the feminine of course) throughout, and we did not want to burden readers with numerous clumsy references to "he or she", "him or her".

We would like to thank all those who have helped us in the preparation of this book: Lord Slynn for kindly agreeing to write the Foreword; Gerald Barling QC and other colleagues at Brick Court Chambers for their comments on drafts and willingness to discuss ideas; our clerks, Ian Moyler and Mark Simpkin for their encouragement and patience; and last but far from least Jane Belford at Palladian without whom this book would not have been begun or finished.

James Flynn and Jemima Stratford
Brick Court Chambers
July 1999

· Table of Cases & Decisions ·

· Table of Statutes ·

Table of OFT Guidelines & DGFT Rules

· Table of EC Treaty Articles ·

· Table of EC Legislation ·

Chapter 1

· **Introduction** ·

1.1   **Overview of the Competition Act**

Competition law is the branch of the law that attempts to preserve and foster the benefits of a free market. Left to their own devices, players in the market may limit competition between themselves or stifle new forms of competition, to their own advantage rather than that of their customers and consumers. Competition law is the means by which the central authorities exercise some control over those market players.

The Competition Act 1998 ("the Act") is the most dramatic change to the competition law of the United Kingdom for a quarter of a century. In 1973, domestic law was affected by the passing of the Fair Trading Act 1973 and also by the United Kingdom's accession to the European common market, as most people then called what is now the European Union (EU). The EC Treaty competition rules were then in their infancy, but have grown in strength and confidence in the intervening years to become one of the most developed and powerful systems in the world. Competition law in the United Kingdom has not kept pace and various proposals to reform it did not secure sufficient support from the government of the day to reach the statute book.[1]

That position will be transformed by the Act. It is due to enter fully into force on 1 March 2000. Legal formalism and regulatory toothlessness is to be replaced by economic realism in assessment of practices and agreements and by sweeping investigatory powers for the regulators, backed by very significant fines for those who are shown to have crossed the line. Firms large and small need to be aware of the Act's provisions and to ensure that their business practices will withstand scrutiny. This Act will reach into every sector of the UK economy[2], and it is not only those who are engaged in "big business" who need fear it. It can apply to small, local markets just as much as to firms with national or international coverage.

---

1 See the section of this chapter on the origins of the Competition Act 1998 below.
2 The Act applies to the whole of the UK, that is, England and Wales, Scotland and Northern Ireland.

The system introduced by the Act is modelled very directly on the EC competition rules. European experience is a guide to the way the Act will apply in the United Kingdom, and the authorities are required to follow EC precedent closely.[3] Some discussion of the EC case law and practice is thus necessary for a proper understanding of the Act.

This book aims to explain the most important provisions of the Act, and to do so in a way that is comprehensible to those whose experience of the EC competition provisions is not extensive.

Structure of the Act

The Act is divided into four parts:

- Part I – Competition
- Part II – Investigations in relation to Articles 85 and 86
- Part III – Monopolies
- Part IV – Supplemental and Transitional.

There are 14 Schedules to the Act numbered as follows:

1 – Exclusions: Mergers and Concentrations

2 – Exclusions: Other Competition Scrutiny

3 – General Exclusions

4 – Professional Rules

5 – Notifications under Chapter I: Procedure

6 – Notifications under Chapter II: Procedure

7 – The Competition Commission

8 – Appeals

9 – Director's Rules

10 – Regulators

11 – Interpretation of Section 55 (confidentiality and disclosure of information)

12 – Minor and Consequential Amendments

---

3 See Chap 2 below on the European Dimension.

13 – Transitional Provisions and Savings

14 – Repeals and Revocations.

All of the Act, and most of the Schedules are reproduced at Appendix 1. However, this book will in the main explain and discuss the reforms which are contained in Part I of the Act and the associated Schedules, as it is this Part of the Act which introduces the new prohibition-based system of competition law into the UK.

Part I of the Act

Part I of the Act is divided into five Chapters. Chapters I and II are entitled "Agreements" and "Abuse of Dominant Position" respectively. They create the new prohibitions, based on Articles 81 and 82 of the EC Treaty (old Articles 85 and 86)[4], and are the core provisions of the new Act. The prohibitions are termed the Chapter I prohibition and the Chapter II prohibition in the Act, and those descriptions will also be used in this work.[5] The other three Chapters of Part I of the Act are:

- Chapter III – Investigation and Enforcement[6]
- Chapter IV – The Competition Commission and Appeals[7]
- Chapter V – Miscellaneous (including provisions on vertical agreements and land agreements,[8] on regulators[9] and on confidentiality[10])

Part II of the Act

Part II of the Act (sections 61-65) gives the High Court the power to issue a warrant authorising European Commission officials and any named officers of the Director General of Fair Trading (DGFT) to enter premises for the purposes of a Commission investigation relating to Article 81 or 82 of the EC Treaty (old Articles 85 and 86). It also creates offences for the intentional obstruction of any person in the exercise of powers under such a warrant. Part II of the Act is therefore

---

4 Arts 85 and 86 have been renumbered Arts 81 and 82 under the consolidated EC Treaty following ratification of the Treaty of Amsterdam. The new numbering system is used throughout this book, with some references to the old numbers appearing in brackets.

5 See Chaps 3 and 4 below.

6 See Chap 6 below.

7 See Chap 7 below.

8 See Chap 3 below.

9 See Chap 9 below.

10 See Chap 5 below.

concerned with UK courts and officials assisting the European Commission in the conduct of its competition investigations, rather than with the reform of domestic competition law. It is discussed further in Chapter 6 on Investigation and Enforcement below.

Part III of the Act

Part III of the Act (sections 66-69) makes certain amendments to the powers of the DGFT under the Fair Trading Act 1973 to conduct monopoly investigations. These amendments are explained in more detail in Chapter 4 on the Chapter II prohibition.

Part IV of the Act

The supplemental and transitional provisions contained in Part IV of the Act (sections 70-76) include section 71 which provides that the power to make regulations or orders under the Act shall be exercisable by statutory instrument, and section 72 in relation to the circumstances in which an officer of a company may be liable under the Act for offences committed by that company.[11] In a significant departure from the previous law, section 73 provides that the provisions of the Act bind the Crown. Thus, government departments may be party to infringements of the prohibitions, at least in circumstances where they may be said to be acting as "undertakings".[12] However, no criminal or other penalty can be imposed on the Crown and the Act does not apply to Her Majesty in her private capacity.[13] There are also restrictions on the DGFT's powers to enter Crown premises in connection with investigations of possible infringements of the Act or of the EC Treaty prohibitions.[14] However, public servants are not immune from criminal or other penalties.[15]

1.2   **Origins of the Competition Act**

Almost all commentators had been agreed for many years that the UK system of competition law was unduly complex and often ineffective.

---

11 See Chap 6 below.
12 See Chaps 3 and 4 below.
13 S 73(1) of the Act.
14 S 73(4)-(8).
15 S 73(2).

Various reform proposals were put forward by the governments of the day, which successively identified and sought to rectify the weaknesses of the existing legislation and procedure.

The reform proposals

Following the publication of a Green Paper in 1988, in 1989 the government published a White Paper entitled "Opening markets: new policy on restrictive trades practices."[16] This proposed far-reaching amendments to the Restrictive Trades Practices Act 1976, replacing existing legislation on anti-competitive agreements with a prohibition-based system similar to Article 81 (old Article 85).

In 1992 the Department of Trade and Industry (DTI) produced a consultation document on "Abuse of market power"[17], which discussed a number of possibilities for reform of the Fair Trading Act 1973 and the Competition Act 1980, both of which concerned the control of anti-competitive conduct. The DTI proposed the introduction of an Article 82-type (old Article 86) prohibition system, but in the spring of 1993 the government announced that it had decided not to proceed with radical reform of these statutes, but rather to introduce only some smaller procedural amendments to the existing system. At the time this announcement disappointed many, business people and lawyers alike.

There was no further progress until 1996, when the DTI published another consultation paper, this time entitled "Tackling cartels and the abuse of market power." This accepted the case for legislation based on Article 81 (old Article 85) in relation to anti-competitive agreements, but rejected any move towards an Article 82-type (old Article 86) prohibition approach for anti-competitive conduct. In the event, there was no room for a Bill in the parliamentary timetable.

Only three months after taking office in May 1997, the Labour Government published a draft Competition Bill in August 1997. The DTI consultation document introducing the Bill was called "A prohibition approach to anti-competitive agreements and abuse of dominant position", and the draft Bill set out two prohibitions based closely on both Articles 81 and 82 (old Articles 85 and 86) of the EC Treaty. It was this draft Bill which, following a period of consultation and extensive debate and amendment in parliament, received Royal Assent as the Competition Act 1998 on 9 November 1998.

---

16 Cm 727, 1989.
17 Cm 2100 (1992).

1.3   **Education and compliance programmes**

Education

The authorities responsible for introducing and for enforcing the new Act recognise that it marks a wholesale reform of UK competition law, and that a significant programme of education and training is required for businesses if infringements are to be kept to a minimum following the entry into force of the Chapter I and Chapter II prohibitions on 1 March 2000.

To this end, the Act itself requires the DGFT to publish general advice and information about the application of the Chapter I and Chapter II prohibitions, and about the enforcement of those prohibitions.[18] To comply with this requirement, the Office of Fair Trading (OFT) has consulted on and published a series of Guidelines on the Act.[19] These are entitled:

- The Major Provisions
- The Chapter I Prohibition
- The Chapter II Prohibition
- Market Definition
- Powers of Investigation
- Concurrent Application to Regulated Industries
- Transitional Arrangements
- Enforcement
- Trade Associations, Professions and Self-Regulating Bodies

The OFT has also promised Guidelines on:

- Assessment of Individual Agreements and Conduct (OFT 414)
- Assessment of Market Power (OFT 415)
- Mergers and Ancillary Restraints (OFT 416)
- The Application of the Competition Act in the Telecommunications Sector (OFT 417)
- Intellectual Property Rights (OFT 418)
- Vertical Agreements and Restraints (OFT 419)
- Land Agreements (OFT 420)
- General Economic Interest (OFT 421)

Some of these Guidelines are already available in draft and may be viewed on the OFT website.

---

18 S 52(1) of the Act.
19 The DGFT was required to consult on the Guidelines under s 52(6)-(8).

In addition, the DGFT has published Procedural Rules, directions governing notifications for early guidance, and Forms N and EG on which notifications to the DGFT must be made.[20] These are reproduced at Appendix 2. Reference to the OFT Guidelines and Rules will be made where relevant throughout this book. Copies of the Guidelines themselves may be obtained from the OFT (Field House, 15-25 Bream's Buildings, London EC4A 1PR, Tel: 0171 211 8000, Fax: 0171 211 8800) and are available on the OFT website at http://www.oft.gov.uk/.

The OFT Guidelines are quite detailed and legalistic in places, so the OFT has also undertaken to publish a series of short booklets which summarise the new legislation in straightforward language. These will be available from the OFT at the address above.

The OFT education programme is aimed at companies, businesses, trade associations and other representative bodies, and will include seminars which it is hoped will be organised by the CBI, the Institute of Directors, chambers of commerce, trade associations, and other similar bodies throughout the country. The OFT has stated that it aims to ensure both that more businesses will comply with the Act, and to encourage those who suffer from anti-competitive activity to complain to the OFT or the relevant sectoral regulators.[21] The OFT is also considering how to reach smaller businesses who may not be attracted to such seminars, and has put forward participation in selected trade fairs as one possibility.[22] A video on the Act, "Competition Matters", has been produced by the OFT, which may be used by businesses as part of their in-house training.[23]

Compliance programmes

The OFT is also actively encouraging businesses, particularly larger and more diverse organisations, to institute what are termed compliance programmes to educate staff at all levels about the Act on an on-going basis. The reasons for having a compliance programme include the level of fines which may be imposed for intentional or negligent infringement of the prohibitions (up to 10% of UK turnover), and the fact that the

---

20 See further Chap 5 on Notification below.
21 For example, speech by Mrs Margaret Bloom, Director of Competition Policy, OFT, to a conference organised by the Centre for the Law of the European Union, University College London, 10 September 1998, now published in *The Europeanisation of UK Competition Law* (eds Green and Robertson) (Hart 1999).
22 See, for example, speech by the DGFT, John S Bridgeman, available on the OFT website.
23 A copy of the video may be obtained from the OFT.

DGFT has stated that having a properly implemented, evaluated and regularly audited compliance programme is highly likely to reduce the level of financial penalty imposed where an infringement does occur.[24]

The OFT will not endorse particular compliance programmes, but it has outlined what it considers to be the essential elements of such a programme. These elements are derived from research which the OFT has conducted into existing compliance programmes, and from consultation with DGIV (the competition Directorate of the European Commission in Brussels) and with the Australian, Canadian and US competition authorities. The four key elements are:

(1) **Support of senior management.** Commitment to compliance by members of an organisation's senior management indicates the great importance which that organisation attaches to compliance, and should make more junior employees more receptive to training. This support should be expressed in writing, and preferably supported by a personal message to staff, perhaps by way of video where a business is sufficiently large to warrant this. If a company has a mission statement, this should include a commitment to compliance with all applicable competition laws, and the DGFT has suggested that directors and senior management might show active involvement by attending compliance training sessions with more junior members of staff.[25]

(2) **Appropriate compliance policy and procedures.** Compliance policy should be directed by the central objective of full compliance with relevant legislation, both by not engaging in anti-competitive behaviour and by refusing to take part in prohibited activities initiated by others. This policy should be clearly set out in written form, possibly in a compliance manual to be given to all staff, which must be updated regularly. This should set out the "do's and don'ts for compliance" in plain English. Employees may be required to sign an undertaking to conduct all business in a compliant manner as part of their contract of employment, and there should be the possibility of internal disciplinary measures against staff who engage in anti-competitive agreements or practices. A business must also have clear procedures for employees to follow where they wish to check the legality of a proposed agreement or course of action. For example, there could

---

24 Speech by John S Bridgeman, 9 March 1999, referred to above.
25 Speech by John S Bridgeman, *ibid.*

be a compliance officer appointed within each department, or a central compliance "help desk".

(3) **Training.** In addition to producing a compliance manual or handbook, a business should arrange training on the relevant law, policy and procedures for all staff who may be involved in activities affected by competition law. Such a training programme might target marketing and sales staff first, and then extend to all other business staff. It should form part of the induction programme for new staff, and "refresher courses" must be given at regular intervals. Training programmes may be provided "in-house" (possibly with the use of the OFT video and other commercially produced training videos), or they may be provided by outside experts such as law firms. Training is likely to be more effective if it includes workshop sessions and case studies, and the OFT have highlighted the possibility of arranging a mock investigative raid to alert staff in a vivid manner to the risks of anti-competitive practices.[26]

(4) **Evaluation.** It is not enough to put a compliance programme in place and leave it to run; it must be evaluated for effectiveness and modified as necessary. Such evaluation could include informal sessions in which employee's knowledge and understanding of the relevant law and procedures are tested, and occasional unannounced audits of certain parts of the business to check for actual or potential infringements.

A compliance programme containing all of the above four elements is likely to prove fairly costly for a business, particularly during its early stages. Nonetheless, the DGFT and OFT are strongly urging businesses to consider the long term savings and benefits of such a programme: avoiding time-consuming investigations; the possibility of significant financial penalties; and adverse publicity where an infringement is found.

1.4 Structure of this book

The book begins by looking at the mechanisms which the Act uses to achieve consistency and harmony with European competition law (Chapter 2). We then describe the two central prohibitions on anti-

---

26 For example, speech by Mrs Margaret Bloom, Director of Competition Policy, OFT, to a conference organised by the Centre for the Law of the European Union, University College London, 10 September 1998 now published in *op cit*, fn 21.

competitive agreements (Chapter 3) and anti-competitive conduct by dominant firms (Chapter 4). Chapters 5 and 6 deal respectively with notifications to the DGFT and with investigations and enforcement. We then describe the new system for appeals to the Competition Commission (Chapter 7). The transitional provisions which apply pending the full introduction of the prohibitions are described in Chapter 8. Finally, Chapter 9 explains how the Act will impact on the regulated industries (telecommunications, gas, electricity, water and the railways).

Chapter 2

· The European Dimension ·

2.1   Introduction

The inspiration for the prohibition system on which the Act is based came from Europe. It is a key feature of the Act that it strives for consistency and harmony with the EC system. This chapter looks at the mechanisms the Act employs to achieve those objectives.

The Act does not implement Articles 81 and 82 EC (old Articles 85 and 86) into the law of the United Kingdom: it sets up a parallel universe. More accurately perhaps, the aim is to replicate the EC system at the UK level, much as settlers and missionaries recreate the legal and societal structures of the mother country or church. Tools are in place to ensure that the UK derivative offshoot does not mutate and that it keeps pace with developments in the original.

The first part of this chapter deals with section 60, the mechanism in the Act designed to ensure consistency of substantive outcome; the second part considers how conflicts will be avoided when jurisdiction overlaps.

2.2   Section 60: keeping faith with the EC Treaty

Section 60, referred to as the "consistency" or "guiding principles" clause, is at once the most creative and the most problematic provision in the Act. It has given rise to more commentary and criticism than any other section, and it is likely that it will also give rise to the most difficult and challenging issues in legal proceedings under the Act.

The purpose of section 60

It begins with a statement of its aim, itself an indication that the section is to be given a "purposive" interpretation (*i.e.* one which gives effect to the stated aim, overlooking textual niceties if necessary). Section 60(1) provides:

> "The purpose of this section is to ensure that so far as is possible (having regard to any relevant differences between the provisions concerned), questions arising under this Part[1] in relation to competition within the United Kingdom are dealt with in a manner which is consistent with the treatment of corresponding questions arising in Community law in relation to competition within the Community."

The lawyer's eye dwells momentarily on the phrases "so far as possible", "relevant differences", "questions ... in relation to competition" and "corresponding questions". Potential arguments suggest themselves as to where the limits of possibility are to be found or whether a difference is always a relevant difference.

Areas of actual difference may be found both in the underlying objectives of the prohibitions and at the textual level. An example of each type of difference is respectively:

- the treatment of vertical agreements (at present caught by EC law, but excluded under the Act which does not have the market integration imperative of the EC Treaty); and
- the wording of the Chapter II prohibition compared with that of Article 82 (old Article 86) (section 18 uses the words "conduct which amounts to" the abuse of a dominant position, which words are not found in Article 82).

It may be doubted whether those differences are relevant differences for the purposes of section 60 such that a court would decide to interpret the Act differently from the way in which the EC provisions had been applied on the same point. In point of fact, despite the possibilities which section 60 suggests, it seems unlikely that there will be any substantial difference in the way the Act and the EC rules are applied and interpreted.

Of more interest perhaps is the meaning of the phrase "questions ... in relation to competition". Does the formulation concern pure competition issues to the exclusion of other EC principles relevant to the determination of competition issues?

The government made its position clear: section 60 is intended to bring in the general principles of Community law as well as the principles used to construe Articles 81 and 82 (old Articles 85 and 86) themselves.[2] Such general principles, not referred to in the EC Treaty

---

1 *i.e.* Part I of the Act (ss 1-60), the part bringing in the EC-style prohibitions.
2 This was clearly stated by Lord Simon of Highbury, Minister for competitiveness in Europe who was in charge of the Bill's progress through the House of Lords, in debates on 25 November 1997 (Hansard cols 960 and 961) and 5 March 1998 (Hansard cols 1364 and 1365).

but read into its application by the European Court (ECJ) as matters of common tradition to the Member States, include, for example, the principle of equality before the law and the principle of proportionality (which could be relevant to the setting of a fine commensurate with the gravity of the infringement). More generally, the European Court has insisted on standards of procedural fairness in situations where the Community institutions have power to take decisions affecting legal rights, and especially where there are financial sanctions. For example, it is axiomatic that a person should have the opportunity to comment on material which will form the basis of a decision adversely affecting his interests.

Thus it is plain that importing EC standards into the interpretation of the UK prohibitions will make inroads into the type of decisions which can be taken and the procedure which can be followed in arriving at them. Lord Simon in the House of Lords hazarded a distinction between "high-level" principles and the detail of the procedure.

Undoubtedly this is a valid distinction. It can readily be seen that the European Court's jurisprudence requires, for example, that there should be a fair hearing, not necessarily one which in all respects resembles the type of hearing which the EC Commission affords. However, it will not always be obvious how the distinction should be drawn in practice. As will be explained in later chapters of this book, the procedure which the Director General of Fair Trading (DGFT) intends to follow will in some respects be quite different from that prescribed for the European Commission in Regulation 17[2a] and other such texts. The difference as such will not be a legitimate basis for complaint by those being investigated, but they will no doubt be alert to the possibility that the difference gives rise to a divergence in standards of legal protection which the European Court would not countenance.

The section 60 obligation

Having set out its purpose in sub-section (1), section 60 then states the substantive obligation. In short, it is to secure consistency with the European Court's case law and to have regard to relevant decisions of the European Commission.

The obligation is said to apply to "the court". That term is defined[3] to include any court or tribunal, which clearly embraces the Competition

---

2a Council Reg 17 of 1962 (JO 204/62, [1959-62] OJ Spec. Ed. 57.
3   In s 60(5).

Commission Appeal Tribunals, the new body set up under the Act to hear appeals from decisions of the DGFT.[4] The obligation of consistency is also applied to the DGFT and the sectoral regulators[5] by section 60(4).

The section 60 obligation thus does not bind the Secretary of State who, as will be seen throughout this book, has extensive order-making powers under the Act. This seems both logical and unobjectionable in principle and law, in that it is for the UK legislator to define the scope of the Act and the extent to which it coheres with EC law.

The consistency obligation is set out in section 60(2) as follows:

> "At any time when the court determines a question arising under this Part[6], it must act (so far as is compatible with the provisions of this Part and whether or not it would otherwise be required to do so[7]) with a view to securing that there is no inconsistency between –
>
> (a) the principles applied, and decision reached, by the court in determining that question; and
>
> (b) the principles laid down by the Treaty and the European Court, and any relevant decision of that Court, as applicable at that time in determining any corresponding question arising in Community law."

Section 60(3) continues:

> "The court must, in addition, have regard to any relevant decision or statement of the Commission."

Possible differences from EC law

As with section 60(1), it is striking that the section 60(2) consistency obligation is phrased with slight equivocation: "so far as is compatible" and "with a view to securing" (rather than, for example, "the court shall ensure") in addition to the double negative of "no inconsistency". It may be doubted whether in practice this hedging about will achieve very much. Inconsistency of outcome with EC law will surely be a valid basis for an appeal under the Act. It will not be enough to show that the DGFT or the Appeal Tribunal tried to secure consistency or acted with consistency in view: they must achieve it, and the circumstances in

---

4 For appeals, see Chap 7 below.

5 For the powers and responsibilities under the Act of sectoral regulators, see Chap 9 below.

6 See fn 1 above.

7 In other words, the obligation goes beyond that arising under s 2(1) of the European Communities Act 1972, a statutory duty to recognise the EC law concepts of direct applicability and direct effect.

which it will be compatible with the Act to achieve a divergent result are likely to be few and rare.

A relatively minor example of a clear difference between the Act and the Court of Justice's case law is the attribution of privilege under the Act to advice from in-house lawyers, remedying what is widely seen as an injustice in the EC system which requires the advice to have come from external independent lawyers if privilege is to be attracted.[8] Clearly, the Act requires documents emanating from the in-house lawyer to be withheld from the DGFT's investigators and bars them from making any use of the material if they should accidentally come across it (for example, such advice may contain the only reference which the investigators have seen to a cartel agreement). Section 60 plainly does not have the result of disapplying that rule in the Act on the ground that EC law would not treat the material as privileged. But the real question on any appeal from the eventual decision taken at the conclusion of his investigation is whether the DGFT applied the Chapter I prohibition consistently with the way in which the EC Commission would have applied Article 81 (old Article 85), albeit making use of different evidence.

A tool for consistency

It seems more profitable to concentrate on the effect of section 60 as a tool for consistency, rather than on its limited potential for driving a wedge between the UK prohibitions and their EC prototypes. The significant overall effect is that it is not possible to understand the prohibitions without some understanding of the effect of the Court of Justice's case law in the interpretation of Articles 81 and 82 (old Articles 85 and 86, as they are called in all the relevant case law to date).

A simple example is the fact that, although the prohibitions are phrased in absolute terms, the ECJ has ruled that only agreements which have a significant or appreciable effect on competition fall within the scope of the Treaty. The Court is most unlikely to resile from that reading of the Treaty, and it would have been the easiest thing in the world for the appreciabilty standard to have been written into the Chapter I prohibition. That course has not been chosen. Readers of the Act are presumed to know their EC case law. The use of the phrase "as applicable at that time" in section 60(2)(b) shows also that developments in the case law have to be taken into account.

---

8 Case 155/79 *A M & S Europe* v *Commission* [1982] ECR 1575.

Developments in the case law of the Court concerning the competition provisions of the European Coal and Steel Community (ECSC) Treaty do not have to be followed, as section 59(1) defines "Treaty" as the treaty establishing the European Community, *i.e.* the EC Treaty. The ECSC provisions are certainly different from the EC provisions, but judgments relating to the ECSC provisions have on occasion blazed the trail for their EC cousins. They can, of course, be cited to the court in the usual way where they contain indications relevant to an open point. Similarly, the obligation relates only to judgments of the ECJ and not to opinions of the Advocates General. This will not and should not stop parties from citing those Opinions in proceedings under the Act.

An illustration which combines both these points is the important opinion of Advocate General Van Gerven in an ECSC case, *Banks*[9], in which he discusses topics such as the possibility of claiming damages for breach of competition law which do not receive detailed consideration elsewhere in the Court's case law to date.

The right to claim damages?

That precise issue (whether the prohibitions under the Act give rise to the possibility of civil damages) is only dealt with in an indirect way in the Act. The Restrictive Trade Practices Act (RTPA) gave an explicit basis for an action in breach of statutory duty for those affected by a contravention of the duty not to implement agreements which should have been registered with the DGFT.[10] No such provision is to be found in the Act.

There is an oblique reference in section 58 to court proceedings which concern an alleged infringement of the Chapter I or Chapter II prohibition, but which are brought otherwise than by the DGFT. In such court proceedings, findings of fact made by the DGFT following a notification or investigation are binding on the parties (unless the court otherwise directs[11]) if no appeal has been brought against the decision in

---

9 Case C-128/92 *H J Banks & Co v British Coal Corporation* [1994] ECR I-1209.

10 See s 35 of the RTPA. This provision had been relatively little used, but oddly is enjoying something of an Indian summer in a number of cases currently pending before the High Court.

11 No hint is given as to the circumstances in which a court might decide to make such a direction, and there is no apparent limitation on its ability to do so. It is envisaged that the DGFT may give the court assistance: s 58(3). There is a clear parallel between this possibility and the offer which the Commission makes in its Notice on co-operation with national courts to assist them in competition cases – the Notice is discussed later in this chapter and is set out in Appendix 4.

the time prescribed[12] or if the finding of fact has been upheld in the course of such an appeal. There is no express reference in section 58 or elsewhere in the Act to such proceedings concerning or including a claim for damages.

And yet there is no doubt that it is intended that the Act should give rise to civil actions. The government's Explanatory and Financial Memorandum, issued when the draft Bill was first published, stated that savings from the abolition of the Restrictive Practices Court would be offset by additional workload on the courts arising from private actions for civil damages and appeals from decisions of the Appeal Tribunals. There are also several parliamentary statements by government ministers affirming that civil actions for breach of the prohibitions were intended.[13]

There was considerable criticism of the lack of an explicit base for such action in the Bill as it passed through Parliament. The response illustrates why the government was coy about including such a basis and how it considers the issue is to be dealt with. At a relatively late stage, the types of decision to be taken into account under sub-paragraphs (2) and (3) of section 60 were expanded to include decisions as to "the civil liability of an undertaking for harm caused by its infringement of Community law".[14] In other words, the intention is that the scope for bringing civil actions under the Act should be the same as that under Articles 81 and 82 (old Articles 85 and 86).

While this is no doubt a sensible aim, and it is both desirable in principle and policy that civil actions will be brought, and beyond question that the courts will entertain them, it is still legitimate to question the rather dogmatic approach which has been taken. There are two obvious difficulties with it.

(1) No one actually knows what the EC position is. The European Court has not yet handed down any decisions directly on the issue. Indeed, its case law is to the effect that the civil law consequences of breach of Article 81 (old Article 85) are a matter for national law.[15] Section 60 thus seems to set up a rather sterile double renvoi.

---

12 For appeals, see Chap 7 below. No time has yet been prescribed within which an appeal must be brought. The ECJ has laid down a rule that a party who could have sought the annulment of a Commission decision in a direct action under Art 230 (old Art 173) may not subsequently raise the issue of its validity in national proceedings: see Case C-188/92 *TWD Textilwerke Deggendorf GmbH* v *Germany* [1994] ECR I-833.

13 See in particular Hansard 25 November 1997 and 18 July 1998.

14 S 60(6)(b).

15 See in particular Case 319/82 *Kerpen* & *Kerpen* [1983] ECR 4173.

(UK law looks to EC law for the answer, but EC law refers the question back to national law.)

(2) Whatever the Court's case law may say now or in the future about the consequences of a breach of Articles 81 or 82 (old Articles 85 and 86), the basis for such consequences in Community law is the direct effect of those articles. Direct effect is a concept which is difficult to apply within a single national legal system. It is usually allied with the Community principle of primacy or supremacy to achieve the result that, provided only that the Community norm is sufficiently precise and unconditional, it can be relied on by the individual against inconsistent domestic law. Bizarre consequences will ensue if protection in respect of infringements of the domestic prohibitions is made to prevail over "inconsistent" rules of English law. This might mean, for example, that the rule against pleading one's own illegality would have to give way. Such a result would go further than would be required in respect of a breach of Article 81 (old Article 85) since EC law leaves the civil law consequences of the nullity of affected obligations to be determined by the national court.

Parties will thus be left in some insecurity as to the appropriate basis on which to bring claims for damages (or other relief such as injunctive relief). Community law claims were usually pleaded as claims for breach of statutory duty (relying on the European Communities Act and dicta of Lord Diplock in *Garden Cottage Foods*[16]) or, in the more recent practice, simply (or alternatively) as claims relying directly on the Treaty articles. In a purely domestic context, without an explicit basis in the legislation for bringing such a claim, it is far from obvious that a competitor is a class of person who the Act intends should benefit from special protection under the Act, in particular since it both specifies the nature of the penalty which should be imposed for breaches of the prohibitions and sets up a detailed review mechanism for the administrative decisions imposing such penalties. Under normal English law principles, then, it is not clear that the courts would construe the Act as conferring the right to bring private damages actions on those alleging injury as a result of breach of the prohibitions.

Clearly, however, it is the courts' duty to find a way through. Whatever the formal or procedural basis of the claim under the Act, the courts will no doubt derive assistance from their own decisions in

---

16 [1984] 1 AC 130.

relation to the availability of damages and injunctions for breaches of Articles 81 and 82 (old Articles 85 and 86).[17] There has been no final award of damages in any case in the United Kingdom under either Article 81 or Article 82, but it is generally recognised that such damages are available in principle.[17a]

A solid line of cases in England established a principle that, whatever might be the position of third parties, the parties to an agreement prohibited under Article 81 could not sue each other for damages in respect of their own performance of that agreement.[18] That issue has now been referred to the European Court of Justice by the Court of Appeal.[19]

Status of European Commission decisions

It should be noted that the obligation of consistency requires the authorities and the courts in effect to follow European Court decisions, but only to "have regard" to decisions and statements of the European Commission (section 60(3)). The Commission cannot pronounce definitively on the law[20], so this seems an appropriate recognition of its place in the hierarchy. Furthermore, its decisions are taken on the basis of the facts and circumstances of individual cases, so can only be of illustrative rather than precedent value.

The reference to statements means most obviously the statements which the Commission makes to explain its policy. These may take the form of notices published in the *Official Journal* or comments made in the annual report on competition policy. The DGFT takes a straitened view of his obligation under section 60(3), saying that it is "limited to decisions or statements which have the authority of the European Commission as a whole".[21] The status of other "statements" of the Commission, such as those made in comfort letters or calls for comments on individual notifications under Article 19(3) of Regulation 17 remains to be seen.

---

17   See *Practitioners' Handbook of EC Law* (Trenton, 1998), Chap 12. The EC Commission procured a survey of national decision on Arts 81 and 82 (old Arts 85 and 86): see *The Application of Articles 85 & 86 of the EC Treaty by National Courts in the Member States* (European Commission, Brussels, 1997).

17a   Indeed, significant sums have been paid in a number of cases to settle claims made under Arts 81 and 82 (old Arts 85 and 86).

18   See two Court of Appeal judgments, *Gibbs Mew* v *Gemmell* [1998] EuLR 588 and *Trent Taverns* v *Sykes* [1999] EuLR 492 (CA) in which the previous authorities are summarised.

19   *Crehan* v *Courage Ltd and others* (27 May 1999, unreported).

20   As it itself recognises: all its interpretative notices include a reference to their being subject to contrary rulings by the ECJ.

21   The Competition Act 1998: The Major Provisions, (OFT 400), para 6.2.

It should also be noted that the reference to decisions and statements knowingly excludes wider legislative measures such as regulations, whether of the Commission or the Council. The most significant use of regulations under the EC Treaty has been in connection first with procedural matters, where, as already noted, there is no intention of following the EC model to the letter, and secondly to bring in the block exemptions from the prohibition in Article 81(1) (old Article 85(1)). In relation to block exemptions, the Act achieves consistency, not directly through section 60, but by the neat device of the "parallel" exemption (described in Chapter 3 below).

Article 234 references

A final question which is raised by section 60 is whether it will be possible to refer questions of interpretation of relevant EC law issues to the European Court of Justice under Article 234 of the EC Treaty (old Article 177). That question breaks into two. The first is whether the European Court would accept a reference at all, given that the Act is not implementing EC law but merely setting up a parallel system. If it would or might, the second issue is which of the agencies involved in the system set up by the Act might be able to make such a reference.

Will references be accepted by the ECJ?

The European Court has vacillated somewhat over the years in its case law on accepting references on questions of EC law where the national system has in some way pledged that it will align itself on the EC rules even where not obliged to do so.[22] The key to the European Court's willingness to accept such references seems to be whether the national court is obliged to apply the ruling on EC law or is free to take a different view.

In *Kleinwort Benson*[23], the European Court was asked by the English Court of Appeal for an interpretation of the Brussels Convention on mutual recognition and enforcement of judgments, but refused to answer the question referred. That was because the national proceedings involved allocation of jurisdiction between England and Scotland, an

---

22 So has the position of the British Government: at a stage when competition law reform was on the Conservative Government's agenda, it seemed that the Government did not want the legislation to give rise to the possibility of references under Art 234 (old Art 177).

23 Case C-346/93 *Kleinwort Benson v City of Glasgow District Council* [1995] ECR I-615.

internal matter governed by the Civil Jurisdiction and Judgments Act 1982 which only required the national court to "have regard"[24] to the ECJ's case law under the Convention itself.

In later cases, despite highly persuasive opinions from Advocate General Jacobs to the effect that national law and Community law are never the same and that the Court should not accept references where the national court is not intending to apply Community law, the Court has said that in principle it is for national courts to decide when a reference on a point of Community law would be helpful to it. Such cases may include situations where the national court is dealing with a purely internal situation to which the national legislator has decided to apply the same treatment as it would receive under Community law.[25]

More recently, the Court had to consider a question on Article 82 (old Article 86) referred by an Austrian court specifically competent to apply national competition law. The relevant provision of Austrian law had a completely different test for dominance from that contained in Article 82 and a completely different enforcement mechanism; however, the provision on abuse was very precisely modelled on Article 82. On this occasion, Advocate General Jacobs recommended to the Court that it should accept the reference on the basis that the referring body, being a court, was entitled and obliged to apply Article 82. The Court did not say explicitly on what basis it was prepared to give an interpretation of Article 82, but stated that the national court might wish to avoid conflict between its domestic competition law and Community competition law. The Court also suggested that it would not accept a reference if it was clear that Community law could have no application to the facts of the case before the national court.[26]

Avoidance of conflict might be said to be the main aim of section 60, but the possibility of it occurring through relevant differences in the respective systems is explicit. Despite its generosity in cases such as *Bronner*, *Leur-Bloem* and *Giloy*, therefore, there must remain a possibility that the qualifying words in section 60 would make the European Court nervous about accepting a reference in connection with proceedings under the Act. The situation might be different if the referring national court might also be applying the EC provisions to the facts of the case.

---

24 Incidentally, the phrase now used in s 60(3) in relation to Commission decisions and statements, as has already been seen.

25 See Case C-28/95 *Leur-Bloem v Inspecteur der Belastingsdienst* [1997] ECR I-4161 and Case C-130/95 *Giloy v HzA Frankfurt am Main* [1997] ECR I-4291, in which Advocate General Jacobs delivered a single opinion.

26 Case C-7/97 *Bronner v Mediaprint*, judgment of 26 November 1998 (not yet reported in ECR).

Who may make a reference?

As to the bodies which might refer, there is of course no doubt that the courts may do so. It seems most likely that the Competition Commission Appeal Tribunals will also be able to make references, although there might be a question under the *Bronner* rationale as to whether they were empowered to apply EC law directly.[27]

Lastly, there has been speculation as to whether the DGFT (and the sectoral regulators) could refer questions, given that recent case law of the European Court may indicate a relaxation of its attitude to references from administrative bodies.[28] The Minister left the issue open in Parliament.[29] In practice, it seems unlikely that the DGFT would wish to make references, so the issue may not be tested.

2.3   Relationship between proceedings under the Act and EC proceedings

The jurisdictional threshold

In practice, many competition cases in the United Kingdom are likely to engage both the prohibitions under the Act and Articles 81 and/or 82 of the EC Treaty (old Articles 85 and 86). This is because the jurisdictional threshold for applicability of Articles 81 and 82 is whether the agreement or conduct in question may "affect trade between Member States", and the EC authorities (both the Commission and the Court) have given a broad interpretation to this phrase. Thus, in an early case on Article 81, the European Court of Justice ruled that effect on trade meant only that:

> "the agreement in question may have an influence, **direct or indirect, actual or potential**, on the pattern of trade between Member States."[30] (emphasis added)

This requirement is met if the agreement alters the normal flow or pattern of trade, or causes trade to develop differently from the way it

---

27 Because their jurisdiction is conferred by the Act, and confined to appeals from decisions of the DGFT made under the Act: see Chap 7 below. Conversely, if Advocate General Jacobs intended to suggest that a national tribunal empowered to hear competition appeals must, as a matter of Community law, apply Community law, further interesting questions might arise as to how the Appeal Tribunals might do so and what would be the effect, especially in areas of divergence between the UK and the EC approaches.

28 See Case C-54/96 *Dorch Consult* [1997] ECR I-4961 where the Court accepted a reference from the Federal Supervisory Board for Public Procurement, against the advice of Advocate General Tesauro.

29 See Lord Simon of Highbury in Hansard 25 November 1997.

30 Case 56/65 *Société Technique Minière* v *Maschinenbau Ulm GmbH* [1966] ECR 235.

would have in the absence of the agreement[31], or where conduct brings about an alteration in the structure of competition within the EU.[32] An effect on inter-state trade may be presumed where the agreement or conduct in question relates directly to cross-border transactions, and may be found even where the parties concerned are all situated in one Member State such as the United Kingdom.[33] For this reason, persons concerned with whether a particular agreement or conduct infringes the prohibitions under the Act, should also begin by considering whether Articles 81 or 82 (old Articles 85 and 86) apply.

Where may competition law issues be decided?

There are four possible fora in which competition law issues may fall to be decided, two for EC law and two for domestic law under the Act.

Law relied upon	Forum	Nature of proceedings	Appeals available
EC law	European Commission	Notification or complaint	To CFI and ECJ in Luxembourg (Arts 229/230 – old Arts 172/173)
EC law	National courts	reliance on Arts 81/82 (old Arts 85/86) in civil action (either offensively – "sword" or defensively – "shield")	To CA/HL. Possibility of reference to Luxembourg (Art 234 – old Art 177)
The Act	OFT	Notification or complaint	To Competition Commission, and to CA/HL on points of law. Possibility of reference to Luxembourg (Art 234)
The Act	National courts	reliance on Chapters I/II in civil action (either offensively – "sword" or defensively – "shield")	To CA/HL. Possibility of reference to Luxembourg (Art 234)

---

31 See, for example, Case 71/74 *Frubo* v *Commission* [1975] ECR 563.
32 Cases 6 & 7/73 *Commercial Solvents* v *Commission* [1974] ECR 223.
33 See, for example, Case 8/72 *Cementhandelaren* v *Commission* [1972] ECR 977 (Art 81 – old Art 85); Case 322/81 *Michelin* v *Commission* [1983] ECR 3461 (Art 82 – old Art 86).

Where the agreement or conduct in question has the necessary effect on trade between Member States, so that its legality could be determined under both EC law and under the Act, it is important to understand the relationship between these possible proceedings. Careful strategic and tactical decisions may be required as to where, and using what law, it would be best to litigate, notify or complain. Such decisions may have important practical consequences on the speed and outcome of any proceedings. Of course it may be possible in a particular case for a party to rely upon both domestic and EC competition law simultaneously in a civil action. However, for the sake of clarity, this analysis principally considers the effect of bringing EC competition proceedings on subsequent proceedings under the Act.

Effect of EC competition proceedings on proceedings under the Act

The supremacy principle

The European Court of Justice has stressed on a number of occasions the importance of avoiding inconsistent decisions arising from the concurrent application to a particular agreement or conduct of both Community law and domestic competition law. If there is a potential conflict between domestic competition law and EC competition law, the basic rule is that Community law must take precedence.[34] This principle is sometimes termed the "supremacy rule".

However, the simultaneous application of stricter national competition law is not necessarily in conflict with Community competition law and policy. The issue is whether such application impairs the effectiveness and uniformity of Community competition rules.[35] The parameters and practical effect of the supremacy principle have still not been fully worked out in the case law of the ECJ. In particular, the question as to whether an agreement granted exemption under Article 81(3) (old Article 85(3)) may nonetheless subsequently be made subject to a national prohibition has not been conclusively determined.[36]

---

34 Case 14/68 *Walt Wilhelm v Bundeskartellamt* [1969] ECR 1, paras 3-9.
35 Cases 253/78 etc *Procureur de la République v Giry and Guerlain* [1980] ECR 2327.
36 In two recent Opinions, Advocate General Tesauro stated that an agreement benefitting from an Art 81(3) (old Art 85(3)) exemption could not be prohibited on the basis of more restrictive national provisions, save possibly in exceptional circumstances: Case C-266/93 *Bundeskartellamt v Volkswagen and VAG Leasing* [1995] ECR I-3477 at 3502; Case C-70/93 *BMW v ALD* [1995] ECR I-3439 at 3456. The judgment of the ECJ in those cases did not address this question, and so there is still no definitive ruling from the ECJ on the point.

The Act has, of course, been drafted with the supremacy principle in mind, and a number of its provisions and procedures are designed to ensure consistency with Community law rulings in the same case. These provisions are referred to in detail below. However, it is relevant to note at this point that section 10(5) of the Act purports to give the DGFT the power to cancel or to impose conditions or obligations subject to which a parallel exemption is to have effect. An agreement benefits from a parallel exemption where it benefits from an Article 81(3) (old Article 85(3)) exemption granted by the European Commission (whether by way of individual or block exemption)[37], and thus it is questionable whether the DGFT may in fact exercise this power consistently with Community law as it stands. However, the Commission's recent papers on Vertical Restraints[37a] and on the Modernisation of Articles 81 and 82[37b] suggest that national authorities could be empowered to withdraw the benefits of a block exemption in certain circumstances.

The Co-operation Notices

Although the national courts of all the Member States, including the UK courts, may apply and enforce Articles 81 and 82 (old Articles 85 and 86) in domestic civil proceedings, only the European Commission has the competence to decide whether an agreement is deserving of an exemption under Article 81(3).[38] This centralised notification system and exclusive jurisdiction of the Commission in relation to Article 81(3) exemptions have led over the years to the Competition Directorate (DGIV) becoming increasingly over-burdened and facing an unacceptable backlog of cases. This so-called "enforcement gap" which has developed provided the main catalyst for the Commission to issue the two Co-operation Notices: the Notice on Co-operation between national courts and the Commission in applying Articles 85 and 86 [new Articles 81 and 82] of the EEC Treaty[39] and the Notice on Co-operation between national competition authorities and the Commission in handling cases falling within the scope of Articles 85 and 86 [new Articles 81 and 82] of the EC Treaty.[40] The same concerns regarding the "enforcement gap" have formed part of the impetus behind the Commission's recent proposals for modernisation of Articles 81 and 82.[40a]

---

37 See further Chap 3 below.
37a OJ 1998 C365/3.
37b Communication 99/027 of 28 April 1999.
38 Art 9(1) of Reg 17 of 1962 (JO 204/62, [1959-62] OJ Spec. Ed. 57).
39 OJ 1993 C39/6, reproduced at Appendix 4.
40 OJ 1997 C313/3, reproduced at Appendix 4.
40a Communication 99/027 of 28 April 1999.

The Notice on Co-operation with national courts outlines the powers of the Commission under Articles 81 and 82 (old Articles 85 and 86), with particular reference to the procedures established under Regulation 17.[41] It then stresses the way in which those powers must be exercised in the light of the limited resources which are at the Commission's disposal.[42] This part of the Notice is derived from a decision of the Court of First Instance (CFI) in *Automec v Commission (No2)*.[43] In that case, the Commission had refused to proceed with a complaint made to it as it considered there to be insufficient "Community interest", and proceedings were pending before the Italian courts which were capable of granting the remedy sought. The CFI approved the stance taken by the Commission, and this decision therefore made clear that the Commission is entitled to prioritise its case load so as to refuse to investigate a case if there is a lack of Community interest in pursuing the investigation.[44]

Part IV of the Notice on Co-operation with national courts is largely derived from the points of principle which emerge from the decision of the ECJ in *Stergios Delimitis v Henniger Brau AG*.[45] The Notice encourages national courts to stay proceedings if the Commission has already begun an examination of the agreement or practice at issue in the case before the national court. A national court should pass judgment on whether an agreement does or does not infringe Article 81 (old Article 85) only if the matter is absolutely clear and gives rise to no doubt. In order to try to assist national courts, the Notice also encourages them to consult with the Commission concerning the existence and timetable of any administrative proceedings, the Commission's view of particular arguments advanced by the parties, and factual information. Any answers given by the Commission to a request for factual information (for example, information on the situation in other Member States, or market analysis resulting from earlier Commission investigations) cannot be definitive and is therefore of limited value. In practice, the UK courts generally prefer to use the Article 234 (old Article 177) reference procedure for the determination of legal issues, and to rely on the parties to produce expert evidence of economic issues.

---

41 OJ 1997 C313/3, reproduced at Appendix 4.
42 *Ibid*, Part III.
43 Case T-24/90 [1992] ECR II-2223.
44 The concept of "lack of Community interest" was subsequently affirmed by the ECJ: Case C-91/95 *Tremblay v Commission* [1996] ECR I-5547. The term "Community interest" is not defined with qualitative or quantitative precision (cf "Community dimension" under the Merger Reg 4064/89).
45 Case C-234/89 [1991] ECR I-935.

The more recent Notice on Co-operation with national competition authorities represents a further Commission initiative aimed at more efficient enforcement of EC competition law. It is intended to complement the Notice on Co-operation with national courts, and resulted from recognition that some undertakings within the EU were reluctant to have recourse to the courts for the enforcement of their competition law rights, and preferred to rely upon the actions of the public administration. This Notice addresses the role of the Member States and·of the Community (Part I), lays down guidelines on case allocation as between the Commission and the national competition authorities, and considers the manner in which it will co-operate with national competition authorities depending on whether the Commission or the national authority which initiates proceedings first (Parts III and IV).

The Notice on Co-operation with national competition authorities contains an unambiguous plea by the Commission for national competition authorities to be empowered to apply Articles 81 and 82 (old Articles 85 and 86) directly.[46] The United Kingdom has not taken the step urged by the Commission. The Act does not give the DGFT the power to apply and enforce EC law directly, although it does contain some provisions designed to assist the Commission in their investigation and enforcement of Articles 81 and 82. These include section 55(3)(a)(ii) which enables the DGFT to disclose to the Commission information gained by investigation under the Act, and Part II of the Act which gives the High Court the power to issue a warrant authorising Commission officials and any named officers of the DGFT to enter premises for the purposes of a Commission investigation relating to Articles 81 or 82.[47]

Compatibility provisions in the Act

The Act contains a number of provisions which reflect the supremacy principle and the procedural practices which have developed from the Co-operation Notices. Section 60, which has been discussed above, is itself in part a recognition of these principles. The following table summarises the most important of the additional compatibility provisions in the Act. They are all explained in greater detail in subsequent chapters.

---

46 See, in particular, para 15 of the Notice at Appendix 4. Currently the national competition authorities which apply Arts 81 and 82 (old Arts 85 and 86) (usually alongside their national competition law) are: Belgium, France, Germany, Greece, Italy, the Netherlands, Portugal and Spain.
47 See further Chap 6 on Investigation and Enforcement below.

Section of the Act	Effect of the provision
10(1)(a)	Agreement benefits from a parallel exemption from the Chapter I prohibition if it falls within an EC block exemption
10(2)	Agreement benefits from a parallel exemption from the Chapter I prohibition if it would fall within an EC block exemption if it affected inter-state trade
10(1)(b)	Agreement benefits from a parallel exemption from the Chapter I prohibition if it has received an individual exemption from the Commission
10(1)(c)	Agreement benefits from a parallel exemption from the Chapter I prohibition if it has the benefit of an exemption under the opposition procedure in a Regulation
10(4)(b)	Parallel exemption ceases to have effect if the relevant Community exemption ceases to have effect
41	Agreement benefits from provisional immunity from penalties if it has been notified to the Commission for an exemption under Art 81(3) (old Art 85(3)). This provisional immunity lapses if the EC immunity is withdrawn. NB does not prevent DGFT from conducting a simultaneous investigation into the agreement, although this is likely to be rare in practice
Schedule 1, paragraph 6	The prohibitions do not apply at all to matters over which the European Commission has exclusive jurisdiction under the Merger Regulation (Reg 4064/89)
Schedule 3, paragraph 4	The prohibitions do not apply to an undertaking entrusted with the operation of services of general economic interest where Art 86(2) (old Art 90(2)) of the EC Treaty would apply
Schedule 3, paragraph 8	The prohibitions do not apply to agreements or conduct relating to a coal or steel product to the extent to which the ECSC Treaty gives the Commission exclusive jurisdiction
Schedule 3, paragraph 9	The Chapter I prohibition does not apply to agreements relating to production of or trade in agricultural products to the extent that they benefit from an exclusion from Art 81(1) (old Art 85(1))

Practical effect of compatibility provisions

The various situations which may arise in practice, and where the compatibility provisions are invoked, can also usefully be summarised as follows.

The situation	The effect
Agreement falls within an EC block exemption	Benefits from a parallel exemption under the Act (s 10(1)(a)).[47a]
Agreement would fall within an EC block exemption if it affected trade between Member States	Benefits from a parallel exemption under the Act (s 10(2)).[47a]
Agreement is granted an individual exemption by the Commission	Benefits from a parallel exemption under the Act (s 10(1)(b)).[47a]
Agreement is granted an exemption under the opposition procedure provided for in certain EC Regulations	Benefits from a parallel exemption under the Act (s 10(1)(c)).[47a]
Commission finds that an agreement infringes Art 81(1) (old Art 85(1) and refuses to grant an exemption, or that conduct infringes Art 82 (old Art 86)	The illegal provisions of the agreement are void and unenforceable (may be severed from agreement to leave part intact and enforceable, depending on the way in which the agreement is drafted). The conduct is illegal. The DGFT must "have regard" to this decision of the Commission (s 60(3)), and is therefore likely to find an infringement of the Chapter I or Chapter II prohibition also. Any penalty imposed under the Act must take account of any fine imposed by the Commission or by any other Member State in respect of the agreement (s 38(9)).
Commission writes a letter stating that as a matter of its internal priorities it will not consider the matter further,	As a general policy, the DGFT will not depart from the Commission's assessment, and is therefore likely to find an infringement of the Chapter I or Chapter II prohibition (OFT

47a The Act purports to give the DGFT the power to cancel the parallel exemption, or to make it subject to conditions or obligations (s 10(5)), but some doubt the legality of this under EC law.

but that it considers that there is an infringement of Art 81(1) (old Art 85(1)) which would not qualify for an exemption or of Art 82 (old Art 86) (a "discomfort letter")	Guidelines on the Chapter I Prohibition, para. 7.12).
Commission find that an agreement does not infringe Art 81(1) (old Art 85(1)) or 82 (old Art 86) (negative clearance)	The DGFT must "have regard" to this decision of the Commission (s 60(3)), and is therefore likely to find that the Chapter I or Chapter II prohibition also has not been infringed. In practice, DGFT likely to issue an administrative letter/comfort letter in response to any notification/complaint.
Commission writes a letter stating that as a matter of its internal priorities it will not consider the matter further, but that it considers that the agreement would be likely to qualify for an exemption (a "comfort letter")	As a general policy, the DGFT will not depart from the Commission's assessment, and is therefore likely to find that the Chapter I prohibition has not been infringed. The DGFT may depart from this policy where (1) the agreement raises particular concerns in relation to competition in the UK (rare), or where (2) the Commission has issued its comfort letter only on the basis that the agreement does not have an appreciable effect on inter-state trade (OFT Guideline on the Chapter I Prohibition, para 7.12). In practice, DGFT likely to issue an administrative letter/comfort letter in response to any notification/complaint.
Agreement or conduct has been notified to the Commission, but no decision has yet been taken or comfort letter/discomfort letter issued	DGFT will generally take no action until the Commission has completed its assessment and informed the parties. However, DGFT may proceed to consider a notification that is already being considered by the Commission where (1) it raises particular concerns in relation to competition in the UK (rare) or (2) it involves important legal, economic or policy developments. (OFT Guidelines on the Chapter I Prohibition, paras 7.9-7.10).
Agreement or conduct was the subject of a complaint to the Commission, but the Commission has taken no action	If the Commission has refused to exercise its powers on grounds of insufficient Community interest, this will usually be of no relevance to the DGFT's exercise of his powers under the Act.

Effect of proceedings under the Act on EC competition proceedings

All of the compatibility provisions referred to above are concerned with the considerable impact of decisions and other actions or inactions of the Commission on proceedings under the Act. In contrast, decisions and other rulings under the Act do not have the same effect on proceedings under Article 81 or 82 (old Articles 85 and 86).

A favourable assessment of an agreement or conduct under the Act does not in any way bind the European Commission in any proceedings brought under Article 81 or 82 (old Articles 85 and 86). For example, the fact that an agreement has been granted automatic exemption from the Chapter I prohibition because it was the subject of a section 21(2) direction under the Restrictive Trade Practices Act 1976[48] does not prevent the Commission from instituting proceedings under Article 81. Even where an agreement has been granted an individual exemption from the Chapter I prohibition on the basis that its pro-competitive effects outweigh the anti-competitive ones, the Commission may still find an infringement of EC competition law. Nonetheless, it seems likely that favourable domestic assessment of an agreement or conduct will weigh in its favour in any subsequent proceedings under Article 81 or 82.

Where should you notify, litigate or complain?

As the analysis set out above will have made clear, there are a number of sometimes competing factors which must be considered and balanced when considering where to notify, litigate or complain. The factors to be taken into account when considering whether to notify an agreement or practice, are discussed in a later chapter.[49] But there is a more fundamental question which must be addressed first in the many cases in which both the Act and EC competition law apply: which law should be invoked?

The Office of Fair Trading (OFT) is keen to encourage those who wish to notify agreements which meet the inter-state trade criterion to do so using EC law and to the European Commission, in order to try to avoid an unmanageable flood of notifications to the OFT. The OFT Guidelines stress that:

---

48 See para 2 of Sched 3 to the Act.
49 Chap 5 on Notifications.

- only the Commission can grant an individual exemption from Article 81(1) (old Article 85(1));
- an exemption from Article 81(1) (old Article 85(1) will result in an automatic parallel exemption under the Act;
- the reverse situation, that is exemption under the Act, will not preclude the application of Article 81(1);
- an exemption granted by the Commission has effect in all Member States of the EU, whereas exemption from the Chapter I prohibition has effect only in the United Kingdom;
- notification to and exemption from the Commission is therefore likely to result in reduced compliance costs;
- notification to the Commission gives an agreement provisional immunity from fines for so long as the Commission has not withdrawn its provisional immunity or determined the matter;
- the DGFT has the power to grant retroactive exemptions in all cases, whereas the Commission generally may only grant an exemption with effect from the date of notification.[50]

The OFT discourages dual notification to both the Commission and the UK authorities, but recognises that there may be some cases in which it could be appropriate. Where a person wishes to notify an agreement or (more unusually) conduct, but is unsure as to whether it has the necessary effect on inter-state trade for the application of Articles 81 and 82 (old Articles 85 and 86), an informal approach may be made to the OFT for guidance.[51] If the Commission subsequently declines jurisdiction on the basis of lack of effect on trade between Member States, or indeed on the basis of insufficient Community interest, a notification could be made to the DGFT. The OFT has indicated that it will try to give priority to such cases and would be likely to grant any exemption with retroactive effect.[52] Where dual notifications are made, the OFT will liaise closely with the Commission to determine where it may most appropriately be determined.[53]

The OFT has not made similar efforts to encourage complaints to be made to the Commission rather than to it under the Act.[54] This is probably because the OFT is keen to use complaints to alert it to anti-competitive agreements or practices which it can then investigate. Since

---

50 OFT Guideline on The Chapter I Prohibition (OFT 401), paras 7.4-7.5. See further Chap 5 on Notifications below.
51 *Ibid*, para 7.6.
52 *Ibid*, para 7.7.
53 *Ibid*, para 7.9.
54 OFT Guideline on The Major Provisions (OFT 400), paras 8.1-8.3.

it is notoriously difficult to interest the Commission in a complaint, and a Commission investigation can be slow even after a case is taken up, it may be advisable to complain to the OFT, at least in the first instance. The Commission and the OFT will only rarely conduct simultaneous investigations into a complaint, and are likely to consult one another to determine the more appropriate authority to assess the agreement or conduct in question.[55]

It is likely that in civil proceedings in which a party seeks to rely upon competition law, whether as a "sword" or as a "shield", many litigants will plead both the Act and EC competition law. Whilst this may be a sensible precaution, at least during the early years of the operation of the Act when its parameters and procedures are still uncertain, the evidential burden of proving an effect on trade between Members States for the purposes of Article 81 or 82 (old Articles 85 and 86) is a significant one which should not be overlooked.[56] It may therefore prove sufficient and less burdensome to rely solely on the Chapter I and II prohibitions contained in the Act. Furthermore, the OFT Guideline indicates that if an agreement is challenged in the UK courts on the basis of its compliance with competition law, the DGFT will endeavour to give priority to any notification of that agreement for exemption, and would probably grant any exemption retroactively.[57] The Commission, on the other hand, has made no such commitment, and notifications for Article 81(3) (old Article 85(3)) exemption may therefore cause considerable delay to domestic court proceedings.

---

55 OFT Guideline on The Chapter I Prohibition (OFT 401), para 7.9.
56 See, for example, *Panayiotou v Sony* [1994] EMLR 229.
57 OFT Guideline on The Chapter I Prohibition (OFT 401), paras 7.5 and 7.7.

Chapter 3

· The Chapter I Prohibition ·

3.1   Introduction

Fashions change. There have been periods in British life, especially between the wars, during which cartels, notably in commodity goods, have seemed a good thing, leading to rational production and orderly delivery, and relieving companies of the need to use up financial and other resources in competing with one another. That view may return. But for the moment and for the foreseeable future, the orthodoxy is that agreements between economic operators significantly limiting competition between them are to be regarded as pernicious, and it is with restrictive agreements that the Act opens.

Section 1 boldly sweeps away the previous legislation concerning such agreements, namely the Restrictive Practices Acts[1] and the Resale Prices Act 1976.

Section 2 ushers in their replacement, a prohibition closely modelled on Article 81 (old Article 85) of the EC Treaty.[2] For the reason that it occurs in "Chapter I" of Part I of the Act, the prohibition introduced by section 2 has been given, in section 2(8), the rather fussy name of "the Chapter I prohibition".

This chapter describes the Chapter I prohibition and the types of agreement to which it applies or which, in one way or another, are removed from its scope. Its structure, following that of Article 81 (old Article 85), is that of an extremely wide prohibition for those agreements which are not excluded from its scope, subject to discretionary exemptions in the hands of a regulator for agreements which afford offsetting benefits. In the EC Treaty system, the regulator is the EC Commission; under the Act, it is the Director General of Fair Trading (DGFT). Section 60 is designed to ensure consistency of outcome, at least to the extent that the Chapter I prohibition is trying to achieve the same object as Article 81.[3]

---

1 *i.e.* the Restrictive Trade Practices Act 1976 (RTPA), the Restrictive Trade Practices Act 1977 and the Restrictive Practices Court Act 1976.

2 For Art 81 (old Art 85), see Appendix 3.

3 See Chap 2 above for discussion of s 60.

There is a clear overlap in the jurisdiction of the EC Commission and the DGFT respectively: agreements may be subject to Article 81 (old Article 85) if they affect trade and competition at the EC level and also to the Chapter I prohibition if they satisfy the equivalent tests under the Act.[3a]

The general principle of the Act is that any agreement which has a Community exemption, of whatever kind, benefits automatically from a co-extensive or, as the Act calls it, a "parallel" exemption from the Chapter I prohibition. Since the EC Commission manages to issue only a handful of individual exemption decisions each year, generally disposing of notifications to it by means of informal "comfort" letter, an effort must be made to accommodate those letters also in the new system, but the Act does not specifically provide for them.

An important preliminary point is that many of the principal terms used in connection with the Chapter I prohibition are not defined in the Act but are to be deduced from EC law by virtue of section 60. This includes essential notions such as "agreement", "undertaking", effect on competition and so on. Vitally, it has been stressed by the Office of Fair Trading (OFT) and the Department of Trade and Industry (DTI) on every conceivable occasion that, just as Article 81 (old Article 85) only applies to agreements which are capable of affecting competition to a significant or "appreciable"[4] degree, so does the Chapter I prohibition.

Thus, to understand the Act, it is essential to have some understanding of EC competition law. The OFT Guideline[5] refers to the EC decisions regarded as relevant by those who are entrusted with implementing the prohibition and so is essential reading for those who may be affected. The Guideline also reveals the OFT's strong encouragement of parties to notify their agreements to the EC Commission in Brussels whenever possible rather than to the DGFT. The EC Commission, conversely, is keen for parties to notify the national competition authorities rather than DG IV whenever possible.[6]

3.2 **The prohibition**

In the absence of a relevant exclusion or exemption, the Chapter I prohibition applies to "agreements between undertakings", "decisions

---

3a See Chap 2 above for a discussion of overlapping jurisdiction.

4 The term preferred by the OFT and DTI, although it is not one to which the ECJ confines itself: the origin of the requirement lies in Case 5/69 *Volk* v *Vervaecke* [1969] ECR 295 in which the European Court said " ... an agreement falls outside the prohibition in Art 81 (old Art 85) when it has only an *insignificant* effect on the markets ..." (emphasis added).

5 The Chapter I Prohibition (OFT 401).

6 See Chap 2 above and also Chap 5 below on Notifications.

by associations of undertakings" and "concerted practices" which "(a) may affect trade within the United Kingdom" and "(b) have as their object or effect the prevention, restriction or distortion of competition within the United Kingdom."[6a]

Territorial scope

The United Kingdom has always been a staunch supporter of theories of limited territorial jurisdiction for antitrust laws.[7]

In case the limited territorial ambitions of the Act are not already clear enough from the wording quoted above, it is also provided that the prohibition applies "only if the agreement, decision or practice is, or is intended to be, implemented in the United Kingdom".[8] This is intended to replicate in UK law the European Court's ruling in *Woodpulp*[9] which comes close to endorsing the so-called "effects doctrine". Under that theory, a competition authority is entitled to take jurisdiction over agreements, wherever made and wherever the parties may be located, whose economic *effects* are felt within its territory.

It is important to remember, however, that for these purposes, "United Kingdom" includes any part of the country;[10] and there is no requirement in the Act that it should be a "significant" part of the country. In contrast, one of the tests under the Fair Trading Act 1973 for regulatory consideration of mergers is a market share of 25% in the United Kingdom or a "substantial" part of it. That definition has led to controversy in cases involving concentration in local markets, such as those for bus services.[11] The Act avoids such difficulties.

The EC case law, to be considered in application of section 60, indicates that effects which are confined to a single Member State will nevertheless be taken to have an effect "within the common market" if it leads to that country becoming less permeable to imports or otherwise leads to or reinforces the partitioning of the common market.

6a　S 2(1).
7　Consider the Protection of Trading Interests Act 1980; cf also the UK's intervention in ECJ cases such as Cases 89/85 etc *Ahlstrom and others* v *Commission* [1988] ECR 5193 ("*Woodpulp*").
8　S 2(3).
9　Cases 89/85 etc *Ahlstrom and others* v *Commission* [1988] ECR 5193. This judgment has given rise to an extensive debate in the literature: see Van Gerven in (1989) Fordham Corporate Law Institute; a heretical view is succinctly expressed by Mann in (1989) ICLQ 375.
10　S 2(7).
11　In *R* v *Monopolies and Mergers Commission ex parte South Yorkshire Transport* [1993] 1 WLR 23, the courts held that "substantial" meant a part which was not insubstantial.

To date, it has not successfully been argued that any particular Member State was too small in comparison with the common market for such effects to fall below the appreciability threshold. It remains to be seen whether, with remorseless enlargement of the European Union, and the addition of other very small states alongside Luxembourg, this position can be maintained.

Important terms in Chapter I prohibition and their meaning in EC law

Several terms in the text of the Chapter I prohibition require some explanation for those unfamiliar with the wording and operation of Article 81 (old Article 85). This explanation will also provide a basic primer of the objectives and scope of the EC prohibition which is reflected in Chapter I.

"*Agreement*": there is nothing legalistic about this term, which goes well beyond the concept of a legally binding contract, to cover informal arrangements and understandings, written, oral or arising by inference from contacts of any kind. A single "agreement" for Article 81 (old Article 85) or Chapter I purposes may arise from a series of agreements or understandings between different parties. At the margin, the concept of "agreement" shades into that of "concerted practice". The European Court of First Instance (CFI) has been increasingly receptive to the Commission's view that there is no need to draw rigorous distinctions between the two concepts.[11a]

"*Concerted practice*": defined by the ECJ as "a form of co-ordination between undertakings which, without having reached the stage at which an agreement properly so-called has been concluded, knowingly substitutes practical co-operation between them for the risks of competition".[12] The OFT Guideline emphasises the requirement for some form of practical co-operation knowingly entered into, and the demonstration of effects on the market stemming from direct or indirect contacts.[13] The argument in EC cases has generally turned on the issue whether an undertaking's behaviour, particularly in an oligopoly, is based on intelligent adaptation to market conditions and anticipation of decisions to be taken by competitors, or reflects some form of common understanding.

11a See Joined Cases T-305/94 etc *LVM and others* v *Commission*, judgment of 20 April 1999 ("PVC 2").

12 Case 47/69 *ICI* v *Commission* [1972] ECR 619.

13 The Chapter I Prohibition (OFT 401), paras 2.11-2.13.

"*Decision*": typically, a decision or recommendation of a trade association, whether or not formally binding on members (for instance, it does not matter whether there is any internal sanction for failure to abide by a recommendation). Depending on the circumstances, a measure may be analysed as a decision of an association or as an agreement or concerted practice between its members.

"*Undertaking*": any economic operator offering goods or services on the market ("entreprise" in French), so not only companies, but also partnerships, sole traders, unincorporated associations and so on. It is important to realise that it is not just the manifestation of the entity actually involved in the agreement which constitutes the relevant "undertaking". The notion encompasses all entities forming a single economic unit, so that parent and subsidiary companies are generally viewed as forming part of one and the same undertaking.[14] Undertakings may be in the private or public sector. The meaning of the term "undertaking" is discussed in more detail in Chapter 4 below.

In two sets of circumstances regularly encountered in practice, an agreement may not qualify as an agreement "between undertakings" for the purposes of the prohibition.

The first is true agency: where the agent is seen as, and only as, an auxiliary of the principal, his acts are attributable to the principal. EC case law, or at least the Commission's decisional practice, on the topic is in an unsatisfactory state. It indicates that this analysis may not hold good where the agent acts for two or more principals who are in competition one with another, especially if the principals have agreed to appoint a common agent. There have also been suggestions that an agent may be regarded as an undertaking in its own right if it has substantial other businesses in addition to the agency in question.

The second case concerns agreements between members of the same corporate group (agreements between parent and subsidiary or between fellow subsidiaries and so on). The European Court's case law is to the effect that agreement between parent and subsidiary will not be caught by Article 81 (old Article 85):

> "if the undertakings form an economic unit within which the subsidiary has no real freedom to determine its course of action on the market, and if the agreements or practices are concerned merely with the internal allocation of tasks as between the undertakings".[15]

---

14 See also the Chapter I Prohibition (OFT 401) para 2.6.
15 See *e.g.* Case 15/74 *Centrafarm* v *Sterling Drug* [1974] ECR 1147; Case C-73/95 P *Viho* v *Commission* [1996] ECR I-5457.

This formulation, contemplating the existence of subsidiaries which *are* free to determine their action on the market, has left the door slightly open for the introduction of a concept equivalent to the "intra-enterprise conspiracy" theory known to US antitrust law. We suggest that undertakings which are linked in such a way as to meet the definition of participating undertakings (see next section below) should not be regarded as capable of making an agreement among themselves for Chapter I purposes, even if *vis-à-vis* third parties each of them may be a separate "undertaking".

"*Association of undertakings*": typically, a trade association, not itself an economic operator on the market. An association may be an association of undertakings although not all its members are themselves undertakings.

Appreciable effect

It is important to realise that an inquiry as to whether an agreement may have an appreciable effect on competition cannot be carried out in the abstract. It has to be performed in the context of a properly defined market and in the light of the relevant economic circumstances.[16]

It is also helpful to bear in mind the distinction between a restriction on *competition* (an economic concept) and a restriction on *conduct* (a concept which lawyers find easier to understand, especially since such restrictions can often be discerned from contractual terms without deeper consideration of the underlying circumstances).

The considerations which will guide the DGFT in deciding whether an agreement has an appreciable effect are set out in the OFT Guideline.[17] The Guideline does not miss the opportunity to stress that agreements without an appreciable effect on competition should **not** be notified. EC experience suggests that undertakings may not be as sanguine as the OFT hopes about taking their own view on this issue. After all, what is being asked of them is not only to form their own view, but also to anticipate the likely view of the OFT and risk substantial fines if they are wrong on that.

The Guideline explains that it is the market share attributable to the parties that will be the prime consideration in assessing the effect of an

---

16 Market definition is considered in detail in Chap 4 below. See also the Guideline on Market Definition (OFT 403).
17 Guideline on the Chapter I Prohibition (OFT 401), paras 2.18-2.22.

agreement on competition, although price-fixing agreements will normally be presumed to have an appreciable effect.

However, it is not only the market shares of the actual (legal) parties to the agreement that need to be taken into consideration. The Guideline notes that the market share will be that of the parties and also the groups to which they belong, that is, the undertakings they control and the undertakings which control them.[18] This is an oblique reference to the definition of "Participating Undertakings" in the EC Commission's Notice on Agreements of Minor Importance[19], which itself drew for inspiration on the EC Merger Regulation.[20] It calls for an examination up and down the control chain starting with the undertakings which are party to the agreement. Undertakings in which the parties have more than a 50% interest (measured by capital, votes, assets or board or management representation) or which they have the right to manage (for instance, under contract) are to be taken into account; likewise undertakings which have such rights over the parties, and so on up the chain.

It is the *combined* market share of the groups thus found which has to be taken into consideration. The Guideline states that the DGFT will not normally consider that there is an appreciable effect if the combined market share does not exceed 25%.[21] This level seems quite high when compared with the thresholds laid down by the EC Commission Notice, which are 5% for horizontal agreements and 10% for vertical agreements. It is closer to levels found in merger control rules.[22] However, the DGFT's analysis will often be made in the context of local markets, such as those for bus services, where a combination of a number of relatively small undertakings may find themselves comfortably exceeding a 25% share.

There will be circumstances in which the parties to an agreement have a combined market share below 25%, but an appreciable effect on competition will nevertheless be found. Conversely, the Guideline makes it clear that even where the market share exceeds 25%, the effect on competition may not be considered to be appreciable:

> "Other factors, for example, the content of the agreement and the structure of the market or markets affected by the agreement, such as

18 *Ibid*, para 2.22.
19 OJ 1997 C372/13, para 12.
20 Council Reg 4064/89 (as amended), Art 5(4).
21 The Chapter I Prohibition (OFT 401), para 2.19.
22 The 25% market share test is used in the Fair Trading Act 1973 to determine whether a merger qualifies for investigation and in EC merger control to define affected markets in upstream or downstream relationships, although a 15% share test is used for horizontal relationships.

entry conditions or the characteristics of buyers and the structure of the buyers' side of the market will be considered in determining whether the agreement has an appreciable effect."[23]

While this is helpful guidance, it clearly illustrates the potential uncertainties with which parties to agreements will be faced.

The Guideline states[24] that the DGFT will generally regard the following types of agreements as being capable of having an appreciable effect even if the parties' combined market share falls below the 25% threshold. They are agreements which:

- directly or indirectly fix prices or share markets;
- impose minimum resale prices;
- form part of a network of similar agreements having a cumulative effect on the relevant market.

A counsel of perfection is that undertakings should avoid all agreements falling within the first two of those categories. The third category is principally relevant to vertical arrangements, which are discussed separately below.

There are two important points on which to end this discussion of appreciability. First, an appreciable effect on competition is a precondition for the applicability of the Chapter I prohibition: no appreciable effect, no prohibition. Secondly, assessing appreciability is essentially an economic exercise: it is a real (or potential) impact on the relevant market which has to be established before the prohibition can bite.

The logical consequence of this is that, just as economic circumstances can change, so can the applicability of the prohibition. An agreement may be innocent when entered into, but may become prohibited subsequently if the parties' market power increases. The converse may also be true: an agreement may be prohibited at inception, but become licit due to changes in economic circumstances. This principle has been established by the English courts in the Article 81 (old Article 85) context.[25]

The conclusion is that a continuous assessment needs to be carried out for groups whose market shares are on the borderline, or where economic conditions in the relevant market change significantly.

---

23 Guideline on the Chapter I Prohibition (OFT 401), para 2.21.
24 *Ibid*, para 2.20.
25 See *Passmore* v *Morland* [1998] EuLR 580 (High Court) and [1999] EuLR 501 (CA).

Principal categories of agreement caught by the prohibition

There is a list, identical to that in Article 81(1) (old 85(1)), of the types of agreement[26] which the prohibition is intended particularly to catch. In short, those types are:

- price fixing;
- market sharing;
- restricting output, development or investment;
- imposing discriminatory trading conditions; and
- tying.

In full, section 2(2) reads as follows:

> "[The Chapter I prohibition] applies, in particular, to agreements, decisions or practices which -
>
> (a) directly or indirectly fix purchase or selling prices or any other trading conditions
>
> (b) limit or control production, markets, technical development or investment;
>
> (c) share markets or sources of supply;
>
> (d) apply dissimilar conditions to equivalent transactions with other trading parties, thereby placing them at a competitive disadvantage;
>
> (e) make the conclusion of contracts subject to acceptance by the other parties of supplementary obligations which, by their nature or according to commercial usage, have no connection with the subject of such contracts."

The list is not exhaustive, so other forms of anti-competitive object or effect may be caught. However, it is not easy to think of examples of undesirable agreements which the general wording of the list would fail to catch.

Conversely, the types of agreement caught by the prohibition may be entirely benign. For example, parties setting up a joint venture may well accept restrictions which can be characterised as restrictions on output or as sharing of markets (and may require individual exemption if they could lead to an appreciable effect on competition[27]). This feature of a

---

26 This term will generally be used in this book to cover also decisions by associations of undertakings and concerted practices, except where there is a relevant difference. The Act makes a similar statement: see sub-ss (5) and (6) of s 2.

27 Although there is an exclusion from Chapter I for agreements setting up joint ventures which satisfy the Fair Trading Act definition of a merger: see Section 3.3 of this chapter on "Exclusions", p 46 below.

prohibition system is easily overlooked. A criticism which can be levelled at the tone of the OFT Guideline is that it stresses the types of undesirable agreement at which the prohibition is aimed without giving very much emphasis to the fact that the undesirability will very much depend on the economic and commercial context in which the restriction is accepted.

That said, the focus of the Guideline is, understandably, on the type of anti-competitive agreements which the DGFT hopes to uncover by use of his enhanced enforcement powers.[28] The primary targets are those agreements, identified above, which are always considered to have an appreciable effect, namely price fixing and market sharing agreements.

Price-fixing and market-sharing

The Guideline sets out various forms of price fixing and market sharing, including agreement on price formulation mechanisms, or subsidiary terms such as discounts or allowances, extra charges such as transport, or credit or guarantee terms. However, all will depend on the circumstances. It has not normally been regarded as infringing behaviour for companies to agree, perhaps through a trade association, a code of conduct regarding late payment or treatment of credit risks, even to the extent of sharing information about customers with a poor record.

Bid-rigging

A particular example of an anti-competitive agreement which the Guideline gives[29] is collusive tendering or "bid-rigging". Such agreements of course defeat the object of tenders, which is to open the processes of contract awarding to competition. It may be no coincidence that the OFT has encountered several examples of bid-rigging in its enforcement activity under the RTPA, such as in the field of local authority contracts for bus services.

Information exchange

The Guideline then turns to consider agreements to exchange information between competitors, either directly or through the medium of a trade association.[30] The position it takes, taking its lead from the

---

28 For enforcement powers, see Chap 6 below.
29 The Chapter I Prohibition (OFT 401), para 3.14.
30 *Ibid*, paras 3.17 *et seq*. For trade associations, see the Guideline on Trade Associations, Professions and Self-Regulating Bodies (OFT 408).

EC Commission, is that information exchange can be pro-competitive or innocent, leading to transparency and to efficiencies. However, the closer such information comes to being of use to the recipient in deciding its future strategy, especially its pricing strategy, the more likely it is to cross the line into illicit sharing of information and facilitating collusion.

Other types of anti-competitive agreement

The Guideline then refers to other types of anti-competitive agreements, such as collective boycotts of suppliers or distributors who deal with competitors, or rebate schemes to incentivise customers to deal with a group of horizontal competitors.[31] Lastly, the OFT notes[31a] that other types of agreements may be caught by the prohibition, such as specialisation agreements and joint ventures for the development of new products and markets. It is disappointing that there is not an immediate mention of the possibility of exemption for such agreements, notably by reference to the relevant EC Commission Notices.[32]

The Guideline gives no examples of the last two items on the "hit-list" in section 2(2), namely agreements imposing discriminatory trading conditions and tying agreements. This undoubtedly reflects enforcement priorities, in that such matters normally arise in vertical agreements about which the OFT is much less concerned. It may also reflect uncertainty as to what exactly the reference to discriminatory trading conditions covers. It is sometimes argued by those who are unhappy with the agreement to which they are a party that others with whom the counterparty deals have better terms and therefore that this element of the prohibition has been breached.[33] In those circumstances, is there an agreement imposing discriminatory trading conditions? If so, which is it: the one which is the subject of the proceedings, or the one with which it is being compared? If the latter, does it affect the validity of the agreement which is the subject of the proceedings? EC law is still struggling with the application of Article 81(old Article 85) to what in reality is unilateral conduct, as for example in the case of directives issued by a supplier to its network of distributors.[34]

---

31   The Chapter I Prohibition (OFT 401), para 3.27.
31a *Ibid*, para 3.28.
32   Including the Notice on the Assessment of Co-operative Joint Ventures (OJ 1993 C43/2) and the notice on the concept of full-function joint ventures (OJ 1998 C66/1).
33   This has been a regular feature of the claims under Art 81 (old Art 85) brought by pub tenants against their brewer or pubco landlord: see *e.g. Gibbs Mew* v *Gemmell* [1998] EuLR 588 (CA) and *Trent Taverns* v *Sykes* [1998] EuLR 571 and [1999] EuLR 492 (CA).
34   See Case T-41/96 *Bayer AG* v *Commission* (pending); interim suspension of Commission decision reported at [1996] ECR II-381.

Voidness

Any agreement caught by the prohibition is "void"[35] in the absence of a relevant exclusion or exemption.

The meaning and consequences of this voidness are to be deduced from EC law pursuant to section 60, given that there is no contrary indication elsewhere in the Act. This is one example where the effect of section 60 becomes rather self-referential.[36] EC law regards the consequences of voidness as a matter essentially for national law. Fortunately, there is some United Kingdom jurisprudence dealing with the domestic consequences of the voidness laid down by Article 81(2) (old Article 85(2)). The approach of the UK courts is explained below.

The European Court has made it clear that it is only the actual restrictions which contravene the prohibition that are to be regarded as void.[37] Those restrictions are unlawful and the national court cannot lend its aid to their enforcement. However, EC law has no objection to any parts of the wider agreement between the parties that do not infringe Article 81 (old Article 85). It is for national law to decide whether the remainder of the contract can survive the striking down of the void restrictions.

At least in cases where they have been faced with a written contract, English law has adopted the approach of taking the censorious "blue pencil" to the text of the contract (that is, the words giving rise to the objectionable restriction are deleted). The court will not re-write the contract or insert additional words. If what is left is an agreement supported by consideration, and not so different from what the parties originally agreed as to make it incredible that they would have consented to the surviving arrangement, then the courts will give effect to the surviving clauses.[38] If not, they will not.[39]

English law has taken the position that agreements which are void under Article 81(2) (old 85(2)) are also illegal agreements, because they

---

35 S 2(4).
36 The issue whether damages are available in respect of a breach of the prohibition is another such example. See Chap 2 above.
37 See *e.g.* Case 56/65 *Société Technique Minière* v *Maschinenbau Ulm* [1966] ECR 235. This is a further indication that the notion of agreement under Art 81 (old Art 85) and Chapter I should not be seen as equivalent to a legal contract.
38 *Chemidus Wavin* v *TERI* [1978] 3 CMLR 514 (CA). Thus, in the pub tenancy cases, the courts have been prepared to hold that, irrespective of whether Art 81 (old Art 85) may affect the validity of the beer tie, they cannot affect the obligation to pay rent under the principal covenants of the lease: see *e.g. Inntrepreneur* v *Boyes* [1993] 2 EGLR 112 (CA) per Ralph Gibson LJ.
39 See *Richard Cound Limited* v *BMW* [1997] EuLR 277.

are prohibited – under Article 81(1) (old 85(1)) – and subject to penalties. Thus the civil consequences go beyond mere unenforceability: they also preclude reliance by either party on his illegality, so that payments made or property transferred pursuant to the illegal agreement cannot be recovered.[40]

Voidness depends on and flows from an agreement's being prohibited: if an agreement ceases to be prohibited, it ceases to be void.[41-42]

3.3   Exclusions

Various types of agreement are excluded from the Chapter I prohibition. These exclusions are to be legally effected either through Orders (Statutory Instruments) made by the Secretary of State pursuant to powers under section 50 of the Act or by Schedules 1-4, which are introduced by section 3 of the Act. There are some significant exclusions rather buried in the Schedules of the Act, especially in Schedule 3, blandly entitled "General Exclusions".

It is important to remember that, in respect of certain of the types of excluded agreement, the DGFT has discretionary power to withdraw the exclusion in specified circumstances.

Some of the categories of exclusion are watertight and fairly easy to identify. Others are much less so and may involve subjective "judgment calls" (for example, as to whether an agreement is a vertical agreement or as to the applicability of the "Article 86(2)" (old Article 90(2)) defence in Schedule 3: see below). This in turn may lead to some potentially excluded agreements nevertheless being notified to the DGFT as a precaution, which is of course not at all the intended result.

Vertical agreements

From the earliest pronouncements of the incoming Labour administration, it was made clear that there would be special treatment for "vertical" agreements as these were not thought to raise the same level of competition concern as horizontal agreements. This was seen as one area in which the new UK system could differ substantially from EC

---

40 See *e.g. Gibbs Mew* v *Gemmell* [1998] EuLR 588 (CA), applying *Tinsley* v *Milligan* [1994] 1 AC 340 and *Boissevain* v *Weil* [1950] AC 327.

41-42 See *Passmore* v *Morland* [1998] EuLR 580 (High Court) and [1999] EuLR 501 (CA).

law. EC law had used competition policy instrumentally, as a tool to promote economic integration within the common market. That was why EC law had attached so much importance to regulating distribution systems which could otherwise perpetuate the barriers between national markets. Since the United Kingdom was already a single market, there was no need to have any regard to the integration imperative. Furthermore, vertical agreements, despite their increasingly recognised pro-competitive effects, had been notified in significant quantities to the EC Commission, a phenomenon which the UK regulators did not want to experience.

Block exemption or exclusion

Section 50 (included at a relatively late stage in the Bill's Parliamentary progress since the Government had been unable to decide on its preferred approach) provides the Secretary of State with a wide choice of instrument for taking vertical agreements outside the scope of the Chapter I prohibition. Which would be deployed would depend in part on progress by the EC Commission in Brussels towards formulating a new approach to vertical restraints, more governed by economic theory rather than by legal concepts. That process is incomplete at the time of writing.[43]

The terms of section 60 allow for significant differences between the UK approach and that of EC law. However, ultimately the policy decision was taken that the Brussels approach to vertical agreements would be shadowed as closely as possible. Essentially, the economists' case has been accepted that vertical agreements only pose regulatory concerns when they are associated with significant market power, either because of the power of the supplier or because there is a substantial network of linked vertical agreements.

Thus the terms of the Statutory Instrument currently proposed under the section 50 powers reflect the latest drafts of the Commission's proposed "wide" block exemption for vertical agreements.[44] The Order[45] defines a vertical agreement as:

---

43 See EC Commission Communication on vertical restraints, OJ 1998 C365/3. The latest position is set out in Annexes C and D to the DTI consultation paper on vertical agreements, cited in fn 44.

44 See Competition Act 1998: Exclusion of Vertical Agreements: Consultation on a draft Order (DTI, February 1999, URN 98/1030). The policy behind the draft is clearly explained in that paper.

45 The text assumes that a Statutory Instrument has been adopted in the terms of the DTI's consultation draft.

"an agreement –

(a) between two or more undertakings, each operating at a different stage of the economic process for the purposes of that agreement, and

(b) in respect of the supply or purchase, or both, of goods for resale or processing or in respect of the marketing of services."

It will be noted that this definition does not extend to the licensing of patents or other intellectual property. Licensing agreements are subject to the prohibition to the extent that they fail to qualify for a parallel exemption (see p 57 *et seq* below).

The approach proposed is to exempt such vertical agreements, provided that they are not price-fixing agreements, and subject to a power for the DGFT to withdraw the benefit of the exclusion in respect of a particular agreement.

Price fixing is defined as occurring when the agreement:

"directly or indirectly, in isolation or in combination with other factors under the control of the parties including the exercise of industrial property rights, has the object or effect of (i) fixing resale prices or minimum resale prices; (ii) fixing maximum resale prices or recommended resale prices which have the same effect as fixed resale prices or fixed minimum resale prices."

The DGFT's power to withdraw the benefit of the exclusion can be exercised if he considers that, without the exclusion, the agreement would be likely to infringe the Chapter I prohibition (so that it must have an appreciable effect on competition) and would not qualify for an individual exemption.

Land agreements

Section 50 refers, in addition to vertical agreements, to "land agreements", intentionally a wide term and one which has no particular meaning in traditional land law. It is well known that the DTI and OFT officials in charge of developing the legislative proposals for what became the Act held extensive discussions with their counterparts in other Member States with experience of enacting and operating Article 81 (old Article 85) look-alike systems. In Ireland, introduction of a prohibition system had led to the notification of hundreds of agreements concerning shopping centres and the like, where leases often contain restrictions on the number of particular kinds of retail outlet which will be allowed in each development. While such restrictions can be characterised as restrictions on competition, it is extremely rare that they should have a sufficiently appreciable effect on competition to attract regulatory scrutiny. It was therefore decided to exclude such agreements from the Chapter I prohibition, naturally with power for the DGFT to claw back[46] the exclusion.

The proposed Order[47] defines "land agreement" as:

> "an agreement between undertakings which creates, alters, transfers or terminates, an interest in land, or an agreement to enter into such an agreement, together with any obligation and restriction which in accordance with Article 3 [of the Order] is to be treated as part of the agreement."

Mergers, concentrations and ancillary restrictions

This exclusion[48] applies to agreements bringing about either a merger as defined in the Fair Trading Act[49] or a "concentration" over which the EC Commission has exclusive jurisdiction, as defined in the EC Merger Regulation.[50] (There is a similar exclusion from the Chapter II prohibition.[51]) The OFT has published a draft Guideline on the scope of the exclusion.[52]

Clearance under the EC Merger Regulation extends to restrictions which are "directly related and necessary" to the bringing about of the concentration itself.[53] Such restrictions are called "ancillary" and are considered in a Commission Notice.[54] That Notice will be useful guidance under the Act since the exclusion for agreements bringing about a Fair Trading Act merger is extended[55] to provisions directly related and necessary to the implementation of the merger.

---

46 A misnomer, in that, since he did not have jurisdiction over it in the first place, he does not claw anything "back".
47 Competition Act 1998: Exclusion of Land Agreements: Consultation on a draft Order (DTI, February 1999, URN 98/1029).
48 S 3(1)(a) and Sched 1.
49 Para 1 of Sched 1. The FTA test is too elaborate to be discussed in detail here. However, note that para 1(4) of Sched 1 provides in effect that the exclusion will apply whatever level of control is being acquired under the merger agreements.
50 Para 6 of Sched 1. This provision may be "belt and braces" since Member States are prohibited from applying their domestic competition laws to concentrations over which the Commission has exclusive jurisdiction: see Art 21.2 of the EC Merger Regulation (Reg 4064/89, as amended).
51 See Chap 4 below.
52 Exclusion for Mergers and Ancillary Restrictions (OFT 416).
53 Art 6.1 of the EC Merger Regulation (Reg 4064/89, as amended).
54 OJ 1990 C203/5.
55 By para 1(2) of Sched 1.

Typically, such provisions include non-competition covenants accepted by the seller and intellectual property licences or temporary supply agreements allowing the acquired business the time to set up its own arrangements. Whether arrangements of that kind are sufficiently connected with the merger or "necessary" for its implementation will depend on the circumstances, including in particular their proposed duration.

The Guideline envisages that the DGFT will consider such matters in deciding whether a restriction is directly related and necessary to a merger.[56] The exercise will be carried out by staff in the OFT's Mergers Secretariat who are responsible for advising the DGFT on whether mergers should be referred to the Competition Commission (reporting side).[57] The Guideline suggests that the parties may be able to negotiate amendments to restrictions associated with mergers so as to satisfy the OFT that they are truly ancillary.[58]

Such arrangements have in the past constituted registrable arrangements under the RTPA. The exclusion for merger agreements under the Act should result in them being reviewed under one statute only.

The DGFT has power to withdraw the exclusion by giving a "direction". This he may do if the parties fail to provide information to him on request, or if he takes the view that the agreement (if not excluded) would infringe the prohibition and that he would be unlikely to give it an unconditional exemption.[59] The Guideline points out that this is only likely to arise where the combined market share of the parties exceeds 25% (*i.e.* the normal appreciability threshold for the application of the Act, as well as one of the alternative jurisdictional tests for mergers under the Fair Trading Act).

There are certain circumstances in which the DGFT cannot withdraw the exclusion[60] and the relevant agreements are therefore said to be "protected". These are: where the Secretary of State has announced that the merger in question will not be referred to the Competition Commission; or a reference has been made and the Commission has found that there is indeed a qualifying merger;[61] or the

---

56 Exclusion for Mergers and Ancillary Restrictions (OFT 416), para 4.8.
57 See Chap 7 below for a description of the Competition Commission.
58 Exclusion for Mergers and Ancillary Restrictions (OFT 416), para 4.21.
59 Para 4 of Sched 1.
60 Para 5 of Sched 1.
61 *i.e.* either the 25% market share or the £70 million assets test under the Fair Trading Act is satisfied.

transaction leads to the acquisition of actual control.[62] The last of these makes it clear that the intention is that the DGFT should be able to investigate "merger" arrangements under which one party has influence over the commercial strategy of the other which falls short of actual control.

There are special rules for newspaper and water industry mergers.[63]

Specific competition régimes

Existing exclusions from the RTPA and Competition Act 1980 in various sectors are preserved and transformed into exclusions from the Chapter I prohibition by Schedule 2 of the Act. The coverage of these exclusions is as follows:

Financial services	the constitution and rules of recognised self-regulating organisations, investment exchanges and clearing houses.
Company law	the operation of a recognised "supervisory body" or "qualifying body" under the Companies Act 1989
Broadcasting	networking arrangements designated by the Independent Television Commission and Channel 3 news arrangements
Environmental protection	producer responsibility obligations under exemption schemes pursuant to the Environment Act 1995.

General exclusions

Schedule 3 contains a mixed bag of exclusions, some of which are fundamental to the operation of the Act. They are as follows (by reference to the numbered paragraphs of Schedule 3).

(1) Planning agreements:	agreements embodying planning obligations under the various Town and Country Planning Acts
(2) "Section 21(2)":	agreements which have been given formal clearance under section 21(2) of the RTPA

---

62 The highest of the three levels of control specified in the Fair Trading Act.
63 See paras 3 and 5(d) respectively of Sched 1.

(*i.e.* have been notified, considered and found unobjectionable by the DGFT, who has so advised the Secretary of State) are excluded from the Chapter I prohibition; however, this exclusion can be clawed back by the DGFT and the transitional period for such agreements can be truncated: this is discussed in Chapter 8 below, dealing with the Act's transitional provisions

(3) EEA regulated markets:

agreements setting up investment exchanges and the like in Member States of the European Economic Area ("EEA") and agreements which included restrictions designed to ensure compliance with the rules of such exchanges

(4) General economic interest:

Art 86(2) (old Art 90(2)) of the EC Treaty shelters undertakings entrusted with the operation of services of "general economic interest" from Treaty rules, in particular the competition rules; this wording is carried over wholesale as an exclusion from both Chapter I and Chapter II, although arguably section 60 would have led to the same result[63a]

(5) Compliance with law:

it is not an infringement of the Chapter I prohibition to make or comply with an agreement entered into so as to comply with a legal obligation; the legal obligation may stem from UK law, directly applicable EU or EEA law, or from the law of another Member State which has legal effect in the United Kingdom

(6) International agreements:

the Secretary of State is given power to exclude individual agreements or categories of agreements from the Chapter I prohibition if he is satisfied that it is necessary to do so

---

63a Chap 9 below treats this issue in more depth (see p 187). An OFT Guideline on the topic has been promised but has yet to emerge.

to avoid conflict with an international obligation of the United Kingdom; the fact that "international obligation" is defined so as to extend to international arrangements concerning civil aviation gives a hint as to what was envisaged

(7) Public policy:

more widely phrased powers for the Secretary of State, allowing the exclusion of individual agreements or categories if he is satisfied that there are "exceptional and compelling reasons of public policy" why the Chapter I prohibition ought not to apply; it seems unlikely that there will be much recourse to this provision; if such measures were taken and challenged, one interesting legal issue would be whether this was to intended to be, or to cater for, a "relevant difference" between the Act and Art 81 (old Art 85), which would preclude either party from relying on section 60 if the result was inconsistent with the European Court's case law under Art 81

(8) Coal and steel:

for the remaining lifetime of the ECSC Treaty (due to expire on 22 July 2002), matters over which the EC Commission has exclusive jurisdiction under that Treaty are excluded from the Chapter I prohibition[64]

(9) Agricultural products:

lastly, there is an exclusion for certain agreements concerning agricultural products which further the aims of the agricultural provisions of the EC Treaty (set out in Art 33 (old Art 39) EC) or which set up production or sale co-operatives so long as there is no requirement to charge "identical" prices; the exclusion is deemed terminated if the EC

---

64 The ECJ has held that only the Commission can establish whether or not there has been an infringement of the ECSC competition rules: neither national courts nor national competition authorities have any jurisdiction over agreements relating to the coal and steel products listed in the ECSC Treaty: see Case C-128/92 *H J Banks & Co* v *British Coal Corporation* [1994] ECR I-1209.

Commission examines an agreement under Regulation 26[65] and concludes that it does not qualify for exclusion from the operation of Art 81(1) (old Art 85(1)); this makes the exclusion rather similar to a parallel exemption.[66] This exclusion can also be clawed back by the DGFT in the same way as the "section 21(2)" exclusion, described above.

Professional rules

The self-regulation of professions and other service providers can involve some restrictions on competition. The rules usually require members of the profession to renounce forms of conduct thought to be unsuitable or incompatible with their professional status.

The RTPA excluded a large number of professions from its scope altogether (so that, for examples, price fixing by lawyers would not have been caught – if it had ever happened). The Act takes a narrower approach.[67] Schedule 4 allows the Secretary of State to "designate" (in effect, to approve) the rules of bodies regulating a number of specified professions.[68] In respect of such rules, once designated, there is no infringement of Chapter I either in making them, in the obligations they impose or in agreeing to abide by them.

The Act is commendably neutral in that it seemingly allows any body which represents professionals to put forward its rule-book for designation. Thus, to the extent that the general law allows, a "break-away" body could set up as a rival to the traditional regulator and still have its rules approved.

The list of designated rules is to be set up, and any amendments to it effected, by Statutory Instrument.[68a] The Secretary of State has to transmit to the DGFT any rules which he designates. The DGFT is

---

65   Which makes provision for the application of the EC competition rules to agriculture.
66   See the section on "Exemptions" below, p 55.
67   See the Guideline on Trade Associations, Professions and Self-Regulating Bodies (OFT 408).
68   The professional services concerned are listed in Part II of Sched 4, as follows, in an order which makes one wonder about the draftsman's priorities (although it is in fact a survival from the RTPA, Schedule 1): Legal; Medical; Dental; Ophthalmic; Veterinary; Nursing; Midwifery; Physiotherapy; Chiropody; Architectural; Accounting and auditing; Insolvency; Patent agency; Parliamentary agency; Surveying; Engineering and technology etc [*sic*]; Educational; Religious.
68a   Sched 4, para 5.

obliged to keep copies, which will be available for inspection and copying by the public, possibly on payment of a fee.[68b]

The DGFT can advise the Secretary of State if he considers that any set of rules, or individual rules, should not be designated or, indeed, that rules which are not designated should be.[69] If the Secretary of State accepts the DGFT's advice, he may revoke a designation.[69a]

Altering the range of exclusions

The Secretary of State is given power to amend the exclusions for mergers[70] or, more significantly, the "general" list in Schedule 3.[71] The amendment can take the form of adding to the list, altering it or removing exclusions from it. However, he may only *amend or remove* from the Schedule 3 exclusions *either* items which he has added to the list or those relating to planning agreements, "section 21(2)", or the EU-related matters of coal and steel or agricultural agreements.[72] Before *adding* to the Schedule 3 categories, he must be satisfied either that the agreements concerned generally do not adversely affect competition or that they are best dealt with under the Chapter II prohibition or the retained monopoly provisions of the Fair Trading Act 1973.[73]

New forms of exclusion can be made subject to the same sort of claw-back power as, for example, the section 21(2) exclusion.[74]

3.4   Exemptions

Agreements that do not fall within the terms of one of the exclusions will face the full force of the prohibition (always assuming an appreciable effect on competition) unless they qualify for an exemption. Exemptions are conferred either automatically (by law, whether via EC law – the parallel exemption – or directly as a matter of United Kingdom law – domestic block exemptions) or on application to the DGFT (individual

---

68b *Ibid*, paras 5 and 7.
69   Sched 4, para 5.
69a Sched 4, para 6.
70   S 3(2).
71   S 3(3).
72   *Ibid*.
73   See Chap 4 below on the DGFT's retained powers under the Fair Trading Act 1973.
74   S 3(5).

exemption or section 11 exemptions – the procedure for notifying agreements for an individual exemption is described in Chapter 5 below[75]).

It is that order of possible exemption (parallel, block or individual) which is the most logical to follow when it is necessary to decide "what to do about" an agreement which an undertaking is proposing to enter into or which an adviser has to examine. That is because it makes sense to see if there is an applicable exemption already in existence before considering whether to go to the trouble and expense of applying for an individual exemption for the agreement. That is the order we will follow, although it is not the order in which the Act sets out the possibilities.

Whatever type of exemption may be relevant, agreements may only have one if, on assessment, they demonstrably afford economic benefits outweighing the restrictions on competition to which they give rise. The criteria for making that assessment, under EC law or under the Act, derive from Article 81(3) (old Article 85(3)). It is helpful to set them out before describing the various types of possible exemption.

The criteria for exemption

The balancing exercise to be performed by the DGFT in deciding whether exemption can be granted is set out in section 9 of the Act. Exemption may be available in respect of an agreement which:

"(a) contributes to –
  (i) improving production or distribution, or
  (ii) promoting technical or economic progress,
while allowing consumers a fair share of the resulting benefit;

but

(b) does not –
  (i) impose on the undertakings concerned restrictions which are not indispensable to the attainment of those objectives; or
  (ii) afford the undertakings concerned the possibility of eliminating competition in respect of a substantial part of the products in question."

As the OFT Guideline points out[76-77], this is taken directly from Article 81(3) (old 85(3)), with the omission of that article's reference to "goods" in connection with improvements to production or distribution. It is clear that Article 81(3) is applicable to services agreements as well as to

---

75 See p 105.
76-77 The Chapter I Prohibition (OFT 401), para 4.9.

goods agreements, so this is a sensible departure from the wording of the EC precedent.

It can be seen that section 9 (like Article 81(3)) requires in each case two positive and two negative conditions to be satisfied before exemption can be granted. An agreement may contribute marvellously to the distribution of goods, but it will not receive an exemption if it allows the parties to eliminate competition on the relevant market or contains restrictions going beyond what is necessary to achieve the claimed benefits.

The conditions themselves are largely self-explanatory. The Guideline[78] sets out some examples and gives an indication of the DGFT's expected approach to these issues. Production or distribution improvements may be effected by lower costs from longer production runs, improvements in product quality and so on. Technical or economic progress may be promoted by efficiency gains from economies of scale, or specialisation in R&D. These improvements are not required to occur overnight, so long as there is a benefit to consumers in addition to the benefits to the parties. "Consumers" are not necessarily final consumers; they may be (indeed perhaps are more likely to be) the customers of the parties. The Guideline emphasises that the views of those for whom benefits are claimed are important considerations in the exemption process and may well be sought directly.[79]

It also emphasises the importance attached to the negative criteria. The DGFT "will look carefully for any restrictions beyond those necessary to securing those benefits";[80] and:

> "if, after an appropriate market analysis, he concludes that [the condition as to the elimination of competition] is not satisfied, there can be no possibility of an exemption. An application for an individual exemption is unlikely to succeed if the parties are unable to show that there will continue to be effective competition in the markets for the goods or services with which the agreement is concerned."[81]

Parallel exemptions

Parallel exemptions[82] are automatic exemptions from the Chapter I prohibition for agreements which are exempted under EC law from the prohibition in Article 81(1) (old Article 85(1)) or which would be so

---

78 The Chapter I Prohibition (OFT 401), paras 4.11-4.16.
79 *Ibid*, para 4.13.
80 *Ibid*, para 4.15.
81 *Ibid*, para 4.16.
82 The term conferred by s 10(3).

exempted if they affected trade between Member States.[83] "Automatic" means that the exemption arises by law and does not have to be applied for.

This concept, which is an attractive and neat invention of the framers of the Act, gives effect to the desire for consistency and avoidance of conflict in the operation of the two systems, UK and EC, which is given specific expression in section 60. It recognises the potential for overlap, or double jeopardy as it is sometimes called, between the two systems and avoids inconsistency in application both when EC law applies and when it does not.

Thus, if an agreement benefits from an exemption under EC law from the operation of Article 81(1) (old 85(1)), it is automatically taken outside the scope of the Chapter I prohibition. That principle applies whether that EC exemption is an individual one or arises from a block exemption, with or without an "opposition" procedure (under which the agreement is deemed cleared if notified to the Commission and not specifically objected to within a specified period).[84]

Likewise, there is also an automatic exemption from the Chapter I prohibition for agreements which do not affect trade between member states – in other words, they fall outside the scope of Article 81(1) (old 85(1)) – but which would be covered by an EC block exemption if they did affect inter-state trade.[85]

It is usually easy enough for the parties to know whether they have an individual EC exemption for their agreement. It may be less easy to know whether they are covered by an EC block exemption.

Experience shows that there are many uncertainties in interpretation of EC block exemptions. For example, it has been unclear for many years whether the standard United Kingdom method of specifying beers in pub leases conforms with the method required by the relevant EC block exemption: judicial authority in this country conflicted with the Commission's view.[86] Likewise there are numerous open issues in the new Technology Transfer Block Exemption.[87]

---

83 The parallel exemption extends also to agreements which are caught by, and exempted from, the prohibition of restrictive agreements in Art 53 of the EEA agreement: this is subject to any modifications which may be prescribed by the Secretary of State: s 10(11). This rather arcane point will not be further discussed here.

84 S 10(1). The "most relevant" EC block exemptions are listed in the Guideline on the Chapter I prohibition (OFT 401), para 4.6. The ones mentioned there are those for specialisation agreements, R&D, exclusive distribution, exclusive purchasing, franchise agreements, motor vehicle distribution and servicing and technology transfer. There are also several block exemptions in the areas of transport and of insurance.

85 S 10(2).

86 *Greenalls Management Ltd* v *Canavan* [1998] EuLR 507 (CA).

87 Discussed in Kinsella, *EU Technology Licensing* (Palladian, 1998).

Since parallel exemption depends on the applicability of an EC exemption, there will be occasions on which these uncertainties will matter. The Act does not specify how they may be dealt with. It is to be expected that the OFT will be reluctant to give a view on whether the parties can claim the benefit of an EC block exemption. The OFT is more likely to urge the parties to approach the EC Commission directly. However, it should be remembered that the Commission cannot give a legally binding ruling on the interpretation of a block exemption[88] and the English Court of Appeal has (correctly) been prepared to take a different view from that taken by the Commission in a published Notice.[89]

Ultimately therefore, the issue whether the parties can claim the benefit of a *parallel exemption* may require a UK court (including the Competition Commission) to refer a question of interpretation of an *EC block exemption* to the European Court under Article 234 (old Article 177) of the EC Treaty.[90] While this is undoubtedly the correct approach as a matter of law, it does go to show that some legal uncertainty is inherent in the concept of parallel exemption.

In principle, the parallel exemption is precisely co-extensive with the relevant EC exemption. Thus, it takes effect from the date on which the EC exemption takes effect and ceases if the EC exemption ceases to apply or is withdrawn.[91]

However, there are elaborate powers for the DGFT to withdraw the benefit of a parallel exemption, even retroactively, or to subject it to conditions.[92] In deciding whether or not to exercise these powers, the DGFT has investigative powers to compel the parties to produce any information he may require.[93] He is also required to consult the public as well as the parties.[94]

It is far from clear in what circumstances the DGFT might wish to exercise these powers. The Guideline[95] refers to agreements which have produced or may produce significantly adverse effects on a market in the United Kingdom or part of it. It is an open question whether and in what circumstances national competition law can be used to override a Community exemption; and the answer may be different as between

---

88 As the Commission itself well recognises: all its Notices are qualified by a statement that interpretation of the law is for the ECJ. See, for example, paras 39 and 47 of the Notice on Co-operation with National Courts, included at Appendix 4 to this book.
89 *Greenalls Management Ltd* v *Canavan* [1998] EuLR 507 (CA).
90 See Chap 2 above, p 20.
91 S 10(4).
92 S 10(5)-(7).
93 S 10(8).
94 See Rule 21 of the DGFT's Procedural Rules (OFT 411).
95 The Chapter I Prohibition (OFT 401), para 4.7.

individually exempted agreements and agreements falling within a block exemption.[96] It follows that section 60 itself might pose an obstacle to the application of these powers, depending on the meaning and content of the words "relevant differences" in that obscurely fascinating provision.

(United Kingdom) block exemptions

If the benefit of a parallel exemption cannot be claimed for the agreement, the next logical step would be to see whether it was covered by a block exemption provided for under UK law. As things stand, however, this seems to be a merely theoretical possibility, as no block exemptions have yet been proposed.[97] A principal reason for the lack of UK block exemptions is the neatness of the concept of parallel exemptions. Since they cover agreements without any inter-state trade effect as well as agreements which do actually fall within Article 81(1) (old Article 85(1)), they avoid the necessity of issuing UK block exemptions which precisely track the EC block exemptions.

That being so, there is no need at this stage for an elaborate discussion of the provisions of the Act under which block exemptions can be issued and their consequences. In brief, the DGFT may recommend[98] to the Secretary of State that he makes[99] a Statutory Instrument block exempting certain categories of agreement which are likely to meet the statutory criteria for exemption.[1] There are detailed provisions as to consultation and the Secretary of State's powers to depart from the DGFT's recommendation.[2]

A block exemption adopted in accordance with these provisions may attach conditions or obligations to the exemption.[3] Breach of such a condition leads automatically to the loss of the exemption.[4] Breach of any such obligation entitles the DGFT to withdraw it.[5] He may in any event be given the power to withdraw (or, as it is often more excitingly

---

96 See Chap 2 above on the relationship between the Act and EC proceedings.
97 At one stage, the DTI was considering whether there was a need for a block exemption for joint development agreements in the gas industry. Present indications are that no such block exemption will be adopted.
98 Under s 6(1).
99 Pursuant to powers conferred by s 6(2).
1 Under s 9, discussed above.
2 S 8.
3 S 6(5).
4 S 6(6)(a).
5 S 6(6)(b).

called, "claw back") the exemption in respect of a particular agreement.[6] United Kingdom block exemptions may include an "opposition" procedure as they are called in those EC block exemptions which employ them.[7] They have been little used to date in EC experience.

Section 11 exemptions

A different sort of exemption by category is provided for in section 11 of the Act which also seems unlikely to be used in the foreseeable future. Article 84 (old Article 88) of the EC Treaty gives reserve powers to Member States to apply Articles 81 and 82 (old Articles 85 and 86) pending the adoption of Regulations under Article 83 (old Article 87) laying down procedures for the application of Articles 81 and 82 by the Community institutions. Since the adoption of Regulation 17, Article 84 (old Article 88) has largely been a dead letter although it does still apply to non-EU air transport and tramp shipping.

Nevertheless, for form's sake, the Act makes provision for exemption to be given from the Chapter I prohibition in respect of agreements over which the United Kingdom authorities retain jurisdiction by virtue of Article 84 (old Article 88).[8] It is open to the Secretary of State to make regulations in effect exempting any such category of agreement from Chapter I.[9] In an uninspired moment, the draftsman decided that an exemption thus issued under section 11 of the Act would be known as "a section 11 exemption".[10]

Individual exemptions

If no parallel or national block exemption is available, an agreement which falls within the scope of Chapter I will require an individual exemption if the full force of the prohibition is to be fended off.

It is a basic aspect of an authorisation system, such as that set up by the Act, that individual exemption has to be applied for, however meritorious the agreement. It is not enough for the parties to take the view that they deserve one. There is no legal duty to notify, but if they believe that their agreement offers the wider benefits which would

---

6 S 6(6)(c).
7 S 7. For EC opposition procedures, see for example the Technology Transfer Regulation, described by Kinsella, *op cit*, fn 87 above.
8 S 11(1).
9 S 11(2).
10 S 11(3).

qualify it for exemption, they must bring those matters to the authorities' attention, and are at risk as to fines if they do not. However, as will be seen, this aspect is somewhat alleviated under the Act in that retroactive exemption can be given (on notification) for deserving agreements. There are also powers for modifying or withdrawing exemptions if circumstances change or if they have been obtained on the basis of misleading information.

Granting individual exemptions

Section 4 gives effect to these basic principles by providing that the DGFT may only grant individual exemption in respect of agreements which have been notified to him and which meet the section 9 criteria. The mechanics of notification are discussed in Chapter 5 below. The form for notification is reproduced in Appendix 2 to this book. The intended approach of the DGFT to the section 9 conditions for exemption has already been discussed above.

It is said in the Guideline that the onus of proving that the conditions are satisfied is on the parties.[11] Technically, that may be right. The real question in each case, however, is the willingness of the regulator to be persuaded.

The DGFT has power to attach conditions or obligations to an individual exemption.[12] No indications are given in the Guideline as to the sort of conditions or obligations which the DGFT envisages. The EC Commission regularly calls for reports and information about the operation of the exempted agreement. It may require a specified proportion of capacity to be made available on reasonable terms to third parties. It may demand to be informed if the parties decide not to license jointly developed technology to third parties or to refuse them membership of an approved association. It seems likely that the DGFT will impose similar sorts of conditions in appropriate cases.

The difference between conditions and obligations can be seen in the consequences of failing to comply with them (discussed below, under "Cancelling or modifying individual exemptions", page 64).

The Act provides that the exemption will have effect for such period as the DGFT considers appropriate[13], and that the period must be specified in the grant of the exemption.[14] This suggests that a permanent

---

11 The Chapter I Prohibition (OFT 401), para 4.10.
12 S 4(3)(a).
13 S 4(3)(b).
14 S 4(4).

exemption cannot be given, which seems consistent both with principle and with EC law.[15]

However, given the slight differences in wording between the relevant parts of the Act and the EC's Regulation 17, there may be some room for argument that the DGFT is not absolutely required to impose a limit on the duration of the exemption. The Guideline points in this direction also, saying that "an individual exemption may be granted subject to conditions or obligations *and/or* for a specified period".[16] In any event, the Act makes clear that, once given, an exemption may be extended on application.[17] This accords with EC practice under which exemptions for some long-standing agreements have been renewed once or more, giving them a life stretching over decades.[18]

An important difference between the Act and the EC system is that exemption under the Act can be fully retroactive, whereas under EC law the exemption cannot normally be backdated beyond the date of notification.[19] The Act provides that individual exemption may have effect from a date earlier than that on which it is granted, without placing any limits on what that date may be.[20] This will allow exemption to be sought after the agreement has been in operation, for example if litigation between the parties is threatened or begun.[21]

The OFT clearly hopes that the availability of fully retroactive exemption will reduce the volume of precautionary notifications. In some circumstances, this hope may be well founded. Certainly the realisation that, under the EC rules, subsequent notification cannot cure the effects of the prohibition (notably that of contractual invalidity) for the period between inception and notification has caused some parties to notify agreements on a precautionary basis to DG IV. This is so particularly if they have doubts about being able to cohabit peacefully with the other parties to the agreement for its duration.

---

15 Art 8.1 of EC Reg 17, JO 204/62, [1959-62] OJ Spec. Ed. 57 (the basic procedural regulation for the application of Arts 81 and 82 – old Arts 85 and 86) provides that individual exemption pursuant to Art 81(3) (old 85(3)) "*shall* be issued for a specified period" (emphasis added).

16 The Chapter I Prohibition (OFT 401), para 4.2; emphasis added.

17 S 4(6), which envisages that the DGFT will issue rules, under s 51, specifying how applications for extension are to be made. The procedure envisaged is set out in Rule 19 of the DGFT's Procedural Rules (OFT 411).

18 See *e.g. National Sulphuric Acid Association,* OJ 1989 L190/22; *Transocean Marine Paint Association,* OJ 1980 L39/73.

19 See Art 6.1 of Reg 17: the date from which exemption takes effect "shall not be earlier than the date of notification". Art 6.2 provides for limited exceptions from this rule, essentially for "pre-accession" agreements and Art 4.2 agreements, essentially those whose effects are confined to one Member State.

20 S 4(5).

21 See Chap 2 above.

However, parties will have to be sure that, in the event of litigation, it will be possible to obtain a retroactive exemption speedily for non-notification to be a sensible course for them to adopt in those circumstances. The Guideline states that the DGFT will endeavour to give priority to applications for individual exemptions in such circumstances.[22] Only experience will tell whether the OFT is capable of delivering on that rather non-committal promise.

Cancelling or modifying individual exemptions

The DGFT is given power to revoke exemptions, or to alter them if circumstances change, or if it transpires that he was not given the full picture when the agreement was notified. These powers will now be examined in more detail.

If the DGFT has reasonable grounds for considering that there has been a material change of circumstances since he granted an individual exemption, he may cancel it, or add, remove or vary conditions or obligations attached to the exemption.[23] It is said that he may exercise this power on his own initiative or on a complaint being made by any person.[24] This suggests that the powers will always be used in an adverse fashion.

However, this power ought, in an appropriate case, be used to loosen the regulatory burden as well as to tighten it. An arrangement may at the outset be exempted, but on condition that, for example, third parties are always able to buy the output of the joint venture company at published prices (the DGFT's power to impose conditions on an individual exemption is mentioned above). That condition could be removed if subsequently competition develops in that product market so that the condition puts the joint venture at a commercial disadvantage. It would therefore have been appropriate for the Act to specify that the power may be exercised on application by the parties to an exempted agreement, just as parties have regularly over the years applied to be released from undertakings given following a merger or from undertakings given to the Restrictive Practices Court.

Whatever the Act says, it is to be expected that such applications from parties would be entertained by the DGFT. The point remains, however, that the prohibition mentality tends to focus on the supposedly restrictive aspects of agreements, and to forget that the width of the

---

22   The Chapter I Prohibition (OFT 401), para 7.13.
23   S 5(1).
24   S 5(7); our emphasis.

prohibition catches harmless and indeed pro-competitive arrangements as well. Section 5(7)[25] is a good example of the product of the inappropriate legislative mindset which may result. It is to be hoped that the DGFT does not become similarly infected.

The DGFT may exercise his power to cancel an exemption or add or vary conditions or obligations in two further situations.

The first is if he has a "reasonable suspicion" that the information on which he based his decision to grant an individual exemption was incomplete, false or misleading in a material particular.[26] (And, of course, the actual provision of such information to the DGFT is a criminal offence.[27]) This is a power which is unlikely to have to be used to any great extent.

The second situation is in the event of a breach of an *obligation* attached to an individual exemption.[28]

Withdrawing or amendment of exemption in these three situations (change of circumstances, exemption based on false or misleading information, breach of obligation) requires a positive act of the DGFT, namely a notice in writing. The notice must specify the time from which the cancellation or the imposition, variation or revocation of a condition or obligation takes effect.[29] If the pretext for the DGFT's action is either of the "culpable" bases (that is, false or misleading information or breach of obligation) the date can be earlier that the date of the notice.[30] In other words, just as exemption can be made fully retroactive, so it can be utterly revoked, leaving the parties exposed to civil proceedings brought by third parties for the period for which they apparently had an exemption.

In contrast, breach of a *condition* attached to an exemption leads automatically to the cancellation of the exemption.[31] No notice from the DGFT is required. This suggests that breach of a condition is more serious than breach of an obligation.[32] The potential for automatic cancellation of the exemption, being a legal consequence, makes it important that conditions be phrased clearly and without the use of

---

25 See fn 24.
26 S 5(2).
27 S 44. The criminal offences which may be committed in connection with the Act are discussed in more detail in Chap 6 below, and in the Guideline on Enforcement (OFT 407).
28 S 5(4).
29 S 5(5).
30 S 5(6).
31 S 5(3), which says that failure to comply with a condition "has the effect of" cancelling the exemption.
32 "Condition" and "obligation" are distinguished, without much clarity, in certain EC block exemptions such as Reg 4056/86 (OJ 1986 L378/4) on maritime transport (Arts 4 and 5).

subjective concepts, so that compliance can be objectively verified. There should be no room for doubt as to whether exemption has been lost or retained.

Chapter 4

Abuse of Dominant · Position: The Chapter II · Prohibition

4.1 The Chapter II prohibition

Scope of the prohibition

Section 18 of the Act prohibits conduct which amounts to the abuse of a dominant position. It is therefore intended to control the behaviour of those who possess market power. This prohibition is referred to in the Act as "the Chapter II prohibition" (s 18(4)), as sections 17-24 of the Act are contained within Chapter II of Part I which is entitled "Abuse of Dominant Position".

Differences from Article 82

Section 18 is closely modelled on Article 82 (old Article 86) of the EC Treaty,[1] but there are some differences between the texts of the two provisions. The most important differences arise from the exclusively national jurisdiction of section 18, as opposed to the Community-wide jurisdiction of Article 82 (old Article 86) of the EC Treaty. Thus, whereas under Article 82 a dominant position must be held "within the common market or in a substantial part of it", under section 18(1) read together with section 18(3) a dominant position need only be held on a market "within the United Kingdom or any part of it".

Not only is the remit of the Act national, as one would expect, but in addition there is no requirement that the dominant position be held in a "substantial" part of the United Kingdom. Furthermore, Article 82 (old Article 86) can only be triggered where the behaviour "may affect trade between Member States", but section 18(1) only requires a possibility of an effect on trade within the United Kingdom or any part of it.

---

1 Art 82 is set out at Appendix 3.

Overall, it can be seen that the Chapter II prohibition could potentially be invoked to control relatively small localised markets within the United Kingdom, and thus there is likely to be an increase in the volume of applications and notifications as compared with activity under pre-existing national and Community competition law.

Article 82 (old Article 86) refers to "any **abuse** by one or more undertaking" whereas section 18 refers positively to "any **conduct** on the part of one or more undertaking". This has led to some suggestion that section 18 is designed to be directed against positive action only, as opposed to simply allowing something to occur. However, and particularly in view of the consistency requirements imposed by section 60 of the Act, it seems more likely that this difference in language is simply due to the different way in which section 18 has been structured.

The key issues

Two central questions arise:

(1) Who is subject to the Chapter II prohibition?

(2) What conduct is prohibited?

These questions, and the issues which arise, will be examined in turn.

4.2 **Who is subject to the Chapter II prohibition?**

Undertakings

Section 18 of the Act is concerned with conduct "on the part of one or more undertakings". The term "undertaking" is not defined in the Act, but it is familiar to competition lawyers as it is used, for example, in Articles 81 and 82 (old Articles 85 and 86) of the EC Treaty. The EC Treaty does not define an "undertaking" either, but case law of the European Court of Justice (ECJ) and decisions of the Commission establish that in principle any natural or legal person, of whatever juridical character, capable of carrying on some commercial or economic activity in the goods or services sector should come within the definition.[1a] The expression has therefore been construed broadly, and held to include:

1a See, for example, the Commission Decisions in *Polypropylene* OJ [1986] L230/1; [1988] 4
    CMLR 347, and in *Distribution of Package Tours during the 1990 World Cup* OJ 1992 L326/31.

- companies;
- partnerships;
- individuals;
- trade associations;
- P&I Clubs;
- agricultural associations;
- state-owned corporations.

Certain bodies have been held not to constitute an undertaking for the purposes of Articles 81 and 82 (old Articles 85 and 86). In particular, Member States, local authorities, and other institutions established by the state have been held not to qualify as an undertaking when exercising their public law powers.[2] On the other hand, those bodies have been regarded as undertakings in the exercise of their commercial activities.[3]

It can therefore be seen that the term "undertaking" in the Chapter II prohibition will be construed widely so as to include almost all natural and legal persons, provided that they are carrying on some commercial or economic activity.

One or more undertakings

Section 18 of the Act prohibits abusive conduct on the part of "one or more" dominant undertakings. This expression opens the door to arguments that two or more undertakings together hold a "collective dominant position" or a "joint dominant position". Thus, even where undertakings may not individually be dominant, certain market structures may permit them together to behave in an abusive manner. This is termed an oligopolistic market.

The concept of joint dominance is still an uncertain one in EC law, and there is particular controversy surrounding the nature of the links (economic or otherwise) which must exist between undertakings for there to be a finding of joint dominance. In the *Italian Flat Glass* case the Court of First Instance (CFI) rejected the Commission's approach to collective dominance, but held:

> "There is nothing, in principle, to prevent two or more independent economic entities from being, on a specific market, united by some economic links that, by virtue of that fact, together they hold a dominant

---

2 See, for example, Cases C-159 & 160/91 *Poucet v Assurances Générales de France* [1993] ECR 637 (French regional social security offices not undertakings).

3 See, for example, *Höfner and Elser v Macrotron* [1991] ECR I-1979 (German Federal Employment Office, in so far as it was providing services to the employment market, was an undertaking).

position vis-à-vis the other operators on the same market. This could be the case, for example, where two or more independent undertakings jointly have, through agreements or licences, a technological lead affording them the power to behave to an appreciable extent independently of their competitors, their customers and ultimately of their consumers."[4]

In a later case, the ECJ stated that for a collective dominant position to exist, the undertakings in the group must be linked in such a way as to adopt the same conduct on the market.[5] Most recently, in a case concerning shipping liner conferences, the CFI stated that it is "settled case law" that Article 82 (old Article 86) is capable of applying to situations where several undertakings together hold a dominant position on the relevant market.[6]

In recognition of the developing nature of the ECJ and CFI jurisprudence in this area, the Office of Fair Trading (OFT) Guideline on the Chapter II Prohibition deals with this issue briefly and states:

> "The links may be structural or they may be such that the undertakings adopt the same conduct on the market."[7]

The need for the DGFT to employ the concept of a collective dominant position may prove to be less frequent than under Community law, as the Competition Act retains the complex monopoly provisions of the Fair Trading Act 1973, under which this type of situation can be referred to the reporting arm of the Competition Commission.[8] However, private parties may wish to involve the principle of collective dominance in support of complaints or claims under the Act.

The requirement of dominance

The Chapter II prohibition only applies to undertakings which hold a dominant position in a market. A dominant undertaking is one which is able to behave "to an appreciable extent independently of its competitors and customers and ultimately of consumers".[9] It is important to bear in mind that dominance itself is not prohibited under the Act or Article 82, only abuse of that dominant position.

---

4 Cases T-68/89 etc *Società Italiano Vetro SpA v Commission* [1992] ECR II–1403 at para 358.
5 Case C-393/92 *Almelo* [1994] ECR I–1477.
6 Joined Cases T-24-26 & 28/93 *Compagnie Maritime Belge v Commission* [1996] ECR II–1201, now on appeal to the ECJ with case number C-395/96P (Opinion of A G Fennelly delivered on 29 October 1998).
7 (OFT 402), para 3.21.
8 See further Section 4.5 of this chapter on complex monopolies below, and Part III of the Act.
9 Case 322/81 *Michelin v Commission* [1983] ECR 3461 at 3503.

Dominance cannot be assessed in a vacuum, and is only a meaningful concept when judged against the background of a properly defined market. Therefore in order to assess whether section 18 of the Act may bite, legal advisers will have to consider a series of issues which will often require complex economic analysis. These may be summarised as follows:

- what is the relevant product market?
- what is the relevant geographic market?
- what is the relevant temporal market?
- what is the undertaking's power on the relevant market as defined?

Often the answers to some of these questions may affect the answers given to others, but it is nonetheless helpful to approach each question in turn. The OFT Guidelines take this course[10], and the ECJ and the Commission have usually dealt with dominance in these separate stages.

The current approach to market definition

In general, competition authorities in Europe, North America and elsewhere have refined the techniques used in market definition in recent years. In particular, the European Commission published a Notice in 1997 on the definition of the relevant market for the purposes of Community competition law[11] which draws heavily on the approach to economic analysis espoused by the United States Department of Justice and Federal Trade Commission in their Horizontal Merger Guidelines (revised 1992). The OFT has indicated in its Guideline on Market Definition[12] that it will generally follow this approach. This is helpful in promoting transparency and increased legal certainty, but market definition nonetheless remains an inexact science.

Methodological tools

A significant technique which the OFT has stated that it will use is sometimes termed the hypothetical monopolist test. This focuses upon whether a hypothetical monopolist could maintain prices above

---

10 See, for example, the OFT Guidelines on Market Definition (OFT 403), on Assessment of Market Power (OFT 415 in draft), and on the Chapter II Prohibition (OFT 402) at paras 3.3-3.18.
11 OJ 1997 C372/5.
12 (OFT 403), para 1.3.

competitive levels. The test was originally developed by United States competition authorities to assess the effects of proposed mergers, and they defined a market as:

> "a product or group of products and a geographic area in which it is produced or sold such that a hypothetical profit-maximising firm, not subject to price regulation, that was the only present and future producer or seller of those products in that area likely would impose at least a 'small but significant and non-transitory' increase in price, assuming the terms of sale of all other products are held constant. A relevant market is a group of products and a geographic area that is no bigger than necessary to satisfy this test."[13]

This test of whether it would be profitable to impose a "small but significant and non-transitory increase in price" is referred to as the "SSNIP" test. Generally a price of 5-10% above competitive levels will be used, although the OFT stresses that this is a rough guide rather than a rule.[14]

However, this test is only a methodological tool, and cannot be applied mechanically. In particular, often a case which arises under the Chapter II prohibition may require market definition where an undertaking is dominant and therefore has already raised prices above competitive levels, such that even they could not profitably raise prices further. In such a case, the competition authorities would need to assess whether the current price is already above competitive levels by looking, for example, for evidence of excess profits.

Precedents

In accordance with the requirement of consistency with Community law laid down under section 60 of the Act, the OFT has acknowledged that in cases where a market has already been investigated and defined by the European Commission or Courts, that market definition will provide an important precedent under the Act.[15] However, the OFT Guidelines point out that competitive conditions may change over time, and the market definition used in a previous case may not always be the correct one to use in future cases. Even within the same geographic area and at the same time, market definition can vary depending upon the parties and the type of the alleged infringement.

---

13 US Horizontal Merger Guidelines (revised 1992), p 7.
14 OFT Guideline on Market Definition (OFT 403), para 3.2.
15 *Ibid*, paras 5.15-5.20.

The relevant product market

Definition of the relevant product or services market is a crucial first step in identifying whether a dominant position exists.[16] In very broad terms, where products can be regarded as interchangeable, they are within the same product market. To assess whether products are interchangeable, it is necessary to consider:

- demand-side substitutability;
- supply-side substitutability.

Demand-side substitutability

This involves consideration of what other products a customer would turn to, where prices of the product or products which are the subject of the inquiry are raised by a small but significant amount above competitive levels. Where such a price rise would cause a significant switch by customers to other products, the so-called "cross-elasticity of demand" is high, and this suggests that the substitute products are within the same market. This test can be repeated by adding the substitute products to the market, until a stage is reached where a small but significant price rise would not cause significant numbers of customers to switch to substitute products. At that point, all of the substitute products which customers would demand will be included within the product market.

In addition to considering cross-elasticities of demand, other factors including a product's intended use, physical characteristics and price may all be relevant to interchangeability.

It is important to note that it is not necessary that all customers, or even a majority of customers, would switch to alternative products. What is essential is that the number of customers likely to switch is sufficiently large to prevent a hypothetical monopolist from maintaining prices above competitive levels.

What period of time would be take into account when considering whether customers would switch to substitute products? The OFT has indicated in its Guideline on Market Definition that "as a rough rule of thumb" if substitution took longer than one year, those products would not be included within the same product market. However, the OFT

---

16 Reference is hereafter to the relevant product market, but the analysis would apply equally to defining the relevant services market in an appropriate case. See generally OFT Guideline on Market Definition (OFT 403), paras 3.1-3.22.

Guideline goes on to state that the answer will vary from "case to case".[17]

Captive customers and chains of substitution

Other considerations which the OFT has stated that it will take into account in considering demand-side substitutability include captive customers and chains of substitution.

As an example of captive customer, the Market Definition Guideline refers to commuters travelling by train. For them, slower buses at a later time of day would not be an acceptable substitute, whereas leisure travellers might be happy to travel later in the day and may view buses as a close substitute for trains.[18] In those circumstances, the authorities would be alert to price discrimination against the "captive" commuter customers.

Chains of substitution are linked products, which may be included in the same product market even where they are not direct substitutes for one another. This is because there is an unbroken chain of substitutable products linking them together.[19]

How demand-side substitutability is assessed

What evidence will the OFT take into account when considering issues of demand-side substitutability for a particular product or products? The Guideline on Market Definition indicates that the following are likely to be important:

- interviews with customers and competitors;
- evidence of the cost to customers of switching products relative to the value of the product;
- patterns in price change and historical evidence of the effects of any previous price changes;
- evidence on price elasticities.[20]

Supply-side substitutability

In some cases it is relevant to consider the degree of substitutability which exists on the supply-side of the market. Where the producer of

---

17 OFT Guideline on Market Definition (OFT 403), para 3.5.
18 *Ibid*, para 3.8.
19 See further *ibid*, paras 3.9-3.12.
20 *Ibid*, para 3.6.

product B can relatively easily switch its machinery and other processes to produce product A, supply-side substitutability will act as a constraint on the ability of the producer of product A to raise prices. This might suggest that products A and B are part of the same market.

Not all competition authorities consider supply-side substitutability at the stage of market definition, but rulings of the ECJ indicate that it should be considered[21], and the OFT has stated in its Guideline that it will include supply-side substitutes within the market definition when it is clear that substitution would take place relatively quickly and easily.[22] Substitution which would take longer than one year would not normally be included within the market.[23]

How supply-side substitutability is assessed

The Guideline on Market Definition indicates that the OFT may consider evidence from the following:

- potential suppliers, who could be asked about substitutability from a technical, cost and timing point of view. Evidence as to the capacity of potential suppliers to switch production might also be relevant;
- consumers, who could be asked whether they would use products supplied by an alternative producer.[24]

The relevant geographic market

The geographic market is the area over which the conditions of competition applying to the product or products concerned are the same for all traders.[25] It is the geographic area over which product substitution would take place. In the case of some products, there are practical, technical or legal reasons why it could not be supplied to a wide geographic market. For example, some heavy goods may be disproportionately expensive to transport in relation to their value, so that no undertaking would attempt to market them far from their place of manufacture. For other products, the market may be national, Community-wide or even world-wide.

---

21 For example, Case 6/72 *Continental Can v Commission* [1973] ECR 215.
22 OFT Guideline on Market Definition (OFT 403), paras 3.18-3.19.
23 *Ibid*, para 3.16.
24 *Ibid*, para 3.20.
25 See, for example, Case 27/76 *United Brands v Commission* [1978] ECR 207 at para 36 *et seq.*

Methodological tools and evidence

Competition authorities use the same methodological tools to examine the relevant geographic market as they apply to the definition of the product market. Thus, both demand-side and supply-side substitutability will be considered, although the OFT has stated in its Market Definition Guideline that retailing markets are more likely to be defined on the demand-side, whereas wholesaling and manufacturing markets are more likely to be defined on the supply-side.[26]

The sources of evidence used to determine the relevant geographic market will also be similar to those employed in defining the relevant product market. Again, the OFT Guideline on Market Definition makes specific reference to chains of substitution, but the OFT also states that other factors including the value of a product, customer mobility and transport costs may be particularly relevant to geographic market definition.[27] Significant imports of a particular product may indicate that the relevant geographic market is international, although this factor is not determinative.[28]

The European Commission's 1997 Notice on the definition of the relevant market for the purposes of Community competition law[29] suggests that the following may be factors in defining the geographic market:

- past evidence of diversion to other areas;
- basic demand characteristics (including national preferences, language, culture, lifestyle and the need for local presence on the market);
- the views of customers and competitors;
- the existing geographic pattern of purchases;
- trade flows and the pattern of shipments.

Scope of geographic markets under the Act

During parliamentary debates on the Competition Act, the Government stated clearly that it intended that the Chapter II prohibition should not be read as limiting the relevant geographic market to the United Kingdom. The relevant market could be defined as being wider than the

---

26 (OFT 403), para 4.2.
27 *Ibid*, paras 4.4, 4.6, 4.8.
28 *Ibid*, paras 4.9-4.10.
29 OJ 1997 C372/5.

United Kingdom. However, neither dominance which existed elsewhere but not in the United Kingdom, would not be caught by the Chapter II prohibition.

The relevant temporal market

As has already been noted above, considerations of time and duration come into the assessment of the product and geographic market. However, there is also the third temporal dimension of market definition, which has received far less attention in the case law of the Commission or the ECJ than product and geographic market definition. Although the temporal market is sometimes presented as an aspect of the product market, it is often helpful to consider it as a separate issue.

Competitive conditions may vary over time, for example during different seasons of the year or at different times of day. Thus in *United Brands v Commission*[30-31] there was evidence that the cross-elasticity for bananas rose and fell according to the season (and the availability of other fresh fruit). The OFT Guideline on Market Definition also refers to peak and off-peak train tickets as possibly being within different temporal markets.[32]

Complements and secondary products

The OFT Guideline on Market Definition highlights two further factors which may be relevant to market definition: complements and secondary products.[33]

Complements are products which are consumed together (such as coffee and milk) or produced together (such as petrol and diesel oil). Complements will be included in the same market when competition to supply one of the products constrains the price charged for the other. The most common situation in which complements become relevant is the market for secondary products.

Secondary products, also termed "after markets", are those which are only purchased if a customer has already purchased a primary

---

30-31 Case 27/76 [1978] ECR 207.
   32 (OFT 403), paras 5.1-5.3.
   33 See generally (OFT 403), paras 5.4-5.11.

product. Typical examples of secondary products include spare parts and servicing for equipment and machinery. The OFT suggests that where secondary products exist there are three possible market definitions:

- a single market, including both the primary and secondary products (*e.g.* cars plus their spare parts);
- multiple markets, where there is one market for the primary product but separate markets for the secondary products which relate to each brand of primary product (*e.g.* Ford spare parts, Fiat spare parts, Rolls Royce spare parts, and so on);
- dual markets, one for the primary product, and one for all brands of secondary product (*e.g.* a market for new cars and a separate market for spare parts for all types of car).[34]

In deciding which market definition is appropriate in a particular case, the OFT has indicated that it will pay particular attention to whether customers consider the whole-life cost of a product before purchasing it. The Guideline on Market Definition notes that customers are more likely to take this whole-life cost approach where the secondary product constitutes a relatively high proportion of the primary product's cost.[35]

Market power

Once the relevant markets have been defined (product, geographic and temporal), it is then necessary to consider whether an undertaking has sufficient market power to be dominant. To reiterate, the test laid down by the ECJ is does the undertaking enjoy a position of economic strength which:

> "enables it to prevent effective competition being maintained on the relevant market by affording it the power to behave to an appreciable extent independently of its competitors, customers and ultimately of its consumers."[36]

The draft OFT Guideline on Assessment of Market Power defines market power as the ability to raise prices above competitive levels.[37]

---

34 *Ibid*, para 5.6.
35 *Ibid*, para 5.8.
36 Case 27/76 *United Brands v Commission* [1978] ECR 207, para 38. See also Case 322/82 *Michelin v Commission* [1983] ECR 3461, para 30.
37 (OFT 415), para 1.1 at footnote 1.

In assessing market power, market shares are usually the most important indicator, but there are a number of other factors which may be taken into account.

Market shares

The larger the market share, the more likely a finding of dominance. In *Hoffman-La Roche v Commission*[38] the ECJ ruled that:

> "... although the importance of the market shares may vary from one market to another the view may legitimately be taken that very large shares are in themselves, and save in exceptional circumstances, evidence of the existence of a dominant position. An undertaking which has a very large market share and holds it for some time ... is by virtue of that share in a position of strength ..."

There are two important points to note from this statement. First that "in exceptional circumstances" even very large market shares may not evidence dominance. For example, it could be that an undertaking with a large market share is charging competitive rates, and that if it were to raise its prices new entrants would immediately come onto the market. Secondly, the ECJ referred to a very large market share held "for some time". It is important to consider not only current market shares, but also changes in the pattern of shares held over time. A very large market share held for only a short amount of time is unlikely to be indicative of dominance in itself.[39]

What is a very large market share? In *AKZO*[40] the ECJ ruled that a market share of 50% could be considered to be very large. Above this level, the onus would usually be on the undertaking concerned to show why it was not dominant on the relevant market. There have been many findings of dominance in relation to undertakings which hold market shares in the region of 40%. At the other end of the scale, where an undertaking has a market share of less than about 25%, it is unlikely to be dominant. The OFT Guidelines state that the Director General of Fair Trading (DGFT) considers it unlikely that an undertaking will be individually dominant if its market share is below 40%, although dominance could be established below that figure if other relevant

---

38 Case 85/76 [1979] ECR 461.
39 See also draft OFT Guideline on Assessment of Market Power (OFT 415), paras 4.2-4.3.
40 Case C-62/86 *AKZO Chemie BV v Commission* [1991] ECR I-3359, para 60.

factors (such as the weak position of competitors in that market) provided strong evidence of dominance.[41]

How market shares are measured

The draft OFT Guideline on Assessment of Market Power indicates that data on market shares may be collected from:

- companies under investigation;
- trade associations;
- customers and suppliers;
- market research reports.[42]

The OFT takes the view that the best indicator of market power will usually be a calculation of market shares using data relating to the value of a company's output, rather than volume of output.[43] The Guideline also expresses the hope that companies will submit data on market shares under alternative market definitions, rather than confining data to the market definition which gives the lowest market share.[44]

Other factors indicating dominance

When assessing market power, it is important to consider whether there are "barriers to entry" which would make it difficult for a new undertaking to enter the relevant market. Barriers to entry could include:

- legal provisions (for example licences or permits);
- technology and technical resources;
- size and strength of both the undertaking and possible new entrants (including so-called first-mover advantages, *i.e.* advantages which an undertaking enjoys from being already active in a market);
- economies of scale and scope;
- intellectual property rights (copyrights, patents and trade marks).

---

41 Draft OFT Guidelines on Assessment of Market Power (OFT 415) at para 2.11 and on the Chapter II Prohibition (OFT 402) at para 3.13.
42 Draft OFT Guideline on Assessment of Market Power (OFT 415), para 4.4.
43 *Ibid*, para 4.5.
44 *Ibid*, paras 4.7-4.8.

The draft OFT Guideline on Assessment of Market Power classifies entry barriers under three groups:

(1) absolute advantages (regulation, intellectual property rights and right to use an essential facility);

(2) strategic or "first-mover" advantages (sunk costs, economies of scale and scope, and access to finance); and

(3) exclusionary behaviour (vertical restraints, predatory behaviour and refusal to supply).[45-46]

Other factors which the OFT are likely to consider when assessing dominance under the Chapter II prohibition include:

- the extent of competition in the market (including the degree of vertical integration or of excess capacity in the market);
- price history and profitability of the businesses in the market;
- customer awareness and inertia.

4.3 What conduct is prohibited?

Examples of abuse

Once it has been established that an undertaking does hold a dominant position on the market as defined, it is necessary to decide whether it has abused that dominant position. Dominant undertakings have a "special responsibility" not to behave in ways which may prejudice competition in general, competitors or consumers.[47] Section 18 may therefore prohibit behaviour which would be wholly unobjectionable were the undertaking in question not dominant.

Section 18(2) of the Act lists examples of conduct which may constitute abuse:

- imposing unfair purchase or selling prices (directly or indirectly);
- imposing other unfair trading conditions;
- limiting production, markets or technical development to the prejudice of consumers;
- applying dissimilar conditions to equivalent transactions with other trading parties, thereby placing them at a competitive disadvantage (*i.e.* discrimination);

45-46 (OFT 415), paras 5.1-5.31.
47 Case 322/81 *Michelin v Commission* [1983] ECR 3461 at 3511.

- making the conclusion of contracts subject to the acceptance of supplementary obligations which have no connection with the subject of the contracts (including tying).

Although these examples represent some of the most common forms of abuse, it is important to remember that the list in section 18(2) is only by way of example; it is not exhaustive. The examples listed mirror exactly those given in Article 82 (old Article 86) of the EC Treaty.

Objective justification

Unlike the Chapter I prohibition, there is no possibility of an exemption from a finding that the Chapter II prohibition has been infringed. Similarly, there is no possibility of an exemption from a finding that Article 82 (old Article 86) of the EC Treaty has been abused.

However, the European Commission and Court have developed the concept of "objective justification", whereby conduct for which there is clear objective justification is not regarded as an abuse even if it restricts competition. Thus, by asking whether there is an objective justification for the particular conduct in question, legitimate commercial behaviour can be distinguished from anti-competitive behaviour which should and does fall within Article 82 (old Article 86). The OFT Guideline on the Chapter II Prohibition indicates that the UK authorities will also adopt this approach.[48] Of course, this is as one would expect given the section 60 requirement for consistency with European law.

When will conduct be held to be objectively justified? This can only be determined on a case by case basis, but could include, for example, a refusal to supply on the ground of poor creditworthiness. In order to be objectively justifiable, any conduct must be proportionate to the aim sought to be achieved. Thus it must be:

(1) capable of achieving that aim; and

(2) must not go beyond what is necessary to achieve that aim.

For example, a refusal to supply unless purchasers also contracted to take after-care servicing (*i.e.* tying) might in some circumstances be objectively justifiable on safety grounds, but only where there was no less restrictive means to achieve the necessary level of safety (for example, by requiring servicing by any one of a number of authorised providers).

---

48 (OFT 402), para 4.3

The burden of proving objective justification lies on the party which has asserted it.

Exclusionary and exploitative abuses

Most types of abuse can be categorised as either exclusionary or exploitative, and some kinds of abusive conduct fall within both categories. **Exclusionary conduct** is conduct aimed at actual or potential competitors, and has the object or effect of reducing or eliminating effective competition on the market. It is sometimes also termed anti-competitive conduct. Examples of exclusionary or anti-competitive conduct include refusal to supply and predatory pricing.

Exploitative conduct is conduct aimed at buyers or sellers of the relevant goods or services, and which exploits the dominant position held by imposing unfair or unreasonable trading conditions. Examples of exploitative conduct include charging excessive prices and discriminatory prices or other terms.

Causation

Does there need to be a link between the dominant position held by an undertaking and its ability to behave in an abusive manner?

The wording of section 18 and of Article 82 (old Article 86) might be thought to suggest that there does need to be such a chain of causation, but in fact the case law of the ECJ has established that there may be a finding of abuse even where an undertaking has not actually exercised or relied upon its market power.[49]

The ECJ has arguably gone even further its recent decision in *Tetra Pak II*[50], where it ruled that in certain circumstances Article 82 (old Article 86) can capture predatory conduct engaged in by a dominant undertaking on a market in which that undertaking is not dominant. On the facts of that case the abusive conduct was practised by Tetra Pak on a product market neighbouring the market of dominance, there were close "associative links" between the two markets, and even on the non-dominant market Tetra Pak was still significantly stronger than any of its rivals and held a "leading" position.

---

49 See, for example, Case 6/72 *Europemballage Corporation and Continental Can Co Inc v Commission* [1973] ECR 215.
50 Case C-333/94P *Tetra Pak International SA v Commission* [1996] ECR I-5951.

The OFT has referred to the *Tetra Pak II* decision in its Guideline on the Chapter II Prohibition.[51] It is to be hoped that reliance on this doctrine will be limited to the (perhaps rare) cases whose features when taken together give rise to the necessary level of association between the dominated market and the market on which the abuse took place.

Excessive pricing

The charging of excessive prices is one of the most obvious forms of exploitative abuse, but it is not always easy to determine what constitutes an excessive price. The European Court of Justice has set out the principles governing the prohibition on unfairly high prices in a series of cases.[52]

General Motors v Commission was the first case in which the ECJ directly considered a Commission decision condemning the excessive pricing of a dominant firm. The Belgian Government had given General Motors the exclusive power to grant test certificates to second-hand imports of Opel cars. This function was held to constitute a separate market, and General Motors' exclusive right meant that it was in a dominant position. The Commission had imposed a fine on General Motors on the ground that it had charged an excessive amount on the import of motor vehicles manufactured in another Member State for the inspection for conformity with the specifications contained in the Belgian approval certificate. Although the ECJ quashed the Commission decision because there was insufficient evidence to support it, nonetheless at paragraphs 11 and 12 of the judgment the Court set out the general principle as follows:

> "It is possible that the holder of the exclusive position referred to above may abuse the market by fixing a price – for a service which it is alone in a position to provide – which is to the detriment of any person acquiring a motor vehicle imported from another Member State and subject to the approval procedure.
>
> Such an abuse might lie, *inter alia*, in the imposition of a price which is **excessive in relation to the economic value of the service provided, ...**"
> (emphasis added)

---

51 (OFT 402), para 4.50.
52 Case 26/75 *General Motors v Commission* [1975] ECR 1367; Case 27/76 *United Brands v Commission* [1978] ECR 207; Case 226/84 *British Leyland v Commission* [1986] ECR 3263; Case 30/87 *Bodson v Pompes Funèbres* [1988] ECR 2479; Case 247/86 *Alsatel v Novosam* [1988] ECR 5987; Case 395/87 *Ministère Public v Tournier* [1989] ECR 2521.

In *United Brands* the ECJ, again quashing a Commission decision based on excessive pricing, indicated that an objective means of determining whether a price had no reasonable relation to the economic value of the product supplied would be a comparison of selling prices with costs of production.

In its Guideline on the Chapter II Prohibition, the OFT has suggested that a price might be viewed as excessive if it had allowed an undertaking consistently to earn profits which significantly exceeded its cost of equity capital.[53] These are termed "supra-normal" profits. However, the Guideline goes on to recognise that there may be many objective justifications for prices which are apparently excessive, and further that undertakings in competitive markets may be able to sustain supra-normal profits for a period of time if they are more efficient or innovative than their competitors. These issues are addressed in greater detail in the draft Guideline on Assessment of Individual Agreements and Conduct.[54]

Following its defeat in the *United Brands* case, the Commission has been reluctant to base Article 82 (old Article 86) decisions on excessive pricing alone, and the OFT Guideline indicates that the UK authorities propose to follow the same course.[55]

Price discrimination

Price discrimination may constitute both an exploitative and an exclusionary abuse. In other words, it may have adverse effects both on consumers and on competitors of a dominant undertaking. In general terms, price discrimination consists of charging dissimilar prices to persons who are in materially the same position, or the same prices to persons who are in a materially dissimilar position.

Different prices will not be considered discriminatory if there is an objective justification for the difference, for example where significant transport costs justify higher prices for products which have to be transported further.

In several cases, the ECJ has ruled that discriminatory pricing was abusive and contrary to Article 82 (old Article 86) where competitor undertakings were placed at an economic disadvantage as a result of the

---

53 (OFT 402), para 4.8.
54 (OFT 414), paras 2.5-2.17.
55 *Ibid*, paras 2.12 and 2.17.

pricing policy. For example, in *AKZO*[56] the Court condemned conduct which involved offering lower prices only to customers who bought from a competitor undertaking; this not only disadvantaged the competitor undertaking, but also other customers who continued to pay AKZO's higher prices.

The ECJ has consistently held that price discrimination based upon the nationality of the seller is abusive and contrary to Article 82 (old Article 86).[57] This is to be expected, given the Community's abhorrence of price discrimination based upon the maintenance of national boundaries. It is to be anticipated that the UK competition authorities and courts would take a similar approach under the Competition Act to unjustified discriminatory pricing as between, say, customers from different parts of the United Kingdom.

However, it is not clear from the case law of the ECJ that a dominant company must always sell on non-discriminatory terms to all purchasers. In particular, the OFT has suggested in its Guideline on the Chapter II Prohibition that price discrimination might be objectively justified in industries where there are high fixed costs and low marginal costs.[58] In such industries, typically the utilities such as water and electricity, the cost of supplying each additional unit of output is small compared to the initial investment needed to start the business. The Guideline suggests that it may be efficient, and not abusive, for such undertakings to charge their customers according to their willingness to pay.[59]

Loyalty discounts, which seek to reward long-term faithful customers, may also be abusive when offered by a dominant company, as they may make it unduly difficult for other undertakings to compete effectively.[60] It is an abuse for a dominant undertaking to include a loyalty obligation in its contracts, even if such a term has been requested by the buyer.[61] Loyalty discounts should not be confused with quantity discounts (*i.e.* discounts for bulk purchases), which may well be objectively justified, so long as they are transparent and available on non-discriminatory terms to all customers.[62]

---

56 Case 62/86 *AKZO v Commission* [1991] ECR I-3359.
57 See, for example, Case 27/76 *United Brands v Commission* [1978] ECR 207 at paras 226 *et seq.*
58 (OFT 402), para 4.15.
59 This ignores the highly regulated nature of all such industries in the UK, which often circumscribes the prices which an undertaking may set. This is acknowledged in the draft Guideline on Assessment of Individual Agreements and Conduct (OFT 414), paras 3.13-3.15.
60 Case 85/76 *Hoffman-La Roche* [1979] ECR 461; see also Case C-31/93P *BPB Industries and British Gypsum v Commission* [1995] ECR I-865.
61 Case C-393/92 *Almelo* [1994] ECR I-1477.
62 Case 322/81 *Michelin v Commission* [1983] ECR 3461, paras 81-85. See also the draft OFT Guideline on Assessment of Individual Agreements and Conduct (OFT 414), paras 5.12-5.13.

Predatory pricing

Predatory pricing is unduly low pricing, which is aimed at stifling competition by rendering it uneconomic. Competition law is concerned to prevent such behaviour, as although customers may benefit from low prices in the short term, the medium to long term effects may be to so weaken or even eliminate competition that excessive prices can then be charged.

How low must prices be to be categorised as predatory? When competition lawyers and economists consider this question, they refer to three kinds of costs. Fixed costs are costs which remain constant whatever the level of output, for example management overheads. Variable costs are costs which change according to the level of output, for example materials and direct labour costs. Fixed and variable costs together equal total cost.

Where prices charged are below the average variable costs of a product (*i.e.* costs which vary depending on the quantities produced), the ECJ has presumed an intention to eliminate competition and therefore held the pricing to be abusive unless that presumption has been rebutted. Where prices are higher than average variable cost but lower than average total cost (*i.e.* the sum of fixed and variable costs), abuse will be found only where there is proof of intention to eliminate a competitor. Where prices are higher than average total costs, there is no evidence of abusive predatory pricing.[63]

These three possibilities can be illustrated as follows:

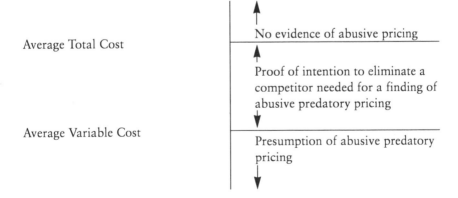

Average Total Cost	No evidence of abusive pricing
	Proof of intention to eliminate a competitor needed for a finding of abusive predatory pricing
Average Variable Cost	Presumption of abusive predatory pricing

---

63 See Case-62/86 *AKZO v Commission* [1991] ECR I–3359, at paras 69-72 and Case C-333/94P *Tetra Pak International SA v Commission ("Tetra Pak II")* [1996] ECR I-5951. See also, most recently, Joined Cases T-24-26 & 28/93 *Compagnie Maritime Belge v Commission* [1996] ECR II–1201, on appeal to the ECJ as Case C-395/96P (Opinion of A G Fennelly delivered on 29 October 1998).

The rules against predatory pricing are not intended to prevent price reductions by a dominant undertaking, or to prevent such a company from responding competitively to a price reduction by others. It is therefore necessary on the facts of any particular case to distinguish between legitimate competitive conduct, and conduct which is properly categorised as predatory or abusive. This can be difficult, particularly in industries which have high fixed costs and very low variable costs.[64] Furthermore, there is often a tension between allowing or even encouraging initial investment to develop a new market, and discouraging new entry otherwise than on the merits.[65]

Refusal to supply

A dominant undertaking must have an objectively justifiable reason for refusing to supply an existing customer, otherwise the refusal is very likely to be held to be abusive.[66] Possible objective justification could include:

- reasonable concerns as to creditworthiness;[67]
- temporary capacity constraints.

The following could not constitute objective justification for refusal to supply:

- the wish on the part of a dominant undertaking to enter a new market itself in substitution for a customer;[68]
- disproportionate retaliation against the commercial or trading practices of a customer.[69]

Where a dominant undertaking refuses to supply not an existing customer, but a new customer, will that refusal also be held to be

---

64 For example, high technology industries such as telecommunications.
65 See further the OFT Guideline on the Chapter II Prohibition (OFT 402), paras 4.18-4.25, and the draft OFT Guideline on Assessment of Individual Agreements and Conduct (OFT 414), paras 4.1-4.17.
66 See, for example, the decision of the ECJ in Cases 6 & 7/73 *Commercial Solvents v Commission* [1974] ECR 223, especially at 250-251.
67 In *Leyland DAF v Automotive Products* [1994] 1 BCLC 245 the Court of Appeal held that refusal by a dominant company to supply products to a customer when that customer had failed to pay for products supplied previously was justified and not contrary to Article 82 (old Art 86).
68 See, for example, Case 311/84 *Centre Belge d'Etude de Marché-Télémarketing v CLT & IPB* [1985] ECR 3261, which concerned a refusal by the Luxembourg state broadcasting company to supply advertising time to any tele-marketing companies other than its own exclusive agent.
69 See, for example, Case 27/76 *United Brands v Commission* [1978] ECR 207 where United Brands discontinued supplies of green bananas to a Danish ripener and distributor.

abusive if not objectively justified? Recent developments in the case law of the Commission and ECJ suggest that in certain carefully defined circumstances it may be. An abuse of dominant position has been found in a series of cases concerned with refusal of access to "essential facilities".

An **essential facility** is a service or piece of infrastructure, without access to which a competitor is unable to compete in some down-stream market, and which facility it is commercially infeasible, economically inefficient and undesirable for the competitor to replicate. For example, several of the essential facilities cases have concerned access to port facilities.[70]

The judgment of the ECJ in a case known as *Magill*[71] gave rise to some concern that the essential facilities doctrine was capable of much wider application, as the Court found an abuse of Article 82 (old Article 86) where a television listing publication was denied access to the information about programming which the three broadcasters used in their own weekly publications. However, subsequent cases have made clear that *Magill* was an unusual case decided on its particular facts. Most recently the decision of the ECJ in the *Bronner*[72] case has put paid to the idea that the essential facilities doctrine may be widely invoked by smaller undertakings against their larger competitors to gain access to desired infrastructure or services.

The essential facilities doctrine is an exceptional one, which is only applicable in a minority of cases. The OFT Guideline on the Chapter II Prohibition suggests that the doctrine may potentially apply to ports, bus stations, utility distribution networks and some telecommunications networks.[73]

Tying

Section 18(2)(d) of the Competition Act refers expressly to tying clauses. Typically, tying occurs where a dominant firm only agrees to supply a product in respect of which it holds a dominant position on condition that the purchaser also agrees to buy another product from

---

70 See, for example, the Commission decision in *Port of Rødby*, OJ 1994 L55/52; [1994] 5 CMLR 457.

71 Joined Cases C-241/91P and C-242/91P *RTE and ITP v Commission* [1995] ECR I-743.

72 Case C-7/97 *Oscar Bronner GmbH & Co KG v Mediaprint Zeitungs- und Zeitschriftenverlag GmbH & Co KG and others*, judgment of 26 November 1998 (not yet reported).

73 (OFT 402), para 4.49. See further the draft OFT Guideline on Assessment of Individual Agreements and Conduct (OFT 414), paras 7.1-7.17.

the firm. Tying may therefore harm not only the purchaser (who is required to take a product which it might not otherwise buy, or which it might buy from another supplier), but also competitors (who lose the opportunity to supply the tied product).

It will be a question of fact in any case whether two separate products are being sold on a tied basis, sometimes referred to as bundling, or whether the two items are merely components of a single product.

Other types of abuse

The five types of abuse outlined above (excessive pricing, price discrimination, predatory pricing, refusal to supply and tying) are only examples of the principal types of abuse which have received most attention in the existing case law of the ECJ. Other respects in which a dominant firm may abuse its position include:

- cross-subsidisation;[74]
- the abuse of intellectual property rights; and
- the imposition of anti-competitive purchasing and distribution conditions on customers.

These last types of abuse are often termed vertical restraints, and have been discussed in more detail in Chapter 3 above on the Chapter I prohibition. However, it is important to note that the Chapter II prohibition may apply to vertical restraints where one of the parties to an agreement is in a dominant position.[75]

4.4 Excluded cases

Section 19 of the Competition Act provides for certain excluded cases to which the Chapter II prohibition does not apply. Section 19 is in similar, but more limited terms to section 3, which provides for excluded agreements to which the Chapter I prohibition does not apply.[76]

The cases from which the Chapter II prohibition is excluded are shown in the table overleaf.

---

74 See further draft OFT Guideline on Assessment of Individual Agreements and Conduct (OFT 414), paras 5.2-5.11.
75 See further *ibid*, paras 6.1-6.33 (especially at 6.29-6.33) for a detailed analysis of the approach which the DGFT will take to vertical restraints where one of the parties to an agreement is dominant.
76 See the discussion at Chap 3 above.

Excluded Case	*Section of the Act*
Conduct which results in a merger within the meaning of the Fair Trading Act 1973	Section 19(1)(a) and Schedule 1, paragraph 2
Conduct which results in a concentration where the EC Merger Regulation (No 4064/89) gives the European Commission exclusive jurisdiction	Section 19(1)(a) and Schedule 1, paragraph 6(2)
Undertakings entrusted with the operation of "services of general economic interest or having the character of a revenue-producing monopoly" if the application of the Chapter II prohibition would obstruct the performance of the tasks assigned to that undertaking	Section 19(1)(b) and Schedule 3, paragraph 4
Conduct engaged in so as to comply with a legal requirement	Section 19(1)(b) and Schedule 3, paragraph 5(2)
Where the Secretary of State makes an order providing for the Chapter II prohibition not to apply in order to avoid a conflict with international obligations	Section 19(1)(b) and Schedule 3, paragraphs 6(4) and (5)
Where the Secretary of State makes an order providing for the Chapter II prohibition not to apply for "exceptional and compelling reasons of public policy"	Section 19(1)(b) and Schedule 3, paragraphs 7(4) and (5)
Conduct which relates to a coal or steel product to the extent that the European Coal and Steel Treaty gives the European Commission exclusive jurisdiction	Section 19(1)(b) and Schedule 3, paragraph 8(3)

The Secretary of State is also given the power at any time to add, amend or remove the exclusions for mergers and concentrations (section 19(2)), for conduct relating to coal and steel products (section 19(3)), and in other circumstances referred to in Schedule 3 to the Act (section

19(4)). In contrast to the Chapter I prohibition, the DGFT does not have the power to provide for additional general exclusions.

Although it is not an exclusion in the strict sense, it is relevant to refer here to the provisional immunity from fines which applies to conduct of minor significance.[77] This provision is designed to prevent the new Act being unduly burdensome on small businesses, and provides that financial penalties cannot be imposed in respect of "conduct of minor significance" unless this immunity is withdrawn by the DGFT.[78] The phrase "conduct of minor significance" is not defined in the Act[79], but during debates in Parliament the Government indicated that the rules will be turnover based, and that the appropriate level of turnover will be in the region of £20-£50 million.[80]

4.5 The Fair Trading Act monopoly provisions

The Competition Act has not repealed all of the competition law legislation which existed in the United Kingdom before 1998. The provisions of the Fair Trading Act 1973 which address scale monopolies and complex monopolies are retained under the Competition Act.[81] This is because these provisions are generally considered to have operated reasonably well, and to perform a useful function which would not otherwise be covered by the Chapter II prohibition and Article 82 (old Article 86). In particular they afford detailed review by the Competition Commission and structural remedies more appropriate for non-abusive conduct.

Scale monopolies

Scale monopolies, also referred to as structural monopolies, exist where at least 25% of the goods or services of any description supplied in the United Kingdom are supplied by or to one person (sections 6(1)(a) and 7(1)(a) of the Fair Trading Act 1973). The scale monopoly provisions also apply where the persons who are supplying or supplied with the

---

77 S 40 of the Act. See also OFT Guideline on the Chapter II Prohibition (OFT 402), paras 2.8-2.9 and Section 6.3 of Chap 6 on fines at p 142 below.

78 S 40(4)-(8).

79 Other than to say that it may be by reference to criteria including turnover and market share (s 40(2)).

80 Hansard, 17 November 1997, col 434.

81 See Part III of the Act, ss 66-69.

goods or services are two or more companies which are part of a single economic unit (sections 6(1)(b) and 7(1)(b)). These provisions therefore apply where one firm or group of firms alone is responsible for at least 25% of the supply or acquisition of a certain type of goods or services.

The OFT Guideline on the Major Provisions stresses that the scale monopoly powers under the Fair Trading Act have only been retained for cases where the prohibitions contained in the Competition Act have been infringed, but where the abuse continues despite enforcement action. The scale monopoly powers will therefore be used where the structural remedies available under the Fair Trading Act are considered necessary to prevent further abuse (for example, by requiring the divestment of parts of a firm's business).[82]

The only exception to this limitation on the use of the scale monopoly powers is for the regulated industries. The OFT Guideline on the Major Provisions states that:

> "Because of the special circumstances of the utility sectors, and the difficulty of establishing competition, the full use of the scale monopoly provisions is retained for the regulated utility sectors. This means that the scale monopoly provisions may be used in respect of those sectors whether or not there has been a prior infringement of the prohibitions in the Competition Act."[83]

There is no indication as to whether this policy will be changed if and when some of the regulated industries become fully competitive.

Complex monopolies

Complex monopolies, also referred to as behavioural monopolies, exist where companies have a collective share of at least 25% of the supply or consumption of goods or services of the same description in the United Kingdom, or a part of the United Kingdom, and where they behave anti-competitively in parallel (sections 6(1)(c) and 7(1)(c) of the Fair Trading Act 1973). Complex monopolies are therefore defined by reference to the behaviour of the firms being investigated (sections 6(2) and 7(2)).

The complex monopoly provisions of the Fair Trading Act enable the DGFT to make a reference to the Competition Commission where a group of businesses (termed an oligopoly) all adopt similar practices which appear to be anti-competitive, but where there is no evidence of

---

82 (OFT 400), paras 13.3-13.4
83 *Ibid*, para 13.5.

an agreement or concerted practice such that the Chapter I prohibition is infringed. In the past references to the Monopolies and Mergers Commission (MMC) were made in relation to alleged complex monopoly situations where, for example, suppliers used identical terms and conditions in sales agreements.

Services relating to the use of land

Section 68 of the Competition Act gives the Secretary of State the power in the future to use secondary legislation to make arrangements relating to the use of land either subject to or excluded from the application of the complex or scale monopoly provisions under the Fair Trading Act. No such legislation has yet been proposed or enacted, and the draft Land Agreements (Competition Act 1998)(Exclusion) Order 1999 published in February 1999 only addresses the exclusion of land agreements from the Chapter I Prohibition.[84]

Reform of monopoly investigations

Part III of the Competition Act makes certain amendments to provisions of the Fair Trading Act 1973. The power of the DGFT to require information about monopoly situations is amended (section 66), and the offences created under the Fair Trading Act are brought into line with the offences created under the Competition Act (section 67).

---

84 See further Chap 3 above.

Chapter 5

· Notification ·

5.1   Notification under the Competition Act

The Act provides for two principal types of notification:

(1) notification for guidance; and

(2) notification for a decision.

These two forms of notification apply to both the Chapter I and Chapter II prohibitions, but the great majority of notifications are very likely to relate to anti-competitive agreements and Chapter I.

The provisions concerning notification are contained in sections 12-16 and Schedule 5 of the Act (Chapter I) and in sections 20-24 and Schedule 6 of the Act (Chapter II). In addition, the Director General of Fair Trading (DGFT) has issued Procedural Rules and an application form (Form N) in connection with the carrying into effect of Part I of the Act, as he is empowered to do under section 51(1) and Schedule 9 to the Act.

Notification is always optional; there is no statutory requirement to notify. It is for the parties to an anti-competitive agreement or those responsible for anti-competitive conduct to decide on the facts of their case whether they wish to notify. Notification does bring with it certain advantages, notably provisional immunity from fines in respect of an agreement from the date when a valid notification is received by the DGFT. There is no provisional immunity from fines in respect of conduct caught by the Chapter II prohibition, and this is one of the reasons why it is expected that most notifications will relate to Chapter I agreements.

The DGFT may in certain circumstances impose interim measures pending completion of his investigation into an agreement or conduct (section 35 of the Act). Although such interim measures may be imposed following notification for guidance or a decision, they are more likely where the DGFT has undertaken an investigation following a third party complaint or on his own initiative. The subject of interim measures is therefore discussed in Chapter 6 on Investigation and Enforcement.

There is a third form of notification, notification for early guidance, which is provided for under the transitional provisions contained in

Schedule 13 of the Act.[1] Agreements made in the interim period, that is, between 9 November 1998 (the enactment date) and 1 March 2000 (the starting date), may be submitted for early guidance as to whether they are likely to infringe the Chapter I prohibition when it comes into force. It is important to stress that notification for guidance or for a decision may only be made **after** the Chapters I and II prohibitions come into force on 1 March 2000.

Each of these three types of notification (for guidance, for a decision and for early guidance) will now be explained in greater detail.

5.2   Notification for guidance

The Chapter I prohibition

A party to an agreement may notify the DGFT of the agreement and apply to him for guidance as to whether or not, in the view of the DGFT, the agreement is likely to infringe the Chapter I prohibition (section 13(1) and (2)). Guidance may more easily be disturbed than a decision (for example, the DGFT may revisit his guidance following receipt of a third party complaint), but it has the important advantage that a notification for guidance will not be published by the DGFT and third parties will not be consulted.

Form N

Notification must be made using Form N, which is reproduced at Appendix 2.[2] Form N is also available for down-loading from the website of the Office of Fair Trading (the OFT) at http://www.oft.gov.uk/. The DGFT has already stated that Form N will be amended from time to time, so it is important to ensure that the current version is obtained (for example from the OFT website or by telephoning the OFT) before compiling any notification.[3]

---

1 See further Chap 8 below.
2 Rule 1 of the DGFT's Procedural Rules (OFT 411, version dated 17 March 1999 submitted to the Secretary of State for approval on 26 February 1999). Form N must be used for notifications concerning both agreements and conduct, and equally for notifications both for guidance and for a decision. Much of what follows concerning Form N therefore applies also to these other forms of notification.
3 Para 5 of the introduction to the DGFT's Procedural Rules published for consultation in November 1998. Since the version of the Procedural Rules submitted to the Secretary of State for approval in February 1999 (OFT 411) did not contain these helpful introductory comments, some reference will be made here to the earlier consultation version.

Where two or more parties to an agreement jointly wish to make a notification, they may together submit a completed Form N.[4] If a legal or other representative is nominated to submit and receive documents on behalf of the notifier(s), proof of authority to act must also be provided.[5]

Section 53 of the Act provides that the DGFT may charge fees for notifications. There are as yet no draft Rules providing for a mechanism for charging fees or laying down the amount payable, (nor any indication as to when these might be published).

Completing Form N

As the notes to Form N acknowledge, it is a check-list of information which must be supplied to the DGFT, rather than an application form which may simply be filled in. The information required is detailed, and is likely to take time and effort to compile. In particular, Sections 6-8 of Part 2 of Form N concern the relevant product and geographic markets, the position of the notifying undertaking in the relevant product and geographic markets and the barriers to market entry and potential competition which exist in the relevant product and geographic markets. The introduction to Part 2 of the Form states that in some cases it may be possible to dispense with the requirement to provide information in all categories, and that this should be discussed with officials at the OFT before making the notification.[6] Since the notification for guidance procedure is exclusively a written one, and the notification for a decision procedure largely so, it is in the interests of a notifying party to submit as detailed an application in Form N as possible.

Form N is modelled on and similar to Form A/B[7] which must be used for notifications to the European Commission for negative clearance or exemption for restrictive agreements. The OFT is anxious to avoid dual notifications to both the Commission and the OFT, but has stated that if simultaneous notification is made Form A/B may be submitted to both authorities, with the addition of information specific to the UK market for the national notification (as required under Section 7.1 of Part 2 of Form N).[8]

---

4 Rule 2.
5 Rule 4(1) and Section 1.2 of Part 2 of Form N.
6 See also Rule 4(4).
7 Provided for under Commission Reg 27 of 1962 (JO 1118/62, [1959-62] OJ Spec Ed 132).
8 Section 3.2 of Part 2 of Form N and OFT Guideline on the Major Provisions (OFT 400), para 7.11.

Confidential information

Information which is regarded by the notifying undertaking as confidential must be clearly marked as such and placed in a separate confidential annex.[9] This annex must also explain why the information should be regarded as confidential. The DGFT's Procedural Rules define confidential information as:

> "(i) commercial information the disclosure of which would, or might, significantly harm the legitimate business interests of the undertaking to which it relates; or
>
> (ii) information relating to the private affairs of an individual the disclosure of which would, or might, significantly harm his interests;"[10]

The identification and protection of confidential information is of considerably more importance in relation to notifications for a decision than notifications for guidance. This is because notifications for guidance will not be published by the DGFT, and third parties will not be consulted. Nonetheless, it would always be advisable for a notifying party to identify confidential information as such, even when making a notification for guidance. The Secretary of State and the DGFT are in any event always under a duty to consider whether the disclosure of any information would be in breach of confidentiality or contrary to the public interest, but it will obviously assist if an applicant has already identified the information for which it seeks to claim confidentiality.[10a]

There are also restrictions imposed on the disclosure of information received under any provision of the Act. These are contained in section 55. They apparently apply to the DGFT's staff and to private firms alike. Essentially, the permission of the person who provided the information and, if different, the person whose affairs it concerns is required before disclosure can be made.[10b] It is a criminal offence to breach the prohibition on disclosure.[10c] However, there are widely phrased exceptions in respect of disclosure to facilitate the performance of the regulatory functions of a long list of government and official bodies.[10d] This list can be extended by the Secretary of State.[10e] Furthermore, disclosure to the European Commission to enable it to

---

9   Rule 4(3), note 1.6 of Part 1 and the introduction to Part 2 of Form N. See also Rule 27 on confidential third party information.
10   Rule 29(1)(b).
10a S 56 of the Act.
10b S 55(2).
10c S 55(8).
10d See s 55(3)(a)(i) and (ii) and Sched 11.
10e S 55(5) and (6).

perform its functions in respect of EC competition law is permitted.[10f]
Likewise, disclosure can apparently be freely made for the purposes of
criminal or civil proceedings[10g] or to comply with an EC obligation.[10h]

Submitting Form N

The original of Form N, plus two further copies must be sent to the
OFT at the address given on Form N.[11] Notifications may also be made
on disk or using other electronic format, but clearance must first be
obtained from the OFT telephone enquiry point (0171 211 8989). An
original or certified copy of any relevant agreement must be submitted
with Form N together with any annexes, and two further certified
copies of these documents should also be sent.[12]

Where the notification relates to a market which is subject to sectoral
regulation[13], Form N should still be submitted to the OFT, but a further
copy of the notification should also be sent to the OFT for each such
regulator.[14] However, a notification will not be deemed incomplete
simply because the notifier fails to send an additional copy of Form N
for a relevant regulator.[15] Rule 8 of the DGFT's Procedural Rules
provides that if he considers that a regulator has concurrent jurisdiction
in relation to a notification, he must send a copy of Form N to the
regulator as soon as practicable and inform the applicant in writing that
he has done so. He must also inform the applicant in writing of which
Director is to exercise jurisdiction in relation to the notification.[16] The
procedures governing notification set out in the Act and in the DGFT's
Procedural Rules must be followed whether jurisdiction is exercised by
the DGFT or by one of the regulators.

Notifying other parties of a Form N notification

Paragraph 2(2) of Schedule 5 to the Act requires that a party to an
agreement who has made an application for guidance or for a decision
must take all reasonable steps to notify all other parties to the agreement

---

10f S 55(a)(ii). Contrast this with the restrictions imposed under Community law on the use by
     national competition authorities of information received from the European Commission:
     Case C-67/91 *Dirrección General de Defensa de la Competencia* v *Asociación Española de
     Banca Privada and others* [1992] ECR I-4785.
10g S 55(3)(a)(iv), (b) and (c).
10h S 55(3)(d).
11   Rule 3(2).
12   Rule 3(1). See also Section 1.3 of Part 1 of Form N and OFT Guideline on the Major
     Provisions (OFT 400), para 7.9.
13   Telecommunications, electricity, water, rail and gas. See further Chap 9 below.
14   Note 1.5 to Part 1 of Form N and Rule 3(3).
15   OFT Guideline on the Major Provisions (OFT 400), para 7.9.
16   Rule 8(2).

of whom he is aware of the fact of the notification and whether it is for guidance or a decision. The DGFT's Procedural Rules further provide that this must be given in writing and within seven working days of the date on which the applicant receives acknowledgement of receipt of his application from the DGFT. A copy of this written notification must be provided to the DGFT.[17]

The effective date of application

The effective date of an application for notification is important for a number of reasons, notably because it determines the beginning of the period of provisional immunity from fines.[18] The DGFT's Procedural Rules provide that the effective date of an application will be the date on which a materially complete Form N is received by the DGFT. Any application received after 6pm on a working day will be treated as received on the next working day.[19] Information which is false or misleading is treated as incorrect or incomplete under the Rules.[20] The DGFT is under a duty to acknowledge receipt without delay (Rule 5(2)), and if he fails for a period of more than one month to inform the applicant that the Form N submitted was materially incomplete, the notification is deemed to have become effective on the date of its receipt by the DGFT (Rule 5(4)).

The duty to provide accurate information in Form N

Even after receipt of Form N has been acknowledged by the DGFT, the notifying party remains under a duty to inform the DGFT or the regulator exercising jurisdiction without delay of any material changes in the facts which have been notified.[21] If such changes in facts are not communicated voluntarily and without delay, the application may be declared ineffective until the changes have been communicated.[21a]

It is an offence under section 44 of the Act to provide information to the DGFT which is false or misleading in a material respect, if the undertaking providing that information knows that it is false or misleading or is reckless as to whether it is. Form N concludes with a declaration that the information which is provided is true to the best of the signatory's knowledge and belief. A person guilty of an offence under section 44 is liable to a fine or imprisonment or both. Under section 72

---

17   Rule 6.
18   S 13(4)(a) of the Act.
19   Rule 5.
20   Rule 4(2).
21   Rule 5(4) and note 1.7 of Part 1 of Form N.
21a Rule 5(6) and (7).

if an offence committed by a body corporate is proved to have been committed with the consent or conivance of an officer of the company or to be attributable to his neglect, the officer may be found guilty.

Giving of guidance

It is important to note that the DGFT is not under an obligation to provide guidance to a notifying party; section 13(2) of the Act provides only that the DGFT **may** provide guidance as to whether or not, in his view, the agreement is likely to infringe the Chapter I prohibition.

If the DGFT considers that the notified agreement is likely to infringe the Chapter I prohibition if it is not exempt, his guidance may further indicate whether the agreement would be likely to be exempt. That guidance may indicate that the agreement is likely to benefit from:

(1) a block exemption;

(2) a parallel exemption;

(3) a section 11 exemption (relating to tramp shipping and non-EU air transport agreements which are the subject of a ruling under Article 84 (old Article 88) of the EC Treaty);

(4) the grant of an individual exemption.[22]

After the DGFT has determined an application, guidance must be given without delay, in writing, and must state the facts and reasons for the DGFT's determination.[23] Agreements which are the subject of notification for guidance are immune from penalties in respect of the period between the effective date of notification and the date on which the application is determined.[24] However, it is open to the DGFT to withdraw that immunity by issuing a provisional decision. Where after preliminary investigation of an application for guidance the DGFT considers it likely that an agreement infringes the Chapter I prohibition and that it would not be appropriate to grant an exemption, he can, having consulted the applicant[25], make a provisional decision which must be notified to the applicant in writing. This has the immediate

---

22 S 13(3). It seems that guidance is not available as to whether there is likely to be no infringement due to the effect of one of the exclusions contained in Scheds 1-4 (agreements) or 1 and 3 (conduct). Contrast the position in respect of notifications for a decision described in the section below. It may be questioned whether this formal distinction will be rigidly observed.
23 Rule 10.
24 S 13(4) and (5) of the Act.
25 Rule 9(1).

effect of removing the immunity conferred by the notification with retrospective effect.[26] This provision mirrors the power of the European Commission under Article 15(6) of Regulation 17 to withdraw provisional immunity from fines, and it is expected that like its European counterpart it will be used only very rarely.

The effect of guidance

Where the DGFT has given favourable guidance stating that an agreement is not likely to infringe the Chapter I prohibition, either because it does not significantly restrict competition or because it would benefit from one of the forms of exemption available, the DGFT can take no further action under Part I of the Act except in specified circumstances.[27] Those circumstances, listed in section 15(2) are when:

- the DGFT has reasonable grounds for believing that there has been a material change of circumstance since he gave the guidance;
- the DGFT has a reasonable suspicion that the information on which he based his guidance was incomplete, false or misleading in a material particular;
- one of the parties to the agreement applies to the DGFT for a decision;
- the DGFT receives a complaint about the agreement from a third party.

Before taking further action, the DGFT must consult the person to whom he gave the guidance.[28]

No penalty can be imposed in respect of any infringement of the Chapter I prohibition by an agreement in respect of which favourable guidance has been given.[29] However, the DGFT can remove this immunity from penalty by giving written notice to the party who sought the guidance where the situation entitles him to take further action in relation to the agreement. Immunity may only be removed with retrospective effect where the DGFT has reasonable suspicion that the information on which he based his guidance and which was provided by a party to the agreement was incomplete, false or misleading in a material particular.[30]

26　Para 3 of Sched 5 to the Act.
27　Ss 15(1) and (2) of the Act.
28　Rule 11(1).
29　S 15(3).
30　S 15(5).

The Chapter II prohibition

Conduct may also be notified for guidance, if one or more parties to it are concerned as to whether it infringes the Chapter II prohibition (section 21(1) and (2) of the Act).

As has been noted above, in practice conduct is rarely likely to be notified to the DGFT for guidance or a decision. This is analogous to the position in relation to notifications under Article 86 of the EC Treaty, which are extremely rare.[31] The main reasons why parties to conduct are unlikely to notify that conduct to the DGFT are:

- there is no provisional immunity from fines following notification of conduct;
- there is no possibility of exemption for conduct which is abusive of a dominant position;
- guidance from the DGFT that conduct is not abusive would not be binding on the courts in any proceedings.

Nonetheless, there will be some cases where there is genuine doubt as to whether certain conduct would be in breach of the Chapter II prohibition, and where those advising an undertaking conclude that notification for guidance would provide desirable legal certainty and a better assessment of the risk of fines.

Form N

As with notification of agreements for guidance, notification of conduct must be made in accordance with Form N.[32] The account of the requirements of Form N set out in relation to the Chapter I prohibition above applies also to notifications of conduct, but with certain changes which arise from the differences between the Chapters I and II prohibitions.

Where joint conduct is in issue, a joint application may be made[33], but if only one person notifies the conduct for guidance he must take all reasonable steps to notify all of the other parties to the conduct of whom he is aware.[34] As with notification under Chapter I, the other parties must be informed of the notification in writing and within seven

---

31 The Competition Directorate of the European Commission, DGIV, made only six negative clearance decisions under Art 82 (old Art 86) in the period from 1962 to July 1998.
32 Rule 1.
33 Rule 2.
34 Para 2(2) of Sched 6 to the Act.

days of the date on which an acknowledgement of receipt from the DGFT is received.

Since notification for guidance under Chapter II does not afford provisional immunity from fines, determining the effective date of notification is of considerably less importance. However, in an appropriate case it might be argued that the fact of notification for negative clearance under Chapter II evidenced a genuine belief that the prohibition had not been infringed, thus justifying a lower fine, if one were to be imposed.

Giving of guidance

Again, the DGFT is under no obligation to provide guidance, but he may provide guidance as to whether or not, in his view, the notified conduct is likely to infringe the Chapter II prohibition (section 21(2) of the Act).

The procedural rules in relation to the giving of guidance described above apply also to Chapter II notifications, but in a much simplified form due to the non-availability of exemptions and of provisional immunity from fines.

The effect of guidance

Section 23 of the Act lays down the effect of guidance from the DGFT that the notified conduct is unlikely to infringe the Chapter II prohibition. It mirrors substantially section 15 which is concerned with Chapter I guidance. Therefore, section 23(2) provides that the DGFT can take no further action under Chapter II in relation to the conduct unless he:

- has reasonable grounds for believing that there has been a material change of circumstance since he gave the guidance;
- has a reasonable suspicion that the information on which he based his guidance was incomplete, false or misleading in a material particular;
- receives a complaint about the agreement from a third party.[35]

Before taking further action, the DGFT must consult the person to whom he gave the guidance.[36]

---

35 Note that the provision for further action where "one of the parties to the agreement applies to the DGFT for a decision" is omitted from s 23(2), which does not contemplate the possibility that a party to joint conduct may wish the DGFT to take further action.
36 Rule 11(2).

As with the Chapter I prohibition, favourable guidance prevents the imposition of any penalty in respect of the notified conduct.[37] However, the DGFT can remove this immunity from penalty where circumstances permit him to take further action by giving written notice to the party who sought the guidance. Once again, immunity may only be removed with retrospective effect where the DGFT has reasonable suspicion that the information on which he based his guidance and which was provided by a party to the conduct was incomplete, false or misleading in a material particular.[38]

5.3   Notification for a decision

The Chapter I prohibition

A party to an agreement may notify the DGFT of that agreement and apply to him for a decision as to:

- whether the Chapter I prohibition has been infringed; and
- if it has not been infringed, whether that is because of the effect of an exclusion or because the agreement is exempt from the prohibition (section 14(1) and (2)).

Notification of an agreement for a decision may include a request for the agreement to be granted an individual exemption (section 14(3)).

Form N

Notification for a decision must be made using the same Form N which is used for notification for guidance.[39] Almost all of the explanation of Form N given in the section on notification for guidance applies also to notification for a decision, and reference should be made to the account set out above. Only a few key points which are of particular relevance to notification for a decision are set out here.

The need clearly to identify and annex separately any confidential information is of great importance if an agreement is notified for a decision. This is because paragraph 5(2) of Schedule 5 to the Act requires the DGFT to arrange for the application for a decision to be published:

> "in such a way as he thinks most suitable for bringing it to the attention of those likely to be affected by it, unless he is satisfied that it will be

---

37 S 23(3).
38 S 23(5).
39 Rule 1 of the DGFT's Procedural Rules (OFT 411). Form N is set out at Appendix 2.

> sufficient for him to seek information from one or more particular person other than the applicant."

Therefore, in most cases, details of the notification will be published, and may come to the attention of business competitors.

Part 4 of Form N has to be completed only by those notifying for a decision, as the information provided in that part of the application forms the basis for any published notice. The notes to Part 4 state that following receipt of a notification for a decision, the DGFT will place details of the notified arrangement on the public register which is maintained at the OFT.[40] The Procedural Rules further require that the register must contain a summary of the nature and objectives of the notified arrangement and an indication of the outcome of the application.[41] These details will also be published on the OFT's website[42], and in a weekly gazette.[43] The information required under Part 4 includes a summary (in no more than 250 words) of the nature and objectives of the notified arrangement(s), and a full description of the goods and services involved (including the Standard Industrial Classification code where available). This information is published without further reference to the parties, and it is therefore of particular importance that no business secrets or other confidential information are included in the answers to Part 4.[44]

Use of comfort letters

As with the giving of guidance, section 14(2) of the Act provides only that the DGFT may make a decision. He is under no duty to reach a decision. OFT officials have already stated publicly that they expect that many of the agreements notified will have no appreciable effect on competition, and that they will be dealt with by way of "administrative letter", equivalent to the so-called comfort letters received from the European Commission.[45] Comfort letters are non-binding letters which the Competition Directorate of the European Commission (DGIV) uses to close the file without a formal decision in many cases. The Act makes no provision for the issuing of administrative letters, but they are

---

40 The register is open to public inspection at the OFT between 10 am and 4.30 pm on every working day.
41 Rule 7(1).
42 Rule 7(2)(b) and note 1.4 of Part 1 of Form N.
43 OFT Guideline on the Major Provisions (OFT 400), para 7.5.
44 The introductory notes to Part 4 of Form N.
45 For example, Margaret Bloom, Director of Competition Policy at the OFT, in a talk to the Euroforum Conference held on 6-7 July 1998.

probably within the power of the DGFT subject to any directions from a court ordering that the application be determined by way of decision.[46]

These informal administrative letters would indicate that in the view of the DGFT the notified agreement does not infringe the Chapter I prohibition, but that he does not intend to proceed to a formal decision. An administrative letter would probably state that provisional immunity from fines continues to apply in respect of the notified agreement, but the DGFT could indicate a time limit for the validity of the letter or reserve the right to re-open the case following a material change in circumstance. Such a letter does not provide the parties with the same certainty as a final decision, or arguably even as guidance, but if the practice of the European Commission is followed in this respect, a great many files will be closed by the issuing of an administrative letter.

The use of administrative letters is designed to prevent the reformed UK competition system from becoming clogged with numerous notifications which are of no real significance from a competition law perspective. The OFT hope that they will thereby be free to concentrate on cases which are of real importance, be it cartels, serious breaches of the Chapter II prohibition, or other cases which will assist in the development of a coherent and comprehensive UK competition law jurisprudence. How successful they will be, of course, remains to be seen.[47] Borrowed directly from the European practice of issuing comfort letters, administrative letters are likely to prove frustrating to some applicants, and sit a little oddly with a system which, unlike the European one, already includes provision for the giving of guidance.

Providing a decision

The DGFT may decide whether the Chapter I prohibition has been infringed, and if it has not been infringed whether that is because of the effect of one of the exclusions contained in Schedules 1-4 to the Act, or because the agreement is exempt from the prohibition.[48] An agreement may also receive "negative clearance", if it does not appreciably prevent, restrict or distort competition contrary to the prohibition

---

46 Such directions may be made pursuant to para 7 of Sched 5 to the Act. See further the section on "Delays and the administrative timetable" below.

47 The experience of some other countries following the introduction of competition law provisions based on Arts 81 and 82 (old Arts 85 and 86) is not greatly encouraging. The Netherlands and Ireland, in particular, suffered from a deluge of notifications, the majority of which did not raise real competition law concerns, immediately following the enactment of reforming legislation.

48 S 14(2).

contained in section 2 of the Act. Unlike section 13(2) of the Act in relation to the giving of guidance, the different types of exemption available (block, parallel, section 11 or individual) are not listed in section 14, but nothing appears to turn on this difference of wording. Furthermore, section 14 refers the possibility of the Chapter I prohibition not being infringed due to the effect of an exclusion, but section 13 does not include this possibility in relation to guidance. However, the important point to note is that it is only following notification for a decision that an agreement may benefit from an individual exemption granted by the DGFT, and that this must be specifically requested in Form N.[49]

Agreements which are the subject of notification for a decision benefit from immunity from penalties from the effective date of notification, in the same way as agreements which are notified for guidance.[50] However, it is again possible for the DGFT to withdraw that immunity by issuing a provisional decision.[51-52]

Consultation and representations

Paragraph 5(3) of Schedule 5 to the Act states that in determining an application for a decision, the DGFT must take into account any representation which he receives from third parties. In order to comply with this duty, the DGFT's Procedural Rules require that following notification for a decision:

- if the DGFT proposes to grant an exemption, whether or not subject to conditions or obligations, he must consult the public;[53]
- if the DGFT proposes to make a decision that the Chapter I prohibition has not been infringed he may (*i.e.* in his discretion) consult the public.[54]

Public consultation will usually occur by way of publication of details of the notification for a decision in the national press and/or in appropriate trade journals.[55] An invitation for further comment will also be published on the register kept at the OFT, in its weekly gazette, and on the OFT website.[56]

---

49 S 14(3) and para 2.4 of Part 2 of Form N.
50 S 14(4) and (5) of the Act.
51-52 Rule 9(1) and para 3 of Sched 5 to the Act. See further "Notification for guidance" section in relation to "Giving of guidance" above, p 101.
53 Rule 12(1)(a).
54 Rule 12(1)(b).
55 Note 1.4 of Part 1 of Form N. See Rule 26.
56 OFT Guideline on the Major Provisions (OFT 400), para 7.6.

Representations from the parties

If the DGFT proposes to make a decision that the Chapter I prohibition has been infringed, he is obliged to give the applicant and any other parties to the agreement an opportunity to make more detailed representations. Rule 14 provides that the DGFT must give written notice of the proposed infringement decision to both the applicant and to any other party to the agreement of whom he is aware, stating the matters to which the DGFT has taken objection, the action he proposes and his reasons for that action. The written notice must also specify a period within which the applicant and other parties to the agreement may make further oral and written representations. In the introductory comments to the draft Procedural Rules, the DGFT described the making of oral representations as "informal hearings", and stated that he did not consider it necessary to prescribe any formal procedures for such hearings. However, where an infringement decision is proposed, the party is given a right to make oral representations to elaborate a written response, and it remains to be seen how informal such hearings will in fact prove to be.[57]

Right to inspect the file

Before the DGFT makes a decision that the Chapter I prohibition has been infringed or grants an individual exemption, he is also required to give the notifying party and any other parties to the agreement of whom he is aware an opportunity to inspect the documents in the DGFT's file relating to the proposed decision.[58] This right to inspect the file does not extend to confidential information or to OFT internal working papers.[59]

These more extensive procedural rights which are afforded to persons in relation to whom the DGFT proposes to take an infringement decision or grant an individual exemption are reminiscent of some of the rights of the defence which have come to form part of the European Commission's procedures over the years. The OFT has confidently asserted that section 60 of the Act does not require the UK authorities to follow the procedural practices of the Commission, but it is not clear

---

57 During debates on the Competition Bill in the House of Commons, the Government argued that because appeals to the Competition Commission may entail a full rehearing on the merits of a case, with the possibility of substitution of a fresh decision for that of the DGFT, there was less need for the availability of oral hearings before the DGFT. The Government no doubt had in mind in part the case law of the European Convention on Human Rights concerning the right to a fair hearing (Art 6), which establishes that procedural unfairness at first instance may be cured if a sufficiently full appeal is available which does comply with the Convention requirements.

58 Rule 14(4).

59 Rule 14(5).

that this is necessarily the case, at least in relation to the rights of the defence which have been developed through the case law of the Court of Justice[60], and with which the DGFT and the UK courts must ensure consistency.[61]

Delays and the administrative timetable

If the DGFT delays unduly in determining an application for a decision, it is open to the applicant to apply to the court for an order that the application be determined without unnecessary further delay.[62] This possibility, which does not exist in relation to notifications for guidance, does not alter the fact that the DGFT is not bound to reach a decision on every notification. Presumably determination of an application by way of administrative letter would have to be accepted by the court and the notifying party as adequate in all but exceptional cases. However, it remains to be seen how the courts will interpret this power to give directions to the DGFT, and to what extent the power will be used.

The issue of delay in the determination of notifications is a much discussed subject at the European level. The Commission is notoriously slow in processing most of its case load, although efforts have been made in recent years, with some success, to reduce the backlog which has built up.[62a] In part due to this experience, there was considerable pressure, particularly during the Committee stage of the Competition Bill in the House of Lords, to impose time limits on the DGFT. A period of three months was proposed within which the DGFT would have to determine an application for a decision. Attempts were also made to impose a positive obligation on the DGFT to give guidance or make a decision, since, as noted above, the Act merely states that he may do so. These proposed amendments were unsuccessful, but Schedule 9 to the

---

60　See, for example, Case 155/79 *A M & S v Commission* [1982] ECR 1575 (legal professional privilege), and Cases 100/80 etc *Musique Diffusion Française v Commission* [1983] ECR 1825 (right to be heard). On 22 December 1998 the Commission adopted a new consolidated Regulation on various hearing procedures, addressing issues including the rights of the defence, the right to be heard and access to the file (Reg (EC) No 2842/98, OJ 1998 L354/18).

61　The Government Minister responsible for the Competition Bill in the House of Lords, Lord Simon of Highbury, confirmed in Committee stage that general principles of Community law (such as proportionality, non-discrimination and fundamental rights) are to be imported into the Act under s 60 (Hansard, 25 November 1997, col 962). See further Chap 2 above, pp 12-13.

62　Para 7 of Sched 5 to the Act.

62a　It is a recognition of this delay which is a major contributing factor to the Commission's revolutionary proposals in its White Paper on Modernisation of the Rules implementing Articles 81 and 82 of the EC Treaty (old Arts 85 and 86) issued on 28 April 1999. See further Preface, pp xv-xvi above.

Act does provide that rules may be made for applications to be dealt with in accordance with a timetable.[63] No such rules have yet been proposed, but the Government stated during the Committee state of the Bill in the House of Commons that a timetable would be introduced "once the regime has bedded down"[64], and the OFT has undertaken to aim to work to a non-binding administrative timetable from the start.[65] In practice, the speed with which notifications for guidance or a decision are processed is likely prove an issue of great significance to persons considering whether to make such a notification.

Notice of a decision

If the DGFT has made a decision as to whether or not an agreement has infringed the Chapter I prohibition, he must without delay give written notice of the decision to the applicant and to any other person who he is aware is a party to the agreement.[66] The written notice must state the facts on which the DGFT bases his decision and his reasons for making it. The DGFT is also bound to publish the decision and his reasons for it, and this notice, like the notice of the original notification, will be placed on the public register of the OFT, on the OFT's website and in its weekly gazette.[67]

The effect of a decision

Section 16 of the Act is similar to section 15 (which deals with guidance), in providing that where the DGFT has given a favourable decision that the notified agreement has not infringed the Chapter I prohibition, he may take no further action under Part I of the Act except in the listed circumstances.[68] However, in only two situations may the DGFT re-open a decision which he has taken:

- where he has reasonable grounds for believing that there has been a material change of circumstance since he gave the decision;

---

63 Para 2(c) of Sched 9 to the Act.
64 Mr McCartney, Hansard, 11 June 1998, cols 370 and 381.
65 For example, Margaret Bloom, Director of Competition Policy in the OFT, stated at a conference organised by the Centre for the Law of the European Union, University College London, on 10 September 1998, that "we will aim to work to an administrative timetable from the start". The papers have been published as *The Europeanisation of UK Competition Law* (eds Green and Robertson) (Hart, 1999).
66 Rule 15(a)(i).
67 Rule 15(b).
68 S 16(1) and (2) of the Act.

- where he has a reasonable suspicion that the information on which he based his decision was incomplete, false or misleading in a material particular.[69]

Thus, unlike guidance, a decision may not be re-visited merely because the DGFT receives a complaint about the agreement from a third party. Before taking further action, the DGFT must consult the person to whom he gave notice of the decision[70], he may consult more widely[70a], and after taking further action he must publish a notice describing the further action which he has taken.[71]

Section 16(3), (4) and (5) of the Act mirrors exactly section 15(3)-(5) in relation to immunity from penalty and the circumstances in which that immunity may be removed. Therefore, section 16(3) provides that no penalty may be imposed under Part I in respect of any infringement of the Chapter I prohibition by an agreement which has received a favourable decision, but section 16(4) and (5) permits the DGFT to remove this immunity if circumstances entitle him to take further action. The DGFT must give written notice to the applicant party, and immunity may only be withdrawn with retrospective effect where the DGFT has reasonable suspicion that a decision was procured through materially incomplete, false or misleading information.

If the DGFT has made a decision that an agreement infringes the Chapter I prohibition, he may give directions to bring the infringement to an end, and he may impose a penalty on any party to the agreement.[72] The enforcement of infringement decisions is dealt with in detail in Chapter 6 below, and it is sufficient to note here that the DGFT's Procedural Rules state that he must give written notice to a person subject to directions or penalty of the factual basis and reasons for it, and that the directions must be published.[73]

Application for extension of individual exemption

Form N must also be used to apply to the DGFT for extension of the period for which an individual exemption has previously been granted.[74] The right to apply for such an extension is provided by section 4(6) of

---

69 S 16(2).
70 Rule 16(1).
70a Rule 16(2).
71 Rule 16(3).
72 Ss 32 and 36 of the Act.
73 Rule 17.
74 S 4(6) of the Act and Rule 19(1).

the Act. The application must be submitted not more than 12 months and not less than three months before the exemption is due to expire, and the DGFT must consult the public if he proposes to grant the application.[75] This public consultation will presumably be carried out in the same way as consultation prior to the grant of the original exemption (*i.e.* publication in the national press and trade journals, on the OFT public register and website, and in the OFT's weekly gazette), although this has not been fully addressed in the Procedural Rules or Guidelines. If the DGFT makes a decision as to whether or not to extend the individual exemption, he must give written notice of his decision to the applicant and publish it, specifying if appropriate the period of any extension granted.[76] Many of the Procedural Rules which apply to notifications for a decision apply also to applications for extension of an individual exemption.[77]

The Chapter II prohibition

Conduct may be notified to the DGFT for a decision as to whether the Chapter II prohibition has been infringed and, if it has not been infringed, whether that is because of the effect of an exclusion (section 22(1) and (2) of the Act). Such notifications are likely to be rare, for the reasons which have been explained in the section on notifications for guidance above.

Form N

Form N must also be used for notifications for a decision in respect of conduct.[78] Reference should be made to the account of Form N given in Section 5.2 on notification for guidance above[78a], and to the additional points made in this section in relation to the Chapter I prohibition about the need for care when annexing confidential information and when completing Part 4 of Form N for publication of the notification.[78b] Paragraph 5(2) of Schedule 6 to the Act requires the DGFT to arrange

---

75   Rule 19(2) and (3).
76   Rule 19(4).
77   Rule 19(5). The relevant parts of the rules concerning joint applications, copies of Form N, the content of applications, the effective date of notification, the public register and concurrent jurisdiction with sectoral regulators all apply also to applications for an extension of an individual exemption.
78   Rule 1 of the DGFT's Procedural Rules. Form N is set out at Appendix 2.
78a See p 96.
78b See p 105.

for the publication of a notification for a decision concerning the Chapter II prohibition in precisely the same terms as apply to the Chapter I prohibition.

Use of comfort letters

Comfort letters, or administrative letters as they are more correctly called and as the OFT has termed them, may also be used by the DGFT instead of reaching a decision as to whether the Chapter II prohibition has been infringed. See further the description of comfort letters relating to the Chapter I prohibition above.[78c]

Providing a decision

The DGFT may only decide whether the notified conduct infringes the Chapter II prohibition, and, if not, whether that is because of the effect of one of the exclusions contained in Schedule 1 or 3 to the Act.[79] There is no possibility of exemption from the Chapter II prohibition, and no question of provisional immunity from fines following notification of conduct for a decision. Apart from these important differences, the basic procedural rules governing the provision of a decision which have already been described apply also to Chapter II notifications.[79a]

Consultation and representations

Paragraph 5(3) of Schedule 6 to the Act imposes the same obligation on the DGFT to take account of any representations received in relation to a notification of conduct for a decision as applies in respect of the notification of agreements.[79b] However, the DGFT's Procedural Rules are simplified for Chapter II notifications and provide only that if the DGFT proposes to make a decision that the Chapter II prohibition has not been infringed he may consult the public. There is no requirement that public consultation take place. Public consultation will again occur by way of publication in the national press and/or in trade journals[80], probably together with the placing of an invitation for comment on the register of the OFT, on its website, and in its weekly gazette.[81]

78c See p 106.
79   S 22(2).
79a See p 107.
79b See p 107.
80   Rule 26(3) and Note 1.4 of Part 1 of Form N.
81   OFT Guideline on the Major Provisions (OFT 400), para 7.6.

Rule 14 of the DGFT's Procedural Rules concerning the opportunity to make representations and inspection of the DGFT's file apply equally to proposed decisions that the Chapter II prohibition has been infringed, and reference should be made to the discussion of these procedural rights set out in relation to notification of agreements for a decision above.[81a]

Delays and the administrative timetable

Paragraph 7 of Schedule 6 to the Act gives the courts the same power to give directions to the DGFT to secure that an application for a decision in respect of conduct be determined without unnecessary further delay as applies to notification of agreements under Schedule 5. The observations made above concerning the lack of a legally binding timetable for the determination of notifications are also relevant to Chapter II notifications.[81b]

Notice of a decision

The requirements as to giving written notice of a decision without delay[82] and as to publication of a decision[83] are the same for Chapter II as for Chapter I notifications. Again, publication will be by way of placing a notice on the public register of the OFT, on its website and in its weekly gazette. Special provision is made for the giving of notice to associations of undertakings[83a], or where it is not reasonably practicable to give written notice to persons other than the applicant.[83b]

The effect of a decision

Section 24 of the Act lays down the effect of a decision from the DGFT that the notified conduct has not infringed the Chapter II prohibition. Like section 16 (Chapter I prohibition), section 24 provides that where the DGFT has given a favourable decision he may take no further action under Part I of the Act with respect to the notified conduct unless:

81a See pp 107-109.
81b See pp 109-110.
82 Rule 15(a).
83 Rule 15(b).
83a Rule 25.
83b Rule 26.

- he has reasonable grounds for believing that there has been a material change of circumstance since he gave his decision;
- he has a reasonable suspicion that the information on which he based his decision was incomplete, false or misleading in a material particular.[84]

The DGFT may not take further action simply on receipt of a third party complaint. Before taking further action, the DGFT must consult the person to whom he gave notice of the decision[85], and after taking further action he must publish a notice describing the further action which he has taken.[86]

Section 24(3)-(5) provides in terms familiar from sections 15 and 16 (Chapter I) and section 23 (Chapter II) for immunity from penalty and the circumstances in which that immunity may be removed. A favourable decision prevents the imposition of any penalty in respect of the notified conduct[87], but this immunity may be removed in circumstances where the DGFT is entitled to take further action and where he gives written notice to the notifying undertaking.[88] This immunity may only be withdrawn retrospectively where the DGFT has reasonable suspicion that the information on which he based his decision and which was provided to him by an undertaking engaging in the conduct was incomplete, false or misleading in a material particular.[89]

The directions which the DGFT may give to bring an infringement to an end and the penalties which may be imposed are discussed in Chapter 6 below.

5.4 Notification for early guidance

Until the Chapter I and II prohibitions come into force on 1 March 2000 applications may only be made for early guidance, and no notifications for guidance or a decision using Form N will be accepted. Furthermore, applications for early guidance may **only** be made in respect of agreements, not conduct, and **only** in respect of agreements made during the interim period (9 November 1998 – 1 March 2000).

---

84 S 24(2).
85 Rule 16(1).
86 Rule 16(3).
87 S 24(3).
88 S 24(4).
89 S 24(5).

Paragraph 7(2) of Schedule 13 to the Act provides that an application may be made to the DGFT in anticipation of the coming into force of section 13 which permits notifications for guidance. Paragraph 7(2) further provides that applications for early guidance will have effect on and after the starting date of 1 March 2000 as if they were applications for guidance made under section 13.

Paragraph 7 of Schedule 13 also allows the DGFT to make "directions" concerning early guidance, and these were published by the OFT in November 1998.[90] Not surprisingly these directions resemble closely, but in a simplified form, the DGFT's Procedural Rules which apply to notifications proper.

Form EG

Notification of an agreement for early guidance must be made to the DGFT using Form EG, which is reproduced at Appendix 2.[91] Form EG is in large part very like Form N, but without the parts of the form relating to the Chapter II prohibition or to notification for a decision.[92]

Two or more parties to an agreement may make a joint application using Form EG[93], and if a joint representative is nominated to act on behalf of some or all of them proof of authority to act must be submitted.[94] There is no fee for submitting an application for early guidance.

Completing Form EG

The information required under Form EG is almost as extensive as that to be provided in Form N, including detailed market information. Form EG refers like Form N to the possibility that in some cases the requirement to provide information in all categories may be dispensed with, and states that this should be discussed with officials before

---

90 Early guidance directions (OFT 412). Both these early guidance directions and Form EG which must be used for early guidance notifications were issued in final form without prior public consultation due to time constraints and are reproduced at Appendix 2.
91 Direction 1 of the early guidance directions.
92 In places, Form EG uses the term "application" in place of "notification" at the equivalent point in Form N. However, the term "notification" is also used at some points in Form EG, and nothing appears to turn on the difference between these two expressions in any event.
93 Direction 2.
94 Directions 2 and 4(1) and Section 1.2 of Part 2 of Form EG.

making the application.[95] There is no possibility of oral hearings in relation to notifications for early guidance.

Form EG contains the same strictures concerning the identification and separation of confidential information as Form N[96], although since there is no publication or consultation concerning notifications for early guidance, the need for confidentiality is not quite as crucial as it is in relation notifications for a decision.[97] If a third party submits confidential information to the DGFT in respect of an agreement which has been notified for early guidance, the DGFT must (if practicable) consult the supplier of the information before disclosing it (for example, to the notifying party).[98]

Like Form N, Form EG permits a copy of Form A/B to be submitted in its place where simultaneous notification is made to the European Commission, but dual notification is of course strongly discouraged.[99]

Submitting Form EG

An original plus two copies of Form EG should be sent to the DGFT and marked for the attention of the Early Guidance Co-ordination Unit.[1] It is also possible to submit notifications for early guidance in electronic format.[2] An original or a certified copy of the notified agreement should also be submitted with Form EG, together with any other relevant documents. Each of these documents should also be sent in triplicate.[3]

The sectoral regulators also have concurrent jurisdiction with the DGFT in relation to notifications for early guidance, and it is therefore necessary to copy Form EG to the relevant regulator in appropriate cases.[4] The provisions of the early guidance directions and Form EG concerning allocation of jurisdiction and notification of the applicant as

---

95 Rule 4(4) and the introductory note to Part 2 of Form EG.
96 For example, note 1.7 of Part 1 and the introduction to Part 2 of Form EG. See also Direction 4(3) and the definition of confidential information at Direction 11(1)(c).
97 Since there are no publication requirements, Form EG does not have an equivalent to Part 4 of Form N which forms the basis of notices concerning notifications for a decision.
98 Direction 10.
99 Section 3.2 of Part 2 of Form EG.
1 Note 1.5 to Part 1 of Form EG and Direction 3(2).
2 See Note 1.7 to Part 1 of Form EG. Applicants should telephone the OFT enquiry point on 0171 211 8989 before making a notification in this way.
3 Note 1.4 to Part 1 of Form EG.
4 Direction 3(3). The regulators listed in Sched 10 to the Act regulate telecommunications, gas, electricity, water and rail. See further Chapter 9 below, p 176.

to which Director is to exercise jurisdiction are in the same terms as those that apply to notifications proper.[5]

Notifying other parties of a Form EG application

Direction 6 of the early guidance directions provides that an applicant must take all reasonable steps to give written notice of the application to all other parties to the agreement of whom he is aware within seven working days of receipt of an acknowledgement from the DGFT. A copy of this notification must also be provided to the DGFT.

The effective date of application

The provisions determining the effective date of an application for early guidance are the same as those for a notification proper[6], but since there is no question of provisional immunity from fines in the case of early guidance the only real significance of this date is to determine whether an application has been made before 1 March 2000, after which it would be treated as notification for guidance. The DGFT is under a duty to acknowledge receipt of Form EG without delay[7], and if he fails for a period of more than one month to inform the applicant that the Form EG submitted was materially incomplete, the notification is deemed to have become effective on the date of its receipt by the DGFT.[8] The notifying party remains under a continuing duty to inform the DGFT or the regulator exercising jurisdiction without delay of any material changes in the facts which have been notified.[9]

The duty to provide accurate information in Form EG

Although section 44 of the Act does not make it an offence to supply false or misleading information to the DGFT in connection with a notification for early guidance, Form EG concludes with a declaration in the same terms as Form N to the effect that all of the information provided is true to the best of the signatory's knowledge and belief.

---

5 Direction 7 and Note 1.6 to Part 1 of Form EG. See the account set out in Section 5.2 on "Notification for guidance" above, pp 99-100.
6 Direction 5.
7 Direction 5(2).
8 Direction 5(5).
9 Direction 5(4) and note 1.8 of Part 1 of Form N.

Giving of early guidance

It is open to the DGFT either to give early guidance before 1 March 2000 or to give guidance proper under section 15 of the Act as if the notification had been made under section 13.[10] Paragraph 7 of Schedule 13 to the Act does not specify the nature of the early guidance which the DGFT may give, but Form EG indicates that he may determine whether:

- the agreement is likely to benefit from one of the exclusions contained in Schedules 1-4 to the Act;
- whether the agreement is likely to qualify for an exemption (individual, if notified for a decision, block, parallel or under section 11 of the Act).[11]

Where the DGFT gives early guidance, he must do so in writing, without delay after determining the application, and stating the factual basis and reasons for his guidance.[12]

The effect of early guidance

If the DGFT has given favourable early guidance to an agreement, stating either that it is unlikely to infringe the Chapter I prohibition or that it is likely to benefit from an exemption, he may only withdraw that guidance before the starting date of 1 March 2000 if he consults the notifying party.[13] An opportunity must be given to that person to make written representations.[14] Where the DGFT does withdraw early guidance, he must give written notice of the withdrawal to the applicant, and give reasons for the withdrawal.[15]

After 1 March 2000 any early guidance which has been given is to have effect as if given following a notification for guidance proper (para 7(4) of Schedule 13 to the Act). This means that early guidance will then bind the DGFT to the same extent as other guidance, and the parties to the agreement will benefit from the immunity from penalties afforded in the case of favourable guidance.

---

10 Para 7(3) of Sched 13 to the Act.
11 Sections 2.1 and 2.2 of Part 2 of Form EG. It is interesting that Form EG refers to early guidance indicating that an agreement is likely to benefit from an exclusion, but s 13 of the Act fails to mention the possibility of guidance relating to an exclusion for notifications proper.
12 Direction 8.
13 Direction 9(1).
14 Direction 11(1)(d).
15 Direction 9(2).

5.5 **Should you notify?**

OFT officials estimate that they will receive approximately 1,000 notifications per year once the new competition regime is working steadily.[16] This forecast may be broken down as follows:

Type of notification	Chapter I – Guidance	Chapter I – Decision	Chapter II – Guidance	Chapter II – Decision
No of expected notifications per year	600	400	Very few	Very few

The OFT also estimates that it is likely to receive around 250 notifications for early guidance.[17]

What factors should you take into account when considering whether to make a notification to the DGFT? For the reasons which have already been set out earlier in this chapter, businesses will rarely wish to notify conduct for guidance or a decision, and it would rarely be in their interests to do so. Finely balanced questions as to whether to notify will, however, arise not infrequently in relation to agreements, and it is with this question that the remainder of this section is concerned.

Each agreement will, of course, have to be considered on its own particular facts, taking into account the need for legal certainty, the risk of infringement proceedings, and the likelihood of penalties. The factors which are likely to weigh both for and against notification are considered in turn.

Factors in favour of notification

The following is a list of the principal factors which may support notification of an agreement for guidance or for a decision.

- Determination of a notification, or even an administrative or comfort letter, will provide the parties to the agreement with

---

16 Source: Margaret Bloom, Director of Competition Policy in the OFT, in a written paper to a conference organised by the Centre for the Law of the European Union, University College London, on 10 September 1998, now published in *The Europeanisation of UK Competition Law* (eds Green and Robertson) (Hart 1999). The OFT's forecasts are based upon a survey of law firms and its experience with filings and complaints under the unreformed competition law regime. Mrs Bloom contrasted these figures with the number of notifications made to the European Commission: 221 in 1997.

17 Source Margaret Bloom, *ibid.*

some degree of legal certainty as to the enforceability of that agreement. Any parts of an agreement which infringe the Chapter I prohibition are void and cannot be enforced.

- If there are reasonable arguments to suggest that the agreement appreciably restricts, prevents or distorts competition, notification provides provisional immunity against fines (which may only be withdrawn by a provisional decision).
- A favourable decision provides immunity from penalty unless and until that immunity is withdrawn. Fines may be up to 10% of UK turnover.
- Individual exemption of an agreement can only be granted following notification for a decision.
- If an agreement is not notified until a complaint is made or investigation initiated, there is no guarantee that the DGFT would subsequently grant any exemption on a retrospective basis. This could leave the parties open to damages actions in respect of the period prior to the notification.
- Notification will be initiated by, at a time convenient to, and on the terms of the notifying party. In contrast, an investigation initiated by the DGFT, possibly following a third party complaint, will have to be dealt with responsively and potentially without as much time to marshall all the possible evidence.
- The fact that an agreement has been notified to the European Commission does not prevent the DGFT from investigating it under the Act (although he will generally avoid simultaneous investigations in both London and Brussels).
- Where an agreement raises particular concerns for the United Kingdom, the DGFT may not necessarily follow the assessment of the European Commission, and domestic notification may be advisable.
- There may be some agreements which the parties consider are likely to be better understood or more favourably considered by the DGFT than by the Commission. Furthermore, a favourable domestic assessment of an agreement, although not binding on the Commission, will weigh in its favour in any proceedings under Article 81 (old Article 85).

Factors against notification

The following is a list of the principal factors which may militate against notification of an agreement for guidance or for a decision.

- In cases where it is reasonably clear that an agreement does not have an appreciable effect on competition, there is no need to notify. If the DGFT concludes that an agreement does not have an appreciable effect on competition, it will not infringe the Chapter I prohibition, and at most the DGFT will determine the notification by the issue of an administrative letter indicating that he would be minded to grant the agreement negative clearance.

- Where an agreement is not in the public eye, and is unlikely to create third party complaints, it may be reasonable to take the risk of not notifying it. This factor will be strongest where there are tenable arguments that the agreement does not appreciably affect competition, so that even if the agreement were subsequently found to infringe the Chapter I prohibition fines would be unlikely and small in any event.

- The DGFT has power to grant exemptions retrospectively, backdating the exemption to the date the agreement began. As a general rule the European Commission does not have this power in relation to Article 81(3) (old Article 85(3)) exemptions, and the possibility of retrospective exemption is an important factor in reducing the risk of not notifying an agreement from the start.

- Notification using Form N (or Form EG during the interim period) will take some time and effort. Expert advice may need to be sought (whether from lawyers, economists or both), and fees may be introduced for making a notification.

- The existence of an outstanding notification may create unhelpful uncertainty for an agreement, and could delay the resolution of related court proceedings. The extent of any delay will depend upon the time taken by the DGFT to determine notifications, but in the absence of a binding timetable a notifying party has little control over the length of the procedure (see further Section 5.3 in relation to delays and the administrative timetable at p 110 above).

- Notification of an agreement for a decision may bring the fact and details of the agreement to the attention of the public, including business rivals.

- An exemption under Chapter I does not provide immunity from proceedings under Article 81 (old Article 85) of the EC Treaty.

- Where an agreement appreciably affects competition and arguably has an actual or potential, direct or indirect, effect on trade between Member States, it may be appropriate to notify it to the European Commission in Brussels. The question as to whether to notify an agreement to the Commission raises another series of competing factors for and against notification, including the delay involved and the effect which a notification would have on any pending or future national court proceedings raising Article 81 (old Article 85) of the EC Treaty. Some of these considerations have already been referred to in Chapter 2 above. If an agreement is notified to the European Commission, this will in many cases remove the need for any domestic notification. Section 41 of the Act provides that if an agreement has been notified to the Commission, and for so long as the agreement benefits from provisional immunity from fines from the Commission, that provisional immunity also applies domestically.

Notification for guidance or for a decision

If a party to an agreement does decide to notify it to the DGFT, it will have to decide whether to notify for guidance or for a decision. The points in favour of notification for guidance, on the one hand, and a decision, on the other, have been referred to in the discussion of these two forms of notification above, but for convenience the principal factors are summarised here. In support of notifications for guidance may be listed in particular:

- Notifications for guidance are not placed on the public register of the OFT, on its website, or published in its weekly gazette. Unwelcome publicity for the agreement can be avoided.
- Nor are notifications for guidance published in the national press or trade journals. There is no third party consultation.
- The outcome of a notification for guidance can remain confidential to the notifying party and any other parties to the agreement.

However, a party to an agreement may wish to notify it for a decision since:

- A decision affords greater legal certainty than guidance.
- A decision may only be re-visited if it was procured through materially incomplete, false or misleading information, or if there is a material change in circumstance. It may not be re-

opened merely because a third party complains to the DGFT about the agreement.

- An individual exemption for an agreement may only be granted following notification for a decision.

Chapter 6

Investigation and Enforcement

6.1 Introduction

More than any other feature of the RTPA[1] régime, it was the lack of adequate investigatory powers that made it unsatisfactory from the perspective of the Director General of Fair Trading (DGFT). Unless the evidence was given to him virtually on a plate, he had little chance of proving the existence of a cartel. The extensive armoury conferred upon him by the Act – closely modelled on the powers of the European Commission under Regulation 17[2], and rivalling those of Her Majesty's Customs and Excise – will more than compensate for the years of frustration and impotence. They are backed up by a range of criminal penalties for those who attempt resistance.

The enforcement machinery under the RTPA was also cumbersome and inadequate. The sanction for a first-time offender was non-pecuniary, taking the form of orders made by the Restrictive Practices Court after sometimes lengthy and complex proceedings. Again, the enforcement powers conferred upon him by the Act will transform the DGFT's effectiveness. It will come as no surprise that they are more or less exact replicas of the powers available to the European Commission. The centrepiece is the possibility of imposing extremely severe fines, called "penalties" in the Act, for intentional or negligent infringement of the prohibitions. They are levied on undertakings, that is, companies and businesses. Infringement of the prohibitions will not itself be an offence (criminal or otherwise) for directors or other officers of undertakings, in contrast with the more draconian system applying in the United States. However, determined failure by an officer of a company to comply with directions issued by the DGFT at the conclusion of an enquiry may expose that officer to personal liability for the DGFT's costs of obtaining a court order against him to secure compliance.[3]

---

1 See Chap 3, fn 1.
2 Reg 17, JO 204/62, [1959-62] OJ Spec Ed 57.
3 See discussion of s 34(2) in Section 6.3 of this chapter, below.

The investigation and enforcement machinery is contained in Chapter III of Part I of the Act. Sections 25-31 deal with investigations and sections 32-41 with enforcement. Sections 42-44 contain the offences relating to failure to co-operate with investigations. They will be discussed below in connection with investigations, which seems more natural than the order of the provisions in the Act. Reference should also be made to the relevant Office of Fair Trading (OFT) Guidelines[4] and to the DGFT's Procedural Rules.[5] The Act also confers special powers on the DGFT to assist the European Commission in investigating suspected breaches of Articles 81 and 82 (old Articles 85 and 86) in the United Kingdom.[6]

6.2   Investigation

Formal and informal investigations

The pre-condition for the use of compulsory investigative powers is that the DGFT must have "reasonable grounds" for suspecting that there has been an infringement of either the Chapter I or Chapter II prohibitions.[7]

The investigations Guideline[8] indicates that the issue whether he has reasonable grounds for suspicion is one for the DGFT's judgement based on actual information available. Such information might be hard information stemming from a complaint or whistle blowing. Earlier drafts of the Guideline indicated that suspicion might be founded on economic evidence of price movements, but that reference to anti-competitive behaviour in a newspaper alone would not be sufficient. In practice, the DGFT will expect to obtain much of his information from complaints. This is one reason why the OFT has been at pains in public pronouncements to emphasise its openness to receive complaints.

It should be noted that there is nothing in the Act to stop the DGFT from seeking to obtain information from companies or individuals without recourse to his compulsory powers. This happens frequently already under the RTPA and under the Fair Trading Act 1973. There is

---

4 Guidelines on Powers of Investigation (OFT 404) and on Enforcement (OFT 407).

5 (OFT 411).

6 Part II of the Act, ss 61-65. These provisions are discussed under the heading "EC Treaty investigations" in Section 6.2 of this chapter, p 137, below.

7 S 25. The equivalent provision in the RTPA, s 36, required the DGFT to have "reasonable cause" to believe that a person was or might be party to a registrable agreement. Some commentators see a significant difference in the phrases used in the two Acts.

8 Guideline on Powers of Investigation (OFT 404), para 2.1.

no penalty for failing to reply but any information supplied must not be misleading, on pain of criminal penalty. The information turned up by informal enquiries is on occasion sufficient to enable the DGFT to open a formal inquiry. This practice may be expected to continue under the Act.[9]

Once the DGFT is able to satisfy himself that he has reasonable grounds for suspecting an infringement of one of the prohibitions, he has in essence two types of investigative power. The first is the power to compel the production of information[10] and the second, the power to enter premises.[11] The latter power sub-divides into two categories, depending on whether or not a warrant has been obtained.

Compelling the production of information

The DGFT's power to require the production of documents and information is exercised by notice in writing.[12] It would be unwise for any addressee of a notice to respond to the DGFT without first taking legal advice.

The notice may require the person to whom it is addressed to produce a specified document or specified information which the DGFT **"considers relates to any matter relevant to the investigation"**.[13] This is widely[14] phrased indeed.

The notice must[15] inform the addressee of the subject matter and purpose of the investigation and also point out the criminal offences[16] committed in the event of failure to deal properly with the notice.

"Document" is defined in the Act as including "information recorded in any form":[17] an obvious example is information held on computer. "Specified" is defined to mean either actually specified or described in the notice or falling within a category which is specified or described in the notice.[18] In other words, the notice may call for a specific document of whose existence the DGFT is already aware, or it

---

9 *Ibid*, para 2.3.
10 Equivalent to that under Art 11 of Reg 17 in the EC regime.
11 Equivalent to that under Art 14 of Reg 17 in the EC regime.
12 S 26(2). The notice may be sent by post or by fax: Guideline on Powers of Investigation (OFT 404), para 3.8.
13 S 26(1).
14 and clumsily.
15 S 26(3).
16 Described under the heading "Offences", p 134, below.
17 S 59(1).
18 S 26(4).

may call generically for the minutes of the marketing committee, or it may ask for sales records for particular periods and so on.

The notice may specify the time and place at which the document or information is to be provided and also the form or manner in which it is to be provided.[19] This means that addressees can be required to put together information that has not hitherto been compiled (and, by necessary implication, produce it in "documentary" form).[20]

There is no restriction as to the persons to whom a notice may be addressed or the number of occasions on which a notice may be sent to them. Notices may therefore be sent to anyone whom the DGFT believes to possess relevant information whether or not they are suspected of participating in any infringement; and the process may be repeated to gather further information or clarify that which has already been obtained. Obvious targets for information requests include competitors, suppliers and customers of the undertakings which are the prime focus of the investigation. Notices could also be sent to complainants.

In relation to documents actually produced, the power extends to taking copies or extracts from any document (for example, entries for particular dates in a diary) and requiring present or former officers or employees of the addressee to give an explanation of the document.[21] If the document is not produced, the addressee can be required to state, to the best of his knowledge and belief, where it is to be found.[22]

Power to enter premises

"Premises" means business premises first of all. However, in a widely phrased exception, domestic premises may also be entered if they are also used in connection with the affairs of the relevant business or if documents relating to the undertaking are kept there. The definition of "premises" also extends to "any" vehicle, in other words private cars as well as company vehicles.[23]

---

19 S 26(5). The DGFT will consider the volume and complexity of the information required and the urgency of the case when setting time limits: see Guideline on Powers of Investigation (OFT 404), para 3.10.

20 The example given in the Guideline is "market share information or to provide a description of a particular market using the knowledge or experience of the sales manager": see Guideline on Powers of Investigation (OFT 404), para 3.7. A better example might be the production of data presented in a format that the company does not habitually use.

21 S 26(6)(a). A person required to give an explanation of a document under this provision may be accompanied by a legal adviser: Rule 13(3) of the DGFT's Procedural Rules (OFT 411). See Hansard, 8 July 1998, col 1182 (Mr Griffiths).

22 S 26(6)(b).

23 "Premises" are defined in s 59(1).

The DGFT has power to enter any such premises either with or without a court warrant.

Entry without a warrant

The power to enter without a warrant may be exercised by an OFT official authorised in writing by the DGFT, known as an "investigating officer".[24] The investigating officer may turn up without notice at the premises of an undertaking which is under suspicion of having infringed either the Chapter I or Chapter II prohibition, but must attempt to give two working days' written notice of the intended visit to any other occupier.[25] On arrival on an unannounced visit, he has to produce his written authorisation and a document explaining the subject matter and purpose of the investigation and the criminal offences committed in the event of failure to co-operate.[26]

The investigating officer may take with him such equipment as appears necessary.[27] This might include computer and recording equipment; since he has no authority to use force, it would not include any equipment for forcing entry to premises.

He can require **any person** on the premises to produce any document[28] which the officer considers "relates to any matter relevant to the investigation" and to provide an explanation of it if the document is produced.[29] This is again extremely widely phrased. Presumably the person producing the document and the person explaining it need not be the same person (a secretary might be asked to produce a document and an executive to explain it). The officer can require any person to state where a document is to be found[30], and he may take copies or extracts from any document produced.[31] Lastly, he can require information held on a computer and which is accessible from the premises (for example, information held on a database physically located somewhere else but which can be accessed from the premises) to be produced in a form in which the officer can take it away (for example, on disc or tape) and in visible and legible form (*i.e.* decoded).[32]

---

24 S 27(1).
25 S 27(2) and (3). He is excused the notice requirement if he has taken all reasonably practicable steps to give notice but has been unable to do so: s 27(3)(b).
26 S 27(4). This information must be set out in the written notice given to those who are not themselves under suspicion of an infringement.
27 S 27(5)(a).
28 As extensively defined: see text to fn 17 above.
29 S 27(5)(b).
30 S 27(5)(c).
31 S 27(5)(d).
32 S 27(5)(e).

Entry with a warrant

The difference between visits, even unannounced, without a warrant and those made under the authority of a court warrant is the level of force and compulsion that a warrant allows. With a warrant, the DGFT's officials may use force to enter the premises, can carry out a search (rather than asking persons on the premises to produce material for them) and may take actual possession of the material rather than copies or extracts.

When may the DGFT apply for a warrant

There are three sets of circumstances in which the DGFT may apply to the court[33] for a warrant before entering premises. Two of them apply when he has attempted to exercise his other powers of investigation (*i.e.* the power to compel the production of material and the power to enter premises without a warrant) but in some way has been unsuccessful. The third allows him to carry out a full surprise search (the so-called "dawn raid"[34]). In each case, he will have to demonstrate (that, is, to the judge's satisfaction) that he has reasonable grounds for suspecting certain matters.

It is not stated in the Act, but clearly applications will be made *ex parte* (that is, without the "target" being present or even aware of the application) so as to preserve the element of surprise. Warrants will be valid for one month from issue.[35] They will state on their face the subject matter and purpose of the DGFT's investigation and also specify the penalties for not co-operating with the enquiry.[36]

In more detail, the three situations in which a warrant may be sought are as follows:

(1) If the DGFT has asked for documents to˙ be produced either by written notice or on a warrant-free visit, and the documents have not been produced, he may apply for a warrant if he has reasonable grounds for suspecting that there are such documents on the premises.[37]

---

33 Warrants will have to be sought from the High Court in England and Wales, and the Court of Session in Scotland.
34 This is the rather picturesque name that antitrust aficionados have given to unannounced visits by competition regulators such as the EC Commission. OFT officials have, however, been at pains to point out that they do not expect to turn up at dawn, if only because most premises are unoccupied then. The normal time for such a "raid" would be at the opening of business. "The investigating officer will normally arrive at the premises during office hours": see Guideline on Powers of Investigation (OFT 404), para 5.10.
35 S 28(6).
36 S 29(1).
37 S 28(1)(a).

(2) He may apply for a warrant if (a) an investigating officer has attempted to enter premises without a warrant but has been unable to do so[38] and (b) there are reasonable grounds for suspecting that documents of the kind whose production the DGFT could compel are to be found on the premises.[39]

(3) The DGFT may apply for a "dawn raid" warrant where there are reasonable grounds for suspecting that there are documents on the premises whose production he could compel **and** that they would not be produced if called for, but would be "concealed, removed, tampered with or destroyed".[40] Unless the undertaking whose premises are to be searched has previous "form" in refusing to co-operate with such enquiries, the question is essentially one of trust. Certainly the OFT Guideline gives no hint of the circumstances in which the DGFT envisages applying for a "dawn raid" warrant.

The effect of a warrant

A warrant issued under section 28 will authorise a named OFT official, together with other officers authorised in writing by the DGFT, to enter the premises using reasonable force[41] and to search them for the documents which were the subject of the application for the warrant.[42] In fact, if the DGFT can satisfy the judge that there may be other documents relevant to the enquiry on the premises, the warrant may be extended to cover those documents even if the DGFT could not compel their production.[43] It may be arguable that this provision is not fully compatible with the rights of defence recognised in Community law and the rights conferred by Article 6 of the European Convention on Human Rights, soon to be introduced into domestic law by the Human Rights Act 1998.[43a]

The warrant entitles the officials to use force only if necessary, so that if on production of the warrant they are allowed entry, they may not use force.[44] They are obliged to endeavour to contact the occupier if no-one is present when they attend to execute the warrant, and also to

---

38 This may arise either because the occupier refuses to allow the officer to enter, despite production of the necessary paperwork, or because, for some physical reason, he has been unable to get in without using force, *e.g.* the premises are unoccupied or the occupier is absent.
39 S 28(1)(c).
40 S 28(1)(b).
41 And the OFT official may take with him the necessary equipment (s 28(4)), which can include tools for forcing entry.
42 S 28(2)(a) and (b).
43 S 28(3).
43a The Human Rights Act 1998 is due to come fully into force on 2 October 2000.
44 In any event, they may not use force against any person.

allow him or his legal adviser a reasonable time to be present when it is executed.[45]

If the official is unable to contact the occupier, he must leave the warrant prominently displayed and must also leave the premises secured as effectively as he found them.[46]

The named official can take copies or extracts of the documents found provided that they "appear to be" of the kind specified in the application. Indeed, he may take possession of them if that appears necessary to preserve them or to prevent them from being tampered with, or if it is not reasonably practicable to copy them on the spot.[47] He can take any other steps that appear to be necessary to preserve the documents. He may also require any person[48] to explain any apparently relevant document or to state where a document may be found. He has the same powers as on a visit without warrant in relation to information stored on computer.[49]

Legal advice

The Act makes provision in respect of legal professional privilege and, rather less satisfactorily, in relation to the right of undertakings to have their lawyers present during inspections by members of the DGFT's staff.

Legal professional privilege

All of the DGFT's investigatory powers (that is, compelling production of documents or information, and carrying out inspections with or without a warrant) are subject to the right of any person concerned not to produce or disclose a privileged communication.[50] Privileged communications are those between a professional legal adviser and his client or any communication made in connection with legal proceedings which would be protected from disclosure in High Court proceedings[51] on grounds of legal professional privilege.[52] As the Guideline points

---

45 S 29(3); see also section on "Legal advice", below.
46 S 29(4) and s 28(5).
47 S 28(2)(b) and (c). The OFT may retain the documents for three months: s 28(7).
48 Presumably a person on the premises, although this is not stipulated in s 28(2)(e).
49 S 28(2)(f).
50 S 30.
51 Or their equivalent in Scotland: s 30(3).
52 S 30(2).

out[53], this exception is wider than that applying in EC competition law, particularly in that the Act protects advice from qualified in-house lawyers.

The right to have a lawyer present

The OFT has said that its practice will "go no further" than that of the European Commission in relation to delaying inspections so as to allow the undertaking's lawyers to be present.[54] The Guideline indicates that consideration **will** be given to delaying the inspection whenever the officials turn up without notice, unless the company has an in-house lawyer on the premises.[55] Presumably this means an in-house lawyer who is actually present at the time of the inspection. Even so, it may not be satisfactory protection for the undertaking concerned since not all lawyers have expertise in competition law.

The Guideline mirrors the DGFT's Procedural Rules.[56] Rule 13 says that the officer will grant a request to allow a reasonable time for the occupier's legal advisers to arrive at the premises if he considers it reasonable to do so **and** if he is satisfied that any conditions he considers it appropriate to attach are being or will be complied with. In so far as that rule applies to inspections made under authority of a warrant, it is incompatible with the clear wording of the Act which requires the opportunity to be given and says nothing about conditions.[57] In relation to other inspections, the Guideline suggests the nature of the conditions which may be required: the sealing of filing cabinets, closing down the undertaking's external e-mail link or allowing OFT officials to occupy certain rooms in the building.[58] The idea plainly is to ensure that the investigation is not hindered by the removal of relevant material and that others outside the premises, such as fellow members of a suspected cartel, are not informed of the inspection.

Offences

The Act creates three groups of criminal offence[59] to back up the DGFT's powers of investigation. In short, they are obstruction, tampering with documents and providing false or misleading information.

---

53 See Guideline on Powers of Investigation (OFT 404), para 6.2.
54 *Ibid*, para 4.10.
55 *Ibid*, paras 4.10 and 4.11.
56 (OFT 411)
57 S 29(3)(b).
58 See Guideline on Powers of Investigation (OFT 404), para 4.11.
59 In ss 42-44.

Liability of company officers

It is important to note that the Act allows proceedings to be brought against officers[60] of a body corporate which has committed any of the offences to be discussed below if the offence has been committed with the consent or connivance of that officer or is attributable to his neglect.[61]

Obstruction

It is an offence not to comply with a requirement imposed by virtue of the DGFT's investigative powers. However, if the OFT officials have not complied with the statutory requirements for the exercise of those powers, it will not be an offence to fail or refuse to obey.[62]

As regards a requirement to produce a document, to provide information, explain a document or state where a document may be found, failure to do so without reasonable excuse[63] is punishable by a fine. Serious cases will be tried on indictment in the county courts where there is no upper limit on the level of fine.[64] The same applies as regards intentional obstruction of an officer during an inspection carried without a warrant.[65]

Intentional obstruction of an inspection carried out under authority of a warrant is, not surprisingly, a more serious offence, which can carry a prison sentence of up to two years as well as an unlimited fine.[66]

Prison terms and unlimited fines can also be imposed for the other two groups of offence, tampering with documents and providing false or misleading information.

Tampering with documents

As regards destruction or falsification of documents, a person commits an offence in recklessly or intentionally destroying or otherwise disposing of documents, or falsifying or concealing them, or causing or permitting any of those actions **if** that person has been required to produce a document under the DGFT's investigatory powers (that is, in

---

60 Meaning a director, manager, secretary or similar officer, or a person purporting to act as such: s 72(3). Likewise a "member" of a body corporate (such as a shareholder or proprietor) who manages its affairs will be exposed to the risk of prosecution.
61 S 72.
62 S 42(4).
63 S 42(2) and (3).
64 S 42(6).
65 S 42(5).
66 S 42(7).

writing or during any type of inspection).[67] Note that getting rid of documents that might be useful in such an enquiry is not an offence, if it is done before any investigation is begun.

False or misleading information

The offence in relation to false or misleading information is committed by any person who knowingly or recklessly provides information to the DGFT which is materially false or misleading **if** the information is provided to the DGFT in connection with any of his functions in relation to the prohibitions.[68] This is not in terms limited to information provided in response to a request made pursuant to the investigatory powers under sections 26-28 of the Act. That in turn suggests that an offence may be committed if false or misleading information is supplied in response to an informal, non-statutory request. The policy logic of this is evident: there should be no scope for lying to the DGFT with impunity so as to put him off the trail.

The moral is that undertakings should take even informal inquiries from the DGFT very seriously indeed.

Self-incrimination

The OFT Guideline recognises that, by virtue of section 60[69], the privilege against self-incrimination developed in EC cases such as *Orkem*[70] will apply to limit the extent to which a person has to respond to enquiries from the DGFT. The DGFT cannot "compel the provision of answers which might involve an admission on [the undertaking's] part of the existence of an infringement which it is incumbent on the [DGFT] to prove".[71] Self-incrimination might be an issue if the question were, for example, whether prices had been fixed multilaterally at a particular meeting. However, the DGFT is of course free to ask who attended the meeting and for any record of it, including the agenda, to be produced. The Guideline, in saying[72] that the DGFT will request documents or information relating **to facts**, suggests a self-denying ordinance: the implication is that the DGFT will not ask the sort of question that might, if answered, lead to self-incrimination. An alternative and

---

67 S 43(1).
68 S 44(1).
69 See Chap 2 above.
70 Case 374/87 [1989] ECR 3283.
71 See Guideline on Powers of Investigation (OFT 404), para 6.4.
72 *Ibid.*

stricter approach would be to ask the question, knowing that no action could be taken if the undertaking refused to reply.

EC Treaty investigations

It should be kept constantly in mind that the Chapter I and II prohibitions are not Articles 81 and 82 (old Articles 85 and 86) although they are closely modelled on them, and that the Act gives the DGFT no power to apply the EC Treaty competition provisions (much to the EC Commission's disappointment). As far as the United Kingdom is concerned, the EC Commission is the only regulator empowered to administer Articles 81 and 82.[73] As a matter of policy, that is likely to remain the position for as long as the Commission is unwilling to share its competence to grant exemptions pursuant to Article 81(3) (old 85(3)).

However, the Act does strengthen the ability of the DGFT to assist in Commission investigations.[74] It enables the DGFT to apply to the High Court or Court of Session for the appropriate warrant if an investigation being conducted by the Commission itself, or by the DGFT at the Commission's request, is being obstructed or is likely to be obstructed. The circumstances in which an investigation is actually being, or can be regarded as likely to be, obstructed are essentially similar to those applying in the case of the DGFT's own investigations of possible Chapter I or II infringements described above.

The Act makes it clear that, when acting in connection with a Commission investigation, the officials authorised by the DGFT will in effect act as a Commission official would. The Guideline makes it clear that this extends to taking the narrower approach to legal privilege for documents which is recognised in EC law.[75]

The provisions relating to EC investigations are backed up by the same offences as apply in connection with failure to co-operate with searches in connection with the Chapter I and II prohibitions described above.

Investigations under the Fair Trading Act 1973

The Act[76] also strengthens the DGFT's position in relation to investigations under the monopoly provisions of the Fair Trading Act

---

73 Except in connection with tramp shipping and air transport between the UK and non-Member States.
74 See Part II of the Act, ss 61-65.
75 See Guideline on Powers of Investigation (OFT 404), para 10.7.
76 In ss 66-69.

1973. These powers have been retained despite the introduction of the Chapter II prohibition, for the policy reasons discussed in Chapter 4 above.

6.3 **Enforcement**

Interim measures

An important power of the DGFT, which can be seen as an adjunct to his investigative powers, is that of taking interim decisions (called "directions" in the Act) to preserve the position pending an investigation.[77] This will inject greater flexibility and rapidity into his armoury. However, experience with the EC provisions suggest that it is a power that will be used sparingly.

The Act seems to envisage that an investigation must actually have been begun before the power to impose interim measures can be exercised. Section 35(1) specifies that the section applies if the DGFT has a "reasonable suspicion" that there has been an infringement of either the Chapter I or the Chapter II prohibition "but has not **completed** his investigation into the matter".[78] Nevertheless, the power can be exercised at an early stage of the investigation, so it perhaps need hardly have got under way. The notion of "reasonable suspicion" is discussed above.

The DGFT can give directions if he considers it necessary to act as a matter of urgency for specified purposes. Those purposes are the prevention of serious, irreparable damage either to a particular person or to a particular category of persons, or more generally for the protection of the public interest.

The Act contains no definition of "public interest". It is doubtful whether the EC case law[79] will be of much assistance here, as the EC Treaty provisions are interpreted in the light of rather different objectives, notably that of achieving an integrated common market which can hardly be said to be relevant to domestic UK competition law.

The DGFT has to give notice to the persons to whom he intends to address what the Guideline[80] inelegantly calls "interim measures directions" so as to enable them to make representations.[81] The notice

---

77 S 35.
78 S 35(1), emphasis added.
79 To be taken into account generally by virtue of s 60: see Chap 2 above.
80 See Guideline on Enforcement (OFT 407), Section 3.
81 S 35(3).

must be in writing and must specify the nature of the direction that the DGFT intends to issue and his reasons for doing so.[82]

The Act makes it clear that an interim measures direction may go so far as to require the addressee to "terminate the agreement or cease the conduct in question".[83] It may be suggested that to require termination or permanent cessation rather than suspension arguably goes further than the notion of an "interim" measure properly permits.

A direction may stay in place for so long as the DGFT has the reasonable suspicion that an infringement has been committed. At the conclusion of his investigation, he may replace the interim measures directions with permanent and final directions, discussed below.

Decisions

At the end of an investigation, the DGFT may conclude that there has been an infringement of the Chapter I or II prohibitions. If so he may "make" a decision to that effect. Before doing so he must give written notice to the person or persons likely to be affected by the decision he proposes and give them an opportunity to make representations.

That much is provided for in section 31 of the Act, which seems to compress into those terse statements the EC requirement for a Statement of Objections and the opportunity for a hearing before a formal decision can be taken. The Guideline on enforcement[84] does not refer at all to the taking (or making) of decisions, or to the nature of the opportunity to make representations that is to be afforded. As noted already, the official line is that there is no need for the actual procedures of the DGFT to be consistent with those of the EC Commission under Regulation 17, and in particular that section 60 does not require such consistency.[85] Nevertheless, it is accepted that section 60 brings in what have been called "high level" principles of EC law (including fundamental rights and rights guaranteed by the European Convention on Human Rights), which may in time oblige the OFT to align its procedures more closely on those of the EC Commission.

Despite the width of the reference to "persons likely to be affected" by a proposed infringement decision in section 31, the Procedural Rules suggest a narrower and more conventional concept: notice will be given

---

82 S 35(4).
83 S 35(6) and (7), referring back to s 32(3) and s 33(3) respectively.
84 Guideline on Enforcement (OFT 407).
85 See *e.g.* Hansard, 5 March 1998, cols 1363 and 1364 (Lord Simon of Highbury).

either to the person who has asked for a decision to be taken (*i.e.* a notifying party) and any other parties known to the DGFT to be party to the agreement or conduct, or if there has been no notification (as would be the case for traditional cartels), to any person known to the DGFT to be party to the agreement or conduct.[86]

The notice must state the matters to which the DGFT has taken objection, the action he proposes and his reasons for it.[87-88] This suggests that the notice will indeed closely resemble a Statement of Objections from the EC Commission.

The consultation version of the DGFT's Procedural Rules stated that the DGFT did not see the need to lay down formal rules for oral representations, but that "where an infringement decision is proposed, the parties may make oral representations to elaborate an written response". Rule 14(3)(c) more generously suggests that any oral or written representations submitted within a period specified in the notice will be taken into consideration. In practice, it is to be expected that most addressees will wish to avail themselves of both; written observations can go into details, oral observations can hit the strongest aspects of the addressee's case and the weakest of the regulator's.

As with the EC procedure, addressees will have access to the DGFT's file in preparing a response to a notice, and that file will not contain confidential material or papers internal to the OFT.[89]

Once taken, it would appear that what is envisaged is a reasoned decision along the lines of those taken by the EC Commission. Rule 15(1) of the DGFT's Procedural Rules requires the DGFT to give notice of his decision to, in effect, the same persons as those to whom he was required to give notice of his intention to take it, "stating the facts on which he bases his decision and his reasons for it". Likewise, Rule 15(2) requires him to publish without delay his decision "and the reasons for making it". The place of publication is not specified, nor in terms does Rule 26(3)[90] apply. However, the Guideline on enforcement says that **directions** (as to which see next section) will be published on the register maintained by the DGFT and also on a website.[91] Since directions following a finding of infringement will normally be embodied in the decision recording the finding where the decision and the directions are

---

86 DGFT's Procedural Rules (OFT 411), Rule 14(1).
87-88 *Ibid*, Rule 14(3).
89 *Ibid*, Rule 14(3)(b), (4) and (5).
90 Which allows the DGFT to publish notices on the OFT's Register, in the London, Edinburgh and Belfast Gazettes and at least one national daily newspaper and appropriate trade journals.
91 Guideline on Enforcement (OFT 407), para 2.6. The website address has not yet been announced.

addressed to the same person[92], it would appear that decisions are to be published in the same manner.

Final directions

Once an infringement decision has been made, the DGFT is able to give directions intended to bring the infringement to an end. His powers are set out in sections 32 and 33 of the Act dealing with infringements of the Chapter I and Chapter II prohibitions respectively. Unsurprisingly, directions must be in writing. The DGFT's Procedural Rules require him, when making directions under sections 32 and 33, to inform the person to whom the direction is addressed of the facts on which it is based and his reasons for giving the direction.[93] He is also required to publish such directions.[94]

In the case of a Chapter I infringement, the direction may in particular require termination or amendment of the agreement.[95] In the case of a Chapter II infringement, the direction may well require the modification or cessation of the offending conduct.[96]

Directions may be addressed to any person the DGFT considers appropriate. The Guideline emphasises that the direction need not be addressed to, or only to, the infringer: it might be addressed to a parent company.[97]

The DGFT is given complete discretion as to the import of the directions. Whereas a Commission decision finding an infringement typically requires the offending agreement or practices to be terminated, the Guideline suggests that the DGFT may go beyond such traditional "cease and desist" orders and require "positive action". The examples given are informing third parties of the end of an infringement and periodic reporting to the DGFT of prices charged.[98]

As already noted, the Guideline indicates that the publication envisaged by the DGFT's Procedural Rules will be on a register maintained by the DGFT and also on a website.

In the event of failure to comply with directions, the DGFT can seek a court order to secure obedience.[99] Failure to comply with the court

---

92 *Ibid*, para 2.4.
93 DGFT's Procedural Rules (OFT 411), Rule 17(1)(a).
94 *Ibid*, Rule 17(2).
95 S 32(3).
96 S 33(3).
97 Guideline on Enforcement (OFT 407), para 2.2.
98 *Ibid*, para 2.3.
99 See generally s 34.

order would be a contempt of court in the normal way. The court order can require the "defaulter" to comply within a specified period. If the direction required action to be taken in the management or administration of an undertaking, the order may require compliance by the undertaking itself or any its officers.[1] The court may order the DGFT's costs of applying for an order to be borne by the person in default or, in a further example of potential individual liability under the Act[2], by any officer of an undertaking who is responsible for the default.[3]

Fines (penalties)

The power to impose fines (or penalties as the Act calls them) is conferred in section 36. The DGFT may impose them on making a decision that there has been an infringement of the Chapter I or Chapter II prohibition.[4] The persons on whom fines may be imposed are the "undertakings"[5] which have committed the infringement.

The absolute level of the fines that may be imposed on infringers under a system modelled on the EC régime is of course one of the most attention-grabbing features of the Act. The EC Commission is empowered under Article 15(2) of Regulation 17 to impose fines for infringements of Articles 81 and 82 (old Articles 85 and 86) of up to 10% of world-wide turnover (not confined to turnover in the market sector in which the infringement has taken place). Likewise, the Act sets an upper limit of 10% of the undertaking's turnover for the penalties it envisages.[6]

No amount of familiarity with the potential levels of EC fines has bred a dismissive attitude amongst those on the receiving end. Practical experience suggests that the prime motivation for the bringing of challenges to Commission decisions before the Court of First Instance (CFI) in Luxembourg is often the amount of the penalty.

It is a small measure of good news, therefore, for those who fear that they may be fined under the Act that the government has announced[7] that the maximum level of fine will be set at 10% of turnover **in the**

---

1 S 34(1).
2 *i.e.* in addition to those described in connection with obstruction of investigations in Section 6.2 of this chapter, p 135, above.
3 S 34(2).
4 S 36(1) and (2).
5 See Chaps 3 and 4 above for the EC law definition of undertakings, brought into the Act via s 60 (for which see Chap 2 above).
6 S 36(8).
7 See Guideline on Enforcement (OFT 407), para 4.12.

United Kingdom in a forthcoming Statutory Instrument.[8] However, since the natural targets of regulatory interest under the Act will be those companies whose activities are largely concentrated on markets within the United Kingdom, this is indeed a small crumb of comfort. Furthermore, it should be remembered that the relevant turnover is total UK turnover, and not just that in the relevant market.

The DGFT is also required to publish guidance as to the appropriate level of penalties for infringements of the prohibitions.[9] He may alter this guidance at any time[10], which allows him to increase "tariffs" if he feels they are not having sufficient deterrent effect.[11] He must then publish revised guidance.[12] In all cases, his guidance must be approved in advance by the Secretary of State[13] and the DGFT is required to consult such persons as he feels appropriate[14] which must include sectoral regulators when the guidance relates to matters over which they exercise concurrent jurisdiction.[15]

Calculation of fines

Although the statutory guidance on penalties has not yet been published, the Guideline on enforcement contains some pointers.

(1) There will be three main components in the calculation: gravity, duration and the existence of aggravating circumstances or mitigation. The level thus indicated may be further adjusted by reference to matters such as deterrent effect, ability to pay "in a specific social context", benefits derived by the offender from the infringement and the economic context in which the infringement was committed.[16]

(2) Genuine compliance programmes which are regularly audited and actively operated may be treated as a mitigating factor.[17]

---

8 To be made under s 36(8). No draft was available at time of writing. The Inland Revenue has given its view that penalties will not be tax deductible: see para 4.13 of the Guideline on Enforcement (OFT 407).

9 S 38(1). He may decide, after consulting the Secretary of State, how this guidance will be published. It is to be hoped that an up-to-date version of the guidance will always be available on the OFT website. No draft guidance was available at time of writing.

10 S 38(2).

11 *Cf* Guideline on Enforcement (OFT 407), para 4.2.

12 S 38(3).

13 S 38(4).

14 S 36(6).

15 S 36(7). For regulators, see Chap 9 below.

16 Guideline on Enforcement (OFT 407), para 4.33.

17 *Ibid*, paras 4.35 and 4.36. See Chap 1 above for more detailed discussion of compliance programmes.

(3) The DGFT will be likely to follow a similar policy as the EC Commission in treating "whistleblowers" relatively leniently.[18] It should be noted that the Commission will only entertain the first party to give it information which it does not already possess as qualifying for possible lenient treatment; and that some companies who came forward with information which the Commission recognised as valuable in leading to the detection and prosecution of a cartel nevertheless received fines which they felt they had to challenge.[19]

When setting penalties for infringements, the DGFT must have regard to the current guidance[20] and also to any penalties or fines imposed by the EC Commission, or court or other body in another Member State in respect of the same agreement or conduct.[21] The same obligation is laid upon the Appeal Tribunal and courts to which an appeal lies from that tribunal.[22] Although it is not specified, the underlying justification must be the possible overlap in jurisdiction between the Act, on the one hand, and Articles 81 and 82 (old Articles 85 and 86) and their national equivalents in other Member States, on the other. If that were not so, it would be equally relevant to take into account fines imposed by other antitrust authorities across the world, such as in the United States, for agreements or conduct whose effects are felt in several jurisdictions. The Act seemingly takes no account of such "third country" double jeopardy.

Notice of the DGFT's intention to impose a penalty has to be given to the intended payer in writing, with an indication of the reasons why the DGFT requires that person to pay a penalty.[23] In the ordinary course, this will be done in the same document that records the finding of infringement and gives directions for bringing it to an end (which will be compendiously referred to in practice as the DGFT's "decision").

The notice has to specify a time for the payment of the fine, which cannot be less than the period within which an appeal may be brought

---

18 For the DGFT's intention to do so, see *ibid*, paras 4.37-4.39. See the Commission's Notice at OJ 1996 C207/4.

19 For example, Stora in the cartonboard cartel proceedings (see Case T-354/94 *Stora Kopparberg Bergslags AB* v *Commission*, judgment of 14 May 1998; on appeal to the ECJ, Case C-286/98P (pending); and Case T-202/98 *Tate & Lyle plc* v *Commission* (pending) in relation to certain marketing practices in the UK sugar market.

20 S 36(8).

21 S 36(9).

22 S 36(9) and (10).

23 S 36(6) and Rule 17(1)(b) of the DGFT's Procedural Rules (OFT 411).

against the imposition of the penalty.[24] The DGFT has indicated that the likely period for payment of fines will be three months.[25]

Once the specified period has passed without an appeal being made, or after determination of any appeal, the DGFT may recover the fine as a civil debt owed to him if it is not paid in full.[26] The sums thus collected by the DGFT are paid into the Consolidated Fund.[27] In other words, they are added to the government's coffers: they are not hypothecated for the OFT.

Fines can be extracted from parent companies of the company that actually committed the infringement: this is because the parent will be part of the same "undertaking". The Guideline indicates that the DGFT will also draw on the European Court's case law concerning liability of successor companies and vendors of infringing businesses.[28]

Intentional or negligent infringements

The Act provides that the DGFT may only require the payment of a penalty if he is satisfied that the infringement has been committed intentionally or negligently.[29] These concepts are expanded on in the Guideline as follows.[30]

Either criterion will be met by action by persons who are authorised to act on behalf of the undertaking even if such action was not known to senior management. Past "form" under the RTPA may be taken as an indicator of intention or negligence. The novelty of the régime set up by the Act will not be an excuse.

Where an agreement has as its object the restriction of competition or has been performed in the knowledge that the result will be, or is reasonably likely to be, a restriction of competition, that will be treated as intentional infringement, whether or not the undertaking concerned knew of the prohibitions. Concealment of the agreement will be taken as a strong indication of intentional infringement.

Negligence will be established when an undertaking knew or ought to have known that its conduct would infringe the prohibition, or when its conduct is inadvertent.

---

24 S 36(6)(b). That period has not yet been set: see Chap 7 below. The period under Art 230 (old Art 173) of the EC Treaty is two months.
25 Guideline on Enforcement (OFT 407), para 4.41.
26 S 37.
27 S 36(9).
28 Guideline on Enforcement (OFT 407), para 4.44.
29 S 36(3).
30 Guideline on Enforcement (OFT 407), paras 4.3-4.11.

Provisional immunity from fines for small agreements and conduct of minor significance

The Act provides for two categories of limited and provisional immunity from fines. The categories are labelled "small agreements" and "conduct of minor significance" and confer immunity from fines in respect of the Chapter I prohibition and the Chapter II prohibition respectively.[31] The details of each category will be spelled out in rules.[32]

Both are likely to be principally determined by turnover. The relevant provisions state that the criteria to be taken into account in the rules may in particular include the combined turnover of the parties to an agreement or the person whose conduct is in question and the share of the market affected by the agreement or conduct.[33] No drafts are available at the time of writing, but it is expected that the criterion used will be one of turnover rather than market share.[34]

The category of small agreements qualifying for immunity excludes price-fixing agreements.[35] "Price fixing agreement" is defined in section 39(9) in terms which exclude agreements as to prices for goods or services supplied to one of the parties but which arguably still leave room for concern about the situation where the terms of an agreement have a significant determinative effect on the prices set by one of the parties, without being what most people would understand to be an illegal price-fixing agreement. Section 39(9) defines a price fixing agreement as:

> "... an agreement which has as its object or effect, or one of its objects or effect, restricting the freedom of a party to the agreement to determine the price to be charged (otherwise than between that party and another party to the agreement) for the product, service or other matter to which the agreement relates."

The EC has long had a Notice setting out the criteria that determine whether an agreement is of minor importance for the application of Article 81 (old Article 85).[36] However, there is no equivalent in relation to Article 82 (old Article 86), although the requirement of effect on inter-state trade and competition will have acted as something of a

---

31 See s 39 (small agreements) and s 40 (conduct of minor importance).
32 That is, by statutory instrument made under the "negative resolution" procedure: see the definition of "prescribed" in s 61(1) and the procedural requirements in s 71.
33 S 39(2) (agreements) and s 40(2) (conduct) respectively.
34 See Guideline on Enforcement (OFT 407), para 4.14 and see Chap 4, Section 4 above.
35 S 39(1)(b).
36 The latest version is at OJ 1997 C372/13.

filter. The proposed immunity for conduct of minor importance would therefore appear to be an innovation on the part of the British legislator.

By an oddly phrased exception, the DGFT's power to impose fines is also removed if he is satisfied that the undertaking concerned acted upon the reasonable (but presumably mistaken) assumption that it was covered by one of the categories of immunity.[37]

However, the DGFT may also withdraw the immunity if, after investigating a particular agreement or conduct, he concludes that it is likely to infringe the relevant prohibition. He must then inform those affected by the withdrawal of immunity of his decision. Withdrawal is prospective only, with effect from a date specified in the notice which the DGFT gives to the parties. He must set the effective date of withdrawal so as to give them sufficient time to secure that that there will be no further infringement of the prohibition.[38]

The DGFT may not require a fine to be paid, despite a finding that the Chapter I prohibition has been infringed, if the agreement in question has been notified to the EC Commission for an exemption under Article 81(3) (old Article 85(3)).[39] It is not sufficient if the agreement has been notified only for negative clearance, for that does not preclude the application of national competition law. This immunity only applies for infringements of the Chapter I prohibition committed **after** notification to the Commission[40] **and** for so long as the Commission does not withdraw provisional immunity for fines for breach of Article 81 (old Article 85) under Article 15(6) of Regulation 17.[41] The Director may continue to investigate the agreement notwithstanding the notification.[42]

Provisional immunity for notified agreements

As in the EC system, notification of an agreement to the DGFT confers provisional immunity from fines. That immunity, and the DGFT's power to withdraw it in certain circumstances, is considered in Chapter 5 above.

---

37 See s 36(4) and (5).
38 See generally s 39(4)-(8) (small agreements) and s 40(4)-(8) (conduct of minor importance).
39 S 41(1).
40 S 41(2).
41 S 41(3). This is apparently the meaning of withdrawing the benefit of "provisional immunity from penalties" referred to in that provision. S 41(5) specifies that the phrase in inverted commas may be given a prescribed meaning in a statutory instrument.
42 S 41(4).

Appeals

Some of the measures which the DGFT is empowered to take by the provisions discussed above in this chapter are subject to appeal to the Competition Commission. Appeals are discussed in Chapter 7 below. In short, decisions finding infringements and imposing penalties are subject to appeal; decisions ordering investigations are not expressly made the subject of rights of appeal. Whether that separation can be rigidly enforced may be put to the test: the European Court accepted the admissibility of the challenges of Hoescht and Orkem to decisions ordering investigations at their premises[43] and this issue may give rise to argument under section 60.

---

43 See Case 46/87 *Hoescht* v *Commission* [1989] ECR 2859 and Case 374/87 *Orkem* v *Commission* [1989] ECR 3283.

Chapter 7

Appeals and the Competition Commission

7.1 Introduction

Increased powers for the competition authorities have to be balanced by increased opportunities for independent scrutiny of the results by a judicial tribunal such scrutiny should be both as to the substantive outcome of a proceeding and also to ensure that the parties' procedural rights were respected in the course of that proceeding. A review mechanism of this kind is of especial importance when the competition authority has been given extremely wide coercive and penalising powers. The coming into force of the Human Rights Act 1998[1] would have ensured that result even if it had not been intended under the Competition Act.

Decisions of the Director General of Fair Trading (DGFT) under the Restrictive Trade Practices Act (RTPA) are currently reviewable in the Restrictive Practices Court, whose functions will be curtailed and run off when the Chapter I prohibition enters fully into force. Regulatory action under the Fair Trading Act or Competition Act 1980, whether taken by the DGFT or the Monopolies and Mergers Commission (MMC)[2], cannot be directly appealed. Only the judicial review mechanism is available for such action. The courts have shown themselves extremely unwilling to differ from the MMC's conclusions.[3]

In a system in which full-scale reviews of administrative action by the DGFT are seen as a necessary concomitant of his enhanced authority, it would have been unreasonable to require the ordinary courts of general jurisdiction to hear the appeals. Appeals in competition law often concern rather arcane arguments and necessitate a thorough consideration of economic issues. A considerable volume of appeals is to be expected, especially in the early years of operation of the Act. The number and

---

1 Current intentions are that this should be on 2 October 2000.
2 This chapter will use that term to avoid confusion between the Competition Commission properly so called, *i.e.* as envisaged under the Act, and the rebranded MMC (see fn 9, below).
3 See *e.g. R v Monopolies and Mergers Commission ex parte Argyll* [1986] 2 All ER 257; *R v Monopolies and Mergers Commission ex parte Service Corporation International* (Buxton J, unreported); and similarly in respect of the Secretary of State's decision after an MMC enquiry, *R v Secretary of State for Trade and Industry ex parte Anderson Strathclyde* [1983] 2 All ER 233.

weight of competition appeals before the European Court of Justice (ECJ) was one of the major pressures leading to the creation of the Court of First Instance (CFI), initially as a specialist antitrust tribunal.[4]

The solution chosen by the Act is to set up a specialised body, the Competition Commission Appeal Tribunals, which will form one wing or "side" of a new institution called the Competition Commission. (The other side, known as the "reporting" side, is made up of functions formerly fulfilled by the MMC, as described below.) It will be possible to appeal from the rulings of an Appeal Tribunal to the Court of Appeal in England and Wales, or the Court of Session in Scotland and the Court of Appeal in Northern Ireland. Further appeal will lie to the House of Lords.

However, as is the case with the Restrictive Practices Court, the specialised court will only hear appeals against administrative decisions of the DGFT, leaving private actions for breach of the prohibitions to be heard by the ordinary courts.[5] It can be said that, if the ordinary courts are not best equipped for dealing with competition appeals, they are likewise handicapped in dealing with private actions raising competition law issues. However, it is in fact a rare private action that raises purely competition issues, without also giving rise to the need to determine wider legal issues such as breach of contract, illegality, causation, measure of damages and so on. Furthermore, there will usually be a need for findings of fact, possibly involving witness evidence, to a degree which is not usual in competition appeals. Nevertheless, it will be important to ensure that developments in the interpretation of the Act by the Appeal Tribunals and by the High Court go hand in hand. Responsibility for achieving consistency will fall to the Court of Appeal and ultimately to the House of Lords.

The system is not "watertight" in another respect, potentially of some significance. Since the types of decision which may be the subject of an appeal to the Appeal Tribunals are individually listed, there may well be other matters which parties will wish to have scrutinised by the courts but which will be considered by the Tribunals to lie outside their jurisdiction. Indications in Parliament were that ministers expected such matters to be the subject of judicial review applications. It remains to be seen how often this will happen or whether traditional judicial review can provide effective remedies which are consistent either with section 60 or with the Human Rights Act.

---

4 The expansion of the CFI's jurisdiction so that it, too, is now a court of general jurisdiction has led to its own problems of delay, an issue which lies outside the scope of this book.
5 See Chap 2, p 16 above.

This chapter first describes the bodies concerned. Then it describes what decisions of the DGFT may be appealed against and by whom. Lastly, it considers how such appeals may be handled by the Appeal Tribunals. Unfortunately, at that point, a measure of uncertainty and speculation is unavoidable. The Act provides only a framework which is to be completed by rules to be made in consultation with the President of the Appeals Tribunals. Not even drafts of the rules were available at the time of writing. It is, however, a reasonable guess that the procedure of the EC Court of First Instance will be a principal influence on the procedure of the Appeal Tribunals.[6]

7.2 **The Competition Commission**

The new body is set up under section 45 of the Act. It is there given its name[7] and will have the functions conferred upon it by the Act.[8] Those functions include the surviving functions of the Monopolies and Mergers Commission (MMC). The Secretary of State is given the necessary powers to effect the transition from MMC to Competition Commission and make any necessary statutory amendments. He did so with effect from 1 April 1999.[9] In practice, all the existing members and staff of the MMC were absorbed wholesale into the Competition Commission and will carry on as its "reporting side", dealing with matters such as merger references and utility licence reviews.[10] References to the MMC in existing statutes are to be taken as references to the Competition Commission.[11]

There are detailed provisions as to the composition and working methods of the Competition Commission as a whole.[12] Many of those provisions relate to the reporting side of the Commission and are not concerned with appeals under the Act. We concentrate on the aspects relevant to appeals.

---

6 The first President of the Appeals Tribunals is to be Christopher Bellamy QC, the British judge at the Court of First Instance at the time of his appointment.

7 S 45(1). Because the legislator has chosen to call the institution a "Commission", it will generally be necessary to give its full name, something of a mouthful, so as to avoid confusion with the European Commission.

8 S 45(2).

9 See s 45(3), (5) and (6). The dissolution of the MMC and the transfer to the Competition Commission was effected by means of two commencement orders (SI 1999 Nos 505 and 506). Some functions currently conducted by the MMC will be abolished by virtue of the repeal by the Act of existing statutes, namely parts of the Fair Trading Act 1973 and the Competition Act 1980.

10 See generally Part V of Sched 7.

11 S 45(4).

12 In Sched 7 to the Act.

There are four categories of member of the Commission, appointed to form panels relating to:

(1) appeals under the Act;

(2) the Commission's "general functions" (*i.e.* the main work of the reporting side);

(3) newspaper mergers; and

(4) functions relating to the water, electricity and telecommunications industries.

However, an individual may be appointed to perform any or all of those functions, so that a single member may sit on appeals, general and/or specialist panels if his terms of appointment so provide.[13]

The Chairman of the Commission as a whole must be taken from the reporting side.[14] The Chairman of the MMC[15] will serve as chairman of the Competition Commission.[16]

The Secretary of State must also appoint (having first consulted the Lord Chancellor or the Lord Advocate) one of the appeal panel members to be President of the Competition Commission Appeal Tribunals (to give the job title in full). The President must have held a legal qualification for at least ten years and appear to the Secretary of State to have "appropriate experience and knowledge of competition law and practice".[17] No member of the Commission may be appointed for more than five years, although members can be re-appointed.[18] It would be possible for the Secretary of State to appoint a President for a shorter period than five years, but not for longer.

The Commission appoints its own staff, save for its secretary who is appointed by the Secretary of State after consultations with both the Chairman and the President.[19] It is governed by the Council, a management board consisting of the Chairman, President, other members of the Commission appointed to the Council by the Secretary of State, and the Secretary of the Commission. The Chairman will have the casting vote.[20]

---

13 See generally para 2 of Sched 7.
14 *Ibid*, para 3(1).
15 Currently Dr Derek Morris, a distinguished economist,
16 Sched 7, para 31.
17 See generally para 4 of Sched 7. Judge Bellamy handsomely satisfies those criteria.
18 *Ibid*, para 6.
19 *Ibid*, para 9. Again, the serving secretary of the MMC automatically becomes secretary of the Commission: para 35.
20 *Ibid*, para 5.

Since an individual may be both an appeal panel member and a reporting panel member, it would technically be possible in the future for the Chairman of the Commission and the President of the Appeal Tribunals to be one and the same person, if he holds the relevant qualifications.

Appeals of the sort with which this chapter is concerned are to be handled as follows.[21]

When the Commission receives an appeal, the President must set up an appeal tribunal to deal with that appeal. An appeal tribunal will consist of three members, drawn from the appeal panel. The chairman of the tribunal will either be the President or one of the legally qualified "panel chairmen" appointed as such by the Secretary of State. The minimum qualification for panel chairmen is seven years standing as a lawyer and, again, "appropriate experience and knowledge of competition law and practice". No qualifications are specified for other appeal panel members, although the President is required to organise such training for them as he considers appropriate.

Before considering the procedure that the Appeal Tribunals may follow, it is convenient to describe what appeals may be brought before them.

7.3 Appeals

Who may appeal?

The Act provides for two categories of appeals:

- by the persons whose agreement (under Chapter I) or conduct (under Chapter II) has been the subject of a decision by the DGFT (which we call "addressees"); and
- by third parties.

Against what?

Addressees

Addressees may appeal against a decision:[22]

(a) determining whether there has been an infringement of the Chapter I prohibition;

---

21 *Ibid*, Part III (paras 23-27).
22 The lettering is taken from s 46(3) where the list of appealable decisions is set out.

(b) determining whether there has been an infringement of the Chapter II prohibition;

(c) whether to grant an individual exemption;

(d) whether to impose conditions or obligations on an individual exemption (an appeal may also be brought in respect of the duration of any such exemption);

(e) whether to extend an individual exemption;

(f) cancelling an exemption;

(g) imposing a penalty (an appeal may also be brought as to the amount of any such penalty).

Addressees may also appeal against directions given in decisions recording infringements of the Chapter I or Chapter II prohibitions or in interim measures decisions.[23]

The Secretary of State may add to the categories of "decisions" which may be appealed against. Given that there are obvious omissions from the list in (a) to (g) above, in particular in relation to procedural matters during the course of an investigation and conditions attaching to parallel or block exemptions, new categories of appealable decision may be necessary sooner than expected.

Third parties

There is no general right for interested third parties to appeal directly against such decisions. The Act provides a less direct route for them. They may apply to the DGFT asking him to withdraw or vary any decision of the types specified above (except (g), a decision as to fines). It seems to be implicit in the enumeration of the matters against which third parties may appeal that there is no possibility of third party appeal in respect of the DGFT's directions relating to infringements.

Against that, however, the Secretary of State is given power to specify other types of "decision" in respect of which third parties may seek revocation or variation.[24]

The Act specifies that third party requests for variation or revocation must be made in writing, specifying the reasons why the decision should be varied or withdrawn.

The procedure to be followed for such applications is set out in Rule 28 of the DGFT's Procedural Rules.[25] The application must be made

---

23 Under ss 32, 33 and 35 respectively. See generally Chap 6 above.
24 S 47(1).
25 (OFT 411).

within a month of the publication of the relevant decision and must state the applicant's reasons for believing that he has a sufficient interest. If the DGFT proposes to accede to the request, he must consult the addressee of the decision. If he grants the application, he must communicate his decision and the reasons for it to the applicant and the addressee, and the decision must be published. The original "addressee" may appeal against that new decision to withdraw or vary the original decision.[26]

If the DGFT rejects the request, he must notify the applicant of his *decision*. That rejection decision is itself an appealable act, which is addressed to the third party applicant[27] (rather than to the addressee of the original decision). There are two grounds on which the DGFT may reject a request to withdraw or vary a decision.

The first is a threshold as to standing, namely that the application fails to establish sufficient interest in the decision complained of. That may be because the applicant does not have "sufficient interest", or does not represent persons having such interest or the persons the applicant represents do not have a sufficient interest.[28] The notion of sufficient interest is not defined: the most obvious parallel is the test of "direct and individual concern" in Article 230 of the EC Treaty (old Article 173), by which the European Court determines the standing of persons wishing to challenge decisions which are not addressed to them. The test is essentially one of the impact of the decision on their legal interests.[29] Whatever test is chosen, it is clearly going to be a legal test rather than a pure matter of administrative discretion in the hands of the DGFT.

The second ground for rejection is substantive, namely that the applicant does not make out a good case ("does not show sufficient reason") why the decision should be varied or revoked.[30]

No suspensive effect

Neither the bringing of an appeal by an addressee, nor the making of an application for revocation or variation by a third party suspends the legal effect of the decision in question.[31]

The exception to that rule is that decisions relating to fines are suspended by the bringing of an appeal.[32] It is not specified whether, as

---

26 S 46(3)(h).
27 S 47(6).
28 S 47(3).
29 See Brealey & Hoskins, *Remedies in EC Law* (Sweet & Maxwell, 2nd ed 1998) pp 280-303.
30 S 47(4).
31 S 46(4) as regards appeals by addressees, s 47(7) as regards third party applications.
32 S 46(4).

under the EC system, an addressee would be required to lodge some form of security in relation to the suspended fine. It is to be hoped either that no such security will be required or that, if it is, the addressee will be indemnified for the cost of the security if it succeeds on appeal in having the decision overturned. It has long been an injustice in the EC system that the Commission refuses to repay the cost of bank guarantees and the like to parties who successfully apply to the ECJ or CFI to have the decision overturned (and the expense of putting up a guarantee or bond cannot be claimed as a recoverable cost in the European Court litigation).

7.4   Procedure

Bringing an appeal

An appeal is launched by the sending of a notice of appeal to the Competition Commission.[33] The notice must set out the grounds of appeal, including the following matters:

- reference to the provision of the Act under which the appeal is brought;
- the errors of fact or law alleged; and
- the extent to which the appellant is challenging an exercise of discretion by the DGFT.[34]

The period within which appeals are to be brought has not yet been fixed.[35] The equivalent under the EC Treaty is the two months period under Article 230 (old Article 173). Experience shows that that is a very tight timetable given that under the EC rules it is necessary to file a fully argued application within that period. Since the Act authorises the tribunal to give permission for the grounds in the notice of appeal to be amended[36] (which could include supplementing them), it may be that a shorter period than two months could be laid down.

Powers of appeal tribunal

Appeals must be determined by an appeal tribunal.[37] As explained above, each tribunal is set up ad hoc and will consist of three members, with a legally qualified chairman.

---

33 Sched 8, para 2(1).
34 Sched 8, para 2(2).
35 See Sched 8, para 6(a).
36 Sched 8, para 2(3).
37 S 48(1).

The tribunal's task is to determine the appeal on the merits by reference to the grounds of appeal set out in the notice of appeal.[38] In principle, therefore, the appellant determines the scope of the appeal and the tribunal will not be required to consider of its own motion whether there are additional grounds on which the decision might be challenged.

EC law suggests that, although in general, it is acceptable for national courts to take a passive role and confine themselves to determining the issues raised by the parties, there are circumstances in which they are required to take a point under the EC competition rules of their own motion, especially where national procedural rules bar the parties from raising the point.[39] It is possible that a similar principle could be brought into the Act through section 60. However, the circumstances in which this might happen in an appeal against an administrative decision rather than in civil proceedings are likely to be unusual.

The powers of the Appeal Tribunal are extremely wide, and go beyond those which the EC Treaty confers upon the European Court. The tribunal may confirm the decision appealed against (that is, it may dismiss the appeal).[40] In doing so, it may nevertheless set aside any finding of fact by the DGFT.[41]

Or it may set the decision aside in whole or part.[42] It then has the power essentially either to send the matter back to the DGFT for reconsideration or to remake the decision itself. It is that latter power which is wider than those entrusted to the EC courts: the CFI and ECJ cannot substitute their own decision for that of the Commission. It is to be expected that the Appeal Tribunals will use this power sparingly, and will use it for adjusting decisions of the DGFT rather than for making wholly different decisions. By definition, wholly different decisions may require a fresh investigation. In that case, it would be more appropriate to remit the matter to the DGFT for him to reconsider.

In detail the Tribunals may:[43]

(a) remit the matter to the DGFT;

(b) impose, cancel or vary the amount of a fine (that power must include the power to increase a fine as well as to reduce it; the European Courts have the same power in the exercise of the

---

38 Sched 8, para 3(1).
39 See Joined Cases C-430 and 431/93 *Van Schijndel* v *SPF* [1995] ECR I-4705 and Case C-312/93 *Peterbroeck* v *Belgium* [1995] ECR I-4599.
40 Sched 8, para 3(2).
41 Sched 8, para 3(4).
42 Sched 8, para 3(2).
43 *Ibid*, adopting the lettering given in the Act.

"unlimited jurisdiction" conferred by Article 229 EC (old Article 172) but have not so far taken the step of increasing a fine);

(c) grant or cancel an individual exemption or attach or vary conditions to which such an exemption may be subject;

(d) give directions or take any other step which the DGFT could have taken;

(e) make any other decision which the DGFT could himself have made.

Accordingly, a decision by the tribunal on appeal is given the same status as a decision by the DGFT, and can be enforced in the same way.[44]

The Act provides for the possibility of majority decisions by the tribunal.[45] In other words, two of the three members must agree (and the legally qualified President or chairman may be outvoted). The tribunal's decision must state whether it is unanimous or is a majority decision.[46] The decision must be recorded in a document giving the tribunal's reasons. The document must be signed and dated by the chairman of the tribunal. The tribunal is bound by the same requirements as the Secretary of State and the DGFT as to public disclosure of information that may be against the public interest, or may harm the interests of an undertaking or a private individual.[47]

One of the President's responsibilities will be to determine how decisions of the tribunals should be published.[48] No doubt they will be available at an Internet site as well as in print. Commercial publishers are known to be gearing up to produce series of reports of the tribunals' decisions. Consideration should be given to publication of the dissenting view (as is standard practice in British courts and not infrequently done in MMC reports where one member of the panel strongly disagrees with the majority view).

Procedural rules

The Act does not contain a more detailed account of the procedure to be followed when a tribunal hears an appeal. It provides that the

---

44 Sched 8, para 3(3). For enforcement of decisions of the DGFT, see Chap 6, p 141 above.
45 Sched 8, para 4(1).
46 Sched 8, para 4(2)(a).
47 Sched 8, para 4(3) requires the tribunal to have regard to s 56 (see Chap 5 above).
48 Sched 8, para 4(4).

Secretary of State may make rules relating to appeals and appeal tribunals.[49] Before doing so, he must consult the President, as well as such other persons he considers appropriate.[50] Since the President's appointment was not announced until some months after the Act was passed, and he did not take up his position immediately, the formal statutory consultation process was not complete at the time this book was written. The President is clearly intended to play a key role in the drawing up of the rules. The Act also provides that the rules adopted may confer functions upon the President.[51]

Nevertheless, the Act contains indications of the type of procedure which may be expected at least to be put out to consultation. Part II of Schedule 8 contains a number of provisions beginning "Rules may provide ...". The Act makes clear, however, that the indications in that part of Schedule 8 are not to restrict the Secretary of State's freedom of manoeuvre.[52]

What follows is therefore the Act's preliminary indication of matters which the rules may well provide for. The Act is careful not to be prescriptive of the solutions which may actually be adopted to deal with the issues raised in the list. The reference to paragraph numbers is to the paragraphs of Schedule 8.

Registrar of Appeal Tribunals (paragraph 5)

The Competition Commission may be authorised to appoint a registrar. The qualifications for such a position may be specified in the rules, as may the functions which a registrar might exercise.

In the European Court system, where the principle of judge-managed litigation is well established, the role of registrar is an important one. The registrars of each of the Court of Justice and the Court of First Instance are in charge of "judicial administration" at those courts. The registrars are given responsibility for ensuring that written pleadings are in proper form and for deciding such matters as extensions of time limits for lodging documents. The registry is the point of contact between the parties and the court.[53]

---

49 S 48(2).
50 *Ibid.*
51 S 48(3).
52 S 48(4).
53 See generally, *e.g.* Plender (ed) *European Courts Practice and Precedents* (Sweet & Maxwell, 1997), Chap 6.

Notice of appeal (paragraph 6)

The period within which appeals must be brought is not specified in the Act, but is left to the rules to determine. As already noted, the equivalent period under Article 230 EC (old Article 173) is two months for the lodging of a fully pleaded application for annulment of a Commission decision.

Likewise, rules are needed to specify the form and contents of a notice of appeal. The Act also refers to rules about the amendment of notices of appeal. The rules of the European Courts do not permit amendment in the form of adding grounds of appeal which were available at the time the appeal was launched. It remains to be seen whether the rules under the Act will allow a bare notice of appeal to be supplemented by more detailed argument or further pleas at a later stage.[53a]

Response to the appeal (paragraph 7)

It is envisaged that the tribunal may reject an appeal in two situations.

(1) The notice "reveals no valid ground of appeal". The grounds on which an appeal may be based are those set out in paragraph 2(2) of Schedule 8 (see "Bringing an appeal" above).

(2) Where the appellant is "vexatious", using similar wording as that found in section 42 of the Supreme Court Act 1981 concerning the restriction of vexatious legal proceedings.[54] This problem may be expected to be comparatively rare in competition litigation.

Pre-hearing reviews and preliminary matters (paragraph 8)

It is envisaged that the tribunal may carry out a "preliminary consideration of proceedings" and exercise various (unspecified) powers at that stage.

The Court of First Instance has the possibility of ordering so-called measures of organisation of procedure.[55] That inelegant phrase is intended to demonstrate the lack of restriction on the measures which may be ordered: production of further documents, offering of witnesses or representatives of the parties or from other organisations, an inspection of a factory or the answering in writing of specific questions

---

53a This is routine practice for example in the European Court of Human Rights.
54 Para 6 describes a situation where the appellant has "habitually and persistently and without any reasonable ground instituted vexatious proceedings" or made vexatious applications.
55 See Art 64 of the CFI's Rules of Procedure.

put by the Court are merely examples of the sort of measure which may be ordered.

That Court has also instituted a practice of holding "informal meetings" attended by the judge-rapporteur,[55a] the Registrar and the parties and their advisers. They are used to discuss the conduct of the hearing, particularly in cartel cases where it may be possible for there to be some common presentation by the applicants of parts of the case or a division of responsibilities for different grounds of the application as between the advocates appearing. The Court may use the opportunity to explain the issues on which it would like to hear argument and those on which it considers itself sufficiently informed from the written pleadings and the documents it has available to it.

The Act does not go into detail about the sort of power which tribunals may exercise in such preliminary reviews, except that it suggests that they could make continuation of the proceedings subject to the lodging of security in the form of a monetary deposit by any party. It should also provide for the consequences of failure to lodge a deposit, and the circumstances in which the deposit would be repaid or paid to another party in the proceedings and so on.

Conduct of the hearing (paragraph 9)

The Act suggests that rules may cover the manner in which appeals are to be conducted and does not make oral hearings a compulsory feature of that process. However, it is clearly to be expected that oral hearings will be provided for as a possibility even if they are not resorted to in every appeal. In fact, it is likely that, except in the rare case that can be regarded as straightforward, there will be a hearing, but that, as with the procedure under the EC Treaty, the written record will be of greater importance.

Likewise, there will be the possibility of examining witnesses, but this can be expected to be rare.

The following matters are listed in paragraph 9(1) of Schedule 8 for consideration in rules as to the conduct of the hearing:

(a) hearings to be in private if necessary, having regard to section 56[55b];

(b) representation of the parties;

(c) requiring persons to attend to give evidence or produce documents and the administration of oaths to such persons;

55a *i.e.* the judge who has been assigned the lead role in a particular case.
55b Concerning disclosure of information see generally Chap 5 above.

(d) the nature of evidence which may be required or admitted before the tribunal and the extent to which it may be oral or written;

(e) the fixing and extension of time limits;

(f) referring matters back to the DGFT if the tribunal considers that they have not been adequately investigated;

(g) ordering the disclosure or production of documents as between the parties;

(h) appointment of experts;

(i) the award of costs or expenses, including the expense of attendance before the tribunal;

(j) the taxing or settlement of costs which the tribunal directs to be paid, and the enforcement of such awards.

To the extent that the rules enable the tribunal to require the attendance of persons upon it, or the production or disclosure of documents, it will be a criminal offence to fail to comply with such an order without a reasonable excuse.[56]

Interest (paragraph 10)

The Act envisages a power in the tribunal to order interest to be paid on fines, and in particular, compound interest if the fine is not reduced, or reduced by less than a specified percentage.

Fees (paragraph 11)

The Act contemplates with equanimity the introduction of a rule charging fees for specified costs of proceedings before the tribunal.

In the EC system, the courts are free, although there is power (not exercised to date) to order parties to repay avoidable costs which they have caused the court to incur, and excessive translation costs.[57]

Withdrawing an appeal (paragraph 12)

It is envisaged that appeals may not be withdrawn without the leave of the tribunal or, in circumstances to be specified, the President or the

---

56 Sched 8, para 9(2).
57 See Art 72 of the ECJ's Rules of Procedure (the corresponding article in the CFI's Rules is 90).

Registrar. The principal reason for such a requirement is to protect the respondent's position as to costs run up in defending an appeal which is then withdrawn before final ruling. The rules may provide for the tribunal to impose conditions on leave to withdraw, for it to publish any decision which it could have made if the proceedings had not been withdrawn, and, interestingly, as to the procedure to be followed if the parties to appeal proceedings agree to settle.

Interim orders (paragraph 13)

There will obviously be a place for interim relief, just as there is pursuant to Articles 242 and 243 (old Articles 185 and 186) in the EC system. This is particularly so for the reason that, as mentioned above, it is specifically provided that the bringing of an appeal will not have the effect of suspending the contested decision. Thus paragraph 13 suggests that rules may provide for the tribunal to make any order on an interim basis that it could grant in its final decision. In particular, such orders may suspend the effect of a decision of the DGFT or vary the conditions or obligations attached to an exemption. More generally, it is suggested that the rules of the tribunal might reflect the powers given to the DGFT to take interim measures under section 35.[58]

Joinder and consolidation (paragraph 14)

Lastly, there is mention of the possibility of joining a person who is not a party to the appeal proceedings and for appeals to be consolidated as the tribunal may think appropriate. These two short suggestions appear to cover the possibility of intervention by interested parties (most obviously, the addressee in the case of third party appeals and vice versa) and for cases to be joined for the purposes of hearing and/or judgment, both well known facets of litigation before the Court of First Instance. In the EC system, an intervener has to demonstrate an interest in the outcome of the particular case and has to support the form of order sought by one of the parties. As to "joinder" of cases, this is frequent in the CFI when a number of applications are received in connection with the same decision of the Commission, most obviously in the case of a decision concerning a multi-party cartel.

---

58 See Chap 6 Investigation and Enforcement, p 138 above.

Substantive review

The Act does not specify in terms the tests which the Appeal Tribunals should apply in reviewing "the merits" of decisions of the DGFT. Once again, it is section 60 which provides the answer, or much of it. The legality of decisions will have to be judged against the standards laid down in the case law of the ECJ and CFI in interpreting and applying Articles 81 and 82 (old Articles 85 and 86).

That will go to the substantive interpretation of those provisions so that, for example, it should not be possible for the DGFT to characterise as a breach of the Chapter II prohibition conduct which would not amount to an abuse of dominant position under Article 82 (old Article 86). Likewise, account will have to be taken of the European Courts' rulings as to matters such as the relevance of valid justifications for parallel conduct that might otherwise appear to support an inference of collusion or the requirements of due process, such as the obligation on the competition authorities to give the parties being investigated a chance to comment on all material intended to be used against them in the final decision and to produce all exculpatory material.

Where the jurisprudence of the European Courts and the Appeals Tribunals may diverge is on pure procedural issues. The distinction between "high-level" principles of EC law and the procedural rules of Regulation 17 and the like should be borne in mind here. It will not be enough for applicants to criticise the DGFT for not following the same procedure as DG IV. They will have to demonstrate an incorrect substantive outcome or a breach of the rights of the defence if the decision is to be overturned by the Appeal Tribunals.

7.5   Further appeals

Decisions of the Competition Commission Appeal Tribunals may themselves be appealed against. Such further appeals will go to the Court of Appeal in England and Wales, and their Scottish and Northern Irish equivalents, the Court of Session and Court of Appeal in Northern Ireland respectively.[59]

Appeals will only lie on points of law[60], as in the EC system under Article 225 (old Article 168A). The exception is that an appeal under

---

59 S 49(4).
60 S 49(1)(a).

the Act can be brought against any decision of an Appeal Tribunal concerning the amount of a penalty.[61]

Unlike the EC system, appeal is not a right: an appeal requires leave, either from the tribunal itself or from the applicable appeal court.[62]

Appeals may be brought either by the parties to the proceedings before the tribunal (which expression presumably includes the interveners) or "at the instance of a person showing a sufficient interest in the matter". There is no definition of "sufficient interest". That is the term used in Article 37 of the EC Statute of the Court of Justice for the standing to intervene in proceedings. It may be suggested that sufficient interest should be interpreted to mean a level of interest which would have allowed the person concerned either to bring an appeal against the DGFT's decision or to intervene in proceedings before the tribunal concerning that decision.

The Act provides that the rules to be made by the Secretary of State concerning appeal proceedings may also concern matters "incidental to or consequent upon" the making of further appeals.[63]

The normal rules will apply as regards further appeal to the House of Lords, that is, leave will have to be obtained from the Court of Appeal or, if refused, sought by way of petition to the House of Lords.

---

61 S 49(1)(b).
62 S 49(2)(b), s 49(4).
63 S 49(3).

Chapter 8

· Transitional Provisions ·

8.1 **Introduction**

The new regime does not come into force overnight. Business is being given a relatively generous period in which to adjust. Schedule 13 of the Act contains detailed arrangements for the transition from the present competition law regime in the United Kingdom to the full entry into force of the system set up by the Act. They have been explained in detail in publications issued by the Office of Fair Trading (OFT)[1] and the Department of Trade and Industry (DTI).[2]

These arrangements are rather complicated at first sight, but become more comprehensible if some key elements are kept in mind.

First, the Schedule lays down two kinds of transitional arrangement. One kind is **permanent** and of continuing effect; the other applies only for an **interim** period.

Secondly, that interim period is defined in the Schedule as the period lying between two critical dates. They are

- the **enactment date**: the day on which the Act received Royal Assent – 9 November 1998; and
- the **starting date**: the day on which the Chapter I and Chapter II prohibitions come into force – 1 March 2000.[3]

Thirdly, for many agreements (in essence, those which are legal when entered into) there is a further period beginning on the starting date during which those agreements may be adjusted to bring them into line with the Chapter I prohibition. That period is, perhaps confusingly, known as the **transitional period**. As explained below, it will generally be one year (capable of extension – and shortening – by the Director

---

1 Competition Act 1998: Transitional Arrangements (OFT 406).
2 A Guide to the New Transitional Schedule in the Competition Bill, Department of Trade and Industry, June 1998.
3 S 76(3) of the Act provides for its provisions to come into effect on days specified by the Secretary of State in an order. 1 March 2000 is the date to which all concerned are committed; it is not set in the Act and could conceivably change. S 76(2) brings into force certain basic provisions (the commencement provision itself, the Secretary of State's powers to make orders in relation to the Act) and the transitional modifications to the RTPA discussed in this chapter.

General of Fair Trading (DGFT)) but will be five years for defined categories of agreement.

Fourthly and lastly, there is no transitional period for the Chapter II prohibition: that applies without modulation from the starting date.

8.2 Purpose of the transitional arrangements

The overriding objective in respect of agreements is that parties should not be simultaneously subject to the rather different and essentially incompatible regimes of the Restrictive Trade Practices Act (RTPA) and Resale Prices Act 1976 (RPA)[4], on the one hand, and the Chapter I prohibition on the other.

Some of the transitional arrangements are in various ways designed to provide a cut-off between the two regimes. For example, agreements which have been the subject of section 21(2) directions under the RTPA (the RTPA version of exemption) are not subject to the Chapter I prohibition at all.[5] This demonstrates that the RTPA will have a half-life well after the starting date and that some of the so-called transitional arrangements are in effect permanently in place. At the other end of the RTPA compliance spectrum, obligations imposed by order of the Restrictive Practices Court pursuant to section 2 or 35 of the RTPA, or undertakings given to that Court, will fall away on the starting date (although the fact that they were made or given may be taken into account in assessing whether any future infringement of the Chapter I prohibition is intentional or negligent[6]).

The "interim" transitional arrangements are designed to smooth the transition, essentially in two ways. The first is lightening of the regulatory burden in the interim period, both on parties to agreements and on the DGFT. Thus, as described below, many types of agreements, while remaining subject to the RTPA, have ceased to be notifiable under it, and the DGFT's obligation to bring proceedings in respect of registered agreements has been relaxed to a discretion. The second

---

4 For simplicity, we do not separately describe the transitional arrangements relating to agreements caught by the RPA; they are in all respects similar to those applying to agreements caught by the RTPA. It should also be pointed out that Sched 13 makes provision in respect of continuing proceedings under the Fair Trading Act 1973 and Competition Act 1980, not discussed in this book: see paras 40-44 of Sched 13 and Section 8 of the Transitional Arrangements Guideline (OFT 406).

5 See Chap 3 above on exclusions from the Chapter I prohibition.

6 See the OFT Guideline on Enforcement (OFT 407), para 4.4.

technique for easing the passage is the provision to parties of forms of guidance from the OFT during the interim and transitional periods.

8.3   Which regime applies?

For most undertakings and most agreements, it is the date on which the agreement is made that will determine which regime applies. For agreements made before the enactment date, it is the RTPA. For agreements made after the starting date, it is the Chapter I regime (as described in Chapter 3 above). For agreements made in between, it is the modified RTPA which will govern the legality of the agreement; during the interim period, the parties may obtain guidance from the OFT as to the agreement's compatibility with the Chapter I prohibition, and the agreement will also benefit from a transitional period after the starting date to enable any necessary adjustments to be made. As already noted, there is no transitional period in respect of conduct: the Chapter II prohibition will be fully in force from the starting date.

8.4   Pre-enactment agreements

Agreements made before the enactment date are subject to the law as it stood immediately before enactment.[7] This may seem an obvious statement, and one which flows from the non-retroactive effect of legislation, but it is important to appreciate the consequences. If such agreements were subject to registration under the RTPA, particulars had to be furnished, even if the date for lodging particulars fell in the interim period. Pre-enactment agreements do not benefit from the alleviated notification regime which applies to agreements made in the interim period. Nor can they be notified to the DGFT for "early guidance" (see below).

8.5   Agreements made in the interim period

The effect of paragraphs 5 and 6 of the Schedule (brought into force by section 76(2) of the Act on the enactment date) is that only price-fixing

---

7 We cannot give a full account of the RTPA and RPA in this book. For a full and up to date treatment, see Green and Robertson, *Commercial Agreements and Competition Law* (2nd ed, 1997).

agreements made in the interim period have to be notified under the RTPA. The DGFT has a discretion (exercised without reference to the Secretary of State[8]) whether or not to bring proceedings in respect of such agreements before the Restrictive Practices Court.[9]

It is a rare cartel which notifies its agreement to the competition authorities and so it might be expected that there will be very few notifications made under the RTPA during the interim period. However, the precise scope of the phrase "price-fixing agreement" (introduced into the RTPA[10] by the Deregulation and Contracting Out Act 1994) is untested and may apply to agreements which have the effect of setting prices in less obviously undesirable ways, for example in joint venture agreements.

The fact that the agreements made during the interim period are not required to be notified does not, of course, prevent the DGFT from investigating. His investigative powers under the RTPA are not curtailed during the interim period, nor is his power to refer matters to the Restrictive Practices Court. The OFT Guideline emphasises this point.[11] Nor are third parties prevented from bringing proceedings if they believe they can show that they have been affected by the implementation of an agreement which has not been notified to the DGFT (see section 35 of the RTPA).

Early guidance

Agreements made in the interim period (but not before) can be submitted to the DGFT for so-called "early guidance" as to whether they are likely to infringe the Chapter I prohibition when it comes into force.

Paragraph 7 of Schedule 13 allows the DGFT to make "directions" concerning the use of this facility. The DGFT's Early Guidance Directions and the form on which such guidance must be sought, Form EG, are set out in Appendix 2 to this book. In effect, the early guidance procedure is the same as the guidance procedure which will apply after

---

8 This is achieved by disapplying s 21(1) and (2) RTPA: see Sched 13, para 6(b).

9 Para 25 of the Schedule contains elaborate provisions in respect of notifiable price-fixing agreements where the deadline for notification would fall on or after the starting date. They should either be notified before the starting date, in which case they will obtain the benefit of a transitional period of one year, or the parties should hold off, in which case the RTPA is disapplied after the starting date despite the agreement's having been made while the RTPA was still in effect *unless* the parties have put the agreement into effect before the starting date.

10 S 27A.

11 Transitional Arrangements (OFT 406), para 2.5.

the starting date. Indeed, early guidance applications outstanding at the starting date will be treated as applications for "true" guidance. This means that the DGFT will be bound by the early guidance in the same way as "true" guidance and the parties will enjoy the same immunities from fines as applicants for true guidance.[12]

Agreements made before the starting date (whether pre-enactment or made in the interim period) cannot be notified for a decision until the starting date. While this is eminently logical, as the prohibition cannot be in force before the starting date, it is to be hoped that the OFT will have received sufficient advance notice through the early guidance procedure of the volume of agreements likely to be notified to it on the starting date.

There is no possibility of seeking early guidance in respect of the Chapter II prohibition.

8.6 **From the starting date**

From 1 March 2000 (a Wednesday), the Chapter I prohibition comes into force. Agreements made **on or after** that date are subject to the prohibition[13] and the procedural rules described elsewhere in this book.

The transitional arrangements for agreements made **before** that date are as follows. The "general rule"[14] is that such agreements have a transitional period of one year from the starting date during which the Chapter I prohibition will not apply to them. During that period, the parties can apply to the DGFT for guidance and/or notify the agreement if they choose. Thereafter (that is, from 1 March 2001) the prohibition will apply to them with full force.

The main determinant of whether an agreement benefits from a transitional period, and if so of what length, is its status under the RTPA as at the starting date.

Agreements which were not subject to the RTPA (including those which were rendered non-notifiable during the interim period) will have a one-year transitional period from the starting date.

Agreements which have been the subject of directions under section 21(2) of the RTPA (essentially, clearance following due notification)

---

12 See Chap 5, p 101, above.

13 With the limited exception of certain agreements made by utilities where the existing arrangements under the RTPA will be retained for a further five years from the starting date. Thus agreements in the electricity, gas and rail sectors which are currently exempt from the application of the RTPA, and similar agreements in the future, will benefit from transitional periods excluding them from the Chapter I prohibition during that period: see paras 27-35 of Sched 13.

14 Para 19 of Sched 13.

will benefit from an indefinite exclusion from the Chapter I prohibition[15], subject to a power for the DGFT to "claw back" individual "section 21(2) agreements".[16] The exclusion will also be lost automatically (and therefore in some cases inadvertently) if there is a "material variation" to the agreement after the starting date.[17]

Agreements which the Restrictive Practices Court has found not to operate against the public interest will benefit from a five-year transitional period (in effect allowing the DGFT to review the matter in the light of the circumstances prevailing at the end of the transitional period if the agreement is still in force then).

Agreements caught by the RTPA but in respect of which no particulars had been furnished or which have been put into effect before particulars were furnished are illegal agreements and enjoy no transitional period.[18]

Any proceedings brought by the DGFT before the Restrictive Practices Court for orders in respect of breaches of the RTPA which are current on the starting date will "fall away",[19] thus subjecting the relevant agreement to the full force of the Chapter I prohibition without any transitional period.

Not all proceedings before the RPC fall away on the starting date. In particular, proceedings to determine whether the restrictions in an agreement are contrary to the public interest may continue if not withdrawn by consent. The treatment of agreements which are the subject of "continuing proceedings"[20] under the RTPA will depend on the outcome of the proceedings.[21] The result is essentially intended to give the same transitional period *from the date the proceedings are concluded* as would have applied if the proceedings had been determined immediately before the starting date. Thus, if the agreement is found not to operate against the public interest, it will have the five-year transitional period;[22] if it is found to operate against the public interest, it will have no transitional period.[23]

---

15 Para 2(1) of Sched 3.
16 See para 2(3)-(9) of Sched 3 and Rule 22 of the DGFT's Procedural Rules.
17 Para 2(2) of Sched 3. Para 4.16 of Transitional Arrangements (OFT 406) considers the criteria to be applied in determining whether a variation is material: in essence the agreement as varied must fall within Chapter I.
18 Para 20 of Sched 13.
19 As will court orders imposed on parties not to breach the RTPA in the future, or undertakings to the like effect given to the Court.
20 As defined in para 15 of Sched 13.
21 Which will include any possible appeal.
22 Para 23(3) of Sched 13.
23 Para 20(4) of Sched 13.

Special provisions giving a transitional period of up to five years, in some case even for agreements made after the starting date, apply to certain agreements in the regulated "utility" sectors[24] and to agreements the subject of declarations or directions under the Financial Services Act 1986 or the Broadcasting Act 1990.[25]

8.7   Altering the transitional period

The DGFT is given power both to extend and to curtail the transitional period in respect of individual agreements (it would appear that he has no power to lengthen or shorten it generally).

Extending the transitional period

The DGFT may extend a transitional period either on his own initiative or on application by a party to the agreement.[26] He can extend a one-year transitional period by up to a further year, and any other period by up to six months;[27] a period can only be extended once.[28]

The Schedule provides that an application by a party for the period to be extended must be made not less than three months before the end of the period[29] (that is, by 30 November 1999 in most cases). It also requires the DGFT to give notice that the period has been extended.[30]

Rule 24 of the DGFT's Procedural Rules[31] lays down the procedure for applying for extension. An application must be in writing and must give reasons why an extension should be granted and what length of extension is being requested. The DGFT has two months in which to respond (thus giving a further month for the parties to apply for guidance or notify for a decision if they wish before the end of the transitional period). If he does not respond within that period, he is deemed to have granted the maximum extension or, if shorter, the extension actually applied for. The DGFT is required to publicise the fact that he has granted an extension.

---

24 See paras 27-35 of Sched 13 and fn 13 above.
25 See para 26 of Sched 13, not further discussed in this work.
26 Para 36(1) and (2) of Sched 13.
27 Para 36(2).
28 Para 36(5).
29 Para 36(1).
30 Para 36(4).
31 (OFT 411).

Extension are not automatic. The OFT Guideline on Transitional Arrangements sets out the DGFT's policy in considering extensions.[32] He is only likely to grant an extension if it seems that the agreement would infringe the Chapter I prohibition "but not seriously". Agreements involving a serious infringement will not be granted any extension. There must be good reasons for requiring an extension: the examples given in the Guideline are that the agreement is being re-negotiated or that it will expire shortly after the end of the original transitional period or (a more general catch-all) the parties have a "legitimate need" for more time to prepare a notification. It is conceivable that an unexpectedly high work load could lead the OFT to take a more generous approach to this power.

Curtailing the transitional period

The DGFT may bring a transitional period to an end for any agreement by giving a "direction". The principal justification for such a direction is that the DGFT considers that the agreement would infringe the Chapter I prohibition but for the transitional period and that he would be unlikely to grant it an unconditional individual exemption.[33] He may have heard of an objectionable agreement through the early guidance procedure, through complaints or from other sources. If he is considering whether to terminate a transitional period, he may seek information by writing to the parties.[34] If they do not provide it within a period (specified as ten days in the Procedural Rules[35]), he may terminate the transitional period for that reason alone.[36]

The DGFT must specify in any direction the date on which is to have effect; that date must be at least 28 days from the date of the direction.[37] The DGFT must send copies of the direction to the parties and to the Secretary of State. The direction will then come into effect on the specified date unless it has been revoked, either by the DGFT himself or by the Secretary of State.[38] This gives the parties the opportunity to make representations to the DGFT, and indeed to the Department of Trade and Industry. If a direction is revoked, the DGFT can only make

---

32 Para 5.2.3.
33 Para 38(3) of Sched 13.
34 Para 38(1) of Sched 13.
35 Rule 23(2).
36 See para 38(2) of Sched 13.
37 Para 39(1) of Sched 13.
38 Para 39(2) and (3) of Sched 13.

another one in respect of the same agreement if he is satisfied that there has been a material change of circumstances.[39]

The DGFT is also given power to terminate the transitional period applying to agreements which in principle are excluded from the Chapter I prohibition but over which the Act gives the DGFT "claw back" powers.[40] There are three such categories of agreement: merger agreements;[41] "section 21(2) agreements";[42] and some agricultural agreements.[43] It seems from this that the legislator considers that such agreements benefit from a transitional period despite being excluded from the Chapter I prohibition until such time as any direction is given. This might follow from a literal interpretation of the "general rule" in paragraph 19(1) of Schedule 13, but it would seem also that the period for such agreements may in practice be less than one year since it will expire one year after the starting date, irrespective of the date of the direction. Any unfairness in this result may be corrected by specifying a longer period before which the direction takes effect.

Continuing effect of the RTPA

Despite its repeal, the RTPA will have a half life. Some of its continuing effects have been described above. The Schedule continually uses the odd expression "even though section [number] of the RTPA is repealed …".

It is important to realise also that it will still be possible for third parties to bring damages actions in civil proceedings in respect of harm caused by registrable agreements which were not duly furnished to the DGFT, so long as the right to bring proceedings had accrued by the starting date.[44]

The register of agreements will also continue in existence. The DGFT's duty to file particulars is clearly reduced, essentially to what might be called unfinished business on the starting date and "continuing proceedings" in the Restrictive Practices Court. The public will have access to the Register, initially in the same way as before the

---

39 Para 39(4) of Sched 13.
40 See para 37(2) of Sched 13. The DGFT has no claw-back powers over other types of agreement excluded under Sched 3. He is given claw-back powers in respect of vertical agreements and land agreements. Exclusions generally are discussed in Chap 3, p 46, above.
41 See Sched 1, especially paras 4 and 5.
42 See fn 15 above and text.
43 See Sched 3, para 9, especially (3)-(8).
44 Para 13(1) of Sched 13.

starting date. The Schedule provides for the Secretary of State to make regulations governing access. The OFT envisages restrictions on access "when the level of requests for access to the register no longer justifies the costs involved".[45]

---

45 Transitional Arrangements (OFT 406), para 7.2.

Chapter 9

· The Regulators ·

9.1   The regulated industries

Certain industries, which have been subject to specific sectoral regulation since their privatisation, are placed by the Competition Act under the dual control of the Director General of Fair Trading (DGFT) and their sectoral regulator for competition law purposes. Section 54 of the Act provides for the DGFT's powers in relation to the Chapter I and Chapter II prohibitions to be exercised concurrently by those sectoral regulators. Schedule 10 to the Act, which is entitled "Regulators", lists the sectoral regulators who are given these concurrent powers, and describes the industries to which the agreements or conduct must relate.[1]

Agreements or conduct relating to	Governing legislation	Name of regulator
Commercial activities connected with telecommunications	Telecommunications Act 1984	Director General of Telecommunications
The conveyance, supply or transportation of gas and activities ancillary thereto	Gas Act 1986	Director General of Gas Supply
Commercial activities connected with the generation, transmission or supply of electricity	Electricity Act 1989	Director General of Electricity Supply[2]
Commercial activities connected with the supply of water or securing a	Water Industry Act 1991	Director General of Water Services

1 For more detailed definitions of the industries to which the agreements or conduct must relate, see the governing legislation for each sector, which is shown in the second column of the table below.

2 The gas and electricity regulators are in the process of merging to form a new joint regulatory office for the gas and electricity industries. The post of Director General of Gas Supply and Director General of Electricity Supply have been held by a single individual, Callum McCarthy, since 1 January 1999.

supply of water or with the provision or securing of sewerage services		
The supply of railway services	Railways Act 1993	Rail Regulator
Commercial activities connected with the generation, transmission or supply of electricity in Northern Ireland	Electricity (Northern Ireland) Order 1992	Director General of Electricity Supply for Northern Ireland
The conveyance, storage or supply of gas in Northern Ireland	Gas (Northern Ireland) Order 1996	Director General of Gas for Northern Ireland

Each of the regulators has an office to support their work, just as the DGFT is supported by the Office of Fair Trading (OFT).[3] Most of these regulators are referred to in their sectoral legislation as "the Director", and the Competition Act provides that in the main, and unless the context otherwise requires, references to the DGFT in Part I of the Act[4] are to be read as including a reference to the various Directors.[5] However, and for the sake of clarity, in this chapter the sectoral regulators will be referred to as regulators and not as directors.

The relationship between competition law and regulation

The regulators of the former state-owned utilities[6] have had some concurrent competition law jurisdiction with the DGFT since their original appointment. They all had concurrent jurisdiction under parts of the Competition Act 1980 in respect of their areas of responsibility.

---

3 The offices are, respectively, the Office of Telecommunications (OFTEL), the Office of Gas Supply (OFGAS), the Office of Electricity Regulation (OFFER), the Office of Water Services (OFWAT), the Office of the Rail Regulator (ORR), and the (Northern Irish) Office for the Regulation of Electricity and Gas (OFREG).

4 That is, ss 1-60 of the Act.

5 Sched 10, paras 2(6) (telecommunications), 3(5) (gas), 4(5) (electricity), 5(8) (water), 7(5) (Northern Ireland electricity), and 8(5) (Northern Ireland gas). The rail regulator is termed "Regulator" in the Railways Act 1993 (see para 6(5) of Sched 10).

6 There are sound arguments to suggest that telecommunications is not a utility proper, but the precise definition of utilities is not of particular importance when seeking to understand the role of the regulators under the Competition Act. The term "utility" will accordingly be used in this wider sense in this chapter.

Furthermore, a number of the licence conditions to which the businesses they regulate are subject concern matters such as price discrimination, the showing of undue preference and other topics which are also addressed by general competition law. Indeed in the telecommunications field the so-called Fair Trading Condition, which is now included in the licences of most public telecommunications operators[7], introduced Article 81 and 82-type provisions (old Articles 85 and 86) very like those now contained in the Chapter I and Chapter II prohibitions.

It has always been argued that the justification for giving the sectoral regulators concurrent powers with the DGFT and other competition authorities lies in the inextricable link between regulation and competition. In many cases sector-specific regulation seeks to achieve, through more intrusive and heavy-handed means, the same ends as general competition law. Indeed, it is now widely accepted, at least in the United Kingdom, that as competition becomes better established in an industry, it is appropriate and beneficial for the regulatory leash to be loosened and for general competition law to take over so far as possible. It must also be acknowledged that a particular case in a regulated industry may raise both questions which are purely concerned with breach of a licence condition, and more general competition law questions. For these reasons, among others, it was decided that the sectoral regulators should continue to have concurrent competition law jurisdiction under the reformed, and more powerful, Competition Act.

9.2   Concurrent powers and duties of the regulators

Source of the regulators' powers

Concurrent powers are given to the regulators to exercise the powers of the DGFT in their respective fields by section 54 and Schedule 10 to the Act. Section 54(4) also provides that the Secretary of State may make regulations to co-ordinate the concurrent exercise of functions under Part I of the Act by more than one person.[8] Although no such regulations have yet been made, section 54(5) indicates the areas which they might cover:

---

7 It was introduced into the Licence of BT in 1996, and subsequently into the licences of most other public telecommunications operators (see OFTEL Press Release 5/98 of 3 February 1998). OFTEL has stated that it will seek to remove the Fair Trading Condition from all licences with effect from 1 March 2000, to coincide with the Act coming into force (draft OFTEL Guideline on Application in the Telecommunications Sector (OFT 417), para 4.11).

8 Part I of the Act is entitled "Competition" and contains ss 1-60.

- the procedure to be followed when determining who is to exercise Part I functions in a particular case;
- the steps which must be taken before certain Part I functions are exercised;
- the procedure for determining, in a particular case, who is to exercise Part I functions (including the possibility of reference for determination to the Secretary of State or other prescribed persons);
- whether Part I functions should be exercised jointly in a particular case (either by the DGFT and one or more regulators, or by two or more regulators), and as to the procedure to be followed in such cases;
- the circumstances in which the exercise of Part I functions by one person should preclude their exercise by anyone else;
- the cases in which the exercise of Part I functions might be transferred to another person;
- the cases in which the person exercising Part I functions in a particular case might appoint another person to so act or might appoint officers of that other person to assist with the case;
- the manner in which notification must be given as to who is exercising Part I functions in a particular case.

It is clear from this list that a complex series of procedures and arrangements are envisaged, and it is therefore regrettable that, like much else in the Act, this has been left to secondary legislation which to date has not even been published in draft. The Department of Trade and Industry (the DTI) has thus far only stated that it intends to seek views on the provision of the Act allowing for these regulations.[9] The guidance which has been provided to date is limited: relevant passages from the DGFT's Procedural Rules;[10] from Form N which must be used for notifications;[11] and from the OFT Guidelines published under section 52 of the Act, in particular those on Concurrent Application to Regulated Industries[12] and on Investigations.[13]

In addition, OFTEL has issued a draft sector specific guideline in conjunction with the DGFT.[14] This addresses in some detail the particular

---

9 See, for example, para 2.5 of the OFT Guideline on Concurrent Application to Regulated Industries (OFT 405).
10 (OFT 411).
11 A copy is included as Appendix 2.
12 (OFT 405).
13 (OFT 404).
14 Application in the Telecommunications Sector (OFT 417). See also draft Guideline on Application in Water and Sewerage Sectors (OFT 422).

features of and issues raised by the telecommunications industry. Reference should be made to that guideline for a more in-depth analysis of the likely application of the Act to the telecommunications sector.

To date the only guidance on whether the DGFT or the relevant regulator will exercise jurisdiction in a particular case provides merely that "in general, an agreement or conduct which falls within the jurisdiction of a regulator will be dealt with by that regulator", but that in some cases the DGFT will deal with a case which falls within a regulated sector.[15] It is also possible for the DGFT and one or more regulators, or for two or more regulators, jointly to exercise jurisdiction in a particular case.[16] The OFT's Guideline on Concurrent Application states that the factors which will be considered when deciding who is best placed to deal with a case will include:

- the sectoral knowledge of a regulator;
- any previous contacts between the parties/complainants and a regulator or the DGFT;
- any recent experience in dealing with the businesses or issues raised by the case.[17]

Even after a case has been assigned to the DGFT or to a particular regulator for investigation and determination, those not handling the case may still be consulted during the course of an investigation. Furthermore, where appropriate a case may subsequently be transferred to another authority, and the persons concerned would be informed of any such change.[18]

The powers of the regulators

The Act gives the regulators power within their designated sector to apply and enforce the prohibitions on anti-competitive agreements and abuse of a dominant position. As section 54(2) of the Act states, Parts II and III of Schedule 10 to the Act provide for functions of the DGFT

---

15 OFT Guideline on Concurrent Application to Regulated Industries (OFT 405) at para 3.1. See also note 1.5 of Part 1 of Form N, and para 2.4 of the draft OFTEL Guideline on Application in the Telecommunications Sector (OFT 417).

16 See s 54(5)(d). This possibility is not referred to explicitly in the final version of the OFT Guideline on Concurrent Application to Regulated Industries (OFT 405) which suggests that the DGFT and the regulators do not intend that joint jurisdiction should be a common occurrence.

17 OFT Guideline on Concurrent Application to Regulated Industries (OFT 405), para 3.1.

18 *Ibid*, para 3.2.

under Part I to be exercisable concurrently by the regulators. Save for the limited exceptions which are described in the next section, the regulators have all of the powers which the DGFT has to investigate, exempt, enforce and fine in relation to the Chapters I and II prohibitions. For example, where it is decided that a regulator is to have jurisdiction in a case, that regulator has the power to:

- consider and determine notifications for guidance and decisions;[19]
- reach provisional decisions concerning breach of the prohibitions;[20]
- grant exemptions following notification of an agreement for a decision;[21]
- consider complaints concerning breach of the prohibitions;[22]
- carry out investigations into suspected breaches of the prohibitions. This includes the power to require the production of documents and information, and the power to search premises;[23]
- impose interim measures to prevent serious and irreparable damage;[24]
- give and enforce directions to bring an infringement to an end;[25]
- impose financial penalties, taking account of the statutory guidance on penalties which is to be issued by the DGFT;[26]
- issue general advice and information as to how the Act applies in his sector.[27]

It is therefore apparent that the persons who may be affected by the regulators' concurrent jurisdiction under the Competition Act will be not only those operating within the regulated industries, but also customers of or non-regulated business competitors of those companies. Such persons may, for example, wish to make a complaint concerning an undertaking which is subject to regulatory control, and

---

19 Ss 12-16 and 20-24 and Scheds 5 and 6 of the Act.
20 Para 3 of Scheds 5 and 6 to the Act.
21 Ss 4 and 14 of the Act.
22 OFT Guideline on the Major Provisions (OFT 400), paras 8.1-8.5.
23 Ss 25-31 of the Act.
24 S 35 of the Act
25 Ss 32-34 of the Act.
26 Ss 36-41 of the Act.
27 S 52(8) of the Act. In preparing any such advice or information regulators must consult the DGFT, the other regulators and such other persons as they consider appropriate. To date, such advice has been issued by OFTEL in the draft Guideline on Application in the Telecommunications Sector (OFT 417) and OFT /OFWAT draft Guideline (see fn 14).

may find that complaint being dealt with by the regulator using his Competition Act powers rather than by the DGFT.

The powers which the regulators do not have

The Act expressly disapplies certain powers of the DGFT in relation to the regulators. The DGFT alone has the power:

- to issue guidance on penalties under section 38(1)-(6) of the Act;
- to issue and amend procedural rules under section 51 of the Act (subject to approval from the Secretary of State).[28]

However, when issuing or amending such guidance or rules, the DGFT must consult the regulators on all matters in respect of which they exercise concurrent jurisdiction.[29]

The duties of the regulators

Each of the regulators is subject to a number of duties which are imposed by the sectoral legislation under which that regulator operates.[30] For example, all of the regulators are under duties to ensure adequate provision of the regulated service throughout the United Kingdom, to promote or facilitate effective competition in their sector, and to protect the interests of customers and consumers. What happens to these duties when the regulators are acting not pursuant to their sectoral legislation, but under their Competition Act powers? Schedule 10 to the Act amends those sectoral statutes so that the regulators may not have regard to their usual duties unless they are general matters to which the DGFT could have regard in exercising powers under the Act.[31] The duty to promote or facilitate effective competition in a particular regulated sector would almost inevitably qualify as such a general matter to which the regulator could continue to have regard.

The Competition Act also amends the relevant pieces of sectoral legislation to provide that a regulator is not under a duty to enforce a

---

28 Sched 10, paras 2(6) (telecommunications), 3(5) (gas), 4(5) (electricity), 5(6) (water), 6(5) (rail), 7(5) (Northern Ireland electricity), and 8(5) (Northern Ireland gas).
29 Ss 38(7) and 51(4).
30 See the table at pp 176-177.
31 Sched 10, paras 2(4) (telecommunications), 3(3) (gas), 4(3) (electricity), 5(4) (water), 6(3) (rail), 7(3) (Northern Ireland electricity), and 8(3) (Northern Ireland gas).

licence condition where he is satisfied that, in a particular case, it is more appropriate to use the powers available under the Act.[32]

Where a regulated person is legally required to enter into an agreement or to engage in conduct so as to comply with statutory obligations (for example, contained in applicable sector-specific legislation) the Chapter I and Chapter II prohibitions do not apply.[33]

Consequential amendments

Since separate and different pieces of legislation govern the regulation of each of the regulated industries, the reformed competition regime requires a number of consequential but minor amendments to be made to those statutes. These have not been included in the version of the Act set out at Appendix 1[34], but it is worth drawing attention to two slightly more significant consequential amendments which are in the part of Schedule 10 that has been reproduced at Appendix 1.

First, because provisions of the Competition Act 1980 concerned with the control of anti-competitive practices are repealed by the 1998 Act[35], the new Act also removes the functions which the regulators previously had under the Competition Act 1980.[36]

Secondly, the amendments made to the Fair Trading Act 1973 by the Competition Act concerning complex and scale monopoly investigations and offences are also given effect for the regulated industries by Schedule 10.[37] However, the DGFT has stated that because of the special circumstances of the regulated industries, and in particular the difficulty of establishing competition in some sectors, the scale monopoly provisions may continue to be used whether or not there has been a prior infringement of one of the prohibitions under the Act. This is different from the position in relation to all other sectors, where it is proposed that use of the scale monopoly provisions should usually be confined to circumstances where abuse continues despite an earlier finding of infringement and enforcement action.[38]

---

32 See, for example, s 16(5) of the Telecommunications Act 1984, as amended by para 9(4) of Sched 10 to the Act.
33 Para 5 of Sched 3 to the Act.
34 Parts IV and V of Sched 10 have been omitted, but may be viewed on the HMSO website at http://www.hmso.gov.uk/acts.
35 S 17 and Sched 12 to the Act.
36 Sched 10, paras 2(1) (telecommunications), 3(1) (gas), 4(1) (electricity), 5(1) (water), 6(1) (rail), 7(1) (Northern Ireland electricity), 8(1) (Northern Ireland gas).
37 Para 1.
38 See further Chap 4 on Abuse of Dominant Position: the Chapter II Prohibition, above, p 67.

It is also relevant to note that Schedule 13 of the Act provides for extended transitional periods for particular agreements in the electricity, gas and railway sectors.[38a]

9.3   **Application of Competition Act by the regulators**

Notifications, complaints and interim measures

The procedures to be followed where a person wishes to make a notification or complaint, or to apply for interim measures, in respect of an agreement or conduct which falls within the remit of one or more of the sectoral regulators, will now be examined in more detail.

Notifications

Notifications of agreements or conduct for guidance or a decision must always be submitted on Form N to the DGFT.[39] However, where the notifying party considers that the notified arrangement falls within one of the regulated industries, at least one further copy of Form N must be submitted to the DGFT in addition to the original plus two copies which are normally required.[40] If the DGFT considers that a regulator has, or may have, concurrent jurisdiction in relation to the notified agreement or conduct, the DGFT must as soon as practicable send a copy of Form N to the regulator(s) concerned, and inform the applicant in writing that this has occurred.[41] Failure to submit additional copies of Form N in a case where a regulator exercises concurrent jurisdiction does not render the notification incomplete and no penalties will accrue.[42]

As soon as is practicable after the receipt of a notification, the DGFT must inform the applicant in writing of which Director (the DGFT or one of the regulators) is to exercise jurisdiction.[43] If an application is later transferred to a different regulator, the applicant must also be informed in writing of that fact.[44] Any material changes in the facts provided in a notification of which the applicant becomes aware, or

---

38a See Sched 13, paras 27-35 and OFT Guideline on Transitional Arrangements (OFT 406), paras 4.8-4.12. See also Chap 8 above.

39   Rules 1 and 8 of the DGFT's Procedural Rules. See further Chap 5 above, p 95.

40   *Ibid*, Rule 3(2) and (3).

41   *Ibid*, Rule 8(1).

42   OFT Guideline on Concurrent Application to Regulated Industries (OFT 405), paras 3.3 and 3.4.

43   Rule 8(2)(a) of the DGFT's Procedural Rules.

44   *Ibid*, Rule 8(2)(b).

ought reasonably to become aware, must be communicated to the regulator(s) exercising jurisdiction without delay.[45] All of the DGFT's Procedural Rules apply to the regulators when exercising jurisdiction under the Act, and reference should be made to Chapter 5 above, for further details of those procedures.

Agreements made during the interim period between 9 November 1998 and 1 March 2000 may only be notified for early guidance.[46] Where the agreement in some way concerns a regulated industry, notification on Form EG should be made to the DGFT but with additional copies for the relevant regulator(s), just as in the case of notifications for guidance proper described above.[47] The procedures concerning notifications for early guidance and the regulators are exactly the same as those which apply to notifications for guidance or a decision.[48]

Complaints

Complaints concerning suspected infringements of the Chapter I or Chapter II prohibitions may be made either to the DGFT or to the regulator(s) for the relevant sector, but should not be sent to both. The OFT Guideline on concurrency stresses that submitting substantially the same complaint to two or more different authorities will not lead to a re-examination of the complaint under the Act.[49] Complaints which concern breaches both of the applicable licence conditions and of the Act will normally be dealt with by the relevant regulator.[50]

There is no form to submit when making a complaint, but guidance concerning the sort of information which should be provided is available from the OFT or from the offices of the various regulators.[51] Complainants will be told as soon as is practicable whether the DGFT and/or one or more of the regulators is handling the cases, and will be informed of any subsequent change in these arrangements.[52]

If further material facts come to light after a complaint has already been dealt with, these facts should be submitted to the DGFT or regulator who first exercised jurisdiction in relation to the matter.[53]

---

45 *Ibid*, Rule 5(5).
46 See further para 7 of Sched 13 to the Act and Section 5.4 of Chap 5 above, p 116.
47 Direction 3(3) of the Early Guidance Directions (OFT 412).
48 See, in particular, Direction 7 of the Early Guidance Directions and note 1.6 to Part 1 of Form EG.
49 OFT Guideline on Concurrent Application to Regulated Industries (OFT 405), para 3.5.
50 *Ibid*, para 3.5.
51 See further paras 8.1-8.5 of the OFT Guideline on the Major Provisions (OFT 400).
52 OFT Guideline on Concurrent Application to Regulated Industries (OFT 405), para 3.5.
53 *Ibid*, para 3.5.

Interim measures

An application for interim measures may also be made, in an appropriate case, to one of the sectoral regulators. Such an application will be dealt with according to the procedures outlined in relation to complaints above.[54] Where a regulator has a reasonable suspicion that the Chapter I or Chapter II prohibition has been infringed in a case over which that regulator is exercising jurisdiction, and where interim measures are considered necessary as a matter of urgency in order to prevent serious, irreparable damage or to protect the public interest, the regulator may give appropriate directions.[55] These directions may in particular require the person concerned to terminate or to modify the agreement or conduct in question.[56]

Issues of particular relevance to the regulated industries

Competition cases which are investigated, determined and enforced by the regulators under the Act are likely to raise many of the same issues which are raised in cases which have no connection with a regulated industry, and which are handled exclusively by the DGFT. However, due to the nature of the regulated industries, and the way in which they are structured and operate under existing sectoral legislation, certain issues may be of particular relevance in such cases. Some of these issues are highlighted below.[57]

Market definition

Market definition is of particular importance in assessing whether an undertaking is dominant for the purposes of the Chapter II prohibition.[58] Since all of the regulated industries formerly operated as state-owned monopolies, there may still be allegations or suspicions of dominance and abuse of that dominance by the now privatised companies. Market definition may prove difficult and controversial in these fast-changing industries.[59]

---

54 OFT Guideline on Concurrent Application to Regulated Industries (OFT 405), para 3.6.
55 S 35 of the Act.
56 See further paras 3.1-3.14 of the OFT Guideline on Enforcement (OFT 407) and Chap 6 above.
57 These, and other issues, are discussed in relation to the telecommunications industry in some detail in the draft OFTEL Guideline on Application to the Telecommunications Sector (OFT 417).
58 See, generally, Chap 4 above.
59 See, for example, paras 5.1-5.29 of the draft OFTEL's Guideline on Application to the Telecommunications Sector (OFT 417).

Essential facilities

Essential facilities are another issue which is particularly likely to arise in cases concerning the regulated industries and the Chapter II prohibition. An essential facility is a service or piece of infrastructure, without access to which a competitor is unable to compete in some down-stream market, and which facility it is commercially infeasible, economically inefficient and undesirable for the competitor to replicate.[60] The OFT Guideline on the Chapter II Prohibition states that utility distribution networks and some telecommunications networks may potentially constitute essential facilities.[61]

Impact of industry-specific EC legislation

The European Community has introduced liberalising and harmonising secondary legislation, mostly in the form of directives, in relation to the regulated industries. This is more comprehensive and advanced in relation to some industries than it is in relation to others[62], but in any case concerning a regulated industry regard may have to be had to that legislation, and to the need for the UK authorities to act consistently with it.[63] Regard must also be had to any relevant Commission Notices or guidelines.[64]

Exclusion for services of general economic interest or having the character of a revenue-producing monopoly

Paragraph 4 of Schedule 3 to the Act provides for an exclusion from the Chapter I and II prohibitions for undertakings entrusted with the operation of services of general economic interest or having the character of a revenue-producing monopoly, in so far as the prohibition

---

60 See the discussion at paras 7.1-7.17 of the draft OFT Guideline on Assessment of Individual Agreements and Conduct (OFT 414), and the most recent ruling of the ECJ on essential facilities in Case C-7/97 *Oscar Bronner* v *Mediaprint and others*, judgment of 26 November 1998 (not yet reported).

61 See further the section on refusal to supply at Chap 4 above, p 88. See also paras 7.51-7.60 of OFTEL's draft Guideline on Application to the Telecommunications Sector (OFT 417).

62 The telecommunications regime is particularly developed at European level, with the so-called Open Network Provision directives and the liberalising directives together making up what has been termed the "1998 Package". The water industry, on the other hand, is an example of an area where there is as yet very little Community legislation, other than in relation to health and environmental standards.

63 It is not clear whether s 60 of the Act would also apply so as to require compliance and consistency with industry-specific EC legislation.

64 For example, the draft OFTEL Guideline on Application to the Telecommunications Sector (OFT 417) contain extensive reference to the 1991 Commission guidelines on the application of EEC competition rules in the telecommunications sector (91/C 233/02) and to the Commission's 1998 Notice on the application of the competition rules to access agreements in the telecommunications sector (98/C 265/02).

would obstruct the performance (in law or in fact) of the particular tasks assigned to that undertaking. Paragraph 4 is taken almost word for word from Article 86(2) (old Article 90(2)) of the EC Treaty, which is addressed to undertakings and which is concerned in particular with the application of the Treaty rules on competition.

The paragraph 4 exclusion may apply to private undertakings such as the regulated industries, but to come within the definition of an undertaking "entrusted with the operation of services of general economic interest" there must have been a law or other act of the public authority specifically imposing a particular obligation or responsibility on that undertaking.[65] The universal service obligations, which require some of the formerly state-owned regulated industries to provide certain basic services to all persons in the United Kingdom at the same price, are an example of services which might be held to be in the general economic interest.[66]

As an exception to the general rules under the Act, and following European jurisprudence on Article 86(2) (old Article 90(2)), the paragraph 4 exclusion will be construed narrowly.[67] It is not sufficient if a restriction of competition makes the provision of a public service easier or less complicated; for the exclusion to apply the undertaking concerned must be able to show that it has no other technically and economically feasible means of performing the task in question.[68]

Of course, even where the paragraph 4, Schedule 3 exclusion does apply, regulators are still free to use their sectoral regulatory powers.

9.4   Concurrency

The Concurrency Working Party

The Concurrency Working Party was formed in 1997 to:

- ensure co-ordination between the sectoral regulators and the DGFT;

---

65 See, for example, Commission Decision in *British Telecommunications*, OJ 1982 L360/36; [1983] 1 CMLR 457, where the public act was a UK Act of Parliament.

66 The draft OFT Guideline on Concurrent Application to Regulated Industries (OFT 405) gave the example at para 4.5 of the requirement on the national postal service to provide a basic letter post service at the same price throughout the country. However, as the Guideline pointed out, the Post Office is not subject to sector-specific regulation. OFTEL's draft Guideline on Application to the Telecommunications Sector (OFT 417) states at para 7.15 that it is "unlikely that the exception would apply to any telecommunications companies" due to the increasingly competitive nature of that sector.

67 Draft OFT Guideline on Concurrent Application to Regulated Industries (OFT 405), paras 4.6-4.7.

68 Case C-127/73 *BRT v SABAM* [1974] ECR 313 and Cases 96/82 etc *IAZ International Belgium SA v Commission* [1983] ECR 3369, cited at para 4.7 of the draft OFT Guideline on Concurrent Application to Regulated Industries (OFT 405).

- consider the practical working arrangements between the regulators and the DGFT, including ensuring that a single issue would not be investigated by more than one authority;
- ensure consistency of approach in casework;
- co-ordinate the use of concurrent powers;
- prepare the OFT Guideline on Concurrency.

The OFT and each of the regulators are represented on the Concurrency Working Party, and it is chaired by a representative of the OFT.[69]

The OFT Guideline on concurrency states that the Working Party will continue to exist after the Act comes into force, and will focus in particular on:[70]

- **General principles and information sharing.** This will include information about complaints received and investigations in progress or contemplated, in particular, in relation to matters which are also capable of being investigated under sector-specific legislation. Matters of general policy and the way in which the Act is interpreted and applied will be discussed, with a view to ensuring consistency in decision-making;
- **Working arrangements.** The Working Party will deal with questions as to who should deal with a particular case only where it raises policy issues or in the event of disagreement between the DGFT and the regulator(s) concerned. In most cases issues of the day-to-day handling of cases which fall within the scope of the jurisdiction of one or more of the regulators will be resolved in more informal discussions between the DGFT and relevant regulator(s);
- **Guidelines.** The Working Party will review and update as necessary the OFT Guideline on concurrency.[71]

Confidentiality

The operation of the Concurrency Working Party, and in particular the information sharing which occurs, raises certain questions as to the disclosure of confidential information.[72]

Section 55 of the Act imposes strict controls on the disclosure of information which has been obtained under or as a result of any of the

---

69 See OFT Guideline on Concurrent Application to Regulated Industries (OFT 405), para 3.7.
70 *Ibid*, para 3.8.
71 The sectoral guidelines will also be updated as appropriate. See, for example, OFTEL's draft Guideline on Application to the Telecommunications Sector (OFT 417) at para 3.11.
72 The OFT Guideline on Concurrent Application to Regulated Industries (OFT 405) expressly acknowledges this tension at para 3.8.

provisions of Part I of the Act, and which relates to the affairs of any individual or to any particular business of an undertaking. Such information may not be disclosed without consent from the relevant persons for the lifetime of that individual or while that business continues to be carried on.[73] However, this restriction does not apply in certain defined circumstances, including to disclosure made for the purpose of facilitating the performance of any relevant functions of a designated person.[74] The expressions "relevant functions" and "designated persons" are both defined in Schedule 11 to the Act. "Relevant functions" includes any function under the Competition Act, and under each of the pieces of legislation governing the regulated industries which are listed in the table at page 176. "Designated persons" includes the DGFT and all of the regulators, but also includes certain other regulatory bodies such as the Independent Television Commission and the Securities and Investments Board.

Will concurrency work?

Representatives of the regulated industries were among the groups that lobbied hard during the debates on the Competition Bill in Parliament, in an attempt to influence its progress through to Royal Assent. A number of these groups forcefully opposed the system of concurrency which has been introduced, arguing it would be sufficient for the regulators to have advisory or possibly investigatory functions under the Act.

Many of the problems foreseen by those opposed to concurrency arise from the fluid nature of the arrangements, which permit regulators to begin an investigation using powers under the Competition Act, and then to "switch horses" to sector-specific powers mid-investigation (or vice versa).[75] Since the regulators will wield the powerful investigatory tools of the DGFT under the Act, but there are currently only limited rights of review under the sectoral regulatory legislation, this could lead to a lack of proper procedural protection and unfairness.[76]

---

73 S 55(1) and (2) of the Act.
74 S 55(3)(a)(i).
75 This possibility is expressly acknowledged in the OFT's Guideline on Concurrent Application to Regulated Industries (OFT 405) at para 3.2.
76 The full nature of appeals available under the Act is stressed at para 3.10 of the OFT Guideline on Concurrent Application to Regulated Industries (OFT 405). See also para 4.4 of the draft OFTEL Guideline on Application to the Telecommunications Sector (OFT 417) which lists OFTEL's views as to the relative advantages and disadvantages of sector specific legislation versus the Competition Act powers from the point of view of complainant and complainee respectively. The possible unfairness of allowing regulators to switch regimes mid-investigation was vividly described by Lord Kingsland during the Report Stage of the debate on the Competition Bill in the House of Lords (Hansard, 23 February 1998, col 493).

Other arguments deployed against concurrency included the wasteful and costly duplication of effort which may occur with the involvement of more than one authority, and the fear of inconsistent application of the Act. Furthermore, it was pointed out that not all regulated industries are the same, or indeed necessarily clearly defined, and that to establish a system of concurrency under the Act may entrench regulation at a time when increasing competition means that it should be reviewed and lessened.

On the other hand, it must be acknowledged that some form of concurrency existed under the un-reformed UK competition regime, and that this was perhaps inevitable due to the close inter-relationship between competition law and regulation. Furthermore, the Community competition regime to some degree treats certain of the regulated industries as special cases (for example, transport). Nonetheless, it seems likely that concurrent application of the Act by the regulators will give rise to a number of substantive and procedural problems over time, and that this may continue to be an area of controversy.

· **Competition Act 1998** ·

Chapter 41

Arrangement of sections

Part I

Competition

Chapter I

Agreements

Introduction

Section
1. Enactments replaced.

The prohibition

2. Agreements etc. preventing, restricting or distorting competition.

Excluded agreements

3. Excluded agreements.

Exemptions

4. Individual exemptions.
5. Cancellation etc. of individual exemptions.
6. Block exemptions.
7. Block exemptions: opposition.
8. Block exemptions: procedure.
9. The criteria for individual and block exemptions.
10. Parallel exemptions.
11. Exemption for certain other agreements.

Notification

12. Requests for Director to examine agreements.
13. Notification for guidance.
14. Notification for a decision.
15. Effect of guidance.
16. Effect of a decision that the Chapter I prohibition has not been infringed.

Offences

Chapter IV

The Competition Commission and appeals

The Commission

Appeals

Chapter V

Miscellaneous

Vertical agreements and land agreements

Director's rules, guidance and fees

Regulators

Confidentiality and immunity from defamation

Findings of fact by Director

Interpretation and governing principles

· Competition Act 1998 ·

1998 Chapter 41

An Act to make provision about competition and the abuse of a dominant position in the market; to confer powers in relation to investigations conducted in connection with Article 85 or 86 of the treaty establishing the European Community; to amend the Fair Trading Act 1973 in relation to information which may be required in connection with investigations under that Act; to make provision with respect to the meaning of "supply of services" in the Fair Trading Act 1973; and for connected purposes.

[9th November 1998]

BE IT ENACTED by the Queen's most Excellent Majesty, by and with the advice and consent of the Lords Spiritual and Temporal, and Commons, in this present Parliament assembled, and by the authority of the same, as follows:—

Part I Competition

Chapter I Agreements

Introduction

Enactments replaced.
   1. The following shall cease to have effect—
   (a)   the Restrictive Practices Court Act 1976 (c. 33),
   (b)   the Restrictive Trade Practices Act 1976 (c. 34),
   (c)   the Resale Prices Act 1976 (c. 53), and
   (d)   the Restrictive Trade Practices Act 1977 (c. 19).

The prohibition

Agreements etc. preventing restricting or distorting competition.
   2.—(1) Subject to section 3, agreements between undertakings, decisions by associations of undertakings or concerted practices which—
   (a)   may affect trade within the United Kingdom, and
   (b)   have as their object or effect the prevention, restriction or distortion of competition within the United Kingdom,
are prohibited unless they are exempt in accordance with the provisions of this Part.

(2) Subsection (1) applies, in particular, to agreements, decisions or practices which—

(a) directly or indirectly fix purchase or selling prices or any other trading conditions;

(b) limit or control production, markets, technical development or investment;

(c) share markets or sources of supply;

(d) apply dissimilar conditions to equivalent transactions with other trading parties, thereby placing them at a competitive disadvantage;

(e) make the conclusion of contracts subject to acceptance by the other parties of supplementary obligations which, by their nature or according to commercial usage, have no connection with the subject of such contracts.

(3) Subsection (1) applies only if the agreement, decision or practice is, or is intended to be, implemented in the United Kingdom.

(4) Any agreement or decision which is prohibited by subsection (1) is void.

(5) A provision of this Part which is expressed to apply to, or in relation to, an agreement is to be read as applying equally to, or in relation to, a decision by an association of undertakings or a concerted practice (but with any necessary modifications).

(6) Subsection (5) does not apply where the context otherwise requires.

(7) In this section "the United Kingdom" means, in relation to an agreement which operates or is intended to operate only in a part of the United Kingdom, that part.

(8) The prohibition imposed by subsection (1) is referred to in this Act as "the Chapter I prohibition".

Excluded agreements

Excluded agreements.

3.—(1) The Chapter I prohibition does not apply in any of the cases in which it is excluded by or as a result of—

(a) Schedule 1 (mergers and concentrations);

(b) Schedule 2 (competition scrutiny under other enactments);

(c) Schedule 3 (planning obligations and other general exclusions); or

(d) Schedule 4 (professional rules).

(2) The Secretary of State may at any time by order amend Schedule 1, with respect to the Chapter I prohibition, by—

(a) providing for one or more additional exclusions; or

(b) amending or removing any provision (whether or not it has been added by an order under this subsection).

(3) The Secretary of State may at any time by order amend Schedule 3, with respect to the Chapter I prohibition, by—

(a) providing for one or more additional exclusions: or

(b) amending or removing any provision—

    (i) added by an order under this subsection; or

    (ii) included in paragraph 1, 2, 8 or 9 of Schedule 3.

(4) The power under subsection (3) to provide for an additional exclusion may be exercised only if it appears to the Secretary of State that agreements which fall within the additional exclusion—

    (a) do not in general have an adverse effect on competition, or

    (b) are, in general, best considered under Chapter II of the Fair Trading Act 1973 (c. 41).

(5) An order under subsection (2)(a) or (3)(a) may include provision (similar to that made with respect to any other exclusion provided by the relevant Schedule) for the exclusion concerned to cease to apply to a particular agreement.

(6) Schedule 3 also gives the Secretary of State power to exclude agreements from the Chapter I prohibition in certain circumstances.

Exemptions

Individual exemptions.

4.—(1) The Director may grant an exemption from the Chapter I prohibition with respect to a particular agreement if—

    (a) a request for an exemption has been made to him under section 14 by a party to the agreement; and

    (b) the agreement is one to which section 9 applies.

(2) An exemption granted under this section is referred to in this Part as an individual exemption.

(3) The exemption—

    (a) may be granted subject to such conditions or obligations as the Director considers it appropriate to impose; and

    (b) has effect for such period as the Director considers appropriate.

(4) That period must be specified in the grant of the exemption.

(5) An individual exemption may be granted so as to have effect from a date earlier than that on which it is granted.

(6) On an application made in such way as may be specified by rules under section 51, the Director may extend the period for which an exemption has effect; but, if the rules so provide, he may do so only in specified circumstances.

Cancellation etc. of individual exemptions.

5.—(1) If the Director has reasonable grounds for believing that there has been a material change of circumstance since he granted an individual exemption, he may by notice in writing—

    (a) cancel the exemption;

    (b) vary or remove any condition or obligation; or

    (c) impose one or more additional conditions or obligations.

(2) If the Director has a reasonable suspicion that the information on which he based his decision to grant an individual exemption was incomplete, false or misleading in a material particular, he may by notice in writing take any of the steps mentioned in subsection (1).

(3) Breach of a condition has the effect of cancelling the exemption.

(4) Failure to comply with an obligation allows the Director, by notice in writing, to take any of the steps mentioned in subsection (1).

(5) Any step taken by the Director under subsection (1), (2) or (4) has effect from such time as may be specified in the notice.

(6) If an exemption is cancelled under subsection (2) or (4), the date specified in the notice cancelling it may be earlier than the date on which the notice is given.

(7) The Director may act under subsection (1), (2) or (4) on his own initiative or on a complaint made by any person.

Block exemptions.

6.—(1) If agreements which fall within a particular category of agreement are, in the opinion of the Director, likely to be agreements to which section 9 applies, the Director may recommend that the Secretary of State make an order specifying that category for the purposes of this section.

(2) The Secretary of State may make an order ("a block exemption order") giving effect to such a recommendation—

    (a) in the form in which the recommendation is made; or

    (b) subject to such modifications as he considers appropriate.

(3) An agreement which falls within a category specified in a block exemption order is exempt from the Chapter I prohibition.

(4) An exemption under this section is referred to in this Part as a block exemption.

(5) A block exemption order may impose conditions or obligations subject to which a block exemption is to have effect.

(6) A block exemption order may provide—

    (a) that breach of a condition imposed by the order has the effect of cancelling the block exemption in respect of an agreement;

    (b) that if there is a failure to comply with an obligation imposed by the order, the Director may, by notice in writing, cancel the block exemption in respect of the agreement;

    (c) that if the Director considers that a particular agreement is not one to which section 9 applies, he may cancel the block exemption in respect of that agreement.

(7) A block exemption order may provide that the order is to cease to have effect at the end of a specified period.

(8) In this section and section 7 "specified" means specified in a block exemption order.

Block exemptions: opposition.

7.—(1) A block exemption order may provide that a party to an agreement which—

    (a) does not qualify for the block exemption created by the order, but

    (b) satisfies specified criteria,

may notify the Director of the agreement for the purposes of subsection (2).

(2) An agreement which is notified under any provision included in a block exemption order by virtue of subsection (1) is to be treated, as from the end of the notice period, as falling within a category specified in a block exemption order unless the Director—

(a) is opposed to its being so treated; and

(b) gives notice in writing to the party concerned of his opposition before the end of that period.

(3) If the Director gives notice of his opposition under subsection (2), the notification under subsection (1) is to be treated as both notification under section 14 and as a request for an individual exemption made under subsection (3) of that section.

(4) In this section "notice period" means such period as may be specified with a view to giving the Director sufficient time to consider whether to oppose under subsection (2).

Block exemptions procedure.

8.—(1) Before making a recommendation under section 6(1), the Director must—

(a) publish details of his proposed recommendation in such a way as he thinks most suitable for bringing it to the attention of those likely to be affected; and

(b) consider any representations about it which are made to him.

(2) If the Secretary of State proposes to give effect to such a recommendation subject to modifications, he must inform the Director of the proposed modifications and take into account any comments made by the Director.

(3) If, in the opinion of the Director, it is appropriate to vary or revoke a block exemption order he may make a recommendation to that effect to the Secretary of State.

(4) Subsection (1) also applies to any proposed recommendation under subsection (3).

(5) Before exercising his power to vary or revoke a block exemption order (in a case where there has been no recommendation under subsection (3)), the Secretary of State must—

(a) inform the Director of the proposed variation or revocation; and

(b) take into account any comments made by the Director.

(6) A block exemption order may provide for a block exemption to have effect from a date earlier than that on which the order is made.

The criteria for individual and block exemptions.

9. This section applies to any agreement which—

(a) contributes to—

(i) improving production or distribution, or

(ii) promoting technical or economic progress,

while allowing consumers a fair share of the resulting benefit; but

(b) does not—

(i) impose on the undertakings concerned restrictions which are not indispensable to the attainment of those objectives; or

(ii) afford the undertakings concerned the possibility of eliminating competition in respect of a substantial part of the products in question.

Parallel exemptions.

10.—(1) An agreement is exempt from the Chapter I prohibition if it is exempt from the Community prohibition—

(a) by virtue of a Regulation,

(b) because it has been given exemption by the Commission, or

(c) because it has been notified to the Commission under the appropriate opposition or objection procedure and—

(i) the time for opposing, or objecting to, the agreement has expired and the Commission has not opposed it; or

(ii) the Commission has opposed, or objected to, the agreement but has withdrawn its opposition or objection.

(2) An agreement is exempt from the Chapter I prohibition if it does not affect trade between Member States but otherwise falls within a category of agreement which is exempt from the Community prohibition by virtue of a Regulation.

(3) An exemption from the Chapter I prohibition under this section is referred to in this Part as a parallel exemption.

(4) A parallel exemption—

(a) takes effect on the date on which the relevant exemption from the Community prohibition takes effect or, in the case of a parallel exemption under subsection (2), would take effect if the agreement in question affected trade between Member States; and

(b) ceases to have effect—

(i) if the relevant exemption from the Community prohibition ceases to have effect; or

(ii) on being cancelled by virtue of subsection (5) or (7).

(5) In such circumstances and manner as may be specified in rules made under section 51, the Director may—

(a) impose conditions or obligations subject to which a parallel exemption is to have effect;

(b) vary or remove any such condition or obligation;

(c) impose one or more additional conditions or obligations;

(d) cancel the exemption.

(6) In such circumstances as may be specified in rules made under section 51, the date from which cancellation of an exemption is to take effect may be earlier than the date on which notice of cancellation is given.

(7) Breach of a condition imposed by the Director has the effect of cancelling the exemption.

(8) In exercising his powers under this section, the Director may require any person who is a party to the agreement in question to give him such information as he may require.

(9) For the purpose of this section references to an agreement being exempt from the Community prohibition are to be read as including references to the prohibition being inapplicable to the agreement by virtue of a Regulation or a decision by the Commission.

(10) In this section—

"the Community prohibition" means the prohibition contained in—

(a) paragraph 1 of Article 85;

(b) any corresponding provision replacing, or otherwise derived from, that provision;

(c) such other Regulation as the Secretary of State may by order specify; and

"Regulation" means a Regulation adopted by the Commission or by the Council.

(11) This section has effect in relation to the prohibition contained in paragraph 1 of Article 53 of the EEA Agreement (and the EFTA Surveillance Authority) as it has effect in relation to the Community prohibition (and the Commission) subject to any modifications which the Secretary of State may by order prescribe.

Exemption for certain other agreements.

11.—(1) The fact that a ruling may be given by virtue of Article 88 of the Treaty on the question whether or not agreements of a particular kind are prohibited by Article 85 does not prevent such agreements from being subject to the Chapter I prohibition.

(2) But the Secretary of State may by regulations make such provision as he considers appropriate for the purpose of granting an exemption from the Chapter I prohibition, in prescribed circumstances, in respect of such agreements.

(3) An exemption from the Chapter I prohibition by virtue of regulations under this section is referred to in this Part as a section 11 exemption.

Notification

Requests for Director to examine agreements.

12.—(1) Sections 13 and 14 provide for an agreement to be examined by the Director on the application of a party to the agreement who thinks that it may infringe the Chapter I prohibition.

(2) Schedule 5 provides for the procedure to be followed—

(a) by any person making such an application; and

(b) by the Director, in considering such an application.

(3) The Secretary of State may by regulations make provision as to the application of sections 13 to 16 and Schedule 5, with such modifications (if any) as may be prescribed, in cases where the Director—

(a) has given a direction withdrawing an exclusion; or

(b) is considering whether to give such a direction.

Notification for guidance.

13.—(1) A party to an agreement who applies for the agreement to be examined under this section must—

(a) notify the Director of the agreement; and

(b) apply to him for guidance.

(2) On an application under this section, the Director may give the applicant guidance as to whether or not, in his view, the agreement is likely to infringe the Chapter I prohibition.

(3) If the Director considers that the agreement is likely to infringe the prohibition if it is not exempt, his guidance may indicate—

(a) whether the agreement is likely to be exempt from the prohibition under—

   (i) a block exemption;

   (ii) a parallel exemption; or

   (iii) a section 11 exemption; or

(b) whether he would be likely to grant the agreement an individual exemption if asked to do so.

(4) If an agreement to which the prohibition applies has been notified to the Director under this section, no penalty is to be imposed under this Part in respect of any infringement of the prohibition by the agreement which occurs during the period—

(a) beginning with the date on which notification was given; and

(b) ending with such date as may be specified in a notice in writing given to the applicant by the Director when the application been determined.

(5) The date specified in a notice under subsection (4)(b) may not be earlier than the date on which the notice is given.

Notification for a decision.

14.—(1) A party to an agreement who applies for the agreement to be examined under this section must—

(a) notify the Director of the agreement; and

(b) apply to him for a decision.

(2) On an application under this section, the Director may make a decision as to—

(a) whether the Chapter I prohibition has been infringed; and

(b) if it has not been infringed, whether that is because of the effect of an exclusion or because the agreement is exempt from the prohibition.

(3) If an agreement is notified to the Director under this section, the application may include a request for the agreement to which it relates to be granted an individual exemption.

(4) If an agreement to which the prohibition applies has been notified to the Director under this section, no penalty is to be imposed under this Part in

respect of any infringement of the prohibition by the agreement which occurs during the period—

    (a) beginning with the date on which notification was given; and

    (b) ending with such date as may be specified in a notice in writing given to the applicant by the Director when the application has been determined.

(5) The date specified in a notice under subsection (4)(b) may not be earlier than the date on which the notice is given.

Effect of guidance.

15.—(1) This section applies to an agreement if the Director has determined an application under section 13 by giving guidance that—

    (a) the agreement is unlikely to infringe the Chapter I prohibition, regardless of whether or not it is exempt;

    (b) the agreement is likely to be exempt under—

        (i) a block exemption;

        (ii) a parallel exemption; or

        (iii) a section 11 exemption; or

    (c) he would be likely to grant the agreement an individual exemption if asked to do so.

(2) The Director is to take no further action under this Part with respect to an agreement to which this section applies, unless—

    (a) he has reasonable grounds for believing that there has been a material change of circumstance since he gave his guidance;

    (b) he has a reasonable suspicion that the information on which he based his guidance was incomplete, false or misleading in a material particular;

    (c) one of the parties to the agreement applies to him for a decision under section 14 with respect to the agreement; or

    (d) a complaint about the agreement has been made to him by a person who is not a party to the agreement.

(3) No penalty may be imposed under this Part in respect of any infringement of the Chapter I prohibition by an agreement to which this section applies.

(4) But the Director may remove the immunity given by subsection (3) if—

    (a) he takes action under this Part with respect to the agreement in one of the circumstances mentioned in subsection (2);

    (b) he considers it likely that the agreement will infringe the prohibition; and

    (c) he gives notice in writing to the party on whose application the guidance was given that he is removing the immunity as from the date specified in his notice.

(5) If the Director has a reasonable suspicion that information—

    (a) on which he based his guidance, and

    (b) which was provided to him by a party to the agreement,

was incomplete, false or misleading in a material particular, the date specified in a notice under subsection (4)(c) may be earlier than the date on which the notice is given.

Effect of a decision that the Chapter I prohibition has not been infringed.

16.—(1) This section applies to an agreement if the Director has determined an application under section 14 by making a decision that the agreement has not infringed the Chapter I prohibition.

(2) The Director is to take no further action under this Part with respect to the agreement unless—

    (a) he has reasonable grounds for believing that there has been a material change of circumstance since he gave his decision; or

    (b) he has a reasonable suspicion that the information on which he based his decision was incomplete, false or misleading in a material particular.

(3) No penalty may be imposed under this Part in respect of any infringement of the Chapter I prohibition by an agreement to which this section applies.

(4) But the Director may remove the immunity given by subsection (3) if—

    (a) he takes action under this Part with respect to the agreement in one of the circumstances mentioned in subsection (2);

    (b) he considers that it is likely that the agreement will infringe the prohibition; and

    (c) he gives notice in writing to the party on whose application the decision was made that he is removing the immunity as from the date specified in his notice.

(5) If the Director has a reasonable suspicion that information—

    (a) on which he based his decision, and

    (b) which was provided to him by a party to the agreement,

was incomplete, false or misleading in a material particular, the date specified in a notice under subsection (4)(c) may be earlier than the date on which the notice is given.

Chapter II Abuse of dominant position

Introduction

Enactments replaced.

17. Sections 2 to 10 of the Competition Act 1980 (c. 21)(control of anti-competitive practices) shall cease to have effect.

The prohibition

Abuse of dominant position.

18.—(1) Subject to section 19, any conduct on the part of one or more undertakings which amounts to the abuse of a dominant position in a market is prohibited if it may affect trade within the United Kingdom.

(2) Conduct may, in particular, constitute such an abuse if it consists in—

    (a) directly or indirectly imposing unfair purchase or selling prices or other unfair trading conditions;

    (b) limiting production, markets or technical development to the prejudice of consumers;

    (c) applying dissimilar conditions to equivalent transactions with other trading parties, thereby placing them at a competitive disadvantage;

    (d) making the conclusion of contracts subject to acceptance by the other parties of supplementary obligations which, by their nature or according to commercial usage, have no connection with the subject of the contracts.

  (3) In this section—

"dominant position" means a dominant position within the United Kingdom; and

"the United Kingdom" means the United Kingdom or any part of it.

  (4) The prohibition imposed by subsection (1) is referred to in this Act as "the Chapter II prohibition".

Excluded cases

Excluded cases.

  19.—(1) The Chapter II prohibition does not apply in any of the cases in which it is excluded by or as a result of—

    (a) Schedule 1 (mergers and concentrations); or

    (b) Schedule 3 (general exclusions).

  (2) The Secretary of State may at any time by order amend Schedule 1, with respect to the Chapter II prohibition, by—

    (a) providing for one or more additional exclusions; or

    (b) amending or removing any provision (whether or not it has been added by an order under this subsection).

  (3) The Secretary of State may at any time by order amend paragraph 8 of Schedule 3 with respect to the Chapter II prohibition.

  (4) Schedule 3 also gives the Secretary of State power to provide that the Chapter II prohibition is not to apply in certain circumstances.

Notification

Requests for Director to consider conduct.

  20.—(1) Sections 21 and 22 provide for conduct of a person which that person thinks may infringe the Chapter II prohibition to be considered by the Director on the application of that person.

  (2) Schedule 6 provides for the procedure to be followed—

    (a) by any person making an application, and

    (b) by the Director, in considering an application.

Notification for guidance.

  21.—(1) A person who applies for conduct to be considered under this section must—

(a) notify the Director of it; and

(b) apply to him for guidance.

(2) On an application under this section, the Director may give the applicant guidance as to whether or not, in his view, the conduct is likely to infringe the Chapter II prohibition.

Notification for a decision.

22.—(1) A person who applies for conduct to be considered under this section must—

(a) notify the Director of it; and

(b) apply to him for a decision.

(2) On an application under this section, the Director may make a decision as to—

(a) whether the Chapter II prohibition has been infringed; and

(b) if it has not been infringed, whether that is because of the effect of an exclusion.

Effect of guidance.

23.—(1) This section applies to conduct if the Director has determined an application under section 21 by giving guidance that the conduct is unlikely to infringe the Chapter II prohibition.

(2) The Director is to take no further action under this Part with respect to the conduct to which this section applies, unless—

(a) he has reasonable grounds for believing that there has been a material change of circumstance since he gave his guidance;

(b) he has a reasonable suspicion that the information on which he based his guidance was incomplete, false or misleading in a material particular; or

(c) a complaint about the conduct has been made to him.

(3) No penalty may be imposed under this Part in respect of any infringement of the Chapter II prohibition by conduct to which this section applies.

(4) But the Director may remove the immunity given by subsection (3) if—

(a) he takes action under this Part with respect to the conduct in one of the circumstances mentioned in subsection (2);

(b) he considers that it is likely that the conduct will infringe the prohibition; and

(c) he gives notice in writing to the undertaking on whose application the guidance was given that he is removing the immunity as from the date specified in his notice.

(5) If the Director has a reasonable suspicion that information—

(a) on which he based his guidance, and

(b) which was provided to him by an undertaking engaging in the conduct,

was incomplete, false or misleading in a material particular, the date specified in a notice under subsection (4)(c) may be earlier than the date on which the notice is given.

Effect of a decision that the Chapter II prohibition has not been infringed.

24.—(1) This section applies to conduct if the Director has determined an application under section 22 by making a decision that the conduct has not infringed the Chapter II prohibition.

(2) The Director is to take no further action under this Part with respect to the conduct unless—

(a) he has reasonable grounds for believing that there has been a material change of circumstance since he gave his decision; or

(b) he has a reasonable suspicion that the information on which he based his decision was incomplete, false or misleading in a material particular.

(3) No penalty may be imposed under this Part in respect of any infringement of the Chapter II prohibition by conduct to which this section applies.

(4) But the Director may remove the immunity given by subsection (3) if—

(a) he takes action under this Part with respect to the conduct in one of the circumstances mentioned in subsection (2);

(b) he considers that it is likely that the conduct will infringe the prohibition; and

(c) he gives notice in writing to the undertaking on whose application the decision was made that he is removing the immunity as from the date specified in his notice.

(5) If the Director has a reasonable suspicion that information—

(a) on which he based his decision, and

(b) which was provided to him by an undertaking engaging in the conduct,

was incomplete, false or misleading in a material particular, the date specified in a notice under subsection (4)(c) may be earlier than the date on which the notice is given.

Chapter III Investigation and enforcement

Investigations

Director's power to investigate.

25. The Director may conduct an investigation if there are reasonable grounds for suspecting—

(a) that the Chapter I prohibition has been infringed; or

(b) that the Chapter II prohibition has been infringed.

Powers when conducting investigations.

26.—(1) For the purposes of an investigation under section 25, the Director may require any person to produce to him a specified document, or to provide him with specified information, which he considers relates to any matter relevant to the investigation.

(2) The power conferred by subsection (1) is to be exercised by a notice in writing.

(3) A notice under subsection (2) must indicate—

(a) the subject matter and purpose of the investigation; and

(b) the nature of the offences created by sections 42 to 44.

(4) In subsection (1) "specified" means—

(a) specified, or described, in the notice; or

(b) falling within a category which is specified, or described, in the notice.

(5) The Director may also specify in the notice—

(a) the time and place at which any document is to be produced or any information is to be provided;

(b) the manner and form in which it is to be produced or provided.

(6) The power under this section to require a person to produce a document includes power—

(a) if the document is produced—

(i) to take copies of it or extracts from it;

(ii) to require him, or any person who is a present or past officer of his, or is or was at any time employed by him, to provide an explanation of the document;

(b) if the document is not produced, to require him to state, to the best of his knowledge and belief, where it is.

Power to enter premises without a warrant.

27.—(1) Any officer of the Director who is authorised in writing by the Director to do so ("an investigating officer") may enter any premises in connection with an investigation under section 25.

(2) No investigating officer is to enter any premises in the exercise of his powers under this section unless he has given to the occupier of the premises a written notice which—

(a) gives at least two working days' notice of the intended entry;

(b) indicates the subject matter and purpose of the investigation; and

(c) indicates the nature of the offences created by sections 42 to 44.

(3) Subsection (2) does not apply—

(a) if the Director has a reasonable suspicion that the premises are, or have been, occupied by—

(i) a party to an agreement which he is investigating under section 25(a); or

(ii) an undertaking the conduct of which he is investigating under section 25(b); or

(b) if the investigating officer has taken all such steps as are reasonably practicable to give notice but has not been able to do so.

(4) In a case falling within subsection (3), the power of entry conferred by subsection (1) is to be exercised by the investigating officer on production of—

(a) evidence of his authorisation; and

(b) a document containing the information referred to in subsection (2)(b) and (c).

(5) An investigating officer entering any premises under this section may—

(a) take with him such equipment as appears to him to be necessary;
(b) require any person on the premises—
> (i) to produce any document which he considers relates to any matter relevant to the investigation; and
> (ii) if the document is produced, to provide an explanation of it;

(c) require any person to state, to the best of his knowledge and belief, where any such document is to be found;
(d) take copies of, or extracts from, any document which is produced;
(e) require any information which is held in a computer and is accessible from the premises and which the investigating officer considers relates to any matter relevant to the investigation, to be produced in a form—
> (i) in which it can be taken away, and
> (ii) in which it is visible and legible.

Power to enter premises under a warrant.

28.—(1) On an application made by the Director to the court in accordance with rules of court, a judge may issue a warrant if he is satisfied that—

(a) there are reasonable grounds for suspecting that there are on any premises documents—
> (i) the production of which has been required under section 26 or 27; and
> (ii) which have not been produced as required;

(b) there are reasonable grounds for suspecting that—
> (i) there are on any premises documents which the Director has power under section 26 to require to be produced; and
> (ii) if the documents were required to be produced, they would not be produced but would be concealed, removed, tampered with or destroyed; or

(c) an investigating officer has attempted to enter premises in the exercise of his powers under section 27 but has been unable to do so and that there are reasonable grounds for suspecting that there are on the premises documents the production of which could have been required under that section.

(2) A warrant under this section shall authorise a named officer of the Director, and any other of his officers whom he has authorised in writing to accompany the named officer—

(a) to enter the premises specified in the warrant, using such force as is reasonably necessary for the purpose;
(b) to search the premises and take copies of, or extracts from, any document appearing to be of a kind in respect of which the application under subsection (1) was granted ("the relevant kind");
(c) to take possession of any documents appearing to be of the relevant kind if—

(i) such action appears to be necessary for preserving the documents or preventing interference with them; or

(ii) it is not reasonably practicable to take copies of the documents on the premises;

(d) to take any other steps which appear to be necessary for the purpose mentioned in paragraph (c)(i);

(e) to require any person to provide an explanation of any document appearing to be of the relevant kind or to state, to the best of his knowledge and belief, where it may be found;

(f) to require any information which is held in a computer and is accessible from the premises and which the named officer considers relates to any matter relevant to the investigation, to be produced in a form—

(i) in which it can be taken away, and

(ii) in which it is visible and legible.

(3) If, in the case of a warrant under subsection (1)(b), the judge is satisfied that it is reasonable to suspect that there are also on the premises other documents relating to the investigation concerned, the warrant shall also authorise action mentioned in subsection (2) to be taken in relation to any such document.

(4) Any person entering premises by virtue of a warrant under this section may take with him such equipment as appears to him to be necessary.

(5) On leaving any premises which he has entered by virtue of a warrant under this section, the named officer must, if the premises are unoccupied or the occupier is temporarily absent, leave them as effectively secured as he found them.

(6) A warrant under this section continues in force until the end of the period of one month beginning with the day on which it is issued.

(7) Any document of which possession is taken under subsection (2)(c) may be retained for a period of three months.

Entry of premises under warrant: supplementary.

29.—(1) A warrant issued under section 28 must indicate—

(a) the subject matter and purpose of the investigation;

(b) the nature of the offences created by sections 42 to 44.

(2) The powers conferred by section 28 are to be exercised on production of a warrant issued under that section.

(3) If there is no one at the premises when the named officer proposes to execute such a warrant he must, before executing it—

(a) take such steps as are reasonable in all the circumstances to inform the occupier of the intended entry; and

(b) if the occupier is informed, afford him or his legal or other representative a reasonable opportunity to be present when the warrant is executed.

(4) If the named officer is unable to inform the occupier of the intended entry he must, when executing the warrant, leave a copy of it in a prominent place on the premises.

(5) In this section—

"named officer" means the officer named in the warrant; and

"occupier", in relation to any premises, means a person whom the named officer reasonably believes is the occupier of those premises.

Privileged communications.

30.—(1) A person shall not be required, under any provision of this Part, to produce or disclose a privileged communication.

(2) "Privileged communication" means a communication—

(a) between a professional legal adviser and his client, or

(b) made in connection with, or in contemplation of, legal proceedings and for the purposes of those proceedings,

which in proceedings in the High Court would be protected from disclosure on grounds of legal professional privilege.

(3) In the application of this section to Scotland—

(a) references to the High Court are to be read as references to the Court of Session; and

(b) the reference to legal professional privilege is to be read as a reference to confidentiality of communications.

Decisions following an investigation.

31.—(1) Subsection (2) applies if, as the result of an investigation conducted under section 25, the Director proposes to make—

(a) a decision that the Chapter I prohibition has been infringed, or

(b) a decision that the Chapter II prohibition has been infringed.

(2) Before making the decision, the Director must—

(a) give written notice to the person (or persons) likely to be affected by the proposed decision; and

(b) give that person (or those persons) an opportunity to make representations.

Enforcement

Directions in relation to agreements.

32.—(1) If the Director has made a decision that an agreement infringes the Chapter I prohibition, he may give to such person or persons as he considers appropriate such directions as he considers appropriate to bring the infringement to an end.

(2) Subsection (1) applies whether the Director's decision is made on his own initiative or on an application made to him under this Part.

(3) A direction under this section may, in particular, include provision—

(a) requiring the parties to the agreement to modify the agreement; or

(b) requiring them to terminate the agreement.

(4) A direction under this section must be given in writing.

Directions in relation to conduct.

33.—(1) If the Director has made a decision that conduct infringes the Chapter II prohibition, he may give to such person or persons as he considers appropriate such directions as he considers appropriate to bring the infringement to an end.

(2) Subsection (1) applies whether the Director's decision is made on his own initiative or on an application made to him under this Part.

(3) A direction under this section may, in particular, include provision—

    (a) requiring the person concerned to modify the conduct in question; or

    (b) requiring him to cease that conduct.

(4) A direction under this section must be given in writing.

Enforcement of directions.

34.—(1) If a person fails, without reasonable excuse, to comply with a direction under section 32 or 33, the Director may apply to the court for an order—

    (a) requiring the defaulter to make good his default within a time specified in the order; or

    (b) if the direction related to anything to be done in the management or administration of an undertaking, requiring the undertaking or any of its officers to do it.

(2) An order of the court under subsection (1) may provide for all of the costs of, or incidental to, the application for the order to be borne by—

    (a) the person in default; or

    (b) any officer of an undertaking who is responsible for the default.

(3) In the application of subsection (2) to Scotland, the reference to "costs" is to be read as a reference to "expenses".

Interim measures.

35.—(1) This section applies if the Director—

    (a) has a reasonable suspicion that the Chapter I prohibition has been infringed, or

    (b) has a reasonable suspicion that the Chapter II prohibition has been infringed,

but has not completed his investigation into the matter.

(2) If the Director considers that it is necessary for him to act under this section as a matter of urgency for the purpose—

    (a) of preventing serious, irreparable damage to a particular person or category of person, or

    (b) of protecting the public interest,

he may give such directions as he considers appropriate for that purpose.

(3) Before giving a direction under this section, the Director must—

    (a) give written notice to the person (or persons) to whom he proposes to give the direction; and

    (b) give that person (or each of them) an opportunity to make representations.

(4) A notice under subsection (3) must indicate the nature of the direction which the Director is proposing to give and his reasons for wishing to give it.

(5) A direction given under this section has effect while subsection (1) applies, but may be replaced if the circumstances permit by a direction under section 32 or (as appropriate) section 33.

(6) In the case of a suspected infringement of the Chapter I prohibition, sections 32(3) and 34 also apply to directions given under this section.

(7) In the case of a suspected infringement of the Chapter II prohibition, sections 33(3) and 34 also apply to directions given under this section.

Penalty for infringing Chapter I or Chapter II prohibition.

36.—(1) On making a decision that an agreement has infringed the Chapter I prohibition, the Director may require an undertaking which is a party to the agreement to pay him a penalty in respect of the infringement.

(2) On making a decision that conduct has infringed the Chapter II prohibition, the Director may require the undertaking concerned to pay him a penalty in respect of the infringement.

(3) The Director may impose a penalty on an undertaking under subsection (1) or (2) only if he is satisfied that the infringement has been committed intentionally or negligently by the undertaking.

(4) Subsection (1) is subject to section 39 and does not apply if the Director is satisfied that the undertaking acted on the reasonable assumption that that section gave it immunity in respect of the agreement.

(5) Subsection (2) is subject to section 40 and does not apply if the Director is satisfied that the undertaking acted on the reasonable assumption that that section gave it immunity in respect of the conduct.

(6) Notice of a penalty under this section must—

    (a) be in writing; and

    (b) specify the date before which the penalty is required to be paid.

(7) The date specified must not be earlier than the end of the period within which an appeal against the notice may be brought under section 46.

(8) No penalty fixed by the Director under this section may exceed 10% of the turnover of the undertaking (determined in accordance with such provisions as may be specified in an order made by the Secretary of State).

(9) Any sums received by the Director under this section are to be paid into the Consolidated Fund.

Recovery of penalties.

37.—(1) If the specified date in a penalty notice has passed and—

    (a) the period during which an appeal against the imposition, or amount, of the penalty may be made has expired without an appeal having been made, or

    (b) such an appeal has been made and determined,

the Director may recover from the undertaking, as a civil debt due to him, any amount payable under the penalty notice which remains outstanding.

(2) In this section—

"penalty notice" means a notice given under section 36; and

"specified date" means the date specified in the penalty notice.

The appropriate level of a penalty.

38.—(1) The Director must prepare and publish guidance as to the appropriate amount of any penalty under this Part.

(2) The Director may at any time alter the guidance.

(3) If the guidance is altered, the Director must publish it as altered.

(4) No guidance is to be published under this section without the approval of the Secretary of State.

(5) The Director may, after consulting the Secretary of State, choose how he publishes his guidance.

(6) If the Director is preparing or altering guidance under this section he must consult such persons as he considers appropriate.

(7) If the proposed guidance or alteration relates to a matter in respect of which a regulator exercises concurrent jurisdiction, those consulted must include that regulator.

(8) When setting the amount of a penalty under this Part, the Director must have regard to the guidance for the time being in force under this section.

(9) If a penalty or a fine has been imposed by the Commission, or by a court or other body in another Member State, in respect of an agreement or conduct, the Director, an appeal tribunal or the appropriate court must take that penalty or fine into account when setting the amount of a penalty under this Part in relation to that agreement or conduct.

(10) In subsection (9) "the appropriate court" means—

    (a) in relation to England and Wales, the Court of Appeal;

    (b) in relation to Scotland, the Court of Session;

    (c) in relation to Northern Ireland, the Court of Appeal in Northern Ireland;

    (d) the House of Lords.

Limited immunity for small agreements.

39.—(1) In this section "small agreement" means an agreement—

    (a) which falls within a category prescribed for the purposes of this section; but

    (b) is not a price fixing agreement.

(2) The criteria by reference to which a category of agreement is prescribed may, in particular, include—

    (a) the combined turnover of the parties to the agreement (determined in accordance with prescribed provisions);

    (b) the share of the market affected by the agreement (determined in that way).

(3) A party to a small agreement is immune from the effect of section 36(1); but the Director may withdraw that immunity under subsection (4).

(4) If the Director has investigated a small agreement, he may make a decision withdrawing the immunity given by subsection (3) if, as a result of his investigation, he considers that the agreement is likely to infringe the Chapter I prohibition.

(5) The Director must give each of the parties in respect of which immunity is withdrawn written notice of his decision to withdraw the immunity.

(6) A decision under subsection (4) takes effect on such date ("the withdrawal date") as may be specified in the decision.

(7) The withdrawal date must be a date after the date on which the decision is made.

(8) In determining the withdrawal date, the Director must have regard to the amount of time which the parties are likely to require in order to secure that there is no further infringement of the Chapter I prohibition with respect to the agreement.

(9) In subsection (1) "price fixing agreement" means an agreement which has as its object or effect, or one of its objects or effects, restricting the freedom of a party to the agreement to determine the price to be charged (otherwise than as between that party and another party to the agreement) for the product, service or other matter to which the agreement relates.

Limited immunity in relation to the Chapter II prohibition.

40.—(1) In this section "conduct of minor significance" means conduct which falls within a category prescribed for the purposes of this section.

(2) The criteria by reference to which a category is prescribed may, in particular, include—

    (a) the turnover of the person whose conduct it is (determined in accordance with prescribed provisions);

    (b) the share of the market affected by the conduct (determined in that way).

(3) A person is immune from the effect of section 36(2) if his conduct is conduct of minor significance; but the Director may withdraw that immunity under subsection (4).

(4) If the Director has investigated conduct of minor significance, he may make a decision withdrawing the immunity given by subsection (3) if, as a result of his investigation, he considers that the conduct is likely to infringe the Chapter II prohibition.

(5) The Director must give the person, or persons, whose immunity has been withdrawn written notice of his decision to withdraw the immunity.

(6) A decision under subsection (4) takes effect on such date ("the withdrawal date") as may be specified in the decision.

(7) The withdrawal date must be a date after the date on which the decision is made.

(8) In determining the withdrawal date, the Director must have regard to the amount of time which the person or persons affected are likely to require in order to secure that there is no further infringement of the Chapter II prohibition.

Agreements notified to the Commission.

41.—(1) This section applies if a party to an agreement which may infringe the Chapter I prohibition has notified the agreement to the Commission for a decision as to whether an exemption will be granted under Article 85 with respect to the agreement.

(2) A penalty may not be required to be paid under this Part in respect of any infringement of the Chapter I prohibition after notification but before the Commission determines the matter.

(3) If the Commission withdraws the benefit of provisional immunity from penalties with respect to the agreement, subsection (2) ceases to apply as from the date on which that benefit is withdrawn.

(4) The fact that an agreement has been notified to the Commission does not prevent the Director from investigating it under this Part.

(5) In this section "provisional immunity from penalties" has such meaning as may be prescribed.

Offences

Offences.

42.—(1) A person is guilty of an offence if he fails to comply with a requirement imposed on him under section 26, 27 or 28.

(2) If a person is charged with an offence under subsection (1) in respect of a requirement to produce a document, it is a defence for him to prove—

    (a) that the document was not in his possession or under his control; and

    (b) that it was not reasonably practicable for him to comply with the requirement.

(3) If a person is charged with an offence under subsection (1) in respect of a requirement—

    (a) to provide information,

    (b) to provide an explanation of a document, or

    (c) to state where a document is to be found,

it is a defence for him to prove that he had a reasonable excuse for failing to comply with the requirement.

(4) Failure to comply with a requirement imposed under section 26 or 27 is not an offence if the person imposing the requirement has failed to act in accordance with that section.

(5) A person is guilty of an offence if he intentionally obstructs an officer acting in the exercise of his powers under section 27.

(6) A person guilty of an offence under subsection (1) or (5) is liable—

    (a) on summary conviction, to a fine not exceeding the statutory maximum;

    (b) on conviction on indictment, to a fine.

(7) A person who intentionally obstructs an officer in the exercise of his powers under a warrant issued under section 28 is guilty of an offence and liable—

(a) on summary conviction, to a fine not exceeding the statutory maximum;

(b) on conviction on indictment, to imprisonment for a term not exceeding two years or to a fine or to both.

Destroying or falsifying documents.

43.—(1) A person is guilty of an offence if, having been required to produce a document under section 26, 27 or 28—

(a) he intentionally or recklessly destroys or otherwise disposes of it, falsifies it or conceals it, or

(b) he causes or permits its destruction, disposal, falsification or concealment.

(2) A person guilty of an offence under subsection (1) is liable—

(a) on summary conviction, to a fine not exceeding the statutory maximum;

(b) on conviction on indictment, to imprisonment for a term not exceeding two years or to a fine or to both.

False or misleading information.

44.—(1) If information is provided by a person to the Director in connection with any function of the Director under this Part, that person is guilty of an offence if—

(a) the information is false or misleading in a material particular, and

(b) he knows that it is or is reckless as to whether it is.

(2) A person who—

(a) provides any information to another person, knowing the information to be false or misleading in a material particular, or

(b) recklessly provides any information to another person which is false or misleading in a material particular,

knowing that the information is to be used for the purpose of providing information to the Director in connection with any of his functions under this Part, is guilty of an offence.

(3) A person guilty of an offence under this section is liable—

(a) on summary conviction, to a fine not exceeding the statutory maximum;

(b) on conviction on indictment, to imprisonment for a term not exceeding two years or to a fine or to both.

Chapter IV The Competition Commission and appeals

The Commission

The Competition Commission.

45.—(1) There is to be a body corporate known as the Competition Commission.

(2) The Commission is to have such functions as are conferred on it by or as a result of this Act.

(3) The Monopolies and Mergers Commission is dissolved and its functions are transferred to the Competition Commission.

(4) In any enactment, instrument or other document, any reference to the Monopolies and Mergers Commission which has continuing effect is to be read as a reference to the Competition Commission.

(5) The Secretary of State may by order make such consequential, supplemental and incidental provision as he considers appropriate in connection with—

(a) the dissolution of the Monopolies and Mergers Commission; and

(b) the transfer of functions effected by subsection (3).

(6) An order made under subsection (5) may, in particular, include provision—

(a) for the transfer of property, rights, obligations and liabilities and the continuation of proceedings, investigations and other matters; or

(b) amending any enactment which makes provision with respect to the Monopolies and Mergers Commission or any of its functions.

(7) Schedule 7 makes further provision about the Competition Commission.

Appeals

Appealable decisions.

46.—(1) Any party to an agreement in respect of which the Director has made a decision may appeal to the Competition Commission against, or with respect to, the decision.

(2) Any person in respect of whose conduct the Director has made a decision may appeal to the Competition Commission against, or with respect to, the decision.

(3) In this section "decision" means a decision of the Director—

(a) as to whether the Chapter I prohibition has been infringed,

(b) as to whether the Chapter II prohibition has been infringed,

(c) as to whether to grant an individual exemption,

(d) in respect of an individual exemption—

(i) as to whether to impose any condition or obligation under section 4(3)(a) or 5(1)(c),

(ii) where such a condition or obligation has been imposed, as to the condition or obligation,

(iii) as to the period fixed under section 4(3)(b), or

(iv) as to the date fixed under section 4(5),

(e) as to—

(i) whether to extend the period for which an individual exemption has effect, or

(ii) the period of any such extension,

(f) cancelling an exemption,

(g) as to the imposition of any penalty under section 36 or as to the amount of any such penalty,

    (h) withdrawing or varying any of the decisions in paragraphs (a) to (f) following an application under section 47(1),

and includes a direction given under section 32, 33 or 35 and such other decision as may be prescribed.

    (4) Except in the case of an appeal against the imposition, or the amount, of a penalty, the making of an appeal under this section does not suspend the effect of the decision to which the appeal relates.

    (5) Part I of Schedule 8 makes further provision about appeals.

Third party appeals.

    47.—(1) A person who does not fall within section 46(1) or (2) may apply to the Director asking him to withdraw or vary a decision ("the relevant decision") falling within paragraphs (a) to (f) of section 46(3) or such other decision as may be prescribed.

    (2) The application must—
      (a) be made in writing, within such period as the Director may specify in rules under section 51; and
      (b) give the applicant's reasons for considering that the relevant decision should be withdrawn or (as the case may be) varied.

    (3) If the Director decides—
      (a) that the applicant does not have a sufficient interest in the relevant decision,
      (b) that, in the case of an applicant claiming to represent persons who have such an interest, the applicant does not represent such persons, or
      (c) that the persons represented by the applicant do not have such an interest,

he must notify the applicant of his decision.

    (4) If the Director, having considered the application, decides that it does not show sufficient reason why he should withdraw or vary the relevant decision, he must notify the applicant of his decision.

    (5) Otherwise, the Director must deal with the application in accordance with such procedure as may be specified in rules under section 51.

    (6) The applicant may appeal to the Competition Commission against a decision of the Director notified under subsection (3) or (4).

    (7) The making of an application does not suspend the effect of the relevant decision.

Appeal tribunals.

    48.—(1) Any appeal made to the Competition Commission under section 46 or 47 is to be determined by an appeal tribunal.

    (2) The Secretary of State may, after consulting the President of the Competition Commission Appeal Tribunals and such other persons as he considers appropriate, make rules with respect to appeals and appeal tribunals.

    (3) The rules may confer functions on the President.

(4) Part II of Schedule 8 makes further provision about rules made under this section but is not to be taken as restricting the Secretary of State's powers under this section.

Appeals on point of law etc.

49.—(1) An appeal lies—

    (a) on a point of law arising from a decision of an appeal tribunal, or

    (b) from any decision of an appeal tribunal as to the amount of a penalty.

(2) An appeal under this section may be made only—

    (a) to the appropriate court;

    (b) with leave; and

    (c) at the instance of a party or at the instance of a person who has a sufficient interest in the matter.

(3) Rules under section 48 may make provision for regulating or prescribing any matters incidental to or consequential upon an appeal under this section.

(4) In subsection (2)—

"the appropriate court" means—

    (a) in relation to proceedings before a tribunal in England and Wales, the Court of Appeal;

    (b) in relation to proceedings before a tribunal in Scotland, the Court of Session;

    (c) in relation to proceedings before a tribunal in Northern Ireland, the Court of Appeal in Northern Ireland;

"leave" means leave of the tribunal in question or of the appropriate court; and

"party", in relation to a decision, means a person who was a party to the proceedings in which the decision was made.

Chapter V Miscellaneous

Vertical agreements and land agreements

Vertical agreements and land agreements.

50.—(1) The Secretary of State may by order provide for any provision of this Part to apply in relation to—

    (a) vertical agreements, or

    (b) land agreements,

with such modifications as may be prescribed.

(2) An order may, in particular, provide for exclusions or exemptions, or otherwise provide for prescribed provisions not to apply, in relation to—

    (a) vertical agreements, or land agreements, in general; or

    (b) vertical agreements, or land agreements, of any prescribed description.

(3) An order may empower the Director to give directions to the effect that in prescribed circumstances an exclusion, exemption or modification is not to apply (or is to apply in a particular way) in relation to an individual agreement.

(4) Subsections (2) and (3) are not to be read as limiting the powers conferred by section 71.

(5) In this section—

"land agreement" and "vertical agreement" have such meaning as may be prescribed; and

"prescribed" means prescribed by an order.

Director's rules, guidance and fees

Rules.

51.—(1) The Director may make such rules about procedural and other matters in connection with the carrying into effect of the provisions of this Part as he considers appropriate.

(2) Schedule 9 makes further provision about rules made under this section but is not to be taken as restricting the Director's powers under this section.

(3) If the Director is preparing rules under this section he must consult such persons as he considers appropriate.

(4) If the proposed rules relate to a matter in respect of which a regulator exercises concurrent jurisdiction, those consulted must include that regulator.

(5) No rule made by the Director is to come into operation until it has been approved by an order made by the Secretary of State.

(6) The Secretary of State may approve any rule made by the Director—

(a) in the form in which it is submitted; or

(b) subject to such modifications as he considers appropriate.

(7) If the Secretary of State proposes to approve a rule subject to modifications he must inform the Director of the proposed modifications and take into account any comments made by the Director.

(8) Subsections (5) to (7) apply also to any alteration of the rules made by the Director.

(9) The Secretary of State may, after consulting the Director, by order vary or revoke any rules made under this section.

(10) If the Secretary of State considers that rules should be made under this section with respect to a particular matter he may direct the Director to exercise his powers under this section and make rules about that matter.

Advice and information.

52.—(1) As soon as is reasonably practicable after the passing of this Act, the Director must prepare and publish general advice and information about—

(a) the application of the Chapter I prohibition and the Chapter II prohibition, and

(b) the enforcement of those prohibitions.

(2) The Director may at any time publish revised, or new, advice or information.

(3) Advice and information published under this section must be prepared with a view to—

(a) explaining provisions of this Part to persons who are likely to be affected by them; and

(b) indicating how the Director expects such provisions to operate.

(4) Advice (or information) published by virtue of subsection (3)(b) may include advice (or information) about the factors which the Director may take into account in considering whether, and if so how, to exercise a power conferred on him by Chapter I, II or III.

(5) Any advice or information published by the Director under this section is to be published in such form and in such manner as he considers appropriate.

(6) If the Director is preparing any advice or information under this section he must consult such persons as he considers appropriate.

(7) If the proposed advice or information relates to a matter in respect of which a regulator exercises concurrent jurisdiction, those consulted must include that regulator.

(8) In preparing any advice or information under this section about a matter in respect of which he may exercise functions under this Part, a regulator must consult—

(a) the Director;

(b) the other regulators; and

(c) such other persons as he considers appropriate.

Fees.

53.—(1) The Director may charge fees, of specified amounts, in connection with the exercise by him of specified functions under this Part.

(2) Rules may, in particular, provide—

(a) for the amount of any fee to be calculated by reference to matters which may include—

(i) the turnover of any party to an agreement (determined in such manner as may be specified);

(ii) the turnover of a person whose conduct the Director is to consider (determined in that way);

(b) for different amounts to be specified in connection with different functions;

(c) for the repayment by the Director of the whole or part of a fee in specified circumstances;

(d) that an application or notice is not to be regarded as duly made or given unless the appropriate fee is paid.

(3) In this section—

(a) "rules" means rules made by the Director under section 51; and

(b) "specified" means specified in rules.

Regulators

Regulators.

54.—(1) In this Part "regulator" means any person mentioned in paragraphs (a) to (g) of paragraph 1 of Schedule 10.

(2) Parts II and III of Schedule 10 provide for functions of the Director under this Part to be exercisable concurrently by regulators.

(3) Parts IV and V of Schedule 10 make minor and consequential amendments in connection with the regulators' competition functions.

(4) The Secretary of State may make regulations for the purpose of coordinating the performance of functions under this Part ("Part I functions") which are exercisable concurrently by two or more competent persons as a result of any provision made by Part II or III of Schedule 10.

(5) The regulations may, in particular, make provision—

    (a) as to the procedure to be followed by competent persons when determining who is to exercise Part I functions in a particular case;

    (b) as to the steps which must be taken before a competent person exercises, in a particular case, such Part I functions as may be prescribed;

    (c) as to the procedure for determining, in a particular case, questions arising as to which competent person is to exercise Part I functions in respect of the case;

    (d) for Part I functions in a particular case to be exercised jointly—

        (i) by the Director and one or more regulators, or

        (ii) by two or more regulators,

    and as to the procedure to be followed in such cases;

    (e) as to the circumstances in which the exercise by a competent person of such Part I functions as may be prescribed is to preclude the exercise of such functions by another such person;

    (f) for cases in respect of which Part I functions are being, or have been, exercised by a competent person to be transferred to another such person;

    (g) for the person ("A") exercising Part I functions in a particular case—

        (i) to appoint another competent person ("B") to exercise Part I functions on A's behalf in relation to the case; or

        (ii) to appoint officers of B (with B's consent) to act as officers of A in relation to the case;

    (h) for notification as to who is exercising Part I functions in respect of a particular case.

(6) Provision made by virtue of subsection (5)(c) may provide for questions to be referred to and determined by the Secretary of State or by such other person as may be prescribed.

(7) "Competent person" means the Director or any of the regulators.

Confidentiality and immunity from defamation

General restrictions on disclosure of information.

    55.—(1) No information which—

    (a) has been obtained under or as a result of any provision of this Part, and

(b) relates to the affairs of any individual or to any particular business of an undertaking,

is to be disclosed during the lifetime of that individual or while that business continues to be carried on, unless the condition mentioned in subsection (2) is satisfied.

(2) The condition is that consent to the disclosure has been obtained from—

> (a) the person from whom the information was initially obtained under or as a result of any provision of this Part (if the identity of that person is known); and
> (b) if different—
>> (i) the individual to whose affairs the information relates, or
>> (ii) the person for the time being carrying on the business to which the information relates.

(3) Subsection (1) does not apply to a disclosure of information—

> (a) made for the purpose of—
>> (i) facilitating the performance of any relevant functions of a designated person;
>> (ii) facilitating the performance of any functions of the Commission in respect of Community law about competition;
>> (iii) facilitating the performance by the Comptroller and Auditor General of any of his functions;
>> (iv) criminal proceedings in any part of the United Kingdom;
> (b) made with a view to the institution of, or otherwise for the purposes of, civil proceedings brought under or in connection with this Part;
> (c) made in connection with the investigation of any criminal offence triable in the United Kingdom or in any part of the United Kingdom; or
> (d) which is required to meet a Community obligation.

(4) In subsection (3) "relevant functions" and "designated person" have the meaning given in Schedule 11.

(5) Subsection (1) also does not apply to a disclosure of information made for the purpose of facilitating the performance of specified functions of any specified person.

(6) In subsection (5) "specified" means specified in an order made by the Secretary of State.

(7) If information is disclosed to the public in circumstances in which the disclosure does not contravene subsection (1), that subsection does not prevent its further disclosure by any person.

(8) A person who contravenes this section is guilty of an offence and liable—

> (a) on summary conviction, to a fine not exceeding the statutory maximum; or
> (b) on conviction on indictment, to imprisonment for a term not exceeding two years or to a fine or to both.

Director and Secretary of State to have regard to certain matters in relation to the disclosure of information.

56.—(1) This section applies if the Secretary of State or the Director is considering whether to disclose any information acquired by him under, or as a result of, any provision of this Part.

(2) He must have regard to the need for excluding, so far as is practicable, information the disclosure of which would in his opinion be contrary to the public interest.

(3) He must also have regard to—

    (a) the need for excluding, so far as is practicable—

        (i) commercial information the disclosure of which would, or might, in his opinion, significantly harm the legitimate business interests of the undertaking to which it relates, or

        (ii) information relating to the private affairs of an individual the disclosure of which would, or might, in his opinion, significantly harm his interests; and

    (b) the extent to which the disclosure is necessary for the purposes for which the Secretary of State or the Director is proposing to make the disclosure.

Defamation.

57. For the purposes of the law relating to defamation, absolute privilege attaches to any advice, guidance, notice or direction given, or decision made, by the Director in the exercise of any of his functions under this Part.

Findings of fact by Director

Findings of fact by Director.

58.—(1) Unless the court directs otherwise or the Director has decided to take further action in accordance with section 16(2) or 24(2), a Director's finding which is relevant to an issue arising in Part I proceedings is binding on the parties if—

    (a) the time for bringing an appeal in respect of the finding has expired and the relevant party has not brought such an appeal; or

    (b) the decision of an appeal tribunal on such an appeal has confirmed the finding.

(2) In this section—

    "a Director's finding" means a finding of fact made by the Director in the course of—

        (a) determining an application for a decision under section 14 or 22, or

        (b) conducting an investigation under section 25;

    "Part I proceedings" means proceedings—

        (a) in respect of an alleged infringement of the Chapter I prohibition or of the Chapter II prohibition; but

        (b) which are brought otherwise than by the Director;

"relevant party" means—

> (a) in relation to the Chapter I prohibition, a party to the agreement which is alleged to have infringed the prohibition; and
>
> (b) in relation to the Chapter II prohibition, the undertaking whose conduct is alleged to have infringed the prohibition.

(3) Rules of court may make provision in respect of assistance to be given by the Director to the court in Part I proceedings.

Interpretation and governing principles

Interpretation.

59.—(1) In this Part—

"appeal tribunal" means an appeal tribunal established in accordance with the provisions of Part III of Schedule 7 for the purpose of hearing an appeal under section 46 or 47;

"Article 85" means Article 85 of the Treaty;

"Article 86" means Article 86 of the Treaty;

"block exemption" has the meaning given in section 6(4);

"block exemption order" has the meaning given in section 6(2);

"the Chapter I prohibition" has the meaning given in section 2(8);

"the Chapter II prohibition" has the meaning given in section 18(4);

"the Commission" (except in relation to the Competition Commission) means the European Commission;

"the Council" means the Council of the European Union;

"the court", except in sections 58 and 60 and the expression "European Court", means—

> (a) in England and Wales, the High Court;
>
> (b) in Scotland, the Court of Session; and
>
> (c) in Northern Ireland, the High Court;

"the Director" means the Director General of Fair Trading;

"document" includes information recorded in any form;

"the EEA Agreement" means the Agreement on the European Economic Area signed at Oporto on 2nd May 1992 as it has effect for the time being;

"the European Court" means the Court of Justice of the European Communities and includes the Court of First Instance;

"individual exemption" has the meaning given in section 4(2);

"information" includes estimates and forecasts;

"investigating officer" has the meaning given in section 27(1);

"Minister of the Crown" has the same meaning as in the Ministers of the Crown Act 1975 (c. 26);

"officer", in relation to a body corporate, includes a director, manager or secretary and, in relation to a partnership in Scotland, includes a partner;

"parallel exemption" has the meaning given in section 10(3);

"person" in addition to the meaning given by the Interpretation Act 1978 (c. 30), includes any undertaking;

"premises" does not include domestic premises unless—

(a) they are also used in connection with the affairs of an undertaking, or

(b) documents relating to the affairs of an undertaking are kept there,

but does include any vehicle;

"prescribed" means prescribed by regulations made by the Secretary of State;

"regulator" has the meaning given by section 54;

"section 11 exemption" has the meaning given in section 11(3); and

"the Treaty" means the treaty establishing the European Community.

(2) The fact that to a limited extent the Chapter I prohibition does not apply to an agreement, because of an exclusion provided by or under this Part or any other enactment, does not require those provisions of the agreement to which the exclusion relates to be disregarded when considering whether the agreement infringes the prohibition for other reasons.

(3) For the purposes of this Part, the power to require information, in relation to information recorded otherwise than in a legible form, includes power to require a copy of it in a legible form.

(4) Any power conferred on the Director by this Part to require information includes power to require any document which he believes may contain that information.

Principles to be applied in determining questions.

60.—(1) The purpose of this section is to ensure that so far as is possible (having regard to any relevant differences between the provisions concerned), questions arising under this Part in relation to competition within the United Kingdom are dealt with in a manner which is consistent with the treatment of corresponding questions arising in Community law in relation to competition within the Community.

(2) At any time when the court determines a question arising under this Part, it must act (so far as is compatible with the provisions of this Part and whether or not it would otherwise be required to do so) with a view to securing that there is no inconsistency between—

(a) the principles applied, and decision reached, by the court in determining that question; and

(b) the principles laid down by the Treaty and the European Court, and any relevant decision of that Court, as applicable at that time in determining any corresponding question arising in Community law.

(3) The court must, in addition, have regard to any relevant decision or statement of the Commission.

(4) Subsections (2) and (3) also apply to—

(a) the Director; and

(b) any person acting on behalf of the Director, in connection with any matter arising under this Part.

(5) In subsections (2) and (3), "court" means any court or tribunal.

(6) In subsections (2)(b) and (3), "decision" includes a decision as to—

(a) the interpretation of any provision of Community law;

(b) the civil liability of an undertaking for harm caused by its infringement of Community law.

Part II Investigations in relation to Articles 85 and 86

Introduction.

61.—(1) In this Part—

"Article 85" and "Article 86" have the same meaning as in Part I;

"authorised officer", in relation to the Director, means an officer to whom an authorisation has been given under subsection (2);

"the Commission" means the European Commission;

"the Director" means the Director General of Fair Trading;

"Commission investigation" means an investigation ordered by a decision of the Commission under a prescribed provision of Community law relating to Article 85 or 86;

"Director's investigation" means an investigation conducted by the Director at the request of the Commission under a prescribed provision of Community law relating to Article 85 or 86;

"Director's special investigation" means a Director's investigation conducted at the request of the Commission in connection with a Commission investigation;

"prescribed" means prescribed by order made by the Secretary of State;

"premises" means—

(a) in relation to a Commission investigation, any premises, land or means of transport which an official of the Commission has power to enter in the course of the investigation; and

(b) in relation to a Director's investigation, any premises, land or means of transport which an official of the Commission would have power to enter if the investigation were being conducted by the Commission.

(2) For the purposes of a Director's investigation, an officer of the Director to whom an authorisation has been given has the powers of an official authorised by the Commission in connection with a Commission investigation under the relevant provision.

(3) "Authorisation" means an authorisation given in writing by the Director which—

(a) identifies the officer;

(b) specifies the subject matter and purpose of the investigation; and

    (c) draws attention to any penalties which a person may incur in connection with the investigation under the relevant provision of Community law.

Power to enter premises: Commission investigations.

62.—(1) A judge of the High Court may issue a warrant if satisfied, on an application made to the High Court in accordance with rules of court by the Director, that a Commission investigation is being, or is likely to be, obstructed.

(2) A Commission investigation is being obstructed if—

    (a) an official of the Commission ("the Commission official"), exercising his power in accordance with the provision under which the investigation is being conducted, has attempted to enter premises but has been unable to do so; and

    (b) there are reasonable grounds for suspecting that there are books or records on the premises which the Commission official has power to examine.

(3) A Commission investigation is also being obstructed if there are reasonable grounds for suspecting that there are books or records on the premises—

    (a) the production of which has been required by an official of the Commission exercising his power in accordance with the provision under which the investigation is being conducted; and

    (b) which have not been produced as required.

(4) A Commission investigation is likely to be obstructed if—

    (a) an official of the Commission ("the Commission official") is authorised for the purpose of the investigation;

    (b) there are reasonable grounds for suspecting that there are books or records on the premises which the Commission official has power to examine; and

    (c) there are also reasonable grounds for suspecting that, if the Commission official attempted to exercise his power to examine any of the books or records, they would not be produced but would be concealed, removed, tampered with or destroyed.

(5) A warrant under this section shall authorise—

    (a) a named officer of the Director,

    (b) any other of his officers whom he has authorised in writing to accompany the named officer, and

    (c) any official of the Commission authorised for the purpose of the Commission investigation,

to enter the premises specified in the warrant, and search for books and records which the official has power to examine, using such force as is reasonably necessary for the purpose.

(6) Any person entering any premises by virtue of a warrant under this section may take with him such equipment as appears to him to be necessary.

(7) On leaving any premises entered by virtue of the warrant the named officer must, if the premises are unoccupied or the occupier is temporarily absent, leave them as effectively secured as he found them.

(8) A warrant under this section continues in force until the end of the period of one month beginning with the day on which it is issued.

(9) In the application of this section to Scotland, references to the High Court are to be read as references to the Court of Session.

Power to enter premises: Director's special investigations.

63.—(1) A judge of the High Court may issue a warrant if satisfied, on an application made to the High Court in accordance with rules of court by the Director, that a Director's special investigation is being, or is likely to be, obstructed.

(2) A Director's special investigation is being obstructed if—

    (a) an authorised officer of the Director has attempted to enter premises but has been unable to do so;

    (b) the officer has produced his authorisation to the undertaking, or association of undertakings, concerned; and

    (c) there are reasonable grounds for suspecting that there are books or records on the premises which the officer has power to examine.

(3) A Director's special investigation is also being obstructed if—

    (a) there are reasonable grounds for suspecting that there are books or records on the premises which an authorised officer of the Director has power to examine;

    (b) the officer has produced his authorisation to the undertaking, or association of undertakings, and has required production of the books or records; and

    (c) the books and records have not been produced as required.

(4) A Director's special investigation is likely to be obstructed if—

    (a) there are reasonable grounds for suspecting that there are books or records on the premises which an authorised officer of the Director has power to examine; and

    (b) there are also reasonable grounds for suspecting that, if the officer attempted to exercise his power to examine any of the books or records, they would not be produced but would be concealed, removed, tampered with or destroyed.

(5) A warrant under this section shall authorise—

    (a) a named authorised officer of the Director,

    (b) any other authorised officer accompanying the named officer, and

    (c) any named official of the Commission,

to enter the premises specified in the warrant, and search for books and records which the authorised officer has power to examine, using such force as is reasonably necessary for the purpose.

(6) Any person entering any premises by virtue of a warrant under this section may take with him such equipment as appears to him to be necessary.

(7) On leaving any premises which he has entered by virtue of the warrant the named officer must, if the premises are unoccupied or the occupier is temporarily absent, leave them as effectively secured as he found them.

(8) A warrant under this section continues in force until the end of the period of one month beginning with the day on which it is issued.

(9) In the application of this section to Scotland, references to the High Court are to be read as references to the Court of Session.

Entry of premises under sections 62 and 63: supplementary.

64.—(1) A warrant issued under section 62 or 63 must indicate—

    (a) the subject matter and purpose of the investigation;

    (b) the nature of the offence created by section 65.

(2) The powers conferred by section 62 or 63 are to be exercised on production of a warrant issued under that section.

(3) If there is no one at the premises when the named officer proposes to execute such a warrant he must, before executing it—

    (a) take such steps as are reasonable in all the circumstances to inform the occupier of the intended entry; and

    (b) if the occupier is informed, afford him or his legal or other representative a reasonable opportunity to be present when the warrant is executed.

(4) If the named officer is unable to inform the occupier of the intended entry he must, when executing the warrant, leave a copy of it in a prominent place on the premises.

(5) In this section—

    "named officer" means the officer named in the warrant; and

    "occupier", in relation to any premises, means a person whom the named officer reasonably believes is the occupier of those premises.

Offences.

65.—(1) A person is guilty of an offence if he intentionally obstructs any person in the exercise of his powers under a warrant issued under section 62 or 63.

(2) A person guilty of an offence under subsection (1) is liable—

    (a) on summary conviction, to a fine not exceeding the statutory maximum;

    (b) on conviction on indictment, to imprisonment for a term not exceeding two years or to a fine or to both.

Part III Monopolies

[*Sections 66-69, not reproduced in this work, amend sections 44, 46, 83 and 137 of the Fair Trading Act 1973 in relation to monopoly investigations, in particular by increasing the DGFT's investigatory powers.*]

Part IV Supplemental and transitional

Contracts as to patented products etc.

70. Sections 44 and 45 of the Patents Act 1977 (c. 37) shall cease to have effect.

Regulations, orders and rules.

71.—(1) Any power to make regulations or orders which is conferred by this Act is exercisable by statutory instrument.

(2) The power to make rules which is conferred by section 48 is exercisable by statutory instrument.

(3) Any statutory instrument made under this Act may—

    (a) contain such incidental, supplemental, consequential and transitional provision as the Secretary of State considers appropriate; and

    (b) make different provision for different cases.

(4) No order is to be made under—

    (a) section 3,

    (b) section 19,

    (c) section 36(8),

    (d) section 50, or

    (e) paragraph 6(3) of Schedule 4,

unless a draft of the order has been laid before Parliament and approved by a resolution of each House.

(5) Any statutory instrument made under this Act, apart from one made—

    (a) under any of the provisions mentioned in subsection (4), or

    (b) under section 76(3),

shall be subject to annulment by a resolution of either House of Parliament.

Offences by bodies corporate etc.

72.—(1) This section applies to an offence under any of sections 42 to 44, 55(8) or 65.

(2) If an offence committed by a body corporate is proved—

    (a) to have been committed with the consent or connivance of an officer, or

    (b) to be attributable to any neglect on his part,

the officer as well as the body corporate is guilty of the offence and liable to be proceeded against and punished accordingly.

(3) In subsection (2) "officer", in relation to a body corporate, means a director, manager, secretary or other similar officer of the body, or a person purporting to act in any such capacity.

(4) If the affairs of a body corporate are managed by its members, subsection (2) applies in relation to the acts and defaults of a member in connection with his functions of management as if he were a director of the body corporate.

(5) If an offence committed by a partnership in Scotland is proved—

    (a) to have been committed with the consent or connivance of a partner, or

    (b) to be attributable to any neglect on his part,

the partner as well as the partnership is guilty of the offence and liable to be proceeded against and punished accordingly.

(6) In subsection (5) "partner" includes a person purporting to act as a partner.

Crown application.

73.—(1) Any provision made by or under this Act binds the Crown except that—

    (a) the Crown is not criminally liable as a result of any such provision;

    (b) the Crown is not liable for any penalty under any such provision; and

    (c) nothing in this Act affects Her Majesty in her private capacity.

(2) Subsection (1)(a) does not affect the application of any provision of this Act in relation to persons in the public service of the Crown.

(3) Subsection (1)(c) is to be interpreted as if section 38(3) of the Crown Proceedings Act 1947 (c. 44) (interpretation of references in that Act to Her Majesty in her private capacity) were contained in this Act.

(4) If, in respect of a suspected infringement of the Chapter I prohibition or of the Chapter II prohibition otherwise than by the Crown or a person in the public service of the Crown, an investigation is conducted under section 25—

    (a) the power conferred by section 27 may not be exercised in relation to land which is occupied by a government department, or otherwise for purposes of the Crown, without the written consent of the appropriate person; and

    (b) section 28 does not apply in relation to land so occupied.

(5) In any case in which consent is required under subsection (4), the person who is the appropriate person in relation to that case is to be determined in accordance with regulations made by the Secretary of State.

(6) Sections 62 and 63 do not apply in relation to land which is occupied by a government department, or otherwise for purposes of the Crown, unless the matter being investigated is a suspected infringement by the Crown or by a person in the public service of the Crown.

(7) In subsection (6) "infringement" means an infringement of Community law relating to Article 85 or 86 of the Treaty establishing the European Community.

(8) If the Secretary of State certifies that it appears to him to be in the interests of national security that the powers of entry—

    (a) conferred by section 27, or

    (b) that may be conferred by a warrant under section 28, 62 or 63,

should not be exercisable in relation to premises held or used by or on behalf of the Crown and which are specified in the certificate, those powers are not exercisable in relation to those premises.

(9) Any amendment, repeal or revocation made by this Act binds the Crown to the extent that the enactment amended, repealed or revoked binds the Crown.

Amendments, transitional provisions, savings and repeals.

74.—(1) The minor and consequential amendments set out in Schedule 12 are to have effect.

(2) The transitional provisions and savings set out in Schedule 13 are to have effect.

(3) The enactments set out in Schedule 14 are repealed.

Consequential and supplementary provision.

75.—(1) The Secretary of State may by order make such incidental, consequential, transitional or supplemental provision as he thinks necessary or expedient for the general purposes, or any particular purpose, of this Act or in consequence of any of its provisions or for giving full effect to it.

(2) An order under subsection (1) may, in particular, make provision—

(a) for enabling any person by whom any powers will become exercisable, on a date specified by or under this Act, by virtue of any provision made by or under this Act to take before that date any steps which are necessary as a preliminary to the exercise of those powers;

(b) for making savings, or additional savings, from the effect of any repeal made by or under this Act.

(3) Amendments made under this section shall be in addition, and without prejudice, to those made by or under any other provision of this Act.

(4) No other provision of this Act restricts the powers conferred by this section.

Short title, commencement and extent.

76.—(1) This Act may be cited as the Competition Act 1998.

(2) Sections 71 and 75 and this section and paragraphs 1 to 7 and 35 of Schedule 13 come into force on the passing of this Act.

(3) The other provisions of this Act come into force on such day as the Secretary of State may by order appoint; and different days may be appointed for different purposes.

(4) This Act extends to Northern Ireland.

Schedules

Schedule I Exclusions: mergers and concentrations

Part I Mergers

Enterprises ceasing to be distinct: the Chapter I prohibition

Sections 3(1)(a) and 19(1)(a).

1.—(1) To the extent to which an agreement (either on its own or when taken together with another agreement) results, or if carried out would result, in any two enterprises ceasing to be distinct enterprises for the purposes of Part V of the Fair Trading Act 1973 (c. 41) ("the 1973 Act"), the Chapter I prohibition does not apply to the agreement.

(2) The exclusion provided by sub-paragraph (1) extends to any provision directly related and necessary to the implementation of the merger provisions.

(3) In sub-paragraph (2) "merger provisions" means the provisions of the agreement which cause, or if carried out would cause, the agreement to have the result mentioned in sub-paragraph (1).

(4) Section 65 of the 1973 Act applies for the purposes of this paragraph as if—

> (a) in subsection (3) (circumstances in which a person or group of persons may be treated as having control of an enterprise), and
>
> (b) in subsection (4) (circumstances in which a person or group of persons may be treated as bringing an enterprise under their control),

for "may" there were substituted "must".

Enterprises ceasing to be distinct: the Chapter II prohibition

2.—(1) To the extent to which conduct (either on its own or when taken together with other conduct)—

> (a) results in any two enterprises ceasing to be distinct enterprises for the purposes of Part V of the 1973 Act), or
>
> (b) is directly related and necessary to the attainment of the result mentioned in paragraph (a),

the Chapter II prohibition does not apply to that conduct.

(2) Section 65 of the 1973 Act applies for the purposes of this paragraph as it applies for the purposes of paragraph 1.

Transfer of a newspaper or of newspaper assets

3.—(1) The Chapter I prohibition does not apply to an agreement to the extent to which it constitutes, or would if carried out constitute, a transfer of a newspaper or of newspaper assets for the purposes of section 57 of the 1973 Act.

(2) The Chapter II prohibition does not apply to conduct (either on its own or when taken together with other conduct) to the extent to which—

> (a) it constitutes such a transfer, or
>
> (b) it is directly related and necessary to the implementation of the transfer.

(3) The exclusion provided by sub-paragraph (1) extends to any provision directly related and necessary to the implementation of the transfer.

Withdrawal of the paragraph 1 exclusion

4.—(1) The exclusion provided by paragraph 1 does not apply to a particular agreement if the Director gives a direction under this paragraph to that effect.

(2) If the Director is considering whether to give a direction under this paragraph, he may by notice in writing require any party to the agreement in

question to give him such information in connection with the agreement as he may require.

(3) The Director may give a direction under this paragraph only as provided in sub-paragraph (4) or (5).

(4) If at the end of such period as may be specified in rules under section 51 a person has failed, without reasonable excuse, to comply with a requirement imposed under sub-paragraph (2), the Director may give a direction under this paragraph.

(5) The Director may also give a direction under this paragraph if—

    (a) he considers—

            (i) that the agreement will, if not excluded, infringe the Chapter I prohibition; and

            (ii) that he is not likely to grant it an unconditional individual exemption; and

    (b) the agreement is not a protected agreement.

(6) For the purposes of sub-paragraph (5), an individual exemption is unconditional if no conditions or obligations are imposed in respect of it under section 4(3)(a).

(7) A direction under this paragraph—

    (a) must be in writing;

    (b) may be made so as to have effect from a date specified in the direction (which may not be earlier than the date on which it is given).

Protected agreements

5. An agreement is a protected agreement for the purposes of paragraph 4 if—

    (a) the Secretary of State has announced his decision not to make a merger reference to the Competition Commission under section 64 of the 1973 Act in connection with the agreement;

    (b) the Secretary of State has made a merger reference to the Competition Commission under section 64 of the 1973 Act in connection with the agreement and the Commission has found that the agreement has given rise to, or would if carried out give rise to, a merger situation qualifying for investigation;

    (c) the agreement does not fall within sub-paragraph (a) or (b) but has given rise to, or would if carried out give rise to, enterprises to which it relates being regarded under section 65 of the 1973 Act as ceasing to be distinct enterprises (otherwise than as the result of subsection (3) or (4)(b) of that section); or

    (d) the Secretary of State has made a merger reference to the Competition Commission under section 32 of the Water Industry Act 1991 (c. 56) in connection with the agreement and the Commission has found that the agreement has given rise to, or would if carried out give rise to, a merger of the kind to which that section applies.

Part II Concentrations subject to EC controls

6.—(1) To the extent to which an agreement (either on its own or when taken together with another agreement) gives rise to, or would if carried out give rise to, a concentration, the Chapter I prohibition does not apply to the agreement if the Merger Regulation gives the Commission exclusive jurisdiction in the matter.

(2) To the extent to which conduct (either on its own or when taken together with other conduct) gives rise to, or would if pursued give rise to, a concentration, the Chapter II prohibition does not apply to the conduct if the Merger Regulation gives the Commission exclusive jurisdiction in the matter.

(3) In this paragraph—

"concentration" means a concentration with a Community dimension within the meaning of Articles 1 and 3 of the Merger Regulation; and

"Merger Regulation" means Council Regulation (EEC) No 4064/89 of 21st December 1989 on the control of concentrations between undertakings as amended by Council Regulation (EC) No 1310/97 of 30th June 1997.

Schedule 2 Exclusions: other competition scrutiny

Section 3(1)(b).

[*This Schedule, not reproduced in this work, amends the legislation applying specific competition rules in the fields of financial services, company law, broadcasting and environmental protection. The thrust of the amendments is to replace references to the RTPA or the Competition Act 1980 with reference to the Competition Act 1998. The amendments concern sections 125-127 of the Financial Services Act 1986, paragraph 9 of Schedule 14 of the Companies Act 1989 (and the equivalent provisions in Northern Ireland), section 194A of the Broadcasting Act 1990 and networking arrangements covered by that Act and section 94 of the Environment Act 1995.*]

Schedule 3 General exclusions

Planning obligations

Sections 3(1)(c) and 19(1)(b).

1.—(1) The Chapter I prohibition does not apply to an agreement—

(a) to the extent to which it is a planning obligation;

(b) which is made under section 75 (agreements regulating development or use of land) or 246 (agreements relating to Crown land) of the Town and Country Planning (Scotland) Act 1997 (c. 8); or

(c) which is made under Article 40 of the Planning (Northern Ireland) Order 1991 (S.I. 1991/1220 (N.I. 11)).

(2) In sub-paragraph (1)(a), "planning obligation" means—

    (a) a planning obligation for the purposes of section 106 of the Town and Country Planning Act 1990 (c. 8); or

    (b) a planning obligation for the purposes of section 299A of that Act.

Section 21(2) agreements

2.—(1) The Chapter I prohibition does not apply to an agreement in respect of which a direction under section 21(2) of the Restrictive Trade Practices Act 1976 is in force immediately before the coming into force of section 2 ("a section 21(2) agreement").

(2) If a material variation is made to a section 21(2) agreement, sub-paragraph (1) ceases to apply to the agreement on the coming into force of the variation.

(3) Sub-paragraph (1) does not apply to a particular section 21(2) agreement if the Director gives a direction under this paragraph to that effect.

(4) If the Director is considering whether to give a direction under this paragraph, he may by notice in writing require any party to the agreement in question to give him such information in connection with the agreement as he may require.

(5) The Director may give a direction under this paragraph only as provided in sub-paragraph (6) or (7).

(6) If at the end of such period as may be specified in rules under section 51 a person has failed, without reasonable excuse, to comply with a requirement imposed under sub-paragraph (4), the Director may give a direction under this paragraph.

(7) The Director may also give a direction under this paragraph if he considers—

    (a) that the agreement will, if not excluded, infringe the Chapter I prohibition; and

    (b) that he is not likely to grant it an unconditional individual exemption.

(8) For the purposes of sub-paragraph (7) an individual exemption is unconditional if no conditions or obligations are imposed in respect of it under section 4(3)(a).

(9) A direction under this paragraph—

    (a) must be in writing;

    (b) may be made so as to have effect from a date specified in the direction (which may not be earlier than the date on which it is given).

EEA Regulated Markets

3.—(1) The Chapter I prohibition does not apply to an agreement for the constitution of an EEA regulated market to the extent to which the agreement relates to any of the rules made, or guidance issued, by that market.

(2) The Chapter I prohibition does not apply to a decision made by an EEA regulated market, to the extent to which the decision relates to any of the market's regulating provisions.

(3) The Chapter I prohibition does not apply to—

    (a) any practices of an EEA regulated market; or

    (b) any practices which are trading practices in relation to an EEA regulated market.

(4) The Chapter I prohibition does not apply to an agreement the parties to which are or include—

    (a) an EEA regulated market; or

    (b) a person who is subject to the rules of that market,

to the extent to which the agreement consists of provisions the inclusion of which is required or contemplated by the regulating provisions of that market.

(5) In this paragraph—

"EEA regulated market" is a market which—

    (a) is listed by an EEA State other than the United Kingdom pursuant to article 16 of Council Directive No. 93/22/EEC of 10th May 1993 on investment services in the securities field; and

    (b) operates without any requirement that a person dealing on the market should have a physical presence in the EEA State from which any trading facilities are provided or on any trading floor that the market may have;

"EEA State" means a State which is a contracting party to the EEA Agreement;

"regulating provisions", in relation to an EEA regulated market, means—

    (a) rules made, or guidance issued, by that market,

    (b) practices of that market, or

    (c) practices which, in relation to that market, are trading practices;

"trading practices", in relation to an EEA regulated market, means practices of persons who are subject to the rules made by that market, and—

    (a) which relate to business in respect of which those persons are subject to the rules of that market, and which are required or contemplated by those rules or by guidance issued by that market; or

    (b) which are otherwise attributable to the conduct of that market as such.

Services of general economic interest etc.

4. Neither the Chapter I prohibition nor the Chapter II prohibition applies to an undertaking entrusted with the operation of services of general economic interest or having the character of a revenue-producing monopoly in so far as the prohibition would obstruct the performance, in law or in fact, of the particular tasks assigned to that undertaking.

Compliance with legal requirements

5.—(1) The Chapter I prohibition does not apply to an agreement to the extent to which it is made in order to comply with a legal requirement.

(2) The Chapter II prohibition does not apply to conduct to the extent to which it is engaged in an order to comply with a legal requirement.

(3) In this paragraph "legal requirement" means a requirement—

    (a) imposed by or under any enactment in force in the United Kingdom;

    (b) imposed by or under the Treaty or the EEA Agreement and having legal effect in the United Kingdom without further enactment; or

    (c) imposed by or under the law in force in another Member State and having legal effect in the United Kingdom.

Avoidance of conflict with international obligations

6.—(1) If the Secretary of State is satisfied that, in order to avoid a conflict between provisions of this Part and an international obligation of the United Kingdom, it would be appropriate for the Chapter I prohibition not to apply to—

    (a) a particular agreement, or

    (b) any agreement of a particular description,

he may by order exclude the agreement, or agreements of that description, from the Chapter I prohibition.

(2) An order under sub-paragraph (1) may make provision for the exclusion of the agreement or agreements to which the order applies, or of such of them as may be specified, only in specified circumstances.

(3) An order under sub-paragraph (1) may also provide that the Chapter I prohibition is to be deemed never to have applied in relation to the agreement or agreements, or in relation to such of them as may be specified.

(4) If the Secretary of State is satisfied that, in order to avoid a conflict between provisions of this Part and an international obligation of the United Kingdom, it would be appropriate for the Chapter II prohibition not to apply in particular circumstances, he may by order provide for it not to apply in such circumstances as may be specified.

(5) An order under sub-paragraph (4) may provide that the Chapter II prohibition is to be deemed never to have applied in relation to specified conduct.

(6) An international arrangement relating to civil aviation and designated by an order made by the Secretary of State is to be treated as an international obligation for the purposes of this paragraph.

(7) In this paragraph and paragraph 7 "specified" means specified in the order.

Public policy

7.—(1) If the Secretary of State is satisfied that there are exceptional and compelling reasons of public policy why the Chapter I prohibition ought not to apply to—

(a) a particular agreement, or

(b) any agreement of a particular description,

he may by order exclude the agreement, or agreements of that description, from the Chapter I prohibition.

(2) An order under sub-paragraph (1) may make provision for the exclusion of the agreement or agreements to which the order applies, or of such of them as may be specified, only in specified circumstances.

(3) An order under sub-paragraph (1) may also provide that the Chapter I prohibition is to be deemed never to have applied in relation to the agreement or agreements, or in relation to such of them as may be specified.

(4) If the Secretary of State is satisfied that there are exceptional and compelling reasons of public policy why the Chapter II prohibition ought not to apply in particular circumstances, he may by order provide for it not to apply in such circumstances as may be specified.

(5) An order under sub-paragraph (4) may provide that the Chapter II prohibition is to be deemed never to have applied in relation to specified conduct.

Coal and steel

8.—(1) The Chapter I prohibition does not apply to an agreement which relates to a coal or steel product to the extent to which the ECSC Treaty gives the Commission exclusive jurisdiction in the matter.

(2) Sub-paragraph (1) ceases to have effect on the date on which the ECSC Treaty expires ("the expiry date").

(3) The Chapter II prohibition does not apply to conduct which relates to a coal or steel product to the extent to which the ECSC Treaty gives the Commission exclusive jurisdiction in the matter.

(4) Sub-paragraph (3) ceases to have effect on the expiry date.

(5) In this paragraph—

"coal or steel product" means any product of a kind listed in Annex I to the ECSC Treaty; and

"ECSC Treaty" means the Treaty establishing the European Coal and Steel Community.

Agricultural products

9.—(1) The Chapter I prohibition does not apply to an agreement to the extent to which it relates to production of or trade in an agricultural product and—

(a) forms an integral part of a national market organisation;

(b) is necessary for the attainment of the objectives set out in Article 39 of the Treaty; or

(c) is an agreement of farmers or farmers' associations (or associations of such associations) belonging to a single member State which concerns—

(i) the production or sale of agricultural products, or

(ii) the use of joint facilities for the storage, treatment or processing of agricultural products,

and under which there is no obligation to charge identical prices.

(2) If the Commission determines that an agreement does not fulfil the conditions specified by the provision for agricultural products for exclusion from Article 85(1), the exclusion provided by this paragraph ("the agriculture exclusion") is to be treated as ceasing to apply to the agreement on the date of the decision.

(3) The agriculture exclusion does not apply to a particular agreement if the Director gives a direction under this paragraph to that effect.

(4) If the Director is considering whether to give a direction under this paragraph, he may by notice in writing require any party to the agreement in question to give him such information in connection with the agreement as he may require.

(5) The Director may give a direction under this paragraph only as provided in sub-paragraph (6) or (7).

(6) If at the end of such period as may be specified in rules under section 51 a person has failed, without reasonable excuse, to comply with a requirement imposed under sub-paragraph (4), the Director may give a direction under this paragraph.

(7) The Director may also give a direction under this paragraph if he considers that an agreement (whether or not he considers that it infringes the Chapter I prohibition) is likely, or is intended, substantially and unjustifiably to prevent, restrict or distort competition in relation to an agricultural product.

(8) A direction under this paragraph—

  (a) must be in writing;

  (b) may be made so as to have effect from a date specified in the direction (which may not be earlier than the date on which it is given).

(9) In this paragraph—

"agricultural product" means any product of a kind listed in Annex II to the Treaty; and

"provision for agricultural products" means Council Regulation (EEC) No. 26/62 of 4th April 1962 applying certain rules of competition to production of and trade in agricultural products.

Schedule 4 Professional rules

Part I Exclusion

General

Section 3(l)(d).

1.—(1) To the extent to which an agreement (either on its own or when taken together with another agreement)—

(a) constitutes a designated professional rule,

(b) imposes obligations arising from designated professional rules, or

(c) constitutes an agreement to act in accordance with such rules,

the Chapter I prohibition does not apply to the agreement.

(2) In this Schedule—

"designated" means designated by the Secretary of State under paragraph 2;

"professional rules" means rules regulating a professional service or the persons providing, or wishing to provide, that service;

"professional service" means any of the services described in Part II of this Schedule; and

"rules" includes regulations, codes of practice and statements of principle.

Designated rules

2.—(1) The Secretary of State must establish and maintain a list designating, for the purposes of this Schedule, rules—

(a) which are notified to him under paragraph 3; and

(b) which, in his opinion, are professional rules.

(2) The list is to be established, and any alteration in the list is to be effected, by an order made by the Secretary of State.

(3) The designation of any rule is to have effect from such date (which may be earlier than the date on which the order listing it is made) as may be specified in that order.

Application for designation

3.—(1) Any body regulating a professional service or the persons who provide, or wish to provide, that service may apply to the Secretary of State for rules of that body to be designated.

(2) An application under this paragraph must—

(a) be accompanied by a copy of the rules to which it relates; and

(b) be made in the prescribed manner.

Alterations

4.—(1) A rule does not cease to be a designated professional rule merely because it is altered.

(2) If such a rule is altered (whether by being modified, revoked or replaced), the body concerned must notify the Secretary of State and the Director of the alteration as soon as is reasonably practicable.

Reviewing the list

5.—(1) The Secretary of State must send to the Director—

(a) a copy of any order made under paragraph 2; and

(b) a copy of the professional rules to which the order relates.

(2) The Director must—
   (a) retain any copy of a professional rule which is sent to him under sub-paragraph (1)(b) so long as the rule remains in force;
   (b) maintain a copy of the list, as altered from time to time; and
   (c) keep the list under review.

(3) If the Director considers—
   (a) that, with a view to restricting the exclusion provided by this Schedule, some or all of the rules of a particular body should no longer be designated, or
   (b) that rules which are not designated should be designated,
he must advise the Secretary of State accordingly.

Removal from the list

6.—(1) This paragraph applies if the Secretary of State receives advice under paragraph 5(3)(a).

(2) If it appears to the Secretary of State that another Minister of the Crown has functions in relation to the professional service concerned, he must consult that Minister.

(3) If it appears to the Secretary of State, having considered the Director's advice and the advice of any other Minister resulting from consultation under sub-paragraph (2), that the rules in question should no longer be designated, he may by order revoke their designation.

(4) Revocation of a designation is to have effect from such date as the order revoking it may specify.

Inspection

7.—(1) Any person may inspect, and take a copy of—
   (a) any entry in the list of designated professional rules as kept by the Director under paragraph 5(2); or
   (b) any copy of professional rules retained by him under paragraph 5(1).

(2) The right conferred by sub-paragraph (1) is to be exercised only—
   (a) at a time which is reasonable;
   (b) on payment of such fee as the Director may determine; and
   (c) at such offices of his as the Director may direct.

Part II Professional services

Legal

8. The services of barristers, advocates or solicitors.

Medical

9. The provision of medical or surgical advice or attendance and the performance of surgical operations.

Dental

10. Any services falling within the practice of dentistry within the meaning of the Dentists Act 1984 (c. 24).

Ophthalmic

11. The testing of sight.

Veterinary

12. Any services which constitute veterinary surgery within the meaning of the Veterinary Surgeons Act 1966 (c. 36).

Nursing

13. The services of nurses.

Midwifery

14. The services of midwives.

Physiotherapy

15. The services of physiotherapists.

Chiropody

16. The services of chiropodists.

Architectural

17. The services of architects.

Accounting and auditing

18. The making or preparation of accounts or accounting records and the examination, verification and auditing of financial statements.

Insolvency

19. Insolvency services within the meaning of section 428 of the Insolvency Act 1986 (c. 45).

Patent agency

20. The services of registered patent agents (within the meaning of Part V of the Copyright, Designs and Patents Act 1988 (c. 48)).

21. The services of persons carrying on for gain in the United Kingdom the business of acting as agents or other representatives for or obtaining European patents or for the purpose of conducting proceedings in relation to applications for or otherwise in connection with such patents before the European Patent Office or the comptroller and whose names appear on the European list (within the meaning of Part V of the Copyright, Designs and Patents Act 1988).

Parliamentary agency

22. The services of parliamentary agents entered in the register in either House of Parliament as agents entitled to practise both in promoting and in opposing Bills.

Surveying

23. The services of surveyors of land, of quantity surveyors, of surveyors of buildings or other structures and of surveyors of ships.

Engineering and technology etc.

24. The services of persons practising or employed as consultants in the field of—
- (a) civil engineering;
- (b) mechanical, aeronautical, marine, electrical or electronic engineering;
- (c) mining, quarrying, soil analysis or other forms of mineralogy or geology;
- (d) agronomy, forestry, livestock rearing or ecology;
- (e) metallurgy, chemistry, biochemistry or physics; or
- (f) any other form of engineering or technology analogous to those mentioned in sub-paragraphs (a) to (e).

Educational

25. The provision of education or training.

Religious

26. The services of ministers of religion.

Schedule 5 Notification under Chapter I: procedure

Terms used

Section 12(2).

1. In this Schedule—
   "applicant" means the person making an application to which this Schedule applies;
   "application" means an application under section 13 or an application under section 14;

"application for guidance" means an application under section 13;
"application for a decision" means an application under section 14;
"rules" means rules made by the Director under section 51; and
"specified" means specified in the rules.

General rules about applications

2.—(1) An application must be made in accordance with rules.

(2) A party to an agreement who makes an application must take all reasonable steps to notify all other parties to the agreement of whom he is aware—

    (a) that the application has been made; and

    (b) as to whether it is for guidance or a decision.

(3) Notification under sub-paragaph (2) must be in the specified manner.

Preliminary investigation

3.—(1) If, after a preliminary investigation of an application, the Director considers that it is likely—

    (a) that the agreement concerned will infringe the Chapter I prohibition, and

    (b) that it would not be appropriate to grant the agreement an individual exemption,

he may make a decision ("a provisional decision") under this paragraph.

(2) If the Director makes a provisional decision—

    (a) the Director must notify the applicant in writing of his provisional decision; and

    (b) section 13(4) or (as the case may be) section 14(4) is to be taken as never having applied.

(3) When making a provisional decision, the Director must follow such procedure as may be specified.

(4) A provisional decision does not affect the final determination of an application.

(5) If the Director has given notice to the applicant under sub-paragraph (2) in respect of an application for a decision, he may continue with the application under section 14.

Procedure on application for guidance

4. When determining an application for guidance, the Director must follow such procedure as may be specified.

Procedure on application for a decision

5.—(1) When determining an application for a decision, the Director must follow such procedure as may be specified.

(2) The Director must arrange for the application to be published in such a way as he thinks most suitable for bringing it to the attention of those likely to be affected by it, unless he is satisfied that it will be sufficient for him to seek information from one or more particular persons other than the applicant.

(3) In determining the application, the Director must take into account any representations made to him by persons other than the applicant.

Publication of decisions

6. If the Director determines an application for a decision he must publish his decision, together with his reasons for making it, in such manner as may be specified.

Delay by the Director

7.—(1) This paragraph applies if the court is satisfied, on the application of a person aggrieved by the failure of the Director to determine an application for a decision in accordance with the specified procedure, that there has been undue delay on the part of the Director in determining the application.

(2) The court may give such directions to the Director as it considers appropriate for securing that the application is determined without unnecessary further delay.

Schedule 6 Notification under Chapter II: procedure

Terms used

Section 20(2).

1. In this Schedule—

"applicant" means the person making an application to which this Schedule applies;

"application" means an application under section 21 or an application under section 22;

"application for guidance" means an application under section 21;

"application for a decision" means an application under section 22;

"other party", in relation to conduct of two or more persons, means one of those persons other than the applicant;

"rules" means rules made by the Director under section 51; and

"specified" means specified in the rules.

General rules about applications

2.—(1) An application must be made in accordance with rules.

(2) If the conduct to which an application relates is conduct of two or more persons, the applicant must take all reasonable steps to notify all of the other parties of whom he is aware—

(a) that the application has been made; and

(b) as to whether it is for guidance or a decision.

(3) Notification under sub-paragraph (2) must be in the specified manner.

Preliminary investigation

3.—(1) If, after a preliminary investigation of an application, the Director considers that it is likely that the conduct concerned will infringe the Chapter II prohibition, he may make a decision ("a provisional decision") under this paragraph.

(2) If the Director makes a provisional decision, he must notify the applicant in writing of that decision.

(3) When making a provisional decision, the Director must follow such procedure as may be specified.

(4) A provisional decision does not affect the final determination of an application.

(5) If the Director has given notice to the applicant under sub-paragraph (2) in respect of an application for a decision, he may continue with the application under section 22.

Procedure on application for guidance

4. When determining an application for guidance, the Director must follow such procedure as may be specified.

Procedure on application for a decision

5.—(1) When determining an application for a decision, the Director must follow such procedure as may be specified.

(2) The Director must arrange for the application to be published in such a way as he thinks most suitable for bringing it to the attention of those likely to be affected by it, unless he is satisfied that it will be sufficient for him to seek information from one or more particular persons other than the applicant.

(3) In determining the application, the Director must take into account any representations made to him by persons other than the applicant.

Publication of decisions

6. If the Director determines an application for a decision he must publish his decision, together with his reasons for making it, in such manner as may be specified.

Delay by the Director

7.—(1) This paragraph applies if the court is satisfied, on the application of a person aggrieved by the failure of the Director to determine an application for a decision in accordance with the specified procedure, that there has been undue delay on the part of the Director in determining the application.

(2) The court may give such directions to the Director as it considers appropriate for securing that the application is determined without unnecessary further delay.

Schedule 7 The Competition Commission

Part I General

Interpretation

Section 45(7).
1. In this Schedule—
"the 1973 Act" means the Fair Trading Act 1973 (c. 41);
"appeal panel member" means a member appointed under paragraph 2(1)(a);
"Chairman" means the chairman of the Commission;
"the Commission" means the Competition Commission;
"Council" has the meaning given in paragraph 5;
"general functions" means any functions of the Commission other than functions—
(a) in connection with appeals under this Act; or
(b) which are to be discharged by the Council;
"member" means a member of the Commission;
"newspaper merger reference" means a newspaper merger reference under section 59 of the 1973 Act;
"President" has the meaning given by paragraph 4(2);
"reporting panel member" means a member appointed under paragraph 2(1)(b);
"secretary" means the secretary of the Commission appointed under paragraph 9; and
"specialist panel member" means a member appointed under any of the provisions mentioned in paragraph 2(1)(d).

Membership of the Commission

2.—(1) The Commission is to consist of—
(a) members appointed by the Secretary of State to form a panel for the purposes of the Commission's functions in relation to appeals;
(b) members appointed by the Secretary of State to form a panel for the purposes of the Commission's general functions;
(c) members appointed (in accordance with paragraph 15(5)) from the panel maintained under paragraph 22;
(d) members appointed by the Secretary of State under or by virtue of—

(i) section 12(4) or 14(8) of the Water Industry Act 1991 (c. 56);

(ii) section 12(9) of the Electricity Act 1989 (c. 29);

(iii) section 13(10) of the Telecommunications Act 1984 (c. 12);

(iv) Article 15(9) of the Electricity (Northern Ireland) Order 1992 (S.I. 1992/231 (N.I. 1)).

(2) A person who is appointed as a member of a kind mentioned in one of paragraphs (a) to (c) of sub-paragraph (3) may also be appointed as a member of either or both of the other kinds mentioned in those paragraphs.

(3) The kinds of member are—

(a) an appeal panel member;

(b) a reporting panel member;

(c) a specialist panel member.

(4) Before appointing a person who is qualified for appointment to the panel of chairmen (see paragraph 26(2)), the Secretary of State must consult the Lord Chancellor or Lord Advocate, as he considers appropriate.

(5) The validity of the Commission's proceedings is not affected by a defect in the appointment of a member.

Chairman and deputy chairmen

3.—(1) The Commission is to have a chairman appointed by the Secretary of State from among the reporting panel members.

(2) The Secretary of State may appoint one or more of the reporting panel members to act as deputy chairman.

(3) The Chairman, and any deputy chairman, may resign that office at any time by notice in writing addressed to the Secretary of State.

(4) If the Chairman (or a deputy chairman) ceases to be a member he also ceases to be Chairman (or a deputy chairman).

(5) If the Chairman is absent or otherwise unable to act, or there is no chairman, any of his functions may be performed—

(a) if there is one deputy chairman, by him;

(b) if there is more than one—

(i) by the deputy chairman designated by the Secretary of State; or

(ii) if no such designation has been made, by the deputy chairman designated by the deputy chairmen;

(c) if there is no deputy chairman able to act—

(i) by the member designated by the Secretary of State; or

(ii) if no such designation has been made, by the member designated by the Commission.

President

4.—(1) The Secretary of State must appoint one of the appeal panel members to preside over the discharge of the Commission's functions in relation to appeals.

(2) The member so appointed is to be known as the President of the Competition Commission Appeal Tribunals (but is referred to in this Schedule as "the President").

(3) The Secretary of State may not appoint a person to be the President unless that person—

    (a) has a ten year general qualification within the meaning of section 71 of the Courts and Legal Services Act 1990 (c. 41),

    (b) is an advocate or solicitor in Scotland of at least ten years' standing, or

    (c) is—

        (i) a member of the Bar of Northern Ireland of at least ten years' standing, or

        (ii) a solicitor of the Supreme Court of Northern Ireland of at least ten years' standing,

and appears to the Secretary of State to have appropriate experience and knowledge of competition law and practice.

(4) Before appointing the President, the Secretary of State must consult the Lord Chancellor or Lord Advocate, as he considers appropriate.

(5) If the President ceases to be a member he also ceases to be President.

The Council

5.—(1) The Commission is to have a management board to be known as the Competition Commission Council (but referred to in this Schedule as "the Council").

(2) The Council is to consist of—

    (a) the Chairman;

    (b) the President;

    (c) such other members as the Secretary of State may appoint; and

    (d) the secretary.

(3) In exercising its functions under paragraphs 3 and 7 to 12 and paragraph 5 of Schedule 8, the Commission is to act through the Council.

(4) The Council may determine its own procedure including, in particular, its quorum.

(5) The Chairman (and any person acting as Chairman) is to have a casting vote on any question being decided by the Council.

Term of office

6.—(1) Subject to the provisions of this Schedule, each member is to hold and vacate office in accordance with the terms of his appointment.

(2) A person is not to be appointed as a member for more than five years at a time.

(3) Any member may at any time resign by notice in writing addressed to the Secretary of State.

(4) The Secretary of State may remove a member on the ground of incapacity or misbehaviour.

(5) No person is to be prevented from being appointed as a member merely because he has previously been a member.

Expenses, remuneration and pensions

7.—(1) The Secretary of State shall pay to the Commission such sums as he considers appropriate to enable it to perform its functions.

(2) The Commission may pay, or make provision for paying, to or in respect of each member such salaries or other remuneration and such pensions, allowances, fees, expenses or gratuities as the Secretary of State may determine.

(3) If a person ceases to be a member otherwise than on the expiry of his term of office and it appears to the Secretary of State that there are special circumstances which make it right for him to receive compensation, the Commission may make a payment to him of such amount as the Secretary of State may determine.

(4) The approval of the Treasury is required for—
(a) any payment under sub-paragraph (1);
(b) any determination of the Secretary of State under sub-paragraph (2) or (3).

The Commission's powers

8. Subject to the provisions of this Schedule, the Commission has power to do anything (except borrow money)—
(a) calculated to facilitate the discharge of its functions; or
(b) incidental or conducive to the discharge of its functions.

Staff

9.—(1) The Commission is to have a secretary, appointed by the Secretary of State on such terms and conditions of service as he considers appropriate.

(2) The approval of the Treasury is required as to those terms and conditions.

(3) Before appointing a person to be secretary, the Secretary of State must consult the Chairman and the President.

(4) Subject to obtaining the approval of—
(a) the Secretary of State, as to numbers, and
(b) the Secretary of State and Treasury, as to terms and conditions of service,
the Commission may appoint such staff as it thinks appropriate.

Procedure

10. Subject to any provision made by or under this Act, the Commission may regulate its own procedure.

Application of seal and proof of instruments

11.—(1) The application of the seal of the Commission must be authenticated by the signature of the secretary or of some other person authorised for the purpose.

(2) Sub-paragraph (1) does not apply in relation to any document which is or is to be signed in accordance with the law of Scotland.

(3) A document purporting to be duly executed under the seal of the Commission—

    (a) is to be received in evidence; and

    (b) is to be taken to have been so executed unless the contrary is proved.

Accounts

12.—(1) The Commission must—

    (a) keep proper accounts and proper records in relation to its accounts;

    (b) prepare a statement of accounts in respect of each of its financial years; and

    (c) send copies of the statement to the Secretary of State and to the Comptroller and Auditor General before the end of the month of August next following the financial year to which the statement relates.

(2) The statement of accounts must comply with any directions given by the Secretary of State with the approval of the Treasury as to—

    (a) the information to be contained in it,

    (b) the manner in which the information contained in it is to be presented, or

    (c) the methods and principles according to which the statement is to be prepared,

and must contain such additional information as the Secretary of State may with the approval of the Treasury require to be provided for informing Parliament.

(3) The Comptroller and Auditor General must—

    (a) examine, certify and report on each statement received by him as a result of this paragraph; and

    (b) lay copies of each statement and of his report before each House of Parliament.

(4) In this paragraph "financial year" means the period beginning with the date on which the Commission is established and ending with March 31st next, and each successive period of twelve months.

Status

13.—(1) The Commission is not to be regarded as the servant or agent of the Crown or as enjoying any status, privilege or immunity of the Crown.

(2) The Commission's property is not to be regarded as property of, or held on behalf of, the Crown.

Part II Performance of the Commission's general functions

Interpretation

14. In this Part of this Schedule "group" means a group selected under paragraph 15.

Discharge of certain functions by groups

15.—(1) Except where sub-paragraph (7) gives the Chairman power to act on his own, any general function of the Commission must be performed through a group selected for the purpose by the Chairman.

(2) The group must consist of at least three persons one of whom may be the Chairman.

(3) In selecting the members of the group, the Chairman must comply with any requirement as to its constitution imposed by any enactment applying to specialist panel members.

(4) If the functions to be performed through the group relate to a newspaper merger reference, the group must, subject to sub-paragraph (5), consist of such reporting panel members as the Chairman may select.

(5) The Secretary of State may appoint one, two or three persons from the panel maintained under paragraph 22 to be members and, if he does so, the group—

    (a) must include that member or those members; and

    (b) if there are three such members, may (if the Chairman so decides) consist entirely of those members.

(6) Subject to sub-paragraphs (2) to (5), a group must consist of reporting panel members or specialist panel members selected by the Chairman.

(7) While a group is being constituted to perform a particular general function of the Commission, the Chairman may—

    (a) take such steps (falling within that general function) as he considers appropriate to facilitate the work of the group when it has been constituted; or

    (b) exercise the power conferred by section 75(5) of the 1973 Act (setting aside references).

Chairmen of groups

16. The Chairman must appoint one of the members of a group to act as the chairman of the group.

Replacement of member of group

17.—(1) If, during the proceedings of a group—

(a) a member of the group ceases to be a member of the Commission,

(b) the Chairman is satisfied that a member of the group will be unable for a substantial period to perform his duties as a member of the group, or

(c) it appears to the Chairman that because of a particular interest of a member of the group it is inappropriate for him to remain in the group,

the Chairman may appoint a replacement.

(2) The Chairman may also at any time appoint any reporting panel member to be an additional member of a group.

Attendance of other members

18.—(1) At the invitation of the chairman of a group, any reporting panel member who is not a member of the group may attend meetings or otherwise take part in the proceedings of the group.

(2) But any person attending in response to such an invitation may not—

(a) vote in any proceedings of the group; or

(b) have a statement of his dissent from a conclusion of the group included in a report made by them.

(3) Nothing in sub-paragraph (1) is to be taken to prevent a group, or a member of a group, from consulting any member of the Commission with respect to any matter or question with which the group is concerned.

Procedure

19.—(1) Subject to any special or general directions given by the Secretary of State, each group may determine its own procedure.

(2) Each group may, in particular, determine its quorum and determine—

(a) the extent, if any, to which persons interested or claiming to be interested in the subject-matter of the reference are allowed—

(i) to be present or to be heard, either by themselves or by their representatives;

(ii) to cross-examine witnesses; or

(iii) otherwise to take part; and

(b) the extent, if any, to which sittings of the group are to be held in public.

(3) In determining its procedure a group must have regard to any guidance issued by the Chairman.

(4) Before issuing any guidance for the purposes of this paragraph the Chairman must consult the members of the Commission.

Effect of exercise of functions by group

20.—(1) Subject to sub-paragraph (2), anything done by or in relation to a group in, or in connection with, the performance of functions to be performed by the group is to have the same effect as if done by or in relation to the Commission.

(2) For the purposes of—

(a) sections 56 and 73 of the 1973 Act,

(b) section 19A of the Agricultural Marketing Act 1958 (c. 47),

(c) Articles 23 and 42 of the Agricultural Marketing (Northern Ireland) Order 1982 (S.I. 1982/1080 (N.I. 12)),

a conclusion contained in a report of a group is to be disregarded if the conclusion is not that of at least two-thirds of the members of the group.

Casting votes

21. The chairman of a group is to have a casting vote on any question to be decided by the group.

Newspaper merger references

22. The Secretary of State must maintain a panel of persons whom he regards as suitable for selection as members of a group constituted in connection with a newspaper merger reference.

Part III Appeals

Interpretation

23. In this Part of this Schedule—

"panel of chairmen" means the panel appointed under paragraph 26; and "tribunal" means an appeal tribunal constituted in accordance with paragraph 27.

Training of appeal panel members

24. The President must arrange such training for appeal panel members as he considers appropriate.

Acting President

25. If the President is absent or otherwise unable to act, the Secretary of State may appoint as acting president an appeal panel member who is qualified to act as chairman of a tribunal.

Panel of tribunal chairmen

26.—(1) There is to be a panel of appeal panel members appointed by the Secretary of State for the purposes of providing chairmen of appeal tribunals established under this Part of this Schedule.

(2) A person is qualified for appointment to the panel of chairmen only if—

(a) he has a seven year general qualification within the meaning of section 71 of the Courts and Legal Services Act 1990 (c. 41),

(b) he is an advocate or solicitor in Scotland of at least seven years' standing, or

(c) he is—

(i) a member of the Bar of Northern Ireland of at least seven years' standing, or

(ii) a solicitor of the Supreme Court of Northern Ireland of at least seven years' standing,

and appears to the Secretary of State to have appropriate experience and knowledge of competition law and practice.

Constitution of tribunals

27.—(1) On receipt of a notice of appeal, the President must constitute an appeal tribunal to deal with the appeal.

(2) An appeal tribunal is to consist of—

(a) a chairman, who must be either the President or a person appointed by him to be chairman from the panel of chairmen; and

(b) two other appeal panel members appointed by the President.

Part IV Miscellaneous

Disqualification of members for House of Commons

28. In Part II of Schedule 1 to the House of Commons Disqualification Act 1975 (c. 24) (bodies of which all members are disqualified) insert at the appropriate place—

"The Competition Commission".

Disqualification of members for Northern Ireland Assembly

29. In Part II of Schedule 1 to the Northern Ireland Assembly Disqualification Act 1975 (c. 25) (bodies of which all members are disqualified) insert at the appropriate place—

"The Competition Commission".

Part V Transitional provisions

Interpretation

30. In this Part of this Schedule—

"commencement date" means the date on which section 45 comes into force; and

"MMC" means the Monopolies and Mergers Commission.

Chairman

31.—(1) The person who is Chairman of the MMC immediately before the commencement date is on that date to become both a member of the Commission and its chairman as if he had been duly appointed under paragraphs 2(1)(b) and 3.

(2) He is to hold office as Chairman of the Commission for the remainder of the period for which he was appointed as Chairman of the MMC and on the terms on which he was so appointed.

Deputy chairmen

32. The persons who are deputy chairmen of the MMC immediately before the commencement date are on that date to become deputy chairmen of the Commission as if they had been duly appointed under paragraph 3(2).

Reporting panel members

33.—(1) The persons who are members of the MMC immediately before the commencement date are on that date to become members of the Commission as if they had been duly appointed under paragraph 2(1)(b).

(2) Each of them is to hold office as a member for the remainder of the period for which he was appointed as a member of the MMC and on the terms on which he was so appointed.

Specialist panel members

34.—(1) The persons who are members of the MMC immediately before the commencement date by virtue of appointments made under any of the enactments mentioned in paragraph 2(1)(d) are on that date to become members of the Commission as if they had been duly appointed to the Commission under the enactment in question.

(2) Each of them is to hold office as a member for such period and on such terms as the Secretary of State may determine.

Secretary

35. The person who is the secretary of the MMC immediately before the commencement date is on that date to become the secretary of the Commission as if duly appointed under paragraph 9, on the same terms and conditions.

Council

36.—(1) The members who become deputy chairmen of the Commission under paragraph 32 are also to become members of the Council as if they had been duly appointed under paragraph 5(2)(c).

(2) Each of them is to hold office as a member of the Council for such period as the Secretary of State determines.

Schedule 8 Appeals

Part I General

Interpretation

Sections 46(5) and 48(4).

1. In this Schedule—

"the chairman" means a person appointed as chairman of a tribunal in accordance with paragraph 27(2)(a) of Schedule 7;

"the President" means the President of the Competition Commission Appeal Tribunals appointed under paragraph 4 of Schedule 7;

"rules" means rules made by the Secretary of State under section 48;

"specified" means specified in rules;

"tribunal" means an appeal tribunal constituted in accordance with paragraph 27 of Schedule 7.

General procedure

2.—(1) An appeal to the Competition Commission must be made by sending a notice of appeal to the Commission within the specified period.

(2) The notice of appeal must set out the grounds of appeal in sufficient detail to indicate—

(a) under which provision of this Act the appeal is brought;

(b) to what extent (if any) the appellant contends that the decision against, or with respect to which, the appeal is brought was based on an error of fact or was wrong in law; and

(c) to what extent (if any) the appellant is appealing against the Director's exercise of his discretion in making the disputed decision.

(3) The tribunal may give an appellant leave to amend the grounds of appeal identified in the notice of appeal.

Decisions of the tribunal

3.—(1) The tribunal must determine the appeal on the merits by reference to the grounds of appeal set out in the notice of appeal.

(2) The tribunal may confirm or set aside the decision which is the subject of the appeal, or any part of it, and may—

(a) remit the matter to the Director,

(b) impose or revoke, or vary the amount of, a penalty,

(c) grant or cancel an individual exemption or vary any conditions or obligations imposed in relation to the exemption by the Director,

(d) give such directions, or take such other steps, as the Director could himself have given or taken, or

(e) make any other decision which the Director could himself have made.

(3) Any decision of the tribunal on an appeal has the same effect, and may be enforced in the same manner, as a decision of the Director.

(4) If the tribunal confirms the decision which is the subject of the appeal it may nevertheless set aside any finding of fact on which the decision was based.

4.—(1) A decision of the tribunal may be taken by a majority.

(2) The decision must—

    (a) state whether it was unanimous or taken by a majority; and

    (b) be recorded in a document which—

        (i) contains a statement of the reasons for the decision; and

        (ii) is signed and dated by the chairman of the tribunal.

(3) When the tribunal is preparing the document mentioned in sub-paragraph (2)(b), section 56 is to apply to the tribunal as it applies to the Director.

(4) The President must make such arrangements for the publication of the tribunal's decision as he considers appropriate.

Part II Rules

Registrar of Appeal Tribunals

5.—(1) Rules may provide for the appointment by the Competition Commission, with the approval of the Secretary of State, of a Registrar of Appeal Tribunals.

(2) The rules may, in particular—

    (a) specify the qualifications for appointment as Registrar; and

    (b) provide for specified functions relating to appeals to be exercised by the Registrar in specified circumstances.

Notice of appeal

6. Rules may make provision—

    (a) as to the period within which appeals must be brought;

    (b) as to the form of the notice of appeal and as to the information which must be given in the notice;

    (c) with respect to amendment of a notice of appeal;

    (d) with respect to acknowledgement of a notice of appeal.

Response to the appeal

7. Rules may provide for the tribunal to reject an appeal if—

    (a) it considers that the notice of appeal reveals no valid ground of appeal; or

    (b) it is satisfied that the appellant has habitually and persistently and without any reasonable ground—

        (i) instituted vexatious proceedings, whether against the same person or against different persons; or

        (ii) made vexatious applications in any proceedings.

Pre-hearing reviews and preliminary matters

8.—(1) Rules may make provision—

   (a) for the carrying-out by the tribunal of a preliminary consideration of proceedings (a "pre-hearing review"); and

   (b) for enabling such powers to be exercised in connection with a pre-hearing review as may be specified.

(2) If rules make provision of the kind mentioned in sub-paragraph (1), they may also include—

   (a) provision for security; and

   (b) supplemental provision.

(3) In sub-paragraph (2) "provision for security" means provision authorising a tribunal carrying out a pre-hearing review under the rules, in specified circumstances, to make an order requiring a party to the proceedings, if he wishes to continue to participate in them, to pay a deposit of an amount not exceeding such sum—

   (a) as may be specified; or

   (b) as may be calculated in accordance with specified provisions.

(4) In sub-paragraph (2) "supplemental provision" means any provision as to—

   (a) the manner in which the amount of such a deposit is to be determined;

   (b) the consequences of non-payment of such a deposit; and

   (c) the circumstances in which any such deposit, or any part of it, may be—

      (i) refunded to the person who paid it; or

      (ii) paid to another party to the proceedings.

Conduct of the hearing

9.—(1) Rules may make provision—

   (a) as to the manner in which appeals are to be conducted, including provision for any hearing to be held in private if the tribunal considers it appropriate because it may be considering information of a kind to which section 56 applies;

   (b) as to the persons entitled to appear on behalf of the parties;

   (c) for requiring persons to attend to give evidence and produce documents and for authorising the administration of oaths to witnesses;

   (d) as to the evidence which may be required or admitted in proceedings before the tribunal and the extent to which it should be oral or written;

   (e) allowing the tribunal to fix time limits with respect to any aspect of the proceedings before it and to extend any time limit (whether or not it has expired);

   (f) for enabling the tribunal to refer a matter back to the Director if it appears to the tribunal that the matter has not been adequately investigated;

    (g) for enabling the tribunal, on the application of any party to the proceedings before it or on its own initiative—

          (i) in England and Wales or Northern Ireland, to order the disclosure between, or the production by, the parties of documents or classes of documents;

          (ii) in Scotland, to order such recovery or inspection of documents as might be ordered by a sheriff;

    (h) for the appointment of experts for the purposes of any proceedings before the tribunal;

    (i) for the award of costs or expenses, including any allowances payable to persons in connection with their attendance before the tribunal;

    (j) for taxing or otherwise settling any costs or expenses directed to be paid by the tribunal and for the enforcement of any such direction.

  (2) A person who without reasonable excuse fails to comply with—

    (a) any requirement imposed by virtue of sub-paragraph (1)(c), or

    (b) any requirement with respect to the disclosure, reduction, recovery or inspection of documents which is imposed by virtue of sub-paragraph (1)(g),

is guilty of an offence and liable on summary conviction to a fine not exceeding level 3 on the standard scale.

Interest

  10.—(1) Rules may make provision—

    (a) as to the circumstances in which the tribunal may order that interest is payable;

    (b) for the manner in which and the periods by reference to which interest is to be calculated and paid.

  (2) The rules may, in particular, provide that compound interest is to be payable if the tribunal—

    (a) upholds a decision of the Director to impose a penalty, or

    (b) does not reduce a penalty so imposed by more than a specified percentage,

but in such a case the rules may not provide that interest is to be payable in respect of any period before the date on which the appeal was brought.

Fees

  11.—(1) Rules may provide—

    (a) for fees to be chargeable in respect of specified costs of proceedings before the tribunal;

    (b) for the amount of such costs to be determined by the tribunal.

  (2) Any sums received in consequence of rules under this paragraph are to be paid into the Consolidated Fund.

Withdrawing an appeal

12. Rules may make provision—
- (a) that a party who has brought an appeal may not withdraw it without the leave of—
  - (i) the tribunal, or
  - (ii) in specified circumstances, the President or the Registrar;
- (b) for the tribunal to grant leave to withdraw the appeal on such conditions as it considers appropriate;
- (c) enabling the tribunal to publish any decision which it could have made had the appeal not been withdrawn;
- (d) as to the effect of withdrawal of an appeal;
- (e) as to any procedure to be followed if parties to proceedings on an appeal agree to settle.

Interim orders

13.—(1) Rules may provide for the tribunal to make an order ("an interim order") granting, on an interim basis, any remedy which the tribunal would have power to grant in its final decision.

(2) An interim order may, in particular, suspend the effect of a decision made by the Director or vary the conditions or obligations attached to an exemption.

(3) Rules may also make provision giving the tribunal powers similar to those given to the Director by section 35.

Miscellaneous

14. Rules may make provision—
- (a) for a person who is not a party to proceedings on an appeal to be joined in those proceedings;
- (b) for appeals to be consolidated on such terms as the tribunal thinks appropriate in such circumstances as may be specified.

Schedule 9 Director's Rules

General

Section 51(2).

1. In this Schedule—

"application for guidance" means an application for guidance under section 13 or 21;

"application for a decision" means an application for a decision under section 14 or 22;

"guidance" means guidance given under section 13 or 21;

"rules" means rules made by the Director under section 51; and

"specified" means specified in rules.

Applications

2. Rules may make provision—
  (a) as to the form and manner in which an application for guidance or an application for a decision must be made;
  (b) for the procedure to be followed in dealing with the application;
  (c) for the application to be dealt with in accordance with a timetable;
  (d) as to the documents and information which must be given to the Director in connection with the application;
  (e) requiring the applicant to give such notice of the application, to such other persons, as may be specified;
  (f) as to the consequences of a failure to comply with any rule made by virtue of sub-paragraph (e);
  (g) as to the procedure to be followed when the application is subject to the concurrent jurisdiction of the Director and a regulator.

Provisional decisions

3. Rules may make provision as to the procedure to be followed by the Director when making a provisional decision under paragraph 3 of Schedule 5 or paragraph 3 of Schedule 6.

Guidance

4. Rules may make provision as to—
  (a) the form and manner in which guidance is to be given;
  (b) the procedure to be followed if—
      (i) the Director takes further action with respect to an agreement after giving guidance that it is not likely to infringe the Chapter I prohibition; or
      (ii) the Director takes further action with respect to conduct after giving guidance that it is not likely to infringe the Chapter II prohibition.

Decisions

5.—(1) Rules may make provision as to—
  (a) the form and manner in which notice of any decision is to be given;
  (b) the person or persons to whom the notice is to be given;
  (c) the manner in which the Director is to publish a decision;
  (d) the procedure to be followed if—
      (i) the Director takes further action with respect to an agreement after having decided that it does not infringe the Chapter I prohibition; or
      (ii) the Director takes further action with respect to conduct after having decided that it does not infringe the Chapter II prohibition.

(2) In this paragraph "decision" means a decision of the Director (whether or not made on an application)—

    (a) as to whether or not an agreement has infringed the Chapter I prohibition, or

    (b) as to whether or not conduct has infringed the Chapter II prohibition,

and, in the case of an application for a decision under section 14 which includes a request for an individual exemption, includes a decision as to whether or not to grant the exemption.

Individual exemptions

6. Rules may make provision as to—

    (a) the procedure to be followed by the Director when deciding whether, in accordance with section 5—

        (i) to cancel an individual exemption that he has granted,

        (ii) to vary or remove any of its conditions or obligations, or

        (iii) to impose additional conditions or obligations;

    (b) the form and manner in which notice of such a decision is to be given.

7. Rules may make provision as to—

    (a) the form and manner in which an application under section 4(6) for the extension of an individual exemption is to be made;

    (b) the circumstances in which the Director will consider such an application;

    (c) the procedure to be followed by the Director when deciding whether to grant such an application;

    (d) the form and manner in which notice of such a decision is to be given.

Block exemptions

8. Rules may make provision as to—

    (a) the form and manner in which notice of an agreement is to be given to the Director under subsection (1) of section 7;

    (b) the procedure to be followed by the Director if he is acting under subsection (2) of that section;

    (c) as to the procedure to be followed by the Director if he cancels a block exemption.

Parallel exemptions

9. Rules may make provision as to—

    (a) the circumstances in which the Director may—

        (i) impose conditions or obligations in relation to a parallel exemption,

        (ii) vary or remove any such conditions or obligations,

  (iii) impose additional conditions or obligations, or
  (iv) cancel the exemption;
 (b) as to the procedure to be followed by the Director if he is acting under section 10(5);
 (c) the form and manner in which notice of a decision to take any of the steps in sub-paragraph (a) is to be given;
 (d) the circumstances in which an exemption may be cancelled with retrospective effect.

Section 11 exemptions

10. Rules may, with respect to any exemption provided by regulations made under section 11, make provision similar to that made with respect to parallel exemptions by section 10 or by rules under paragraph 9.

Directions withdrawing exclusions

11. Rules may make provision as to the factors which the Director may take into account when he is determining the date on which a direction given under paragraph 4(1) of Schedule 1 or paragraph 2(3) or 9(3) of Schedule 3 is to have effect.

Disclosure of information

12.—(1) Rules may make provision as to the circumstances in which the Director is to be required, before disclosing information given to him by a third party in connection with the exercise of any of the Director's functions under Part I, to give notice, and an opportunity to make representations, to the third party.

(2) In relation to the agreement (or conduct) concerned, "third party" means a person who is not a party to the agreement (or who has not engaged in the conduct).

Applications under section 47

13. Rules may make provision as to—
 (a) the period within which an application under section 47(1) must be made;
 (b) the procedure to be followed by the Director in dealing with the application;
 (c) the person or persons to whom notice of the Director's response to the application is to be given.

Enforcement

14. Rules may make provision as to the procedure to be followed when the Director takes action under any of sections 32 to 41 with respect to the enforcement of the provisions of this Part.

Schedule 10 Regulators

Part I Monopolies

Sections 54 and 66(5).

1. The amendments of the Fair Trading Act 1973 (c. 41) made by sections 66 and 67 of this Act are to have effect, not only in relation to the jurisdiction of the Director under the provisions amended, but also in relation to the jurisdiction under those provisions of each of the following—

    (a) the Director General of Telecommunications;

    (b) the Director General of Electricity Supply;

    (c) the Director General of Electricity Supply for Northern Ireland;

    (d) the Director General of Water Services;

    (e) the Rail Regulator;

    (f) the Director General of Gas Supply; and

    (g) the Director General of Gas for Northern Ireland.

Part II The Prohibitions

Telecommunications

2.—(1) In consequence of the repeal by this Act of provisions of the Competition Act 1980 (c. 21), the functions transferred by subsection (3) of section 50 of the Telecommunications Act 1984 (c. 12) (functions under 1973 and 1980 Acts) are no longer exercisable by the Director General of Telecommunications.

(2) Accordingly, that Act is amended as follows.

(3) In section 3 (general duties of Secretary of State and Director), in subsection (3)(b), for "section 50" substitute "section 50(1) or (2)".

(4) In section 3, after subsection (3A), insert—

    "(3B) Subsections (1) and (2) above do not apply in relation to anything done by the Director in the exercise of functions assigned to him by section 50(3) below ("Competition Act functions").

    (3C) The Director may nevertheless, when exercising any Competition Act function, have regard to any matter in respect of which a duty is imposed by subsection (1) or (2) above ("a general matter"), if it is a matter to which the Director General of Fair Trading could have regard when exercising that function; but that is not to be taken as implying that, in relation to any of the matters mentioned in subsection (3) or (3A) above, regard may not be had to any general matter."

(5) Section 50 is amended as follows.

(6) For subsection (3) substitute—

    "(3) The Director shall be entitled to exercise, concurrently with the Director General of Fair Trading, the functions of that Director under the provisions of Part I of the Competition Act 1998 (other than sections 38(1) to (6) and 51), so far as relating to—

(a) agreements, decisions or concerted practices of the kind mentioned in section 2(1) of that Act, or

(b) conduct of the kind mentioned in section 18(1) of that Act,

which relate to commercial activities connected with telecommunications.

(3A) So far as necessary for the purposes of, or in connection with, the provisions of subsection (3) above, references in Part I of the Competition Act 1998 to the Director General of Fair Trading are to be read as including a reference to the Director (except in sections 38(1) to (6), 51, 52(6) and (8) and 54 of that Act and in any other provision of that Act where the context otherwise requires)."

(7) In subsection (4), omit paragraph (c) and the "and" immediately after it.

(8) In subsection (5), omit "or (3)".

(9) In subsection (6), for paragraph (b) substitute—

"(b) Part I of the Competition Act 1998 (other than sections 38(1) to (6) and 51),".

(10) In subsection (7), omit "or the 1980 Act".

Gas

3.—(1) In consequence of the repeal by this Act of provisions of the Competition Act 1980, the functions transferred by subsection (3) of section 36A of the Gas Act 1986 (c. 44) (functions with respect to competition) are no longer exercisable by the Director General of Gas Supply.

(2) Accordingly, that Act is amended as follows.

(3) In section 4 (general duties of Secretary of State and Director), after subsection (3), insert—

"(3A) Subsections (1) to (3) above and section 4A below do not apply in relation to anything done by the Director in the exercise of functions assigned to him by section 36A below ("Competition Act functions").

(3B) The Director may nevertheless, when exercising any Competition Act function, have regard to any matter in respect of which a duty is imposed by any of subsections (1) to (3) above or section 4A below, if it is a matter to which the Director General of Fair Trading could have regard when exercising that function."

(4) Section 36A is amended as follows.

(5) For subsection (3) substitute—

"(3) The Director shall be entitled to exercise, concurrently with the Director General of Fair Trading, the functions of that Director under the provisions of Part I of the Competition Act 1998 (other than sections 38(1) to (6) and 51), so far as relating to—

(a) agreements, decisions or concerted practices of the kind mentioned in section 2(1) of that Act, or

(b) conduct of the kind mentioned in section 18(1) of that Act,

which relate to the carrying on of activities to which this subsection applies.

(3A) So far as necessary for the purposes of, or in connection with, the provisions of subsection (3) above, references in Part I of the Competition Act 1998 to the Director General of Fair Trading are to be read as including a reference to the Director (except in sections 38(1) to (6), 51, 52(6) and (8) and 54 of that Act and in any other provision of that Act where the context otherwise requires)."

(6) In subsection (5)—

    (a) for "transferred by", in each place, substitute "mentioned in";

    (b) after paragraph (b), insert "and";

    (c) omit paragraph (d) and the "and" immediately before it.

(7) In subsection (6), omit "or (3)".

(8) In subsection (7), for paragraph (b) substitute—

    "(b) Part I of the Competition Act 1998 (other than sections 38(1) to (6) and 51),".

(9) In subsection (8)—

    (a) omit "or under the 1980 Act";

    (b) for "or (3) above" substitute "above and paragraph 1 of Schedule 10 to the Competition Act 1998".

(10) In subsection (9), omit "or the 1980 Act".

(11) In subsection (10), for the words from "transferred" to the end substitute "mentioned in subsection (2) or (3) above."

Electricity

4.—(1) In consequence of the repeal by this Act of provisions of the Competition Act 1980 (c. 21), the functions transferred by subsection (3) of section 43 of the Electricity Act 1989 (c. 29) (functions with respect to competition) are no longer exercisable by the Director General of Electricity Supply.

(2) Accordingly, that Act is amended as follows.

(3) In section 3 (general duties of Secretary of State and Director), after subsection (6), insert—

"(6A) Subsections (1) to (5) above do not apply in relation to anything done by the Director in the exercise of functions assigned to him by section 43(3) below ("Competition Act functions").

(6B) The Director may nevertheless, when exercising any Competition Act function, have regard to any matter in respect of which a duty is imposed by any of subsections (1) to (5) above ("a general matter"), if it is a matter to which the Director General of Fair Trading could have regard when exercising that function; but that is not to be taken as implying that, in the exercise of any function mentioned in subsection (6) above, regard may not be had to any general matter."

(4) Section 43 is amended as follows.

(5) For subsection (3) substitute—

"(3) The Director shall be entitled to exercise, concurrently with the Director General of Fair Trading, the functions of that Director under the provisions of Part I of the Competition Act 1998 (other than sections 38(1) to (6) and 51), so far as relating to—

(a) agreements, decisions or concerted practices of the kind mentioned in section 2(1) of that Act, or

(b) conduct of the kind mentioned in section 18(1) of that Act,

which relate to commercial activities connected with the generation, transmission or supply of electricity.

(3A) So far as necessary for the purposes of, or in connection with, the provisions of subsection (3) above, references in Part I of the Competition Act 1998 to the Director General of Fair Trading are to be read as including a reference to the Director (except in sections 38(1) to (6), 51, 52(6) and (8) and 54 of that Act and in any other provision of that Act where the context otherwise requires)."

(6) In subsection (4), omit paragraph (c) and the "and" immediately after it.

(7) In subsection (5), omit "or (3)".

(8) In subsection (6), for paragraph (b) substitute—

"(b) Part I of the Competition Act 1998 (other than sections 38(1) to (6) and 51),".

(9) In subsection (7), omit "or the 1980 Act".

Water

5.—(1) In consequence of the repeal by this Act of provisions of the Competition Act 1980 (c. 21), the functions exercisable by virtue of subsection (3) of section 31 of the Water Industry Act 1991 (c. 56) (functions of Director with respect to competition) are no longer exercisable by the Director General of Water Services.

(2) Accordingly, that Act is amended as follows.

(3) In section 2 (general duties with respect to water industry), in subsection (6)(a) , at the beginning, insert "subject to subsection (6A) below".

(4) In section 2, after subsection (6), insert—

"(6A) Subsections (2) to (4) above do not apply in relation to anything done by the Director in the exercise of functions assigned to him by section 31(3) below ("Competition Act functions").

(6B) The Director may nevertheless, when exercising any Competition Act function, have regard to any matter in respect of which a duty is imposed by any of subsections (2) to (4) above, if it is a matter to which the Director General of Fair Trading could have regard when exercising that function."

(5) Section 31 is amended as follows.

(6) For subsection (3) substitute—

"(3) The Director shall be entitled to exercise, concurrently with the Director General of Fair Trading, the functions of that Director under the provisions of Part I of the Competition Act 1998 (other than sections 38(l) to (6) and 51), so far as relating to—

(a) agreements, decisions or concerted practices of the kind mentioned in section 2(1) of that Act, or

(b) conduct of the kind mentioned in section 18(1) of that Act,

which relate to commercial activities connected with the supply of water or securing a supply of water or with the provision or securing of sewerage services."

(7) In subsection (4)—

(a) for "to (3)" substitute "and (2)";

(b) omit paragraph (c) and the "and" immediately before it.

(8) After subsection (4), insert—

"(4A) So far as necessary for the purposes of, or in connection with, the provisions of subsection (3) above, references in Part I of the Competition Act 1998 to the Director General of Fair Trading are to be read as including a reference to the Director (except in sections 38(1) to (6), 51, 52(6) and (8) and 54 of that Act and in any other provision of that Act where the context otherwise requires)."

(9) In subsection (5), omit "or in subsection (3) above".

(10) In subsection (6), omit "or in subsection (3) above".

(11) In subsection (7), omit "or (3)".

(12) In subsection (8), for paragraph (b) substitute—

"(b) Part I of the Competition Act 1998 (other than sections 38(1) to (6) and 51),".

(13) In subsection (9), omit "or the 1980 Act".

Railways

6.—(1) In consequence of the repeal by this Act of provisions of the Competition Act 1980 (c. 21), the functions transferred by subsection (3) of section 67 of the Railways Act 1993 (c. 43) (respective functions of the Regulator and the Director etc) are no longer exercisable by the Rail Regulator.

(2) Accordingly, that Act is amended as follows.

(3) In section 4 (general duties of the Secretary of State and the Regulator), after subsection (7), insert—

"(7A) Subsections (1) to (6) above do not apply in relation to anything done by the Regulator in the exercise of functions assigned to him by section 67(3) below ("Competition Act functions").

(7B) The Regulator may nevertheless, when exercising any Competition Act function, have regard to any matter in respect of which a duty is imposed by any of subsections (1) to (6) above, if it is a matter to which the Director General of Fair Trading could have regard when exercising that function."

(4) Section 67 is amended as follows.

(5) For subsection (3) substitute—

"(3) The Regulator shall be entitled to exercise, concurrently with the Director, the functions of the Director under the provisions of Part I of the Competition Act 1998 (other than sections 38(1) to (6) and 51), so far as relating to—

    (a) agreements, decisions or concerted practices of the kind mentioned in section 2(1) of that Act, or

    (b) conduct of the kind mentioned in section 18(1) of that Act, which relate to the supply of railway services.

(3A) So far as necessary for the purposes of, or in connection with, the provisions of subsection (3) above, references in Part I of the Competition Act 1998 to the Director are to be read as including a reference to the Regulator (except in sections 38(1) to (6), 51, 52(6) and (8) and 54 of that Act and in any other provision of that Act where the context otherwise requires)."

(6) In subsection (4), omit paragraph (c) and the "and" immediately after it.

(7) In subsection (6)(a), omit "or (3)".

(8) In subsection (8), for paragraph (b) substitute—

    "(b) Part I of the Competition Act 1998 (other than sections 38(1) to (6) and 51),".

(9) In subsection (9)—

    (a) omit "or under the 1980 Act";

    (b) for "or (3) above" substitute "above and paragraph 1 of Schedule 10 to the Competition Act 1998".

Part III The prohibitions: Northern Ireland

[*Part III of Schedule 10, not reproduced in this work, provides for amendments to the Electricity (Northern Ireland) Order 1992 and to the Gas (Northern Ireland) Order 1996 in similar terms to the amendments to the Electricity Act 1989 and the Gas Act 1986 at Part II, paragraph 4 of the Schedule.*]

Part IV Utilities: Minor and consequential amendments

[*Not reproduced in this work.*]

Schedule 11 Interpretation of section 55

Relevant functions

Section 55(4).

    1. In section 55(3) "relevant functions" means any function under—

        (a) Part I or any enactment repealed in consequence of Part I;

        (b) the Fair Trading Act 1973 (c. 41) or the Competition Act 1980 (c. 21);

        (c) the Estate Agents Act 1979 (c. 38);

        (d) the Telecommunications Act 1984 (c. 12);

(e) the Gas Act 1986 (c. 44) or the Gas Act 1995 (c. 45)

(f) the Gas (Northern Ireland) Order 1996 (S.I. 1996/275 (N.I. 2));

(g) the Airports Act 1986 (c. 31) or Part IV of the Airports (Northern Ireland) Order 1994 (S.I. 1994/426 (N.I. 1));

(h) the Financial Services Act 1986 (c. 60);

(i) the Electricity Act 1989 (c. 29) or the Electricity (Northern Ireland) Order 1992 (S.I. 1992/231 (N.I. 1));

(j) the Broadcasting Act 1990 (c. 42) or the Broadcasting Act 1996 (c. 55);

(k) the Courts and Legal Services Act 1990 (c. 41);

(1) the Water Industry Act 1991 (c. 56), the Water Resources Act 1991 (c. 57), the Statutory Water Companies Act 1991 (c. 58), the Land Drainage Act 1991 (c. 59) and the Water Consolidation (Consequential Provisions) Act 1991 (c. 60);

(m) the Railways Act 1993 (c. 43);

(n) the Coal Industry Act 1994 (c. 21);

(o) the EC Competition Law (Articles 88 and 89) Enforcement Regulations 1996 (S.I. 1996/2199);

(p) any subordinate legislation made (whether before or after the passing of this Act) for the purpose of implementing Council Directive No. 91/440/EEC of 29th July 1991 on the development of the Community's railways, Council Directive No. 95/18/EC of 19th June 1995 on the licensing of railway undertakings or Council Directive No. 95/19/EC of 19th June 1995 on the allocation of railway infrastructure capacity and the charging of infrastructure fees.

Designated persons

2. In section 55(3) "designated person" means any of the following—

(a) the Director;

(b) the Director General of Telecommunications;

(c) the Independent Television Commission;

(d) the Director General of Gas Supply;

(e) the Director General of Gas for Northern Ireland;

(f) the Civil Aviation Authority;

(g) the Director General of Water Services;

(h) the Director General of Electricity Supply;

(i) the Director General of Electricity Supply for Northern Ireland;

(j) the Rail Regulator;

(k) the Director of Passenger Rail Franchising;

(1) the International Rail Regulator;

(m) the Authorised Conveyancing Practitioners Board;

(n) the Scottish Conveyancing and Executry Services Board;

(o) the Coal Authority;

(p) the Monopolies and Mergers Commission;

    (q) the Competition Commission;

    (r) the Securities and Investments Board;

    (s) any Minister of the Crown or any Northern Ireland department.

Schedule 12 Minor and consequential amendments

Section 74(1).

[*Not reproduced in this work.*]

Schedule 13 Transitional provisions and savings

Part I General

Interpretation

Section 74(2).

    1.—(1) In this Schedule—

    "RPA" means the Resale Prices Act 1976 (c. 53);

    "RTPA" means the Restrictive Trade Practices Act 1976;

    "continuing proceedings" has the meaning given by paragraph 15;

    "the Court" means the Restrictive Practices Court;

    "Director" means the Director General of Fair Trading;

    "document" includes information recorded in any form;

    "enactment date" means the date on which this Act is passed;

    "information" includes estimates and forecasts;

    "interim period" means the period beginning on the enactment date and ending immediately before the starting date;

    "prescribed" means prescribed by an order made by the Secretary of State;

    "regulator" means any person mentioned in paragraphs (a) to (g) of paragraph 1 of Schedule 10;

    "starting date" means the date on which section 2 comes into force;

    "transitional period" means the transitional period provided for in Chapters III and IV of Part IV of this Schedule.

    (2) Sections 30, 44, 51, 53, 55, 56, 57 and 59(3) and (4) and paragraph 12 of Schedule 9 ("the applied provisions") apply for the purposes of this Schedule as they apply for the purposes of Part I of this Act.

    (3) Section 2(5) applies for the purposes of any provisions of this Schedule which are concerned with the operation of the Chapter I prohibition as it applies for the purposes of Part I of this Act.

    (4) In relation to any of the matters in respect of which a regulator may exercise powers as a result of paragraph 35(1), the applied provisions are to have effect as if references to the Director included references to the regulator.

    (5) The fact that to a limited extent the Chapter I prohibition does not apply to an agreement, because a transitional period is provided by virtue of

this Schedule, does not require those provisions of the agreement in respect of which there is a transitional period to be disregarded when considering whether the agreement infringes the prohibition for other reasons.

General power to make transitional provision and savings

2.—(1) Nothing in this Schedule affects the power of the Secretary of State under section 75 to make transitional provisions or savings.

(2) An order under that section may modify any provision made by this Schedule.

Advice and information

3.—(1) The Director may publish advice and information explaining provisions of this Schedule to persons who are likely to be affected by them.

(2) Any advice or information published by the Director under this paragraph is to be published in such form and manner as he considers appropriate.

Part II During the interim period

Block exemptions

4.—(1) The Secretary of State may, at any time during the interim period, make one or more orders for the purpose of providing block exemptions which are effective on the starting date.

(2) An order under this paragraph has effect as if properly made under section 6.

Certain agreements to be non-notifiable agreements

5. An agreement which—
  (a) is made during the interim period, and
  (b) satisfies the conditions set out in paragraphs (a), (c) and (d) of section 27A(1) of the RTPA,
is to be treated as a non-notifiable agreement for the purposes of the RTPA.

Application of RTPA during the interim period

6. In relation to agreements made during the interim period—
  (a) the Director is no longer under the duty to take proceedings imposed by section 1(2)(c) of the RTPA but may continue to do so;
  (b) section 21 of that Act has effect as if subsections (1) and (2) were omitted; and
  (c) section 35(1) of that Act has effect as if the words "or within such further time as the Director may, upon application made within that time, allow" were omitted.

Guidance

7.—(1) Sub-paragraphs (2) to (4) apply in relation to agreements made during the interim period.

(2) An application may be made to the Director in anticipation of the coming into force of section 13 in accordance with directions given by the Director and such an application is to have effect on and after the starting date as if properly made under section 13.

(3) The Director may, in response to such an application—

(a) give guidance in anticipation of the coming into force of section 2; or

(b) on and after the starting date, give guidance under section 15 as if the application had been properly made under section 13.

(4) Any guidance so given is to have effect on and after the starting date as if properly given under section 15.

Part III On the starting date

Applications which fall

8.—(1) Proceedings in respect of an application which is made to the Court under any of the provisions mentioned in sub-paragraph (2), but which is not determined before the starting date, cease on that date.

(2) The provisions are—

(a) sections 2(2), 35(3), 37(1) and 40(1) of the RTPA and paragraph 5 of Schedule 4 to that Act;

(b) section 4(1) of the RTPA so far as the application relates to an order under section 2(2) of that Act; and

(c) section 25(2) of the RPA.

(3) The power of the Court to make an order for costs in relation to any proceedings is not affected by anything in this paragraph or by the repeals made by section 1.

Orders and approvals which fall

9.—(1) An order in force immediately before the starting date under—

(a) section 2(2), 29(1), 30(1), 33(4), 35(3) or 37(1) of the RTPA; or

(b) section 25(2) of the RPA,

ceases to have effect on that date.

(2) An approval in force immediately before the starting date under section 32 of the RTPA ceases to have effect on that date.

Part IV On and after the starting date

Chapter I General

Duty of Director to maintain register etc.

10.—(1) This paragraph applies even though the relevant provisions of the RTPA are repealed by this Act.

(2) The Director is to continue on and after the starting date to be under the duty imposed by section 1(2)(a) of the RTPA to maintain a register in respect of agreements—

    (a) particulars of which are, on the starting date, entered or filed on the register;

    (b) which fall within sub-paragraph (4);

    (c) which immediately before the starting date are the subject of proceedings under the RTPA which do not cease on that date by virtue of this Schedule; or

    (d) in relation to which a court gives directions to the Director after the starting date in the course of proceedings in which a question arises as to whether an agreement was, before that date—

        (i) one to which the RTPA applied;

        (ii) subject to registration under that Act;

        (iii) a non-notifiable agreement for the purposes of that Act.

(3) The Director is to continue on and after the starting date to be under the duties imposed by section 1(2)(a) and (b) of the RTPA of compiling a register of agreements and entering or filing certain particulars in the register, but only in respect of agreements of a kind referred to in paragraph (b), (c) or (d) of sub-paragraph (2).

(4) An agreement falls within this sub-paragraph if—

    (a) it is subject to registration under the RTPA but—

        (i) is not a non-notifiable agreement within the meaning of section 27A of the RTPA, or

        (ii) is not one to which paragraph 5 applies;

    (b) particulars of the agreement have been provided to the Director before the starting date; and

    (c) as at the starting date no entry or filing has been made in the register in respect of the agreement.

(5) Sections 23 and 27 of the RTPA are to apply after the starting date in respect of the register subject to such modifications, if any, as may be prescribed.

(6) In sub-paragraph (2)(d) "court" means—

    (a) the High Court;

    (b) the Court of Appeal;

    (c) the Court of Session;

    (d) the High Court or Court of Appeal in Northern Ireland; or

    (e) the House of Lords.

RTPA section 3 applications

11.—(1) Even though section 3 of the RTPA is repealed by this Act, its provisions (and so far as necessary that Act) are to continue to apply, with such modifications (if any) as may be prescribed—

    (a) in relation to a continuing application under that section; or

(b) so as to allow an application to be made under that section on or after the starting date in respect of a continuing application under section 1(3) of the RTPA.

(2) "Continuing application" means an application made, but not determined, before the starting date.

RTPA section 26 applications

12.—(1) Even though section 26 of the RTPA is repealed by this Act, its provisions (and so far as necessary that Act) are to continue to apply, with such modifications (if any) as may be prescribed, in relation to an application which is made under that section, but not determined, before the starting date.

(2) If an application under section 26 is determined on or after the starting date, this Schedule has effect in relation to the agreement concerned as if the application had been determined immediately before that date.

Right to bring civil proceedings

13.—(1) Even though section 35 of the RTPA is repealed by this Act, its provisions (and so far as necessary that Act) are to continue to apply in respect of a person who, immediately before the starting date, has a right by virtue of section 27ZA or 35(2) of that Act to bring civil proceedings in respect of an agreement (but only so far as that right relates to any period before the starting date or, where there are continuing proceedings, the determination of the proceedings).

(2) Even though section 25 of the RPA is repealed by this Act, the provisions of that section (and so far as necessary that Act) are to continue to apply in respect of a person who, immediately before the starting date, has a right by virtue of subsection (3) of that section to bring civil proceedings (but only so far as that right relates to any period before the starting date or, where there are continuing proceedings, the determination of the proceedings).

Chapter II Continuing proceedings

The general rule

14.—(1) The Chapter I prohibition does not apply to an agreement at any time when the agreement is the subject of continuing proceedings under the RTPA.

(2) The Chapter I prohibition does not apply to an agreement relating to goods which are the subject of continuing proceedings under section 16 or 17 of the RPA to the extent to which the agreement consists of exempt provisions.

(3) In sub-paragraph (2) "exempt provisions" means those provisions of the agreement which would, disregarding section 14 of the RPA, be—

(a) void as a result of section 9(1) of the RPA; or

(b) unlawful as a result of section 9(2) or 11 of the RPA.

(4) If the Chapter I prohibition does not apply to an agreement because of this paragraph, the provisions of, or made under, the RTPA or the RPA are to continue to have effect in relation to the agreement.

(5) The repeals made by section 1 do not affect—

(a) continuing proceedings; or

(b) proceedings of the kind referred to in paragraph 11 or 12 of this Schedule which are continuing after the starting date.

Meaning of "continuing proceedings"

15.—(1) For the purposes of this Schedule "continuing proceedings" means proceedings in respect of an application made to the Court under the RTPA or the RPA, but not determined, before the starting date.

(2) But proceedings under section 3 or 26 of the RTPA to which paragraph 11 or 12 applies are not continuing proceedings.

(3) The question whether (for the purposes of Part III, or this Part, of this Schedule) an application has been determined is to be decided in accordance with sub-paragraphs (4) and (5).

(4) If an appeal against the decision on the application is brought, the application is not determined until—

(a) the appeal is disposed of or withdrawn; or

(b) if as a result of the appeal the case is referred back to the Court—

(i) the expiry of the period within which an appeal ("the further appeal") in respect of the Court's decision on that reference could have been brought had this Act not been passed; or

(ii) if later, the date on which the further appeal is disposed of or withdrawn.

(5) Otherwise, the application is not determined until the expiry of the period within which any party to the application would have been able to bring an appeal against the decision on the application had this Act not been passed.

RTPA section 4 proceedings

16. Proceedings on an application for an order under section 4 of the RTPA are also continuing proceedings if—

(a) leave to make the application is applied for before the starting date but the proceedings in respect of that application for leave are not determined before that date; or

(b) leave to make an application for an order under that section is granted before the starting date but the application itself is not made before that date.

RPA section 16 or 17 proceedings

17. Proceedings on an application for an order under section 16 or 17 of the RPA are also continuing proceedings if—

(a) leave to make the application is applied for before the starting date but the proceedings in respect of that application for leave are not determined before that date; or

(b) leave to make an application for an order under section 16 or 17 of the RPA is granted before the starting date, but the application itself is not made before that date.

Continuing proceedings which are discontinued

18.—(1) On an application made jointly to the Court by all the parties to any continuing proceedings, the Court must, if it is satisfied that the parties wish it to do so, discontinue the proceedings.

(2) If, on an application under sub-paragraph (1) or for any other reason, the Court orders the proceedings to be discontinued, this Schedule has effect (subject to paragraphs 21 and 22) from the date on which the proceedings are discontinued as if they had never been instituted.

Chapter III The transitional period

The general rule

19.—(1) Except where this Chapter or Chapter IV provides otherwise, there is a transitional period, beginning on the starting date and lasting for one year, for any agreement made before the starting date.

(2) The Chapter I prohibition does not apply to an agreement to the extent to which there is a transitional period for the agreement.

(3) The Secretary of State may by regulations provide for sections 13 to 16 and Schedule 5 to apply with such modifications (if any) as may be specified in the regulations, in respect of applications to the Director about agreements for which there is a transitional period.

Cases for which there is no transitional period

20.—(1) There is no transitional period for an agreement to the extent to which, immediately before the starting date, it is—

(a) void under section 2(1) or 35(1)(a) of the RTPA;

(b) the subject of an order under section 2(2) or 35(3) of the RTPA; or

(c) unlawful under section 1, 2 or 11 of the RPA or void under section 9 of that Act.

(2) There is no transitional period for an agreement to the extent to which, before the starting date, a person has acted unlawfully for the purposes of section 27ZA(2) or (3) of the RTPA in respect of the agreement.

(3) There is no transitional period for an agreement to which paragraph 25(4) applies.

(4) There is no transitional period for—

(a) an agreement in respect of which there are continuing proceedings, or

(b) an agreement relating to goods in respect of which there are continuing proceedings,

to the extent to which the agreement is, when the proceedings are determined, void or unlawful.

Continuing proceedings under the RTPA

21. In the case of an agreement which is the subject of continuing proceedings under the RTPA, the transitional period begins—

(a) if the proceedings are discontinued, on the date of discontinuance;

(b) otherwise, when the proceedings are determined.

Continuing proceedings under the RPA

22.—(1) In the case of an agreement relating to goods which are the subject of continuing proceedings under the RPA, the transitional period for the exempt provisions of the agreement begins—

(a) if the proceedings are discontinued, on the date of discontinuance;

(b) otherwise, when the proceedings are determined.

(2) In sub-paragraph (1) "exempt provisions" has the meaning given by paragraph 14(3).

Provisions not contrary to public interest

23.—(1) To the extent to which an agreement contains provisions which, immediately before the starting date, are provisions which the Court has found not to be contrary to the public interest, the transitional period lasts for five years.

(2) Sub-paragraph (1) is subject to paragraph 20(4).

(3) To the extent to which an agreement which on the starting date is the subject of continuing proceedings is, when the proceedings are determined, found by the Court not to be contrary to the public interest, the transitional period lasts for five years.

Goods

24.—(1) In the case of an agreement relating to goods which, immediately before the starting date, are exempt under section 14 of the RPA, there is a transitional period for the agreement to the extent to which it consists of exempt provisions.

(2) Sub-paragraph (1) is subject to paragraph 20(4).

(3) In the case of an agreement relating to goods—

(a) which on the starting date are the subject of continuing proceedings, and

(b) which, when the proceedings are determined, are found to be exempt under section 14 of the RPA, there is a transitional period for the agreement, to the extent to which it consists of exempt provisions.

(4) In each case, the transitional period lasts for five years.

(5) In sub-paragraphs (1) and (3) "exempt provisions" means those provisions of the agreement which would, disregarding section 14 of the RPA, be—

(a) void as a result of section 9(1) of the RPA; or

(b) unlawful as a result of section 9(2) or 11 of the RPA.

Transitional period for certain agreements

25.—(1) This paragraph applies to agreements—

(a) which are subject to registration under the RTPA but which—

    (i) are not non-notifiable agreements within the meaning of section 27A of the RTPA, or

    (ii) are not agreements to which paragraph 5 applies; and

(b) in respect of which the time for furnishing relevant particulars as required by or under the RTPA expires on or after the starting date.

(2) "Relevant particulars" means—

(a) particulars which are required to be furnished by virtue of section 24 of the RTPA; or

(b) particulars of any variation of an agreement which are required to be furnished by virtue of sections 24 and 27 of the RTPA.

(3) There is a transitional period of one year for an agreement to which this paragraph applies if—

(a) relevant particulars are furnished before the starting date; and

(b) no person has acted unlawfully (for the purposes of section 27ZA(2) or (3) of the RTPA) in respect of the agreement.

(4) If relevant particulars are not furnished by the starting date, section 35(1)(a) of the RTPA does not apply in relation to the agreement (unless sub-paragraph (5) applies).

(5) This sub-paragraph applies if a person failing within section 27ZA(2) or (3) of the RTPA has acted unlawfully for the purposes of those subsections in respect of the agreement.

Special cases

26.—(1) In the case of an agreement in respect of which—

(a) a direction under section 127(2) of the Financial Services Act 1986 (c. 60) ("the 1986 Act") is in force immediately before the starting date, or

(b) a direction under section 194A(3) of the Broadcasting Act 1990 (c. 42) ("the 1990 Act") is in force immediately before the starting date,

the transitional period lasts for five years.

(2) To the extent to which an agreement is the subject of a declaration—

(a) made by the Treasury under section 127(3) of the 1986 Act, and

(b) in force immediately before the starting date,

the transitional period lasts for five years.

(3) Sub-paragraphs (1) and (2) do not affect the power of—

(a) the Treasury to make a declaration under section 127(2) of the 1986 Act (as amended by Schedule 2 to this Act),

(b) the Secretary of State to make a declaration under section 194A of the 1990 Act (as amended by Schedule 2 to this Act),

in respect of an agreement for which there is a transitional period.

Chapter IV The utilities

General

27. In this Chapter "the relevant period" means the period beginning with the starting date and ending immediately before the fifth anniversary of that date.

Electricity

28.—(1) For an agreement to which, immediately before the starting date, the RTPA does not apply by virtue of a section 100 order, there is a transitional period—

(a) beginning on the starting date; and

(b) ending at the end of the relevant period.

(2) For an agreement which is made at any time after the starting date and to which, had the RTPA not been repealed, that Act would not at the time at which the agreement is made have applied by virtue of a section 100 order, there is a transitional period—

(a) beginning on the date on which the agreement is made; and

(b) ending at the end of the relevant period.

(3) For an agreement (whether made before or after the starting date) which, during the relevant period, is varied at any time in such a way that it becomes an agreement which, had the RTPA not been repealed, would at that time have been one to which that Act did not apply by virtue of a section 100 order, there is a transitional period—

(a) beginning on the date on which the variation is made; and

(b) ending at the end of the relevant period.

(4) If an agreement for which there is a transitional period as a result of sub-paragraph (1), (2) or (3) is varied during the relevant period, the transitional period for the agreement continues if, had the RTPA not been repealed, the agreement would have continued to be one to which that Act did not apply by virtue of a section 100 order.

(5) But if an agreement for which there is a transitional period as a result of sub-paragraph (1), (2) or (3) ceases to be one to which, had it not been repealed,

the RTPA would not have applied by virtue of a section 100 order, the transitional period ends on the date on which the agreement so ceases.

(6) Sub-paragraph (3) is subject to paragraph 20.

(7) In this paragraph and paragraph 29—

"section 100 order" means an order made under section 100 of the Electricity Act 1989; and

expressions which are also used in Part I of the Electricity Act 1989 have the same meaning as in that Part.

Electricity: power to make transitional orders

29.—(1) There is a transitional period for an agreement (whether made before or after the starting date) relating to the generation, transmission or supply of electricity which—

(a) is specified, or is of a description specified, in an order ("a transitional order") made by the Secretary of State (whether before or after the making of the agreement but before the end of the relevant period); and

(b) satisfies such conditions as may be specified in the order.

(2) A transitional order may make provision as to when the transitional period in respect of such an agreement is to start or to be deemed to have started.

(3) The transitional period for such an agreement ends at the end of the relevant period.

(4) But if the agreement—

(a) ceases to be one to which a transitional order applies, or

(b) ceases to satisfy one or more of the conditions specified in the transitional order,

the transitional period ends on the date on which the agreement so ceases.

(5) Before making a transitional order, the Secretary of State must consult the Director General of Electricity Supply and the Director.

(6) The conditions specified in a transitional order may include conditions which refer any matter to the Secretary of State for determination after such consultation as may be so specified.

(7) In the application of this paragraph to Northern Ireland, the reference in sub-paragraph (5) to the Director General of Electricity Supply is to be read as a reference to the Director General of Electricity Supply for Northern Ireland.

Gas

30.—(1) For an agreement to which, immediately before the starting date, the RTPA does not apply by virtue of section 62 or a section 62 order, there is a transitional period—

(a) beginning on the starting date; and

(b) ending at the end of the relevant period.

(2) For an agreement which is made at any time after the starting date and to which, had the RTPA not been repealed, that Act would not at the time at which the agreement is made have applied by virtue of section 62 or a section 62 order, there is a transitional period—

(a) beginning on the date on which the agreement is made; and

(b) ending at the end of the relevant period.

(3) For an agreement (whether made before or after the starting date) which, during the relevant period, is varied at any time in such a way that it becomes an agreement which, had the RTPA not been repealed, would at that time have been one to which that Act did not apply by virtue of section 62 or a section 62 order, there is a transitional period—

(a) beginning on the date on which the variation is made; and

(b) ending at the end of the relevant period.

(4) If an agreement for which there is a transitional period as a result of sub-paragraph (1), (2) or (3) is varied during the relevant period, the transitional period for the agreement continues if, had the RTPA not been repealed, the agreement would have continued to be one to which that Act did not apply by virtue of section 62 or a section 62 order.

(5) But if an agreement for which there is a transitional period as a result of sub-paragraph (1), (2) or (3) ceases to be one to which, had it not been repealed, the RTPA would not have applied by virtue of section 62 or a section 62 order, the transitional period ends on the date on which the agreement so ceases.

(6) Sub-paragraph (3) also applies in relation to a modification which is treated as an agreement made on or after 28th November 1985 by virtue of section 62(4).

(7) Sub-paragraph (3) is subject to paragraph 20.

(8) In this paragraph and paragraph 31—

"section 62" means section 62 of the Gas Act 1986 (c. 44);

"section 62 order" means an order made under section 62.

Gas: power to make transitional orders

31.—(1) There is a transitional period for an agreement of a description falling within section 62(2)(a) and (b) or section 62(2A)(a) and (b) which—

(a) is specified, or is of a description specified, in an order ("a transitional order") made by the Secretary of State (whether before or after the making of the agreement but before the end of the relevant period); and

(b) satisfies such conditions as may be specified in the order.

(2) A transitional order may make provision as to when the transitional period in respect of such an agreement is to start or to be deemed to have started.

(3) The transitional period for such an agreement ends at the end of the relevant period.

(4) But if the agreement—

(a) ceases to be one to which a transitional order applies, or

(b) ceases to satisfy one or more of the conditions specified in the transitional order,

the transitional period ends on the date when the agreement so ceases.

(5) Before making a transitional order, the Secretary of State must consult the Director General of Gas Supply and the Director.

(6) The conditions specified in a transitional order may include—

(a) conditions which are to be satisfied in relation to a time before the coming into force of this paragraph;

(b) conditions which refer any matter (which may be the general question whether the Chapter I prohibition should apply to a particular agreement) to the Secretary of State, the Director or the Director General of Gas Supply for determination after such consultation as may be so specified.

Gas: Northern Ireland

32.—(1) For an agreement to which, immediately before the starting date, the RTPA does not apply by virtue of an Article 41 order, there is a transitional period—

(a) beginning on the starting date; and

(b) ending at the end of the relevant period.

(2) For an agreement which is made at any time after the starting date and to which, had the RTPA not been repealed, that Act would not at the time at which the agreement is made have applied by virtue of an Article 41 order, there is a transitional period—

(a) beginning on the date on which the agreement is made; and

(b) ending at the end of the relevant period.

(3) For an agreement (whether made before or after the starting date) which, during the relevant period, is varied at any time in such a way that it becomes an agreement which, had the RTPA not been repealed, would at that time have been one to which that Act did not apply by virtue of an Article 41 order, there is a transitional period—

(a) beginning on the date on which the variation is made; and

(b) ending at the end of the relevant period.

(4) If an agreement for which there is a transitional period as a result of sub-paragraph (1), (2) or (3) is varied during the relevant period, the transitional period for the agreement continues if, had the RTPA not been repealed, the agreement would have continued to be one to which that Act did not apply by virtue of an Article 41 order.

(5) But if an agreement for which there is a transitional period as a result of sub-paragraph (1), (2) or (3) ceases to be one to which, had it not been repealed, the RTPA would not have applied by virtue of an Article 41 order, the transitional period ends on the date on which the agreement so ceases.

(6) Sub-paragraph (3) is subject to paragraph 20.

(7) In this paragraph and paragraph 33—

"Article 41 order" means an order under Article 41 of the Gas (Northern Ireland) Order 1996 (S.I. 1996/275 (N.I. 2));

"Department" means the Department of Economic Development.

Gas: Northern Ireland - power to make transitional orders

33.—(1) There is a transitional period for an agreement of a description falling within Article 41(1) which—

(a) is specified, or is of a description specified, in an order ("a transitional order") made by the Department (whether before or after the making of the agreement but before the end of the relevant period); and

(b) satisfies such conditions as may be specified in the order.

(2) A transitional order may make provision as to when the transitional period in respect of such an agreement is to start or to be deemed to have started.

(3) The transitional period for such an agreement ends at the end of the relevant period.

(4) But if the agreement—

(a) ceases to be one to which a transitional order applies, or

(b) ceases to satisfy one or more of the conditions specified in the transitional order,

the transitional period ends on the date when the agreement so ceases.

(5) Before making a transitional order, the Department must consult the Director General of Gas for Northern Ireland and the Director.

(6) The conditions specified in a transitional order may include conditions which refer any matter (which may be the general question whether the Chapter I prohibition should apply to a particular agreement) to the Department for determination after such consultation as may be so specified.

Railways

34.—(1) In this paragraph—

"section 131" means section 131 of the Railways Act 1993 (c. 43) ("the 1993 Act");

"section 131 agreement" means an agreement—

(a) to which the RTPA does not apply immediately before the starting date by virtue of section 131(1); or

(b) in respect of which a direction under section 131(3) is in force immediately before that date;

"non-exempt agreement" means an agreement relating to the provision of railway services (whether made before or after the starting date) which is not a section 131 agreement; and

"railway services" has the meaning given by section 82 of the 1993 Act.

(2) For a section 131 agreement there is a transitional period of five years.

(3) There is a transitional period for a non-exempt agreement to the extent to which the agreement is at any time before the end of the relevant period required or approved—

    (a) by the Secretary of State or the Rail Regulator in pursuance of any function assigned or transferred to him under or by virtue of any provision of the 1993 Act;

    (b) by or under any agreement the making of which is required or approved by the Secretary of State or the Rail Regulator in the exercise of any such function; or

    (c) by or under a licence granted under Part I of the 1993 Act.

(4) The transitional period conferred by sub-paragraph (3)—

    (a) is to be taken to have begun on the starting date; and

    (b) ends at the end of the relevant period.

(5) Sub-paragraph (3) is subject to paragraph 20.

(6) Any variation of a section 131 agreement on or after the starting date is to be treated, for the purposes of this paragraph, as a separate non-exempt agreement.

The regulators

35.—(1) Subject to sub-paragraph (3), each of the regulators may exercise, in respect of sectoral matters and concurrently with the Director, the functions of the Director under paragraph 3, 7, 19(3), 36, 37, 38 or 39.

(2) In sub-paragraph (1) "sectoral matters" means—

    (a) in the case of the Director General of Telecommunications, the matters referred to in section 50(3) of the Telecommunications Act 1984 (c. 12);

    (b) in the case of the Director General of Gas Supply, the matters referred to in section 36A(3) and (4) of the Gas Act 1986 (c. 44);

    (c) in the case of the Director General of Electricity Supply, the matters referred to in section 43(3) of the Electricity Act 1989 (c. 29);

    (d) in the case of the Director General of Electricity Supply for Northern Ireland, the matters referred to in Article 46(3) of the Electricity (Northern Ireland) Order 1992 (S.I. 1992/231 (N.I. 1));

    (e) in the case of the Director General of Water Services, the matters referred to in section 31(3) of the Water Industry Act 1991 (c. 56);

    (f) in the case of the Rail Regulator, the matters referred to in section 67(3) of the Railways Act 1993, (c. 43);

    (g) in the case of the Director General of Gas for Northern Ireland, the matters referred to in Article 23(3) of the Gas (Northern Ireland) Order 1996 (S.I. 1996/275 (N.I. 2)).

(3) The power to give directions in paragraph 7(2) is exercisable by the Director only but if the Director is preparing directions which relate to a matter in respect of which a regulator exercises concurrent jurisdiction, he must consult that regulator.

(4) Consultations conducted by the Director before the enactment date, with a view to preparing directions which have effect on or after that date, are to be taken to satisfy sub-paragraph (3).

(5) References to enactments in sub-paragraph (2) are to the enactments as amended by or under this Act.

Chapter V Extending the transitional period

36.—(1) A party to an agreement for which there is a transitional period may apply to the Director, not less than three months before the end of the period, for the period to be extended.

(2) The Director may (on his own initiative or on an application under sub-paragraph (1))—

- (a) extend a one-year transitional period by not more than twelve months;
- (b) extend a transitional period of any period other than one year by not more than six months.

(3) An application under sub-paragraph (1) must—

- (a) be in such form as may be specified; and
- (b) include such documents and information as may be specified.

(4) If the Director extends the transitional period under this paragraph, he must give notice in such form, and to such persons, as may be specified.

(5) The Director may not extend a transitional period more than once.

(6) In this paragraph—

"person" has the same meaning as in Part I; and

"specified" means specified in rules made by the Director under section 51.

Chapter VI Terminating the transitional period

General

37.—(1) Subject to sub-paragraph (2), the Director may by a direction in writing terminate the transitional period for an agreement, but only in accordance with paragraph 38.

(2) The Director may not terminate the transitional period, nor exercise any of the powers in paragraph 38, in respect of an agreement which is excluded from the Chapter I prohibition by virtue of any of the provisions of Part I of this Act other than paragraph 1 of Schedule 1 or paragraph 2 or 9 of Schedule 3.

Circumstances in which the Director may terminate the transitional period

38.—(1) If the Director is considering whether to give a direction under paragraph 37 ("a direction"), he may in writing require any party to the agreement concerned to give him such information in connection with that agreement as he may require.

(2) If at the end of such period as may be specified in rules made under section 51, a person has failed, without reasonable excuse, to comply with a

requirement imposed under sub-paragraph (1), the Director may give a direction.

(3) The Director may also give a direction if he considers—

    (a) that the agreement would, but for the transitional period or a relevant exclusion, infringe the Chapter I prohibition; and

    (b) that he would not be likely to grant the agreement an unconditional individual exemption.

(4) For the purposes of sub-paragraph (3) an individual exemption is unconditional if no conditions or obligations are imposed in respect of it under section 4(3)(a).

(5) In this paragraph—

    "person" has the same meaning as in Part I;

    "relevant exclusion" means an exclusion under paragraph 1 of Schedule 1 or paragraph 2 or 9 of Schedule 3.

Procedural requirements on giving a paragraph 37 direction

39.—(1) The Director must specify in a direction under paragraph 37 ("a direction") the date on which it is to have effect (which must not be less than 28 days after the direction is given).

(2) Copies of the direction must be given to—

    (a) each of the parties concerned, and

    (b) the Secretary of State,

not less than 28 days before the date on which the direction is to have effect.

(3) In relation to an agreement to which a direction applies, the transitional period (if it has not already ended) ends on the date specified in the direction unless, before that date, the direction is revoked by the Director or the Secretary of State.

(4) If a direction is revoked, the Director may give a further direction in respect of the same agreement only if he is satisfied that there has been a material change of circumstance since the revocation.

(5) If, as a result of paragraph 24(1) or (3), there is a transitional period in respect of provisions of an agreement relating to goods—

    (a) which immediately before the starting date are exempt under section 14 of the RPA, or

    (b) which, when continuing proceedings are determined, are found to be exempt under section 14 of the RPA,

the period is not affected by paragraph 37 or 38.

Part V The Fair Trading Act 1973

References to the Monopolies and Mergers Commission

40.—(1) If, on the date on which the repeal by this Act of a provision mentioned in sub-paragraph (2) comes into force, the Monopolies and Mergers Commission has not completed a reference which was made to it before that date, continued consideration of the reference may include consideration of a question which could not have been considered if the provision had not been repealed.

(2) The provisions are—

(a) sections 10(2), 54(5) and 78(3) and paragraph 3(1) and (2) of Schedule 8 to the Fair Trading Act 1973 (c. 41);
(b) section 11(8)(b) of the Competition Act 1980 (c. 21);
(c) section 14(2) of the Telecommunications Act 1984 (c. 12);
(d) section 45(3) of the Airports Act 1986 (c. 31);
(e) section 25(2) of the Gas Act 1986 (c. 44);
(f) section 13(2) of the Electricity Act 1989 (c. 29);
(g) section 15(2) of the Water Industry Act 1991 (c. 56);
(h) article 16(2) of the Electricity (Northern Ireland) Order 1992 (S.I. 1992/231 (N.I. 1));
(i) section 14(2) of the Railways Act 1993 (c. 43);
(j) article 36(3) of the Airports (Northern Ireland) Order 1994 (S.I. 1994/426 (N.I. 1));
(k) article 16(2) of the Gas (Northern Ireland) Order 1996 (S.I. 1996/275 (N.I. 2)).

Orders under Schedule 8

41.—(1) In this paragraph—

"the 1973 Act" means the Fair Trading Act 1973 (c. 41);

"agreement" means an agreement entered into before the date on which the repeal of the limiting provisions comes into force;

"the order" means an order under section 56 or 73 of the 1973 Act;

"the limiting provisions" means sub-paragraph (1) or (2) of paragraph 3 of Schedule 8 to the 1973 Act (limit on power to make orders under paragraph 1 or 2 of that Schedule) and includes any provision of the order included because of either of those sub-paragraphs; and

"transitional period" means the period which—

(a) begins on the day on which the repeal of the limiting provisions comes into force; and

(b) ends on the first anniversary of the starting date.

(2) Sub-paragraph (3) applies to any agreement to the extent to which it would have been unlawful (in accordance with the provisions of the order) but for the limiting provisions.

(3) As from the end of the transitional period, the order is to have effect in relation to the agreement as if the limiting provisions had never had effect.

Part III of the Act

42.—(1) The repeals made by section 1 do not affect any proceedings in respect of an application which is made to the Court under Part III of the Fair Trading Act 1973 (c. 41), but is not determined, before the starting date.

(2) The question whether (for the purposes of sub-paragraph (1)) an application has been determined is to be decided in accordance with sub-paragraphs (3) and (4).

(3) If an appeal against the decision on the application is brought, the application is not determined until—

(a) the appeal is disposed of or withdrawn; or

(b) if as a result of the appeal the case is referred back to the Court—

(i) the expiry of the period within which an appeal ("the further appeal") in respect of the Court's decision on that reference could have been brought had this Act not been passed; or

(ii) if later, the date on which the further appeal is disposed of or withdrawn.

(4) Otherwise, the application is not determined until the expiry of the period within which any party to the application would have been able to bring an appeal against the decision on the application had this Act not been passed.

(5) Any amendment made by Schedule 12 to this Act which substitutes references to a relevant Court for references to the Court is not to affect proceedings of the kind referred to in sub-paragraph (1).

Part VI The Competition Act 1980

Undertakings

43.—(1) Subject to sub-paragraph (2), an undertaking accepted by the Director under section 4 or 9 of the Competition Act 1980 (c. 21) ceases to have effect on the coming into force of the repeal by this Act of that section.

(2) If the undertaking relates to an agreement which on the starting date is the subject of continuing proceedings, the undertaking continues to have effect for the purposes of section 29 of the Competition Act 1980 until the proceedings are determined.

Application of sections 25 and 26

44. The repeals made by section 1 do not affect—

(a) the operation of section 25 of the Competition Act 1980 in relation to an application under section 1(3) of the RTPA which is made before the starting date;

(b) an application under section 26 of the Competition Act 1980 which is made before the starting date.

Part VII Miscellaneous

[*Not reproduced in this work.*]

Schedule 14 Repeals and revocations

Part I Repeals

Section 74(3).

Chapter	Short title	Extent of repeal
1973 c. 41.	The Fair Trading Act 1973.	Section 4. Section 10(2). Section 45. Section 54(5). Section 78(3). In section 81(1), in the words before paragraph (a), from "and the Commission to "of this Act)"; in paragraph (b), "or the Commission, as the case may be" and "or of the Commission"; in subsection (2), "or the Commission" and "or of the Commission" and in subsection (3), from "and, in the case," to "85 of this Act", and "or the Commission, as the case may be,". In section 83, in subsection (1) "Subject to subsection (1A) below" and subsection (1A). In section 135(1), in the words before paragraph (a) and in paragraph (b), "or the Commission", and paragraph (a). Schedule 3. In Schedule 8, paragraph 3(1) and (2).
1976 c. 33.	The Restrictive Practices Court Act 1976.	The whole Act.
1976 c. 34.	The Restrictive Trade Practices Act 1976.	The whole Act.

Chapter	Short title	Extent of repeal
1976 c. 53.	The Resale Prices Act 1976.	The whole Act.
1976 c. 76.	The Energy Act 1976.	Section 5.
1977 c. 19.	The Restrictive Trade Practices Act 1977.	The whole Act.
1977 c. 37.	The Patents Act 1977.	Sections 44 and 45.
1979 c. 38.	The Estate Agents Act 1979.	In section 10(3), "or the Restrictive Trade Practices Act 1976."
1980 c. 21.	The Competition Act 1980.	Sections 2 to 10. In section 11(8), paragraph (b) and the "and" immediately before it. In section 13(1), from "but the giving" to the end. In section 15, subsections (2)(b), (3) and (4). Section 16(3). In section 17, "8(1)" in subsections (1) and (3) to (5) and in subsection (2) "8(1) or". In section 19(3), paragraph (d). In section 19(5)(a), "or in anything published under section 4(2)(a) above". Section 22. Sections 25 to 30. In section 31, subsection (2) and "10" in subsection (3). Section 33(3) and (4).
1984 c. 12.	The Telecommunications Act 1984.	Section 14(2). In section 16(5), the "or" immediately after paragraph (a). In section 50(4), paragraph (c) and the "and" immediately after it.

Chapter	Short title	Extent of repeal
1984 c. 12. *contd.*	The Telecommunications Act 1984.—*contd.*	In section 50(5), "or (3)". In section 50(7), "or the 1980 Act". In section 95(1), "or section 10(2)(a) of the 1980 Act". In section 95(2), paragraph (c) and the "or" immediately before it. In section 95(3), "or the 1980 Act". In section 101(3), paragraphs (d) and (e).
1986 c. 31.	The Airports Act 1986	Section 45(3). In section 54(1), "or section 10(2)(a) of the 1980 Act". In section 54(3), paragraph (c) and the "or" immediately before it. In section 54(4), "or the 1980 Act". In section 56(a)(ii), "or the 1980 Act".
1986 c. 44.	The Gas Act 1986.	Section 25(2). In section 27(1), "or section 10(2)(a) of the Competition Act 1980". In section 27(3)(a), from "or" to "competition reference". In section 27(6), "or the said Act of 1980". In section 28(5), the "or" immediately after paragraph (aa). In section 36A(5), paragraph (d) and the "and" immediately before it. In section 36A(6), "or (3)". In section 36A(8), "or under the 1980 Act".

Chapter	Short title	Extent of repeal
1986 c. 44.— *contd.*	The Gas Act 1986.— *contd.*	In section 36A(9), "or the 1980 Act". In section 42(3), paragraphs (e) and (f).
1986 c. 60.	The Financial Services Act 1986.	Section 126.
1987 c. 43.	The Consumer Protection Act 1987.·	In section 38(3), paragraphs (e) and (f).
1987 c. 53.	The Channel Tunnel Act 1987.	In section 33(2), paragraph (c) and the "and" immediately before it. In section 33(5), paragraphs (b) and (c).
1988 c. 54.	The Road Traffic (Consequential Provisions) Act 1988.	In Schedule 3, paragraph 19.
1989 c. 15.	The Water Act 1989.	In section 174(3), paragraphs (d) and (e).
1989 c. 29.	The Electricity Act 1989.	Section 13(2). In section 15(1), paragraph (b) and the "or" immediately before it. In section 15(2), paragraph (c) and the "or" immediately before it. In section 15(3), "or the 1980 Act". In section 25(5), the "or" immediately after paragraph (b). In section 43(4), paragraph (c) and the "and" immediately after it. In section 43(5), "or (3)". In section 43(7), "or the 1980 Act". In section 57(3), paragraphs (d) and (e).

Chapter	Short title	Extent of repeal
1989 c. 40.	The Companies Act 1989.	In Schedule 20, paragraphs 21 to 24.
1990 c. 42.	The Broadcasting Act 1990.	In section 193(2), paragraph (c) and the "and" immediately before it. In section 193(4), "or the Competition Act 1980".
1991 c. 56.	The Water Industry Act 1991.	In section 12(5), "or the 1980 Act". Section 15(2). In section 17(1), paragraph (b) and the "or" immediately before it. In section 17(2), paragraph (c) and the "or" immediately before it. In section 17(4), "or the 1980 Act". In section 31(4), paragraph (c) and the "and" immediately before it. In section 31(5), "or in subsection (3) above". In section 31(6), "or in subsection (3) above". In section 31(7), "or (3)". In section 31(9), "or the 1980 Act". In Part II of Schedule 15, the entries relating to the Restrictive Trade Practices Act 1976 and the Resale Prices Act 1976.
1991 c. 57.	The Water Resources Act 1991.	In Part II of Schedule 24, the entries relating to the Restrictive Trade Practices Act 1976 and the Resale Prices Act 1976.

Chapter	Short title	Extent of repeal
1993 c. 21.	The Osteopaths Act 1993.	In section 33(4), paragraph (b) and the "or" immediately before it. In section 33(5), "or section 10 of the Act of 1980".
1993 c. 43.	The Railways Act 1993.	Section 14(2). In section 16(1), paragraph (b) and the "or" immediately before it. In section 16(2), paragraph (c) and the "or" immediately before it. In section 16(5), "or the 1980 Act". In section 67(4), paragraph (c) and the "and" immediately after it. In section 67(6)(a), "or (3)". In section 67(9), "or under the 1980 Act". Section 131. In section 145(3), paragraphs (d) and (e).
1994 c. 17.	The Chiropractors Act 1994.	In section 33(4), paragraph (b) and the "or" immediately before it. In section 33(5), "or section 10 of the Act of 1980".
1994 c. 21.	The Coal Industry Act 1994.	In section 59(4), paragraphs (e) and (f).
1994 c. 40.	The Deregulation and Contracting Out Act 1994.	Sections 10 and 11. In section 12, subsections (1) to (6). In Schedule 4, paragraph 1. In Schedule 11, in paragraph 4, sub-paragraphs (3) to (6).
1996 c. 55.	The Broadcasting Act 1996.	Section 77(2).

Part II Revocations

[*Not reproduced in this work.*]

OFT Early Guidance
· Directions, Form EG ·
and Form N

Early Guidance: Directions given by the Director General of Fair Trading under paragraph 7(2) of Schedule 13 to the Act

Form of application

1. A person who wishes to apply under paragraph 7(2) of Schedule 13 for guidance in relation to an agreement shall in all cases submit Form EG to the Director General of Fair Trading.

Joint applications

2. Where a joint application is made, Form EG shall be submitted to the Director General of Fair Trading by or on behalf of all the applicants, and a joint representative may be nominated in the application as authorised to submit and receive documents on behalf of some or all of the applicants.

Copies

3.—(1) Documents submitted as part of Form EG shall be either originals or true copies, and the applicant shall certify that each copy is a true copy of the original.

(2) Subject to paragraph (3) below, two copies of the information submitted as Form EG, in addition to the original, shall be submitted to the Director General of Fair Trading.

(3) If, in the applicant's opinion, one or more regulators has or may have concurrent jurisdiction with the Director General of Fair Trading under paragraph 7 of Schedule 13, one extra copy of the information submitted as Form EG shall be submitted to the Director General of Fair Trading for each such regulator.

Content of applications

4.—(1) Where the declaration which is submitted as part of Form EG is signed by a solicitor or other representative of an applicant, the information submitted as Form EG shall include written proof of that representative's authority to act on that applicant's behalf.

(2) The information submitted as Form EG shall, subject to paragraph (4) below, be correct and complete, and for these purposes information which is false or misleading shall be treated as incorrect or incomplete.

(3) If the applicant considers that any information contained in the application is confidential, in the sense given to that word by direction 11 below, he shall set out that information in a separate annex to the application marked "confidential information" and explain why it should be treated as such.

(4) The Director may dispense with the obligation to submit any particular information, including any document, forming part of Form EG if he considers that such information or document is unnecessary for the examination of the case.

Effective date of application

5.—(1) Except where paragraph (3) below applies, an application shall have effect on the date on which it is received by the Director General of Fair Trading; an application received after 6.00 p.m. on a working day shall be treated as received on the next working day.

(2) The Director General of Fair Trading shall acknowledge receipt of an application to the applicant without delay.

(3) Where the Director finds that the information submitted as Form EG is incomplete in a material respect he shall, without delay, inform the applicant in writing of that fact; in such cases, the application, if otherwise made in accordance with these directions, shall have effect on the date on which the complete information is received by that Director, and information received after 6.00 p.m. on a working day shall be treated as received on the next working day.

(4) Material changes in the facts contained in an application of which the applicant knows, or ought reasonably to know, shall be communicated voluntarily and without delay:

  (a) to the director who is exercising jurisdiction under paragraph 7 of Schedule 13 in relation to the application; or

  (b) where the applicant has not yet been informed of which Director that is, to the Director General of Fair Trading.

(5) If, on the expiry of the period of one month following the date on which an application has been received by the Director General of Fair Trading, the Director has not informed the applicant, under paragraph (3) above, that the application is incomplete in a material respect, the application, if made in accordance with these directions, shall be deemed to have become effective on the date of its receipt by the Director General of Fair Trading.

Notification of application to other parties

6.—(1) A party to an agreement who makes an application under paragraph 7(2) of Schedule 13 shall take all reasonable steps to:

(a) give written notification to all the other parties to the agreement of whom he is aware that the application has been made; and

(b) give such notification within seven working days of the date on which the applicant receives acknowledgement of receipt of his application by the Director General of Fair Trading.

(2) The applicant shall provide a copy of such notification as is given under paragraph (1) above to the Director General of Fair Trading.

Concurrent jurisdiction

7.—(1) If the Director General of Fair Trading considers that a regulator has or may have concurrent jurisdiction under paragraph 7 of Schedule 13 to give guidance in response to an application made under paragraph 7(2) of Schedule 13, he shall:

(a) as soon as practicable, send a copy of the information submitted as Form EG to the regulator; and

(b) inform the applicant in writing that he has done so.

(2) As soon as practicable, the Director General of Fair Trading shall inform the applicant in writing of which Director is to exercise jurisdiction under paragraph 7 of Schedule 13 in relation to the application; if, subsequently, the application is transferred to a different Director who is to exercise such jurisdiction instead, the applicant shall be informed in writing of that fact.

Giving of guidance

8. Where the Director gives guidance to the applicant under sub-paragraph 7(3)(a) of Schedule 13, he shall do so in writing without delay after determining the application, stating the facts on which he bases the guidance and his reasons for it.

Withdrawal of guidance

9.—(l) If, having given guidance under sub-paragraph 7(3)(a) of Schedule 13 to the effect that:

(a) the agreement is unlikely to infringe the Chapter I prohibition, regardless of whether or not it is exempt; or

(b) the agreement is likely to be exempt under:
  (i) a block exemption;
  (ii) a parallel exemption; or
  (iii) a section 11 exemption; or

(c) he would be likely to grant the agreement an individual exemption if asked to do so,

the Director proposes to withdraw that guidance before the date on which section 2 comes into force, he shall consult the person to whom he gave the guidance.

(2) Where the Director withdraws such guidance as is referred to in paragraph (1) above, he shall do so by giving written notice of the withdrawal to the person to whom he gave the guidance, stating his reasons for the withdrawal.

Confidential third party information

10.—(1) If a person who is not a party to the agreement to which an application made under paragraph 7(2) of Schedule 13 relates gives information to the Director in connection with the exercise of the Director's functions under paragraph 7 of Schedule 13 in relation to that agreement, and that person considers that any of the information is confidential, in the sense given to that word by direction 11 below, he shall set out the part of the information which he considers to be confidential in that sense in a separate annex marked "confidential information" and explain why it should be treated as such.

(2) The Director shall, if he proposes to disclose any of the information contained in an annex provided in accordance with paragraph (1) above, consult the person who provided the information if it is practicable to do so.

Interpretation

11.—(1) In these directions:-
   (a) a reference to "the applicant" is to be construed as being a reference to the applicant or to his duly authorised representative if written proof of the representative's authority to act on the applicant's behalf is included in the information submitted as Form EG;
   (b) "a block exemption" is to be construed by reference to section 6;
   (c) information is confidential if it is:
      (i) commercial information the disclosure of which would, or might, significantly harm the legitimate business interests of the undertaking to which it relates; or
      (ii) information relating to the private affairs of an individual the disclosure of which would, or might, significantly harm his interests;
   (d) where the Director, if he proposes to take action, is required to consult a person, he shall:
      (i) give written notice to the person in question, stating the action he proposes and his reasons for it; and
      (ii) inform that person that any written representations made to the Director within the period specified in the notice will be considered;
   (e) a reference to "the Director" is to be construed as being a reference to the Director General of Fair Trading or to any regulator;
   (f) "Form EG" means the information, including any document, required to be provided by such form as is from time to time issued by the Director General of Fair Trading;

(g) "an individual exemption" is to be construed by reference to section 4;

(h) "a parallel exemption" is to be construed by reference to section 10;

(i) "regulator" has the meaning given by section 59;

(j) "a section 11 exemption" is to be construed by reference to section 11; and

(k) "working day" means any day which is not Saturday, Sunday, an official holiday on which the Office of Fair Trading is closed, or any other day on which that office is closed.

(2) References in these directions to the "Act" are to the Competition Act 1998 and references to numbered sections or schedules are to the sections or schedules so numbered in the Act.

Form EG for Applications for Early Guidance under paragraph 7 of Schedule 13 to the Competition Act

Part 1: Notes

1.1 *Guidance in anticipation of the coming into force of Chapter I of the Act ("early guidance") is available for agreements made during the period beginning on 9 November 1998 (enactment date) and ending immediately before 1 March 2000 (the date on which the Chapter I prohibition comes into force). It may be applied for under paragraph 7 of Schedule 13 to the Act. Early guidance is not available in respect of the Chapter II prohibition. This form cannot be used for notifications made on or after 1 March 2000; Form N must be used for such notifications.*

1.2 *Although this document is described as 'a Form', it is essentially a check-list of information which must be supplied to the Director General of Fair Trading to enable him to determine an application for early guidance. Before completing the Form, reference should be made to the Early Guidance Directions of the Director General of Fair Trading issued on 26 November 1998.*

1.3 *The information must be correct and complete for the application to be effective.*

1.4 *The Form must be supplied in original version plus two copies, together with either an original or a certified copy, plus two further copies, of the agreement(s) and any relevant Annexes.*

1.5 *All applications for early guidance should be sent to the Director General of Fair Trading and marked for the attention of the "Early Guidance Co-ordination Unit".*

1.6 *The Act is enforced by the Director General of Fair Trading and, in relation to the regulated utility sectors shown in question 3.5 below, concurrently with the sector regulators; these have concurrent jurisdiction with the Director General to give early guidance. If any positive answer is given [to] question 3.5, provide one further copy of the Form and attachments for each relevant regulator who may have concurrent jurisdiction. A copy of the Form (together with its Annexes and copies of agreements) should also be sent to the relevant regulator(s), if the agreement being notified may fall within their sector(s). In general, the relevant regulator will deal with the application. If the Director General considers that a regulator has, or may have, concurrent jurisdiction in relation to an agreement in respect of which an application for early guidance has been submitted, he will send a copy of the Form EG to the regulator(s) and inform the notifying party that he has done so.*

1.7 *Indicate clearly to which section of the Form any additional pages relate. The application must include the form of receipt at Part 3. Information which is regarded by the undertaking or undertakings as confidential should be clearly identified as such and placed in a separate identified annex. An explanation of why such information is regarded as confidential should also be provided. Applications may also be made on disk or using other electronic format: please telephone the enquiry point at the Office of Fair Trading on 0171 211 8989 before using this facility.*

1.8 *The Director General, or, if the applicant has been informed that a regulator is dealing with the application, that regulator, must be informed of any material changes which occur after application has been made and which may affect any information given in this Form.*

Part 2: Information to be provided by the undertaking notifying the agreement

Number sections as below. In some cases, it may be possible to dispense with the requirement to provide information in all categories. This should be discussed with officials before making the application. Information which is regarded by the undertaking(s) as confidential should be clearly identified as such and placed in a separate identified annex.

1. *The undertaking(s) submitting the application*

    1.1 The identity of the undertaking submitting the application (full name and address, name of representative, telephone and fax numbers, and brief description of the undertaking or association of undertakings). For a partnership, sole trader or other unincorporated body trading under a business name, give the name(s) and address(es) of the proprietor(s) or partners. Please quote any reference which should be used;

    1.2 if acting on behalf of another undertaking, state in what capacity, eg solicitor;

Where the Form is signed by a solicitor or other representative, proof of authority to act on behalf of the undertaking submitting the application must be provided.

    1.3 if the application is submitted by or on behalf of more than one undertaking, indicate whether a joint representative has been appointed. If so, give the details as requested in 1.1. above in respect of the joint representative. If not, give the details in respect of any representatives who have been authorised to act on behalf of each, or either, of the parties to the agreement, indicating who they represent;

    1.4 the Standard Industrial Classification code for the relevant good(s) or service(s), if known. If the code is not known, describe the goods or services involved as fully and accurately as possible;

The directions issued by the Director General require a party to an agreement who makes an application for early guidance in respect of that agreement to take all reasonable steps to notify all other parties to the agreement of whom he is aware that the application has been made. In exceptional cases, it may not be practicable to inform all non-notifying parties to the notified agreement that it has been notified, if, for example, an agreement is concluded with a large number of undertakings. The notification to such other undertakings must be made (a) in writing; and (b) within seven working days of the applicant receiving the Director General's acknowledgment of receipt of his application. The applicant must send a copy of such notification to the Director General.

- 1.5 the full names, addresses (by registered office, where appropriate, and principal place of business, if different), telephone and fax numbers, nature of business, and brief description of any other parties to the agreement, decision or concerted practice ('the arrangement') being notified;
- 1.6 details of the steps to be taken to inform any other such parties that the application has been made and indicate whether the remaining parties have received a copy of the application with confidential information and business secrets deleted. State the reasons, if it is not practicable to inform other parties of the application in accordance with the requirements outlined above.

2.   Purpose of the application

The Chapter I prohibition will not apply unless the arrangement has an 'appreciable effect' on competition and an application for early guidance will not normally be appropriate when that is not the case. Further information is given in the guideline **The Competition Act 1998: the Chapter I prohibition.**

- 2.1 whether the arrangement that is the subject of the application is considered to be of a type which would benefit from any exclusion from the Chapter I prohibition. Specify the exclusion: give reasons why you are unsure whether the arrangement will be covered by the exclusion and why an application for early guidance is considered appropriate;
- 2.2 specify why it is considered that the Chapter I prohibition is likely to be infringed and whether the arrangement is likely to qualify (or in the case of an individual exemption, is likely to qualify if notified) for an exemption (individual, UK block exemption, parallel, or under section 11 of the Act);

3.   Jurisdiction

In general, when an arrangement is also caught by Article 85 of the EC Treaty, the Director General considers that the EC Commission is the more appropriate authority to whom notification should be made (see the guideline **The Competition Act 1998: the Chapter I prohibition***).*

- 3.1 why the arrangement is considered to be not caught by Article 85(1);

3.2 whether the arrangement is the subject of an application to the European Commission. If so, it would assist consideration of the application if three copies of the completed Form A/B and supporting documents, and one further copy if information has been given in response to question 3.5 below, were attached. It is unnecessary to repeat information given on Form A/B, but information specific to the UK market will be necessary (following the format in question 7.1) to the extent that it has not been given on Form A/B, and should be provided separately. Supply three copies of any 'comfort' letter received from the European Commission;

3.3 whether the arrangement is the subject of an application to any other national competition authority;

3.4 if the arrangement relates to transport by rail, road, inland waterway or to services ancillary to transport and is the subject of an application to the European Commission under Regulation 1017/68, it would similarly assist consideration of the application if three copies of the completed Form II and any supporting documents and one further copy if information has been given in response to question 3.5 below were attached;

3.5 whether the arrangement being notified relates to any one or more of:
 a commercial activities connected with telecommunications;
 b the shipping, conveyance or supply of gas and activities ancillary thereto;
 c commercial activities connected with the generation, transmission or supply of electricity;
 d commercial activities connected with the supply of water or securing a supply of water or with the provision or securing of sewerage services;
 e commercial activities connected with the generation, transmission or supply of electricity in Northern Ireland;
 f the conveyance, storage or supply of gas in Northern Ireland;
 g the supply of railway services.
 Identify the sector regulator or regulators who may have concurrent jurisdiction with the Director General of Fair Trading to deal with the application for early guidance;

3.6 names and addresses, telephone and fax numbers, date and the details, including case references, of any previous contacts with the Office of Fair Trading, a regulator, any other national competition authority, or the EC Commission, and of any proceedings in any national court in the European Community, relating to the arrangement being notified and of any relevant previous arrangements.

4. *Details of the arrangement*

4.1 a brief description of the arrangement being notified (nature, content, purpose, date(s) and duration);

    4.2 if written, attach either an original or a certified copy, together with two further copies, of the most recent version of the text of the arrangement being notified (technical details contained in know-how agreements, for example, may be omitted but omissions should be indicated); if not written, provide a full description;

    4.3 identify any provisions in the arrangement which may restrict the parties in their freedom to take independent commercial decisions or to act on those decisions;

    4.4 if the application relates to a standard contract, the number expected to be concluded.

5. Information on the parties to the arrangement and the groups to which they belong

    5.1 for each undertaking identified in 1.5 above, the name of a contact, together with his or her address, telephone and fax numbers, and position held in the undertaking;

    5.2 the corporate groups to which each undertaking belongs and the product and/or services market(s) in which the groups are active (hereafter called 'the relevant product market'); include one copy of the most recent consolidated annual report and accounts (or equivalent for unincorporated bodies) for each undertaking;

    5.3 for each of the parties to the arrangement, provide a list of all undertakings belonging to the same group which are active in the same relevant product market(s), and those active in markets neighbouring the relevant product markets - that is, those which are not regarded by the consumer as fully interchangeable or substitutable for products in the defined relevant product market, as defined in question 6.1 below.

6. The relevant product and geographic markets

A relevant product market comprises all those products and/or services regarded by the consumer of the product or service as interchangeable or substitutable by reason of their characteristics, prices or intended use. The following factors are among those normally considered when determining the relevant product market and should be taken into account, together with any others considered relevant:

- *the degree of physical similarity between the products/services in question;*
- *any differences in end-use to which the goods are or may be put;*
- *differences in price between the products/services;*
- *the cost of switching between two potentially competing products/services; and*
- *established consumer preferences for one type or category of product/service.*

The relevant geographic market is the area in which the undertakings concerned are involved in the supply of products or services in which the conditions of competition are appreciably different from neighbouring areas. The following factors are among those normally considered when determining the relevant geographic market and should be taken into account, together with any others considered relevant:

- *the nature and characteristics of the products or services concerned;*
- *the existence of entry barriers or consumer preferences;*
- *appreciable differences of the undertakings' market share or substantial price differences between neighbouring areas; and*
- *transport costs.*

6.1 In the light of the relevant factors given above (which are not exhaustive), explain the definitions of the relevant product and geographic markets which should be considered, with full reasons, in particular stating the specific products or services directly or indirectly affected by the application and other goods or services that may be viewed as substitutable, with reasons. If the relevant geographic market is considered to be an area smaller, or larger, than the whole of the United Kingdom, [state] the boundaries considered applicable, with reasons. Give reasons for all assumptions or findings, and explain how the factors outlined above have been taken into account. Further details are in the guideline **The Competition Act 1998: Market Definition;**

6.2 provide a copy of the most recent in-house long-term market studies assessing or analysing the relevant markets (including any commissioned by the undertakings from outside consultants), and give references of any external studies of the relevant product market, and, where possible, include a copy of any such studies.

7. The position of the undertakings in the relevant product markets

The information required under this section relates to both the relevant geographic market and the relevant product market, for the groups of the parties as a whole. Market shares may be calculated either on the basis of value or volume. Justification for the figures provided must be given by reference to the sales or turnover of each of the undertakings in question. The source or sources of information should be given, and, where possible, a copy of the document from which information has been taken.

7.1 for each of the previous three calendar or financial years, as available, give:

a details of the market shares of each undertaking in the goods or services in the relevant product and geographic markets, as identified in 6.1 above, and, if different, in the UK, and in the European Community;

  b estimates of market shares in the relevant product and geographic markets for each of the five main competitors of each of the undertakings, giving the undertaking's name, address, telephone and fax number, and, where possible, a contact name;

  c identify the five main customers of each of the undertakings in the relevant product and geographic markets, giving the undertaking's name, address, telephone and fax number, and, where possible, a contact name;

  d details of the undertakings' interests in, and arrangements with, any other companies competing in the relevant product and geographic market, together with details of their market shares, if known.

8. *Market entry and potential competition in the relevant product and geographic markets*

8.1 For all relevant product and geographic markets:

  a describe the factors influencing entry into the relevant product market(s): that is, the barriers which exist to prevent undertakings not presently manufacturing goods within the relevant product market(s) from entering the market(s), taking account of, in particular but not exclusively, the extent to which:
  - entry is regulated by the requirements of government authorisation or standard–setting, in any form, and any legal or regulatory controls on entry to the market(s);
  - entry is influenced by the availability of raw materials;
  - entry is influenced by the length of existing contracts between suppliers and customers;
  - research and development and licensing patents, know-how and other rights are important;

  b describe the factors influencing entry in geographic terms: that is, the barriers that exist to prevent undertakings already producing and/or marketing goods within the relevant product market(s) outside the relevant geographic market(s) from extending sales into the relevant geographic market(s), taking account of, in particular but not exclusively, the importance of:
  - trade barriers imposed by law, such as tariffs, quotas etc;
  - local geographical specifications or technical requirements;
  - procurement policies;
  - the existence of adequate and available local distribution and retailing facilities;
  - transport costs;
  - strong consumer preference for local brands or products;

  c in respect of new entrants in both product and geographic terms, state whether any new undertakings have entered the product market(s) in geographic areas where the undertakings sell, during the last three years. Identify the undertakings concerned by name, address, telephone and fax numbers and, where possible, a contact name, with best estimates of market shares of each in the relevant product and geographic markets.

9.   *Negative clearance*

9.1   state reasons for seeking 'negative clearance' (that is, that the Director General should conclude that the arrangement will not be covered by the Chapter I prohibition). Indicate, for example, which provision or effects of the arrangement may breach the prohibition, and state the reasons why it is considered that the arrangements do not have the object or effect of preventing, restricting or distorting competition within the UK to an appreciable extent.

10.   *Exemption*

The criteria which will be taken into account in considering applications for exemption are set out in section 9 of the Act.

10.1   if guidance on exemption from the Chapter I prohibition is sought, explain how the arrangements contribute to improving production or distribution and/or promoting technical or economic progress, and how consumers will be allowed a fair share of those benefits. Explain how each restrictive provision in the arrangements is indispensable to these objectives, and how the arrangements do not eliminate competition in respect of a substantial part of the relevant product or geographic market concerned.

11.   *Transitional periods*

11.1   if the arrangement is considered to benefit from any transitional periods during which the Chapter I prohibition does not apply, indicate the duration of the relevant transitional periods by reference to Schedule 13 to the Act.

12.   *Other information*

12.1   state:
a   whether this application should be considered as urgent. If so, give reasons;
b   any other information you consider may be helpful.

The application must conclude with the following declaration which is to be signed by or on behalf of all the applicants or notifying undertakings. Unsigned applications are invalid.

DECLARATION

The undersigned declare that all the information given above and in the .... pages annexed hereto is correct to the best of their knowledge and belief, and that all estimates are identified as such and are their best estimates of the underlying facts.

Place and date ....

Signatures ....

....

Status ....

....

.... name(s) in block capitals.

Part 3: Acknowledgement of receipt

This Form will be returned to the address inserted below if the top half is completed by the undertaking lodging it.

to be completed by the undertaking making the application

To: .... (name and address of applicant)

....

....

Your application dated ....

concerning ....

under reference ....

involving the following undertakings:

1. ....

2. .... [and others]

---

to be completed by the Office of Fair Trading

was received on ....

and registered under reference number

....

Please quote this number in all correspondence

In the event that this application is not complete in a material respect, you will be informed within one month of its receipt. If you are not informed within that time that it is considered to be incomplete, it is deemed to be effective on the date of its receipt.

Form N for notifications for guidance or decision under Chapters I and II of the Competition Act 1998

Formal Consultation Draft

Part 1: Notes

1.1   *Although this document is described as 'a Form', it is essentially a checklist of information which must be supplied to the Director General of Fair Trading to enable him to determine a notification. Before completing the Form, reference should be made to the Procedural Rules of the Director General of Fair Trading.*

1.2   *The information must be correct and complete for the notification to be effective.*

1.3   *The Form must be supplied in original version plus two copies, together with either an original or a certified copy, plus two further copies, of any relevant agreement and Annexes.*

1.4   *All notifications for guidance or a decision under Chapter I or Chapter II of the Act should be sent to the Director General of Fair Trading. He will place details of all notifications for decision (although not for guidance) on the public register maintained by him at the Office of Fair Trading and on the Office's Internet website. Details of the notification for decision may subsequently be published in suitable trade and/or national press, where it is considered appropriate to do so.*

1.5   *The Act is enforced by the Director General of Fair Trading and, in relation to the regulated utility sectors shown in question 3.5 below, concurrently with the sector regulators; if any positive answer is given to that question, provide one further copy of the Form and attachments for each relevant regulator who may have concurrent jurisdiction. A copy of the Form (together with its Annexes and copies of agreements) should also be sent to the relevant regulator(s), if the agreement or conduct being notified may fall within their sector(s). In general, the relevant regulator will deal with the notification. If the Director General considers that a regulator has, or may have, concurrent jurisdiction in relation to an agreement or conduct in respect of which a notification has been submitted, he will send a copy of the Form N to the regulator(s) and inform the notifying party that he has done so.*

1.6   *Indicate clearly to which section of the Form any additional pages relate. The notification must include the form of receipt at Part 3.* **Information which is regarded by the undertaking or undertakings as confidential should be clearly identified as such and placed in a separate identified annex, explaining why the information should be regarded as confidential.** *Notifications may also be made on disk or using other electronic format: please telephone the enquiry point at the Office of Fair Trading on 0171 211 [8989] before using this facility.*

1.7 *The Director General must be informed of any changes which occur after notification has been made and which may affect any information given in this Form.*

Complaints

1.8 *Complaints may be sent either to the Director General of Fair Trading or direct to the relevant regulator. There is no form to complete to make a complaint; further information on making complaints is contained in the guideline* **The Competition Act 1998: the Major Provisions.**

Part 2: Information to be provided by the undertaking notifying the agreement or conduct

Number sections as below. In some cases, it may be possible to dispense with the requirement to provide information in all categories. This should be discussed with officials before making the notification. **Information which is regarded by the undertaking(s) as confidential should be clearly identified as such and placed in a separate identified annex.**

1. The undertaking(s) submitting the notification

1.1 The identity of the undertaking submitting the notification (full name and address, name of representative, telephone and fax numbers, and brief description of the undertaking or association of undertakings). For a partnership, sole trader or other unincorporated body trading under a business name, give the name(s) and address(es) of the proprietor(s) or partners. Please quote any reference which should be used;

1.2 if acting on behalf of another undertaking, state in what capacity, eg solicitor;

Where the Form is signed by a solicitor or other representative, proof of authority to act on behalf of the undertaking submitting the notification must be provided.

1.3 if the notification is submitted by or on behalf of more than one undertaking, give the details of the representative(s) as requested in 1.1. above. Indicate whether the representative has been appointed on a joint basis. If not, give the details in respect of representatives who have been authorised to act on behalf of each or either of the parties to the agreement, indicating who they represent;

1.4 the Standard Industrial Classification code for the relevant good(s) or service(s), if known. If the code is not known, describe the goods or services involved as fully and accurately as possible;

Schedules 5 and 6 to the Act require a party to an agreement or conduct who makes a notification for guidance or a decision in respect of that agreement or conduct to take all reasonable steps to notify all other parties to the agreement or conduct of whom he is aware that the notification has been made and whether it is for guidance or a decision. In exceptional cases, it may not be practicable to inform all non-notifying parties to the notified agreement or conduct that it has been notified, if, for example, an agreement is concluded with a large number of undertakings. The notification to such other undertakings must be made (a) in writing; and (b) within seven working days of the notifying undertaking receiving the Director General's acknowledgment of receipt.

1.5 the full names, addresses (by registered office, where appropriate, and principal place of business, if different), telephone and fax numbers, nature of business, and brief description of any other parties to the agreement, decision or concerted practice ('the arrangement') or conduct being notified;

1.6 details of the steps to be taken to inform any other such parties that the notification has been made and indicate whether the remaining parties have received a copy of the notification with confidential information and business secrets deleted. State the reasons, if it is not practicable to inform other parties of the notification in accordance with the requirements outlined above.

2. Purpose of the notificaton

The Chapter I prohibition does not apply unless the arrangement has an 'appreciable effect' on competition, and notification will not normally be appropriate when that is not the case. Further information is given in the guideline **The Competition Act 1998: the Chapter I prohibition.** *The concept of appreciability does not apply to the Chapter II prohibition.*

2.1 whether the notification is being made under Chapter I, Chapter II or both;

2.2 whether it is for guidance or a decision;

if for guidance as to whether the Chapter I prohibition has been infringed:

2.3 specify why it is considered that the Chapter I prohibition has been infringed and whether the arrangement qualifies (or in the case of an individual exemption, would qualify if notified) for an exemption (individual, UK block exemption, parallel, or under section 11 of the Act);

or

if for a decision as to whether the Chapter I prohibition has been infringed:

2.4 whether an individual exemption is requested, and, if so, the date from which it is required to have effect, if different from the date of notification, giving reasons;

2.5 if the notification is for an extension of an individual exemption, state the date of expiry of the existing exemption and the reason why an extension is sought. Enclose a copy of the decision letter granting the exemption;

2.6 whether the arrangement or conduct that is the subject of the notification is considered to benefit from any exclusion from the Chapter I or Chapter II prohibitions. Specify the exclusion: give reasons why you are unsure whether the arrangement or conduct is covered by the exclusion and why notification is considered appropriate;

3. Jurisdiction

In general, when an arrangement is also caught by Article 85 of the EC Treaty, the Director General considers that the EC Commission is the more appropriate authority to whom notification should be made (see the guideline **The Competition Act 1998: the Chapter I prohibition**).

3.1 why the arrangement is considered to be not caught by Article 85(1);

3.2 whether the arrangement or conduct is the subject of a notification to the European Commission. If so, it would assist consideration of the notification if three copies of the completed Form A/B and supporting documents, and one further copy if information has been given in response to question 3.5 below, were attached. It is unnecessary to repeat information given on Form A/B, but information specific to the UK market will be necessary (following the format in question 7.1) to the extent that it has not been given on Form A/B, and should be provided separately. Supply three copies of any 'comfort' letter received from the European Commission;

3.3 whether the arrangement or conduct is the subject of a notification to any other national competition authority;

3.4 if the arrangement relates to transport by rail, road, inland waterway or to services ancillary to transport and is the subject of a notification to the European Commission under Regulation 1017/68, it would similarly assist consideration of the notification if three copies of the completed Form II and any supporting documents and one further copy if information has been given in response to question 3.5 below were attached;

3.5 whether the arrangement or conduct being notified relates to any one or more of:

a commercial activities connected with telecommunications;

b the shipping, conveyance or supply of gas and activities ancillary thereto;

c commercial activities connected with the generation, transmission or supply of electricity;

    d commercial activities connected with the supply of water or securing a supply of water or with the provision or securing of sewerage services;

    e commercial activities connected with the generation, transmission or supply of electricity in Northern Ireland;

    f the conveyance, storage or supply of gas in Northern Ireland;

    g the supply of railway services.

    Identify the sector regulator or regulators who may have concurrent jurisdiction with the Director General of Fair Trading to deal with the notification;

3.6 names and addresses, telephone and fax numbers, date, details and case references of any previous contacts with the Office of Fair Trading, a regulator, any other national competition authority, or the EC Commission, and of any proceedings in any national court in the European Community, relating to the arrangement or conduct being notified and of any relevant previous arrangements or conduct.

4. *Details of the arrangement or conduct*

4.1 a brief description of the arrangement or conduct being notified (nature, content, purpose, date(s) and duration);

4.2 if written, attach either an original or a certified copy, together with two further copies, of the most recent version of the text of the arrangement being notified (technical details contained in know-how agreements, for example, may be omitted but omissions should be indicated); if not written, provide a full description;

4.3 identify any provisions in the arrangement which may restrict the parties in their freedom to take independent commercial decisions or to act on those decisions;

4.4 if the notification relates to a standard contract, the number expected to be concluded.

5. *Chapter I notifications: information on the parties to the arrangement and the groups to which they belong*

5.1 for each undertaking identified in 1.5 above, the name of a contact, together with his or her address, telephone and fax numbers, and position held in the undertaking;

5.2 the corporate groups to which each undertaking belongs and the product and/or services market(s) in which the groups are active (hereafter called 'the relevant product market'); include one copy of the most recent consolidated annual report and accounts (or equivalent for unincorporated bodies) for each undertaking;

5.3 for each of the parties to the arrangement, provide a list of all undertakings belonging to the same group which are active in the same relevant product market(s), and those active in markets neighbouring the relevant product markets – that is, those which are not regarded by the consumer as fully interchangeable or substitutable for products in the defined relevant product market, as defined in question 6.1 below.

6.   The relevant product and geographic markets

A relevant product market comprises all those products and/or services regarded by the consumer of the product or service as interchangeable or substitutable by reason of their characteristics, prices or intended use. The following factors are among those normally considered when determining the relevant product market and should be taken into account, together with any others considered relevant:

– *the degree of physical similarity between the products/services in question;*
– *any differences in end-use to which the goods are or may be put;*
– *differences in price between the products/services;*
– *the cost of switching between two potentially competing products/services; and*
– *established consumer preferences for one type or category of product/ service.*

The relevant geographic market is the area in which the undertakings concerned are involved in the supply of products or services in which the conditions of competition are appreciably different from neighbouring areas. The following factors are among those normally considered when determining the relevant geographic market and should be taken into account, together with any others considered relevant:

– *the nature and characteristics of the products or services concerned;*
– *the existence of entry barriers or consumer preferences;*
– *appreciable differences of the undertakings' market share or substantial price differences between neighbouring areas; and*
– *transport costs.*

6.1 In the light of the relevant factors given above (which are not exhaustive), explain the definitions of the relevant product and geographic markets which should be considered, with full reasons, in particular stating the specific products or services directly or indirectly affected by the notification and other goods or services that may be viewed as substitutable, with reasons. If the relevant geographic market is considered to be an area smaller, or larger, than the whole of the United Kingdom, [state] the boundaries considered applicable, with reasons. Give reasons for all assumptions or findings, and explain how the factors outlined above have been taken into account. Further details are in the guideline *The Competition Act 1998: Market Definition*;

6.2 provide a copy of the most recent in-house long-term market studies assessing or analysing the relevant markets (including any commissioned by the undertakings from outside consultants), and give references of any external studies of the relevant product market, and, where possible, include a copy of any such studies.

7. The position of the undertakings in the relevant product markets

The information required under this section relates to both the relevant geographic market and the relevant product market, for the groups of the parties as a whole. Market shares may be calculated either on the basis of value or volume. Justification for the figures provided must be given by reference to the sales or turnover of each of the undertakings in question. The source or sources of information should be given, and, where possible, a copy of the document from which information has been taken.

7.1 for each of the previous three calendar or financial years, as available, give:

a details of the market shares of each undertaking in the goods or services in the relevant product and geographic markets, as identified in 6.1 above, and, if different, in the UK, and in the European Community;

b estimates of market shares in the relevant product and geographic markets for each of the five main competitors of each of the undertakings, giving the undertaking's name, address, telephone and fax number, and, where possible, a contact name;

c identify the five main customers of each of the undertakings in the relevant product and geographic markets, giving the undertaking's name, address, telephone and fax number, and, where possible, a contact name;

d details of the undertakings' interests in, and arrangements with, any other companies competing in the relevant product and geographic market, together with details of their market shares, if known.

8. Market entry and potential competition in the relevant product and geographic markets

8.1 For all relevant product and geographic markets:

a describe the factors influencing entry into the relevant product market(s): that is, the barriers which exist to prevent undertakings not presently manufacturing goods within the relevant product market(s) from entering the market(s), taking account of, in particular but not exclusively, the extent to which:

– entry is regulated by the requirements of government authorisation or standard-setting, in any form, and any legal or regulatory controls on entry to the market(s);

- entry is influenced by the availability of raw materials;
- entry is influenced by the length of existing contracts between suppliers and customers;
- research and development and licensing patents, know–how and other rights are important;

b describe the factors influencing entry in geographic terms: that is, the barriers that exist to prevent undertakings already producing and/or marketing goods within the relevant product market(s) outside the relevant geographic market(s) from extending sales into the relevant geographic market(s), taking account of, in particular but not.exclusively, the importance of:

- trade barriers imposed by law, such as tariffs, quotas etc;
- local geographical specifications or technical requirements;
- procurement policies;
- the existence of adequate and available local distribution and retailing facilities;
- transport costs;
- strong consumer preference for local brands or products;

c in respect of new entrants in both product and geographic terms, state whether any new undertakings have entered the product market(s) in geographic areas where the undertakings sell, during the last three years. Identify the undertakings concerned by name, address, telephone and fax numbers and, where possible, a contact name, with best estimates of market shares of each in the relevant product and geographic markets.

9. Negative clearance

9.1   state reasons for seeking 'negative clearance' (that is, that the Director General should conclude that the arrangement or conduct is not covered by either the Chapter I or the Chapter II prohibition). Indicate, for example, which provision or effects of the arrangement or conduct may breach the relevant prohibition, and state the reasons why it is considered that the arrangements do not have the object or effect of preventing, restricting or distorting competition within the UK to an appreciable extent, or why the undertaking does not have, or its behaviour does not abuse, a dominant position.

10. Exemption

The criteria which are taken into account in considering notifications for exemption are set out in section 9 of the Act.

10.1   if exemption from the Chapter I prohibition is sought, explain how the arrangements contribute to improving production or distribution and/or promoting technical or economic progress, and how consumers will be allowed a fair share of those benefits. Explain how each restrictive provision in the arrangements is indispensable to these objectives, and how the arrangements do not eliminate competition in respect of a substantial part of the relevant product or geographic market concerned.

11. Transitional periods

11.1 if the arrangement is considered to benefit from any transitional periods during which the Chapter I prohibition does not apply, indicate the duration of the relevant transitional periods by reference to Schedule 13 to the Act.

12. Other information

12.1 state:

a whether this notification should be considered as urgent. If so, give reasons;

b details of trade publications in which advertisements seeking the views of third parties might be placed;

c any other information you consider may be helpful.

12.2 [fees payable ....]

Under section 44 of the Act, it is an offence, punishable by a fine or imprisonment or both, to provide information which is false or misleading in a material particular if the undertaking or person providing it knows that it is false or misleading, or is reckless as to whether it is. If the undertaking is a body corporate, under section 72 of the Act its officers may be guilty of an offence

The notification must conclude with the following declaration which is to be signed by or on behalf of all the applicants or notifying undertakings. Unsigned notifications are invalid.

DECLARATION

The undersigned declare that all the information given above and in the .... pages annexed hereto is correct to the best of their knowledge and belief, and that all estimates are identified as such and are their best estimates of the underlying facts.

Place and date ....

Signatures ....

....

Status ....

....

.... name(s) in block capitals.

Part 3: Acknowledgement of receipt

This Form will be returned to the address inserted below if the top half is completed by the undertaking lodging it.

to be completed by the undertaking making the notification

To: .... (name and address of applicant)

....

....

Your notification dated ....

concerning ....

under reference ....

involving the following undertakings:

1. ....

2. .... [and others]

___

to be completed by the Office of Fair Trading

was received on ....

and registered under reference number

....
Please quote this number in all correspondence

In the event that this notification is not complete in a material respect, you will be informed within one month of its receipt. If you are not informed within that time that it is considered to be incomplete, it is deemed to be effective on the date of its receipt.

Part 4 – To be completed by the undertaking making the notification

Public Register Entry: Decision cases only

Following receipt of a notification for a decision, the Director General will place the details on the public register maintained at:

> The Office of Fair Trading
> [Field House
> Breams Buildings
> London EC4A IPR]

The Director General is required to seek comments from third parties on application[s] for a decision; he may therefore publish a notice inviting comments on the notification. The public register entry and published notice will be made without further reference to the parties. You are therefore asked to provide the information which may be used for this purpose. It is important that the answers to these questions do not contain any business secrets or other confidential information.

1. state the names of the parties to the arrangement(s) or conduct notified, as in questions 1.1 and 1.5 above;
2. give a short summary (no more than 250 words) of the nature and objectives of the arrangement(s);
3. the Standard Industrial Classification code for the relevant good(s) or service(s), if known. If the code is not known, describe the goods or services involved as fully and accurately as possible.

· **EC Treaty Articles** ·

Article 81 (old Article 85)

1. The following shall be prohibited as incompatible with the common market: all agreements between undertakings, decisions by associations of undertakings and concerted practices which may affect trade between Member States and which have as their object or effect the prevention, restriction or distortion of competition within the common market, and in particular those which:

(a) directly or indirectly fix purchase or selling prices or any other trading conditions;
(b) limit or control production, markets, technical development, or investment;
(c) share markets or sources of supply;
(d) apply dissimilar conditions to equivalent transactions with other trading partners, thereby placing them at a competitive disadvantage;
(e) make the conclusion of contracts subject to acceptance by the other parties of supplementary obligations which, by their nature or according to commercial usage, have no connection with the subject of such contracts.

2. Any agreements or decisions prohibited pursuant to this Article shall be automatically void.

3. The provisions of paragraph 1 may, however, be declared inapplicable in the case of:

– any agreement or category of agreements between undertakings;
– any decision or category of decisions by associations of undertakings;
– any concerted practice or category of concerted practices;

which contributes to improving the production or distribution of goods or to promoting technical or economic progress, while allowing consumers a fair share of the resulting benefit, and which does not:

(a) impose on the undertakings concerned restrictions which are not indispensable to the attainment of these objectives;
(b) afford such undertakings the possibility of eliminating competition in respect of a substantial part of the products in question.

Article 82 (old Article 86)

Any abuse by one or more undertakings of a dominant position within the common market or in a substantial part of it shall be prohibited as incompatible with the common market insofar as it may affect trade between Member States.

Such abuse may, in particular, consist in:

(a) directly or indirectly imposing unfair purchase or selling prices or other unfair trading conditions;
(b) limiting production, markets or technical development to the prejudice of consumers;
(c) applying dissimilar conditions to equivalent transactions with other trading partners, thereby placing them at a competitive disadvantage;
(d) making the conclusion of contracts subject to acceptance by the other parties of supplementary obligations which, by their nature or according to commercial usage, have no connection with the subject of such contracts.

Article 86 (old Article 90)

1. In the case of public undertakings and undertakings to which Member States grant special or exclusive rights, Member States shall neither enact nor maintain in force any measure contrary to the rules contained in this Treaty, in particular to those rules provided for in Article 12 and Articles 81 to 89.

2. Undertakings entrusted with the operation of services of general economic interest or having the character of a revenue-producing monopoly shall be subject to the rules contained in this Treaty, in particular to the rules on competition insofar as the application of such rules does not obstruct the performance, in law or in fact, of the particular tasks assigned to them. The development of trade must not be affected to such an extent as would be contrary to the interests of the Community.

3. The Commission shall ensure the application of the provisions of this Article and shall, where necessary, address appropriate directives or decisions to Member States.

Article 234 (old Article 177)

The Court of Justice shall have jurisdiction to give preliminary rulings concerning:

(a) the interpretation of this Treaty;
(b) the validity and interpretation of acts of the institutions of the Community and of the ECB;
(c) the interpretation of the statutes of bodies established by an act of the Council, where those statutes so provide.

Where such a question is raised before any court or tribunal of a Member State, that court or tribunal may, if it considers that a decision on the question is necessary to enable it to give judgment, request the Court of Justice to give a ruling thereon.

Where any such question is raised in a case pending before a court or tribunal of a Member State against whose decisions there is no judicial remedy under national law, that court or tribunal shall bring the matter before the Court of Justice.

Appendix 4

EC Commission
Co-operation Notices

Notice on cooperation between national courts and the Commission in applying Articles 85 and 86 of the EEC Treaty*

(93/C 39/05)

I. Introduction

1. The abolition of internal frontiers enables firms in the Community to embark on new activities and Community consumers to benefit from increased competition. The Commission considers that these advantages must not be jeopardized by restrictive or abusive practices of undertakings and that the completion of the internal market thus reaffirms the importance of the Community's competition policy and competition law.

2. A number of national and Community institutions have contributed to the formulation of Community competition law and are responsible for its day-to-day application. For this purpose, the national competition authorities, national and Community courts and the Commission each assume their own tasks and responsibilities, in line with the principles developed by the case-law of the Court of Justice of the European Communities.

3. If the competition process is to work well in the internal market, effective cooperation between these institutions must be ensured. The purpose of this Notice is to achieve this in relations between national courts and the Commission. It spells out how the Commission intends to assist national courts by closer cooperation in the application of Articles 85 and 86 of the EEC Treaty in individual cases.

II. Powers

4. The Commission is the administrative authority responsible for the implementation and for the thrust of competition policy in the Community and for this purpose has to act in the public interest. National courts, on the other hand, have the task of safeguarding the subjective rights of private individuals in their relations with one another.[1]

---

* OJ C 39, 13.2.1993, p. 6.

1 Case C 234/89 *Delimitis* v *Henninger Bräu* [1991] ECR 1-935, para 44; Case T-24/90 *Automec* v *Commission* [1992] ECR II-2223, paras 73 and 85.

5. In performing these different tasks, national courts and the Commission possess concurrent powers for the application of Article 85(l) and Article 86 of the Treaty. In the case of the Commission, the power is conferred by Article 89 and by the provisions adopted pursuant to Article 87. In the case of the national courts, the power derives from the direct effect of the relevant Community rules. In BRT v Sabam, the Court of Justice considered that 'as the prohibitions of Articles 85(l) and 86 tend by their very nature to produce direct effects in relations between individuals, these Articles create direct rights in respect of the individuals concerned which the national courts must safeguards'.[2]

6. In this way, national courts are able to ensure, at the request of the litigants or on their own initiative, that the competition rules will be respected for the benefit of private individuals. In addition, Article 85(2) enables them to determine, in accordance with the national procedural law applicable, the civil law effects of the prohibition set out in Article 85.[3]

7. However, the Commission, pursuant to Article 9 of Regulation No 17,[4] has sole power to exempt certain types of agreements, decisions and concerted practices from this prohibition. The Commission may exercise this power in two ways. It make take a decision exempting a specific agreement in an individual case. It may also adopt regulations granting block exemptions for certain categories of agreements, decisions or concerted practices, where it is authorized to do so by the Council, in accordance with Article 87.

8. Although national courts are not competent to apply Article 85(3), they may nevertheless apply the decisions and regulations adopted by the Commission pursuant to that provision. The Court has on several occasions confirmed that the provisions of a regulation are directly applicable.[5] The Commission considers that the same is true for the substantive provisions of an individual exemption decision.

9. The powers of the Commission and those of national courts differ not only in their objective and content, but also in the ways in which they are exercised. The Commission exercises its powers according to the procedural rules laid down by Regulation No 17, whereas national courts exercise theirs in the context of national procedural law.

10. In this connection, the Court of Justice has laid down the principles which govern procedures and remedies for invoking directly applicable Community law.

---

2 Case 127/73 *BRT* v *Sabam* [19741 ECR 51, para 16.

3 Case 56/65 *LTM* v *MBU* [1966] ECR 337, Case 48/72 *Brasserie De Haecht* v *Wilkin-Janssen* [1973] ECR 77; Case 319/82 *Ciments et Bétons* v *Kerpen & Kerpen* [1983] ECR 4173.

4 Council Regulation No 17 of 6 February 1962: First Regulation implementing Articles 85 and 86 of the Treaty (OJ 13, 21.2.1962, p. 204/62; Special Edition 1959-62, p. 87).

5 Case 63/75 *Fonderies Roubaix* v *Fonderies Roux* [1976] ECR 111; Case C-234/89 *Delimitis* v *Henninger Bräu* [1991] ECR 1-935.

"Although the Treaty has made it possible in a number of instances for private persons to bring a direct action, where appropriate, before the Court of Justice, it was not intended to create new remedies in the national courts to ensure the observance of Community law other than those already laid down by national law. On the other hand ... it must be possible for every type of action provided for by national law to be available for the purpose of ensuring observance of Community provisions having direct effect, on the same conditions concerning the admissibility and procedure as would apply were it a question of ensuring observance of national law."[6]

11. The Commission considers that these principles apply in the event of breach of the Community competition rules; individuals and companies have access to all procedural remedies provided for by national law on the same conditions as would apply if a comparable breach of national law were involved. This equality of treatment concerns not only the definitive finding of a breach of competition rules, but embraces all the legal means capable of contributing to effective legal protection. Consequently, it is the right of parties subject to Community law that national courts should take provisional measures, that an effective end should be brought, by injunction, to the infringement of Community competition rules of which they are victims, and that compensation should be awarded for the damage suffered as a result of infringements, where such remedies are available in proceedings relating to similar national law.

12. Here the Commission would like to make it clear that the simultaneous application of national competition law is compatible with the application of Community law, provided that it does not impair the effectiveness and uniformity of Community competition rules and the measures taken to enforce them. Any conflicts which may arise when national and Community competition law are applied simultaneously must be resolved in accordance with the principle of the precedence of Community law.[7] The purpose of this principle is to rule out any national measure which could jeopardize the full effectiveness of the provisions of Community law.

III. The exercise of powers by the Commission

13. As the administrative authority responsible for the Community's competition policy, the Commission must serve the Community's general interest. The administrative resources at the Commission's disposal to perform its task are necessarily limited and cannot be used to deal with all the cases brought to its attention. The Commission is therefore obliged, in general, to

---

6 Case 158/80 *Rewe v Hauptzollamt Kiel* [1981] ECR 1805, para 44; see also Case 33/76 *Rewe v Landwirtschaftskammer Saarland* [1976] ECR 1989; Case 79/83 *Harz v Deutsche Tradax* [1984] ECR 1921; Case 199/82 *Amministrazione delle Finanze dello Stato v San Giorgio* [1983] ECR 3595.
7 Case 14/68 *Walt Wilhelm and Others v Bundeskartellamt* [1969] ECR 1; Joined Cases 253/78 and 1 to 3/79 *Procureur de la République v Giry and Guerlain* [1980] ECR 2327.

take all organizational measures necessary for the performance of its task and, in particular, to establish priorities.[8]

14. The Commission intends, in implementing its decision-making powers, to concentrate on notifications, complaints and own-initiative proceedings having particular political, economic or legal significance for the Community. Where these features are absent in a particular case, notifications will normally be dealt with by means of comfort letter and complaints should, as a rule, be handled by national courts or authorities.

15. The Commission considers that there is not normally a sufficient Community interest in examining a case when the plaintiff is able to secure adequate protection of his rights before the national courts.[9] In these circumstances the complaint will normally be filed.

16. In this respect the Commission would like to make it clear that the application of Community competition law by the national courts has considerable advantages for individuals and companies:

– the Commission cannot award compensation for loss suffered as a result of an infringement of Article 85 or Article 86. Such claims may be brought only before the national courts. Companies are more likely to avoid infringements of the Community competition rules if they risk having to pay damages or interest in such an event,

– national courts can usually adopt interim measures and order the ending of infringements more quickly than the Commission is able to do,

– before national courts, it is possible to combine a claim under Community law with a claim under national law. This is not possible in a procedure before the Commission,

– in some Member States, the courts have the power to award legal costs to the successful applicant. This is never possible in the administrative procedure before the Commission.

IV. Application of Articles 85 and 86 by national courts

17. The national court may have to reach a decision on the application of Articles 85 and 86 in several procedural situations. In the case of civil law proceedings, two types of action are particularly frequent: actions relating to contracts and actions for damages. Under the former, the defendant usually relies on Article 85(2) to dispute the contractual obligations invoked by the plaintiff. Under the latter, the prohibitions contained in Articles 85 and 86 are generally relevant in determining whether the conduct which has given rise to the alleged injury is illegal.

---

8 Case T-24/90 *Automec* v *Commission* [1992] ECR II-2223, para 77.
9 Case T-24/90, cited above, paras 91 to 94.

18. In such situations, the direct effect of Article 85(l) and Article 86 gives national courts sufficient powers to comply with their obligation to hand down judgment. Nevertheless, when exercising these powers, they must take account of the Commission's powers in order to avoid decisions which could conflict with those taken or envisaged by the Commission in applying Article 85(l) and Article 86, and also Article 85(3).[10]

19. In its case-law the Court of Justice has developed a number of principles which make it possible for such contradictory decisions to be avoided.[11] The Commission feels that national courts could take account of these principles in the following manner.

1. Application of Article 85(l) and (2) and Article 86

20. The first question which national courts have to answer is whether the agreement, decision or concerted practice at issue infringes the prohibitions laid down in Article 85(l) or Article 86. Before answering, this question, national courts should ascertain whether the agreement, decision or concerted practice has already been the subject of a decision, opinion or other official statement issued by an administrative authority and in particular by the Commission. Such statements provide national courts with significant information for reaching a judgment, even if they are not formally bound by them. It should be noted in this respect that not all procedures before the Commission lead to an official decision, but that cases can also be closed by comfort letters. Whilst it is true that the Court of Justice has ruled that this type of letter does not bind national courts, it has nevertheless stated that the opinion expressed by the Commission constitutes a factor which the national courts may take into account in examining whether the agreements or conduct in question are in accordance with the provisions of Article 85.[12]

21. If the Commission has not ruled on the same agreement, decision or concerted practice, the national courts can always be guided, in interpreting the Community law in question, by the case-law of the Court of Justice and the existing decisions of the Commission. It is with this in view that the Commission has, in a number of general notices,[13] specified categories of agreements that are not caught by the ban laid down in Article 85(l).

---

10 Case C-234/89 *Delimitis* v *Henninger Bräu* [1991] ECR I-935, para 47.
11 Case 48/72 *Brasserie de Haecht* v *Wilkin-Janssen* [1973] ECR 77; Case 127/73 *BRT* v *Sabam* [1974] ECR 51; Case C-234/89 *Delimitis* v *Henninger Bräu* [1991] ECR 1-935.
12 Case 99/79 *Lancôme* v *Etos* [1980] ECR 2511, para 11.
13 See the Notices on:
   – exclusive dealing contracts with commercial agents (OJ 139, 24.12.1962, p. 2921/62),
   – agreements, decisions and concerted practices in the field of cooperation between enterprises (OJ C 75, 29.7.1968, p. 3, as corrected in OJ C 84, 28.8.1968, p. 14),
   – assessment of certain subcontracting agreements (OJ C 1, 3.1.1979, p. 2),
   – agreements of minor importance (OJ C 231, 12.9.1986, p. 2).

22. On these bases, national courts should generally be able to decide whether the conduct at issue is compatible with Article 85(l) and Article 86. Nevertheless, if the Commission has initiated a procedure in a case relating to the same conduct, they may, if they consider it necessary for reasons of legal certainty, stay the proceedings while awaiting the outcome of the Commission's action.[14] A stay of proceedings may also be envisaged where national courts wish to seek the Commission's views in accordance with the arrangements referred to in this Notice.[15] Finally, where national courts have persistent doubts on questions of compatibility they may stay proceedings in order to bring the matter before the Court of Justice, in accordance with Article 177 of the Treaty.

23. However, where national courts decide to give judgment and find that the conditions for applying Article 85(l) or Article 86 are not met, they should pursue their proceedings on the basis of such a finding, even if the agreement, decision or concerted practice at issue has been notified to the Commission. Where the assessment of the facts shows that the conditions for applying the said Articles are met, national courts must rule that the conduct at issue infringes Community competition law and take the appropriate measures, including those relating to the consequences that attach to infringement of a statutory prohibition under the civil law applicable.

2. Application of Article 85(3)

24. If the national court concludes that an agreement, decision or concerted practice is prohibited by Article 85(l), it must check whether it is or will be the subject of an exemption by the Commission under Article 85(3). Here several situations may arise.

25. (a) The national court is required to respect the exemption decisions taken by the Commission. Consequently, it must treat the agreement, decision or concerted practice at issue as compatible with Community law and fully recognize its civil law effects. In this respect mention should be made of comfort letters in which the Commission services state that the conditions for applying Article 85(3) have been met. The Commission considers that national courts may take account of these letters as factual elements.

26. (b) Agreements, decisions and concerted practices which fall within the scope of application of a block exemption regulation are automatically exempted from the prohibition laid down in Article 85(l) without the need for a Commission decision or comfort letter.[16]

---

14 Case 127/73 *BRT* v *Sabam* [1974] ECR 51, paragraph 21. The procedure before the Commission is initiated by an authoritative act. A simple acknowledgement of receipt cannot be considered an authoritative act as such; Case 48/72 *Brasserie de Haecht* v *Wilkin-Janssen* [1973] ECR 77, paragraphs 16 and 17.
15 Case C-234/89 *Delimitis* v *Henninger Bräu* [1991] ECR 1-935, paragraph 53, Part V of this Notice.
16 A list of the relevant regulations and of the official explanatory comments relating to them is given in the Annex to this Notice.

27. (c) Agreements, decisions and concerted practices which are not covered by a block exemption regulation and which have not been the subject of an individual exemption decision or a comfort letter must, in the Commission's view, be examined in the following manner.

28. The national court must first examine whether the procedural conditions necessary for securing exemption are fulfilled, notably whether the agreement, decision or concerted practice has been duly notified in accordance with Article 4(1) of Regulation No 17. Where no such notification has been made, and subject to Article 4(2) of Regulation No 17, exemption under Article 85(3) is ruled out, so that the national court may decide, pursuant to Article 85(2), that the agreement, decision or concerted practice is void.

29. Where the agreement, decision or concerted practice has been duly notified to the Commission, the national court will assess the likelihood of an exemption being granted in the case in question in the light of the relevant criteria developed by the case-law of the Court of Justice and the Court of First Instance and by previous regulations and decisions of the Commission.

30. Where the national court has in this way ascertained that the agreement, decision or concerted practice at issue cannot be the subject of an individual exemption, it will take the measures necessary to comply with the requirements of Article 85(1) and (2). On the other hand, if it takes the view that individual exemption is possible, the national court should suspend the proceedings while awaiting the Commission's decision. If the national court does suspend the proceedings, it nevertheless remains free, according to the rules of the applicable national law, to adopt any interim measures it deems necessary.

31. In this connection, it should be made clear that these principles do not apply to agreements, decisions and concerted practices which existed before Regulation No 17 entered into force or before that Regulation became applicable as a result of the accession of a new Member State and which were duly notified to the Commission. The national courts must consider such agreements, decisions and concerted practices to be valid so long as the Commission or the authorities of the Member States have not taken a prohibition decision or sent a comfort letter to the parties informing them that the file has been closed.[17]

32. The Commission realizes that the principles set out above for the application of Articles 85 and 86 by national courts are complex and sometimes insufficient to enable those courts to perform their judicial function properly. This is particularly so where the practical application of Article 85(1) and Article 86 gives rise to legal or economic difficulties, where the Commission has initiated a procedure in the same case or where the agreement,

---

17 Case 48/72 *Brasserie de Haecht* v *Wilkin-Janssen* [1973] ECR 77; Case 59/77 *De Bloos* v *Bouyer* [1977] ECR 2359; Case 99/79, *Lancôme* v *Etos* [1980] ECR 2511.

decision or concerted practice concerned may become the subject of an individual exemption within the meaning of Article 85(3). National courts may bring such cases before the Court of Justice for a preliminary ruling, in accordance with Article 177. They may also avail themselves of the Commission's assistance according to the procedures set out below.

V. Cooperation between national courts and the Commission

33. Article 5 of the EEC Treaty establishes the principle of constant and sincere cooperation between the Community and the Member States with a view to attaining the objectives of the Treaty, including implementation of Article 3(f), which refers to the establishment of a system ensuring that competition in the common market is not distorted. This principle involves obligations and duties of mutual assistance, both for the Member States and for the Community institutions. The Court has thus ruled that, under Article 5 of the EEC Treaty, the Commission has a duty of sincere cooperation vis-à-vis judicial authorities of the Member States, who are responsible for ensuring that Community law is applied and respected in the national legal system.[18]

34. The Commission considers that such cooperation is essential in order to guarantee the strict, effective and consistent application of Community competition law. In addition, more effective participation by the national courts in the day-to-day application of competition law gives the Commission more time to perform its administrative task, namely to steer competition policy in the Community.

35. In the light of these considerations, the Commission intends to work towards closer cooperation with national courts in the following manner.

36. The Commission conducts its policy so as to give the parties concerned useful pointers to the application of competition rules. To this end, it will continue its policy in relation to block exemption regulations and general notices. These general texts, the case-law of the Court of Justice and the Court of First Instance, the decisions previously taken by the Commission and the annual reports on competition policy are all elements of secondary legislation or explanations which may assist national courts in examining individual cases.

37. If these general pointers are insufficient, national courts may, within the limits of their national procedural law, ask the Commission and in particular its Directorate-General for Competition for the following information.

First, they may ask for information of a procedural nature to enable them to discover whether a certain case is pending before the Commission, whether a case has been the subject of a notification, whether the Commission has officially

---

18 Case C-2/88 *Imm., Zwartveld* [1990] ECR I-3365, paragraph 18; Case C-234/89 *Delimitis* v *Henninger Bräu* [1991] ECR 1-935, paragraph 53.

initiated a procedure or whether it has already taken a position through an official decision or through a comfort letter sent by its services. If necessary, national courts may also ask the Commission to give an opinion as to how much time is likely to be required for granting or refusing individual exemption for notified agreements or practices, so as to be able to determine the conditions for any decision to suspend proceedings or whether interim measures need to be adopted.[19] The Commission, for its part, will endeavour to give priority to cases which are the subject of national proceedings suspended in this way, in particular when the outcome of a civil dispute depends on them.

38. Next, national courts may consult the Commission on points of law. Where the application of Article 85(l) and Article 86 causes them particular difficulties, national courts may consult the Commission on its customary practice in relation to the Community law at issue. As far as Articles 85 and 86 are concerned, these difficulties relate in particular to the conditions for applying these Articles as regards the effect on trade between Member States and as regards the extent to which the restriction of competition resulting from the practices specified in these provisions is appreciable. In its replies, the Commission does not consider the merits of the case. In addition, where they have doubts as to whether a contested agreement, decision or concerted practice is eligible for an individual exemption, they may ask the Commission to provide them with an interim opinion. If the Commission says that the case in question is unlikely to qualify for an exemption, national courts will be able to waive a stay of proceedings and rule on the validity of the agreement, decision or concerted practice.

39. The answers given by the Commission are not binding on the courts which have requested them. In its replies the Commission makes it clear that its view is not definitive and that the right for the national court to refer to the Court of Justice, pursuant to Article 177, is not affected. Nevertheless, the Commission considers that it gives them useful guidance for resolving disputes.

40. Lastly, national courts can obtain information from the Commission regarding factual data: statistics, market studies and economic analyses. The Commission will endeavour to communicate these data, within the limits laid down in the following paragraph, or will indicate the source from which they can be obtained.

41. It is in the interests of the proper administration of justice that the Commission should answer requests for legal and factual information in the shortest possible time. Nevertheless, the Commission cannot accede to such requests unless several conditions are met. First, the requisite data must actually be at its disposal. Secondly, the Commission may communicate this data only in so far as permitted by the general principle of sound administrative practice.

---

19 See paragraphs 22 and 30 of this Notice.

42. For example, Article 214 of the Treaty, as spelt out in Article 20 of Regulation No 17 for the purposes of the competition rules, requires the Commission not to disclose information of a confidential nature. In addition, the duty of sincere cooperation deriving from Article 5 is one applying to the relationship between national courts and the Commission and cannot concern the position of the parties to the dispute pending before those courts. As amicus curiae, the Commission is obliged to respect legal neutrality and objectivity. Consequently, it will not accede to requests for information unless they come from a national court, either directly, or indirectly through parties which have been ordered by the court concerned to provide certain information. In the latter case, the Commission will ensure that its answer reaches all the parties to the proceedings.

43. Over and above such exchange of information, required in specific cases, the Commission is anxious to develop as far as possible a more general information policy. To this end, the Commission intends to publish an explanatory booklet regarding the application of the competition rules at national level.

44. Lastly, the Commission also wishes to reinforce the effect of national competition judgments. To this end, it will study the possibility of extending the scope of the Convention on jurisdiction and the enforcement of judgments in civil and commercial matters to competition cases assigned to administrative courts.[20] It should be noted that, in the Commission's view, competition judgments are already governed by this Convention where they are handed down in cases of a civil and commercial nature.

VI. Final remarks

45. This Notice does not relate to the competition rules governing the transport sector.[21] Nor does it relate to the competition rules laid down in the Treaty establishing the European Coal and Steel Community.

46. This Notice is issued for guidance and does not in any way restrict the rights conferred on individuals or companies by Community law.

47. This Notice is without prejudice to any interpretation of the Community competition rules which may be given by the Court of Justice of the European Communities.

---

20 Convention of 27 September 1968 (OJ L 304, 30.10.1978, p. 77).

21 Regulation No 141/62 of the Council of 26 November 1962 exempting transport from the application of Council Regulation No 17 (OJ 124, 28.11,1962, p. 2751/62), as amended by Regulations Nos 165/65/EEC (OJ 210, 11.12.1965, p. 3141/65) and 1002/67/EEC (OJ 306, 16.12.1967, p. 1); Regulation (EEC) No 1017/68 of the Council of 19 July 1968 applying rules of competition to transport by rail, road and inland waterway (OJ L 175, 23.7.1968, p. 1); Council Regulation (EEC) No 4056/86 of 22 December 1986 laying down detailed rules for the application of Articles 85 and 86 of the Treaty to maritime transport (OJ L 378, 31.12.1986, p. 4), Council Regulation (EEC) No 3975/87 of 14 December 1987 laying down the procedure for the application of the rules on competition to undertakings in the air transport sector (OJ L 374, 31.12.1987, p. 1).

48. A summary of the answers given by the Commission pursuant to this Notice will be published annually in the Competition Report.

ANNEX Block Exemptions

A. *Enabling Council Regulations*

I. Vertical agreements
(see under B.I and B.II)
Council Regulation No 19/65/EEC of 2 March 1965 on the application of Article 85(3) of the Treaty to certain categories of agreements and concerted practices (OJ, Special Edition 1965-66, p. 35).

II. Horizontal agreements
(see under B.III)
Council Regulation (EEC) No 2821/71 of 20 December 1971 on the application of Article 85(3) of the Treaty to categories of agreements, decisions and concerted practices (OJ, Special Edition 1971-Ill, p. 1032), modified by Regulation (EEC) No 2743/72 of 19 December 1972 (OJ, Special Edition 1972, 28-30.12.1972, p. 60).

B. *Commission Block Exemption Regulations and explanatory notices*

I. Distribution agreements
1. Commission Regulation (EEC) No 1983/83 of 22 June 1983 concerning exclusive distribution agreements (OJ L 173, 30.6.1983, p. 1).
2. Commission Regulation (EEC) No 1984/83 of 22 June 1983 concerning exclusive purchasing agreements (OJ L 173, 30.6.1983, p. 5).
3. Commission Notice concerning Commission Regulations (EEC) No 1983/83 and (EEC) No 1984/83 (OJ C 101, 13.4.1984, p. 2).
4. Commission Regulation (EEC) No 123/85 of 12 December 1984 concerning motor vehicle distribution and servicing agreements (OJ L 15, 18.1.1985, p. 16).
5. Commission Notice concerning Regulation (EEC) No 123/85 (OJ C 17, 18.1.1985, p. 4).
6. Commission Notice on the clarification of the activities of motor vehicle intermediaries (OJ C 329, 18.12.1991, p. 20).

II. Licensing and franchising agreements
1. Commission Regulation (EEC) No 2349/84 of 23 July 1984 concerning patent licensing agreements (OJ L 219, 16.8.1984, p. 15; corrigendum OJ L 280, 22.10.1985, p. 32).
2. Commission Regulation (EEC) No 4087/88 of 30 November 1988 concerning franchising agreements (OJ L 359, 28.12.1988, p. 46).
3. Commission Regulation (EEC) No 556/89 of 30 November 1988 concerning know-how licensing agreements (OJ L 61, 4.3.1989, p. 1).

III. Cooperative agreements

1. Commission Regulation (EEC) No 417/85 of 19 December 1984 concerning specialization agreements (OJ L 53, 22.2.1985, p. 1).
2. Commission Regulation (EEC) No 418/85 of 19 December 1984 concerning research and development agreements (OJ L 53, 22.2.1985, p. 5).

Commission Notice on cooperation between national competition authorities and the Commission in handling cases falling within the scope of Articles 85 or 86 of the EC Treaty*

(97/C 313/03)

I. Role of the Member States and of the Community

1. In competition policy the Community and the Member States perform different functions. Whereas the Community is responsible only for implementing the Community rules, Member States not only apply their domestic law but also have a hand in implementing Articles 85 and 86 of the EC Treaty.

2. This involvement of the Member States in Community competition policy means that decisions can be taken as closely as possible to the citizen (Article A of the Treaty on European Union). The decentralized application of Community competition rules also leads to a better allocation of tasks. If, by reason of its scale or effects, the proposed action can best be taken at Community level, it is for the Commission to act. Otherwise, it is for the competition authority of the Member State concerned to act.

3. Community law is implemented by the Commission and national competition authorities, on the one hand, and national courts, on the other, in accordance with the principles developed by the Community legislature and by the Court of Justice and the Court of First Instance of the European Communities.

It is the task of national courts to safeguard the rights of private persons in their relations with one another.[1] Those rights derive from the fact that the prohibitions in Articles 85(1) and 86[2] and the exemptions granted by regulation[3] have been recognized by the Court of Justice as being directly applicable. Relations between national courts and the Commission in applying Articles 85 and 86 were spelt out in a Notice published by the Commission in 1993.[4] This Notice is the counterpart, for relations with national authorities, to that of 1993 on relations with national courts.

4. As administrative authorities, both the Commission and national competition authorities act in the public interest in performing their general task of monitoring and enforcing the competition rules.[5] Relations between them are

---

* OJ 1997 C313/3.
1 Case T-24/90 *Automec* v *Commission* ("Automec II") [1993] ECR II-2223, para 85.
2 Case 127/73 *BRT* v *SABAM* [1974] ECR 51, para 16.
3 Case 63/75 *Fonderies Roubaix-Wattrelos* v *Fonderies A Roux* [1976] ECR 111.
4 Notice on cooperation between national courts and the Commission in applying Articles 85 and 86 of the EEC Treaty (OJ C 39, 13. 2. 1993, p. 6).
5 *Automec II*, see footnote 1; para 85.

determined primarily by this common role of protecting the general interest. Although similar to the Notice on cooperation with national courts, this Notice accordingly reflects this special feature.

5. The specific nature of the role of the Commission and of national competition authorities is characterized by the powers conferred on those bodies by the Council regulations adopted under Article 87 of the Treaty. Article 9(1) of Regulation No 17[6] thus provides: 'Subject to review of its decision by the Court of Justice[7], the Commission shall have sole power to declare Article 85(1) inapplicable pursuant to Article 85(3) of the Treaty'. And Article 9(3) of the same Regulation provides: 'As long as the Commission has not initiated any procedure under Article 2[8], 3[9] or 6[10], the authorities of the Member States shall remain competent to apply Article 85(1) and Article 86 in accordance with Article 88 of the Treaty.'

It follows that, provided their national law has conferred the necessary powers on them, national competition authorities are empowered to apply the prohibitions in Articles 85(1) and 86. On the other hand, for the purposes of applying Article 85(3), they do not have any powers to grant exemptions in individual cases; they must abide by the decisions and regulations adopted by the Commission under that provision. They may also take account of other measures adopted by the Commission in such cases, in particular comfort letters, treating them as factual evidence.

6. The Commission is convinced that enhancing the role of national competition authorities will boost the effectiveness of Articles 85 and 86 of the Treaty and, generally speaking, will bolster the application of Community competition rules throughout the Community. In the interests of safeguarding and developing the single market, the Commission considers that those provisions should be used as widely as possible. Being closer to the activities and businesses that require monitoring, national authorities are often in a better position than the Commission to protect competition.

7. Cooperation must therefore be organized between national authorities and the Commission. If this cooperation is to be fruitful, they will have to keep in close and constant touch.

8. The Commission proposes to set out in this Notice the principles it will apply in future when dealing with the cases described herein. The Notice also seeks to induce firms to approach national competition authorities more often.

---

6 Council Regulation No 17 of 6 February 1962: First Regulation implementing Articles 85 and
    86 of the Treaty; OJ 13, 21. 2. 1962, p. 204/62 (English Special Edition 1959-62, p. 87).
7 Now by the Court of First Instance and, on appeal, by the Court of Justice.
8 Negative clearance.
9 Termination of infringements – prohibition decisions.
10 Decisions pursuant to Article 85(3).

9. This Notice describes the practical cooperation which is desirable between the Commission and national authorities. It does not affect the extent of the powers conferred by Community law on either the Commission or national authorities for the purpose of dealing with individual cases.

10. For cases falling within the scope of Community law, to avoid duplication of checks on compliance with the competition rules which are applicable to them, which is costly for the firms concerned, checks should wherever possible be carried out by a single authority (either a Member State's competition authority or the Commission). Control by a single authority offers advantages for businesses.

Parallel proceedings before the Commission, on the one hand, and a national competition authority, on the other, are costly for businesses whose activities fall within the scope both of Community law and of Member States' competition laws. They can lead to the repetition of checks on the same activity, by the Commission, on the one hand, and by the competition authorities of the Member States concerned, on the other.

Businesses in the Community may therefore in certain circumstances find it to their advantage if some cases falling within the scope of Community competition law were dealt with solely by national authorities. In order that this advantage may be enjoyed to the full, the Commission thinks it is desirable that national authorities should themselves apply Community law directly or, failing that, obtain, by applying their domestic law, a result similar to that which would have been obtained had Community law been applied.

11. What is more, in addition to the resulting benefits accruing to competition authorities in terms of mobilization of their resources, cooperation between authorities reduces the risk of divergent decisions and hence the opportunities for those who might be tempted to do so to seek out whichever authority seemed to them to be the most favourable to their interests.

12. Member States' competition authorities often have a more detailed and precise knowledge than the Commission of the relevant markets (particularly those with highly specific national features) and the businesses concerned. Above all, they may be in a better position than the Commission to detect restrictive practices that have not been notified or abuses of a dominant position whose effects are essentially confined to their territory.

13. Many cases handled by national authorities involve arguments based on national law and arguments drawn from Community competition law. In the interests of keeping proceedings as short as possible, the Commission considers it preferable that national authorities should directly apply Community law themselves, instead of making firms refer to the Community-law aspects of their cases to the Commission.

14. An increasing number of major issues in the field of Community competition law have been clarified over the last thirty years through the case-law of the Court of Justice and the Court of First Instance and through decisions taken on questions of principle and the exemption regulations adopted by the Commission. The application of that law by national authorities is thereby simplified.

15. The Commission intends to encourage the competition authorities of all Member States to engage in this cooperation. However, the national legislation of several Member States does not currently provide competition authorities with the procedural means of applying Articles 85(1) and 86. In such Member States conduct caught by the Community provisions can be effectively dealt with by national authorities only under national law.

In the Commission's view, it is desirable that national authorities should apply Articles 85 or 86 of the Treaty, if appropriate in conjunction with their domestic competition rules, when handling cases that fall within the scope of those provisions.

16. Where authorities are not in a position to do this and hence can apply only their national law to such cases, the application of that law should 'not prejudice the uniform application throughout the common market of the Community rules on cartels and of the full effect of the measures adopted in implementation of those rules'.[11] At the very least, the solution they find to a case falling within the scope of Community law must be compatible with that law, Member States being forbidden, given the primacy of Community law over national competition law[12] and the obligation to cooperate in good faith laid down in Article 5 of the Treaty[13], to take measures capable of defeating the practical effectiveness of Articles 85 and 86.

17. Divergent decisions are more likely to be reached where a national authority applies its national law rather than Community law. Where a Member State's competition authority applies Community law, it is required to comply with any decisions taken previously by the Commission in the same proceedings. Where the case has merely been the subject of a comfort letter then, according to the Court of Justice, although this type of letter does not bind national courts, the opinion expressed by the Commission constitutes a factor which the national courts may take into account in examining whether the agreements on conduct in question are in accordance with the provisions of Article 85.[14] In the Commission's view, the same holds true for national authorities.

---

11 Case 14/68 *Walt Wilhelm and Others* v *Bundeskartellamt* [1969] ECR 1, para 4.
12 *Walt Wilhelm*, see footnote 11; para 6; Case 66/86 *Ahmed Saaed Flugreisen and Others* v *Zentrale Zur Bekämpfung Unlauteren Wettbewerbs* [1989] ECR 803, para 48.
13 Case C-165/91 *Van Munster* v *Rijksdienst voor Pensioenen* [1994] ECR I-4661, para 32.
14 Case 99/79 *Lancôme* v *Etos* [1980] ECR 2511, para 11, cited in the abovementioned Notice on Cooperation between National Courts and the Commission in applying Articles 85 and 86.

18. Where an infringement of Articles 85 or 86 is established by Commission decision, that decision precludes the application of a domestic legal provision authorizing what the Commission has prohibited. The objective of the prohibitions in Articles 85(1) and 86 is to guarantee the unity of the common market and the preservation of undistorted competition in that market. They must be strictly complied with if the functioning of the Community regime is not to be endangered.[15]

19. The legal position is less clear as to whether national authorities are allowed to apply their more stringent national competition law where the situation they are assessing has previously been the subject of an individual exemption decision of the Commission or is covered by a block exemption Regulation. In *Walt Wilhelm*, the Court stated that the Treaty 'permits the Community authorities to carry out certain positive, though indirect, actions with a view to promoting a harmonious development of economic activities within the whole Community' (paragraph 5 of the judgment). In *Bundeskartellamt* v *Volkswagen and VAG Leasing*[16], the Commission contended that national authorities may not prohibit exempted agreements. The uniform application of Community law would be frustrated every time an exemption granted under Community law was made to depend on the relevant national rules. Otherwise, not only would a given agreement be treated differently depending on the law of each Member State, thus detracting from the uniform application of Community law, but the full effectiveness of an act giving effect to the Treaty – which an exemption under Article 85(3) undoubtedly is – would also be disregarded. In the case in point, however, the Court did not have to settle the question.

20. If the Commission's Directorate-General for Competition sends a comfort letter in which it expresses the opinion that an agreement or a practice is incompatible with Article 85 of the Treaty but states that, for reasons to do with its internal priorities, it will not propose to the Commission that it take a decision thereon in accordance with the formal procedures laid down in Regulation No 17, it goes without saying that the national authorities in whose territory the effects of the agreement or practice are felt may take action in respect of that agreement or practice.

21. In the case of a comfort letter in which the Directorate-General for Competition expresses the opinion that an agreement does restrict competition within the meaning of Article 85(1) but qualifies for exemption under Article 85(3), the Commission will call upon national authorities to consult it before they decide whether to adopt a different decision under Community or national law.

---

15 Fourth Report on Competition Policy 1974, point 45.
16 Case C-266/93 [1995] ECR I-3477; see also the Opinion of Advocate-General Tesauro in the same case, para 51.

22. As regards comfort letters in which the Commission expresses the opinion that, on the basis of the information in its possession, there is no need for it to take any action under Article 85(1) or Article 86 of the Treaty, 'that fact cannot by itself have the result of preventing the national authorities from applying to those agreements' or practices 'provisions of national competition law which may be more rigorous than Community law in this respect. The fact that a practice has been held by the Commission not to fall within the ambit of the prohibition contained in Article 85(1) and (2)' or Article 86, 'the scope of which is limited to agreements' or dominant positions 'capable of affecting trade between Member States, in no way prevents that practice from being considered by the national authorities from the point of view of the restrictive effects which it may produce nationally'. (Judgment of the Court of Justice in *Procureur de la République* v *Giry and Guerlain*[17]).

II. Guidelines on case allocation

23. Cooperation between the Commission and national competition authorities has to comply with the current legal framework. First, if it is to be caught by Community law and not merely by national competition law, the conduct in question must be liable to have an appreciable effect on trade between Member States. Secondly, the Commission has sole power to declare Article 85(1) of the Treaty inapplicable under Article 85(3).

24. In practice, decisions taken by a national authority can apply effectively only to restrictions of competition whose impact is felt essentially within its territory. This is the case in particular with the restrictions referred to in Article 4(2)(1) of Regulation No 17, namely agreements, decisions or concerted practices the only parties to which are undertakings from one Member State and which, though they do not relate either to imports or to exports between Member States, may affect intra-Community trade.[18] It is extremely difficult from a legal standpoint for such an authority to conduct investigations outside its home country, such as when on-the-spot inspections need to be carried out on businesses, and to ensure that its decisions are enforced beyond its national borders. The upshot is that the Commission usually has to handle cases involving businesses whose relevant activities are carried on in more than one Member State.

25. A national authority having sufficient resources in terms of manpower and equipment and having had the requisite powers conferred on it, also needs to be able to deal effectively with any cases covered by the Community rules which it proposes to take on. The effectiveness of a national authority's action

---

17 Joined Cases 253/78 and 1 to 3/79 *Procureur de la République* v *Giry and Guerlain* [1980] ECR 2327, para 18.
18 It is possible that an agreement, 'although it does not relate either to imports or to exports between Member States' within the meaning of Article 4 of Regulation No 17, 'may affect trade between Member States' within the meaning of Article 85(1) of the Treaty (judgment of the Court of Justice in Case 43/69 *Bilger* v *Jehle* [1970] ECR 127, para 5).

is dependent on its powers of investigation, the legal means it has at its disposal for settling a case – including the power to order interim measures in an emergency – and the penalties it is empowered to impose on businesses found guilty of infringing the competition rules. Differences between the rules of procedure applicable in the various Member States should not, in the Commission's view, lead to outcomes which differ in their effectiveness when similar cases are being dealt with.

26. In deciding which cases to handle itself, the Commission will take into account the effects of the restrictive practice or abuse of a dominant position and the nature of the infringement.

In principle, national authorities will handle cases the effects of which are felt mainly in their territory and which appear upon preliminary examination unlikely to qualify for exemption under Article 85(3). However, the Commission reserves the right to take on certain cases displaying a particular Community interest.

Mainly national effects

27. First of all, it should be pointed out that the only cases at issue here are those which fall within the scope of Articles 85 and 86.

That being so, the existing and foreseeable effects of a restrictive practice or abuse of a dominant position may be deemed to be closely linked to the territory in which the agreement or practice is applied and to the geographic market for the goods or services in question.

28. Where the relevant geographic market is limited to the territory of a single Member State and the agreement or practice is applied only in that State, the effects of the agreement or practice must be deemed to occur mainly within that State even if, theoretically, the agreement or practice is capable of affecting trade between Member States.

Nature of the infringement: cases that cannot be exempted

29. The following considerations apply to cases brought before the Commission, to cases brought before a national competition authority and to cases which both may have to deal with.

A distinction should be drawn between infringements of Article 85 of the Treaty and infringements of Article 86.

30. The Commission has exclusive powers under Article 85(3) of the Treaty to declare the provisions of Article 85(1) inapplicable. Any notified restrictive practice that *prima facie* qualifies for exemption must therefore be examined by the Commission, which will take account of the criteria developed in this area by the Court of Justice and the Court of First Instance and also by the relevant regulations and its own previous decisions.

31. The Commission also has exclusive responsibility for investigation of complaints against decisions it has taken under its exclusive powers, such as a decision to withdraw an exemption previously granted by it under Article 85(3).[19]

32. No such limitation exists, however, on implementation of Article 86 of the Treaty. The Commission and the Member States have concurrent competence to investigate complaints and to prohibit abuses of dominant positions.

Cases of particular significance to the Community

33. Some cases considered by the Commission to be of particular Community interest will more often be dealt with by the Commission even if, inasmuch as they satisfy the requirements set out above (points 27-28 and 29-32), they can be dealt with by a national authority.

34. This category includes cases which raise a new point of law, that is to say, those which have not yet been the subject of a Commission decision or a judgment of the Court of Justice or Court of First Instance.

35. The economic magnitude of a case is not in itself sufficient reason for its being dealt with by the Commission. The position might be different where access to the relevant market by firms from other Member States is significantly impeded.

36. Cases involving alleged anti-competitive behaviour by a public undertaking, an undertaking to which a Member State has granted special or exclusive rights with the meaning of Article 90(1) of the Treaty, or an undertaking entrusted with the operation of services of general economic interest or having the character of a revenue-producing monopoly within the meaning of Article 90(2) of the Treaty may also be of particular Community interest.

III. Cooperation in cases which the Commission deals with first

37. Cases dealt with by the Commission have three possible origins: own-initiative proceedings, notifications and complaints. By their very nature, own-initiative proceedings do not lend themselves to decentralized processing by national competition authorities.

38. The exclusivity of the Commission's powers to apply Article 85(3) of the Treaty in individual cases means that cases notified to the Commission under Article 4(1) of Regulation No 17 by parties seeking exemption under Article 85(3) cannot be dealt with by a national competition authority on the Commission's initiative. According to the case-law of the Court of First Instance, these exclusive powers confer on the applicant the right to obtain from the Commission a decision on the substance of his request for exemption.[20]

---

19 *Automec II*, see footnote 1; para 75.
20 Case T-23/90 *Peugeot v Commission* [1991] ECR II-653, para 47.

39. National competition authorities may deal, at the Commission's request, with complaints that do not involve the application of Article 85(3), namely those relating to restrictive practices which must be notified under Articles 4(1), 5(1) and 25 of Regulation No 17 but have not been notified to the Commission and those based on alleged infringement of Article 86 of the Treaty. On the other hand, complaints concerning matters falling within the scope of the Commission's exclusive powers, such as withdrawal of exemption, cannot be usefully handled by a national competition authority.[21]

40. The criteria set out at points 23 to 36 above in relation to the handling of a case by the Commission or a national authority, in particular as regards the territorial extent of the effects of a restrictive practice or dominant position (points 27-28), should be taken into account.

Commission's right to reject a complaint

41. It follows from the case-law of the Court of First Instance that the Commission is entitled under certain conditions to reject a complaint which does not display sufficient Community interest to justify further investigation.[22]

42. The Commission's resultant right to reject a complaint stems from the concurrent competence of the Commission, national courts and – where they have the power – national competition authorities to apply Articles 85(1) and 86 and from the consequent protection available to complainants before the courts and administrative authorities. With regard to that concurrent competence, it has been consistently held by the Court of Justice and the Court of First Instance that Article 3 of Regulation No 17 (the legal basis for the right to lodge a complaint with the Commission for alleged infringement of Article 85 or Article 86) does not entitle an applicant under that Article to obtain from the Commission a decision within the meaning of Article 189 of the Treaty as to whether or not the alleged infringement has occurred.[23]

Conditions for rejecting a complaint

43. The investigation of a complaint by a national authority presupposes that the following specific conditions, derived from the case-law of the Court of First Instance, are met.

44. The first of these conditions is that, in order to assess whether or not there is a Community interest in having a case investigated further, the Commission must first undertake a careful examination of the questions of fact and law set

---

21 *Automec II*, see footnote 1; para 75.
22 *Automec II*, see footnote 1; para 85; cited in Case T-114/92 *BEMIM* v *Commission* [1995] ECR II-147, para 80, and in Case T-77/95 *SFEI and Others* v *Commission* [1997] ECR II-1, paras 29 and 55.
23 See in particular Case 125/78 *GEMA* v *Commission* [1979] ECR 3173, para 17, and Case T-16/91 *Rendo and Others* v *Commission* [1992] ECR II-2417, para 98.

out in the complaint.[24] In accordance with the obligation imposed on it by Article 190 of the Treaty to state the reasons for its decisions, the Commission has to inform the complainant of the legal and factual considerations which have induced it to conclude that the complaint does not display a sufficient Community interest to justify further investigation. The Commission cannot therefore confine itself to an abstract reference to the Community interest.[25]

45. In assessing whether it is entitled to reject a complaint for lack of any Community interest, the Commission must balance the significance of the alleged infringement as regards the functioning of the common market, the probability of its being able to establish the existence of the infringement, and the extent of the investigative measures required for it to perform, under the best possible conditions, its task of making sure that Articles 85 and 86 are complied with.[26] In particular, as the Court of First Instance held in *BEMIM*[27], where the effects of the infringements alleged in a complaint are essentially confined to the territory of one Member State and where proceedings have been brought before the courts and competent administrative authorities of that Member State by the complainant against the body against which the complaint was made, the Commission is entitled to reject the complaint for lack of any sufficient Community interest in further investigation of the case, provided however that the rights of the complainant can be adequately safeguarded. As to whether the effects of the restrictive practice are localized, such is the case in particular with practices to which the only parties are undertakings from one Member State and which, although they do not relate either to imports or to exports between Member States, within the meaning of point 1 of Article 4(2) of Regulation No 17[28], are capable of affecting intra-Community trade. As regards the safeguarding of the complainant's rights, the Commission considers that the referral of the matter to the national authority concerned needs must [sic] protect them quite adequately. On this latter point, the Commission takes the view that the effectiveness of the national authority's action depends notably on whether that authority is able to take interim measures if it deems it necessary, without prejudice to the possibility, found in the law of certain Member States, that such measures may be taken with the requisite degree of effectiveness by a court.

Procedure

46. Where the Commission considers these conditions to have been met, it will ask the competition authority of the Member State in which most of the effects of the contested agreement or practice are felt if it would agree to investigate

---

24 *Automec II*, see footnote 1; para 82.
25 *Automec II*, see footnote 1; para 85.
26 *Automec II*, see footnote 1; para 86, cited in *BEMIM*, para 80.
27 See footnote 22; para 86.
28 See footnote 18.

and decide on the complaint. Where the competition authority agrees to do so, the Commission will reject the complaint pending before it on the ground that it does not display sufficient Community interest and will refer the matter to the national competition authority, either automatically or at the complainant's request. The Commission will place the relevant documents in its possession at the national authority's disposal.[29]

47. With regard to investigation of the complaint, it should be stressed that, in accordance with the ruling given by the Court of Justice in Case C-67/91[30] (the 'Spanish banks' case), national competition authorities are not entitled to use as evidence, for the purposes of applying either national rules or the Community competition rules, unpublished information contained in replies to requests for information sent to firms under Article 11 of Regulation No 17 or information obtained as a result of any inspections carried out under Article 14 of that Regulation. This information can nevertheless be taken into account, where appropriate, to justify instituting national proceedings.[31]

IV. Cooperation in cases which a national authority deals with first

Introduction

48. At issue here are cases falling within the scope of Community competition law which a national competition authority handles on its own initiative, applying Articles 85(1) or 86, either alone or in conjunction with its national competiion rules, or, where it cannot do so, its national rules alone. This covers all cases within this field which a national authority investigates before the Commission – where appropriate – does so, irrespective of their procedural origin (own-initiative proceedings, notification, complaint, etc.). These cases are therefore those which fulfil the conditions set out in Part II (Guidelines on case allocation) of this Notice.

49. As regards cases which they deal with under Community law, it is desirable that national authorities should systematically inform the Commission of any proceedings they initiate. The Commission will pass on this information to the authorities in the other Member States.

50. This cooperation is especially necessary in regard to cases of particular significance to the Community within the meaning of points 33-36. This

---

29 However, in the case of information accompanied by a request for confidentiality with a view to protecting the informant's anonymity, an institution which accepts such information is bound, under Article 214 of the Treaty, to comply with such a condition (Case 145/83 *Adams* v *Commission* [1985] ECR 3539). The Commission will thus not divulge to national authorities the name of an informant who wishes to remain anonymous unless the person concerned withdraws, at the Commission's request, his request for anonymity *vis-à-vis* the national authority which may be dealing with his complaint.

30 Case C-67/91 *Dirección General de Defensa de la Competencia* v *Asociación Española de Banca Privada (AEB) and Others* [1992] ECR I-4785, operative part.

31 See footnote 30; paras 39 and 43.

category includes (a) all cases raising a new point of law, the aim being to avoid decisions, whether based on national law or on Community law, which are incompatible with the latter; (b) among cases of the utmost importance from an economic point of view, only those in which access by firms from other Member States to the relevant national market is significantly impeded; and (c) certain cases in which a public undertaking or an undertaking treated as equivalent to a public undertaking (within the meaning of Article 90(1) and (2) of the Treaty) is suspected of having engaged in an anti-competitive practice. Each national authority must determine, if necessary after consulting the Commission, whether a given case fits into one of these sub-categories.

51. Such cases will be investigated by national competition authorities in accordance with the procedures laid down by their national law, whether they are acting with a view to applying the Community competition rules or applying their national competition rules.[32]

52. The Commission also takes the view that, like national courts to which competition cases involving Articles 85 or 86 have been referred, national competition authorities applying those provisions are always at liberty, within the limits of their national procedural rules and subject to Article 214 of the Treaty, to seek information from the Commission on the state of any proceedings which the Commission may have set in motion and as to the likelihood of its giving an official ruling, pursuant to Regulation No 17, on cases which they are investigating on their own initiative. Under the same circumstances, national competition authorities may contact the Commission where the concrete application of Article 85(1) or of Article 86 raises particular difficulties, in order to obtain the economic and legal information which the Commission is in a position to supply to them.[33]

53. The Commission is convinced that close cooperation with national authorities will forestall any contradictory decisions. But if, 'during national proceedings, it appears possible that the decision to be taken by the Commission at the culmination of a procedure still in progress concerning the same agreement may conflict with the effects of the decision of the national authorities, it is for the latter to take the appropriate measures' (Walt Wilhelm) to ensure that measures implementing Community competition law are fully effective. The Commission takes the view that these measures should generally consist in national authorities staying their proceedings pending the outcome of the proceedings being conducted by the Commission. Where a national authority applies its national law, such a stay of proceedings would be based on the principles of the primacy of Community law (*Walt Wilhelm*)[34] and legal certainty, and where it applies Community law, on the principle of legal

---

32 See footnote 30; para 32.
33 Case C-234/89 *Delimitis* v *Henninger Bräu* [1991] ECR I-935, para 53.
34 See footnote 11; paras 8, 9 and 5 respectively.

certainty alone. For its part, the Commission will endeavour to deal as a matter of priority with cases subject to national proceedings thus stayed. A second possibility may, however, be envisaged, whereby the Commission is consulted before adopting the national decision. The consultations would consist, due regard being had to the judgment in the *Spanish banks* case, in exchanging any documents preparatory to the decisions envisaged, so that Member States' authorities might be able to take account of the Commission's position in their own decision without the latter having to be deferred until such time as the Commission's decision has been taken.

Procedure

In respect of complaints

54. Since complainants cannot force the Commission to take a decision as to whether the infringement they allege has actually occurred, and since the Commission is entitled to reject a complaint which lacks a sufficient Community interest, national competition authorities should not have any special difficulty in handling complaints submitted initially to them involving matters that fall within the scope of the Community competition rules.

In respect of notifications

55. Although they form a very small percentage of all notifications to the Commission, special consideration needs to be given to notifications to the Commission of restrictive practices undergoing investigation by a national authority made for dilatory purposes. A dilatory notification is one where a firm, threatened with a decision banning a restrictive practice which a national authority is poised to take following an investigation under Article 85(1) or under national law, notifies the disputed agreement to the Commission and asks for it to be exempted under Article 85(3) of the Treaty. Such a notification is made in order to induce the Commission to initiate a proceeding under Articles 2, 3 or 6 of Regulation No 17 and hence, by virtue of Article 9(3) of that Regulation, to remove from Member States' authorities the power to apply the provisions of Article 85(1). The Commission will not consider a notification to be dilatory until after it has contacted the national authority concerned and checked that the latter agrees with its assessment. The Commission calls upon national authorities, moreover, to inform it of their own accord of any notifications they receive which, in their view, are dilatory in nature.

56. A similar situation arises where an agreement is notified to the Commission with a view to preventing the imminent initiation of national proceedings which might result in the prohibition of that agreement.[35]

---

35 With respect to agreements not subject to notification pursuant to point 1 of Article 4(2) of Regulation No 17, points 56 and 57 of this Notice also apply *mutatis mutandis* to express requests for exemption.

57. The Commission recognises, of course, that a firm requesting exemption is entitled to obtain from it a decision on the substance of its request (see point 38). However, if the Commission takes the view that such notification is chiefly aimed at suspending the national proceedings, given its exclusive powers to grant exemptions it considers itself justified in not examining it as a matter of priority.

58. The national authority which is investigating the matter and has therefore initiated proceedings should normally ask the Commission for its provisional opinion on the likelihood of its exempting the agreement now notified to it. Such a request will be superfluous where, 'in the light of the relevant criteria developed by the case-law of the Court of Justice and the Court of First Instance and by previous regulations and decisions of the Commission, the national authority has ascertained that the agreement, decision or concerted practice at issue cannot be the subject of an individual exemption'.[36]

59. The Commission will deliver its provisional opinion on the likelihood of an exemption being granted, in the light of a preliminary examination of the questions of fact and law involved, as quickly as possible once the complete notification is received. Examination of the notification having revealed that the agreement in question is unlikely to qualify for exemption under Article 85(3) and that its effects are mainly confined to one Member State, the opinion will state that further investigation of the matter is not a Commission priority.

60. The Commission will transmit this opinion in writing to the national authority investigating the case and to the notifying parties. It will state in its letter that it will be highly unlikely to take a decision on the matter before the national authority to which it was referred has taken its final decision and that the notifying parties retain their immunity from any fines the Commission might impose.

61. In its reply, the national authority, after taking note of the Commission's opinion, should undertake to contact the Commission forthwith if its investigation leads it to a conclusion which differs from that opinion. This will be the case if, following its investigation, the national authority concludes that the agreement in question should not be banned under Article 85(1) of the Treaty or, if that provisions cannot be applied, under the relevant national law. The national authority should also undertake to forward a copy of its final decision on the matter to the Commission. Copies of the correspondence will be sent to the competition authorities of the other Member States for information.

62. The Commission will not itself initiate proceedings in the same case before the proceedings pending before the national authority have been completed; in accordance with Article 9(3) of Regulation No 17, such action would have the effect of taking the matter out of the hands of the national authority. The

---

36 Points 29 and 30 of the Notice on cooperation between national courts and the Commission.

Commission will do this only in quite exceptional circumstances – in a situation where, against all expectations, the national authority is liable to find that there has been no infringement of Articles 85 or 86 or of its national competition law, or where the national proceedings are unduly long drawn-out.

63. Before initiating proceedings the Commission will consult the national authority to discover the factual or legal grounds for that authority's proposed favourable decision or the reasons for the delay in the proceedings.

V. Concluding remarks

64. This Notice is without prejudice to any interpretation by the Court of First Instance and the Court of Justice.

65. In the interests of effective, consistent application of Community law throughout the Union, and legal simplicity and certainty for the benefit of undertakings, the Commission calls upon those Member States which have not already done so to adopt legislation enabling their competition authority to implement Articles 85(1) and 86 of the Treaty effectively.

66. In applying this Notice, the Commission and the competent authorities of the Member States and their officials and other staff will observe the principle of professional secrecy in accordance with Article 20 of Regulation No 17.

67. This Notice does not apply to competition rules in the transport sector, owing to the highly specific way in which cases arising in that sector are handled from a procedural point of view.[37]

68. The actual application of this Notice, especially in terms of the measures considered desirable to facilitate its implementation, will be the subject of an annual review carried out jointly by the authorities of the Member States and the Commission.

69. This Notice will be reviewed no later than at the end of the fourth year after its adoption.

---

37 Council Regulation No 141/62 of 26 November 1962 exempting transport from the application of Council Regulation No 17 (OJ 124, 28. 11. 1962, p. 2753; English Special Edition 1959-62, p. 291), as amended by Regulations Nos 165/65/EEC (OJ 210, 11. 12. 1965, p. 314) and 1002/67/EEC (OJ 306, 16. 12. 1967, p. 1); Council Regulation (EEC) No 1017/68 of 19 July 1968 applying rules of competition to transport by rail, road and inland waterway (OJ L 175, 23. 7. 1968, p. 1; English Special Edition 1968 I, p. 302); Council Regulation (EEC) No 4056/86 of 22 December 1986 laying down detailed rules for the application of Articles 85 and 86 of the Treaty to maritime transport (OJ L 378, 31. 12. 1986, p. 4); Council Regulation (EEC) No 3975/87 of 14 December 1987 laying down the procedure for the application of the rules on competition to undertakings in the air transport sector (OJ L 374, 31. 12. 1987, p. 1); and Commission Regulation (EC) No 870/95 of 20 April 1995 on the application of Article 85(3) of the Treaty to certain categories of agreements, decisions and converted practices between liner shipping companies (consortia) pursuant to Council Regulation (EEC) No 479/92 (OJ L 89, 21. 4. 1995, p. 7).

· Index ·